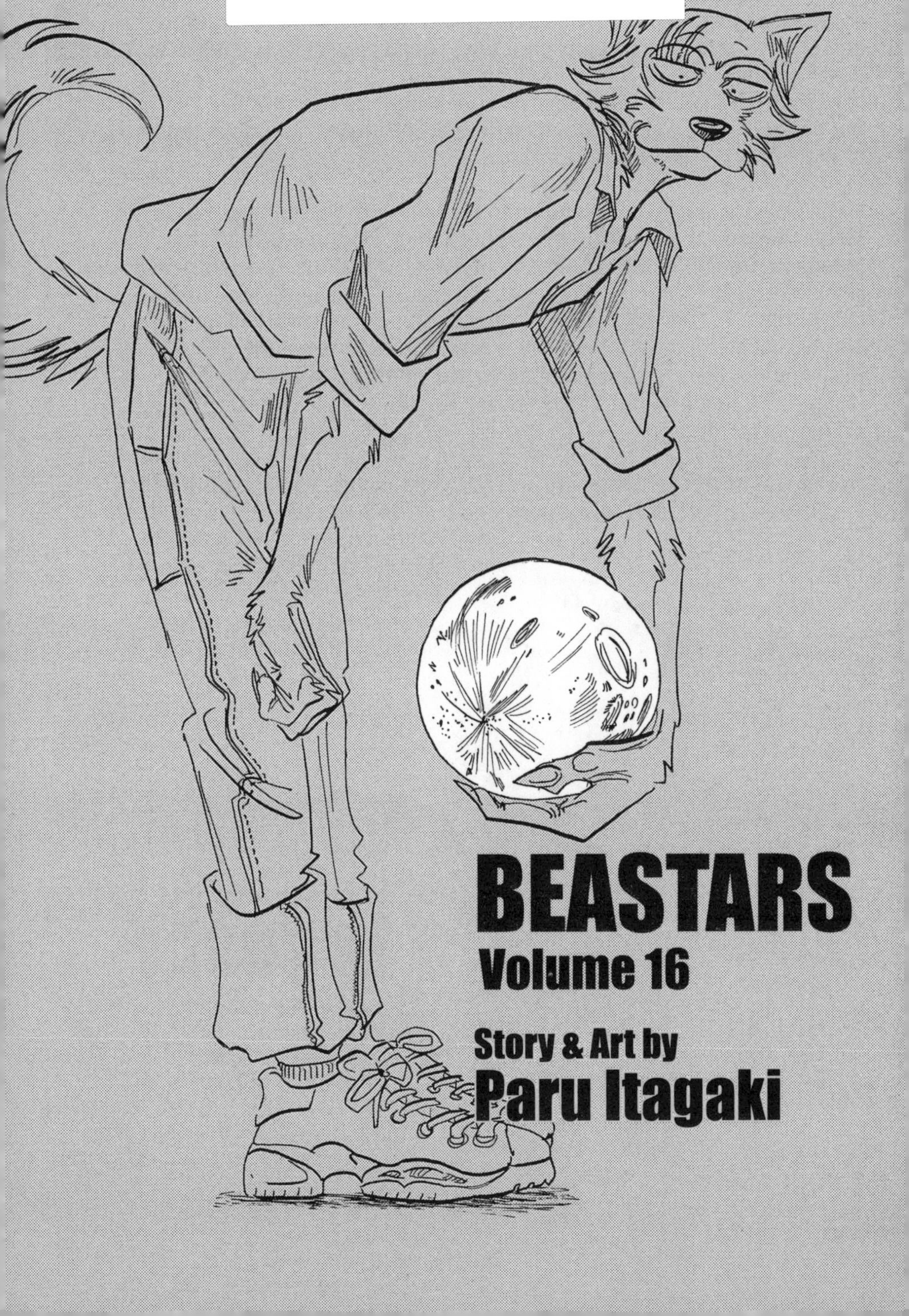

BEASTARS

Volume 16

Story & Art by
Paru Itagaki

STORY & CAST OF CHARACTERS

Legoshi has been designated a registered meat offender after consensually eating his friend Louis's leg to give him the strength to defeat Riz, the bear who murdered their friend Tem. Now Legoshi has dropped out of school and is working at Bebebe, an udon noodle shop. Legoshi's feelings for Haru deepen after he has dinner with her family. But not only is he a carnivore, his criminal record also stands in the way of them ever getting married.

When Beastar Yahya asks Legoshi to help him capture elephant-poacher Melon, despite Legoshi's doubts about Yahya's moral compass, he agrees to assist him in exchange for having his criminal record erased. Legoshi is also curious to meet Melon because he is half-carnivore, half-herbivore. Legoshi and Yahya go undercover at a masked ball and apprehend Melon. Legoshi believes Melon is like the children he and Haru might have one day, so he takes pity on him and sets him free. Instead of being grateful, Melon shoots Legoshi in the chest, critically wounding him.

As Legoshi hovers between life and death, he meets his late mother, mixed-species Leanno, who committed suicide when Legoshi was young. She tries to explain to her son why she became so depressed, telling him about her fears of being rejected by a society that wouldn't accept mixed-species beasts.

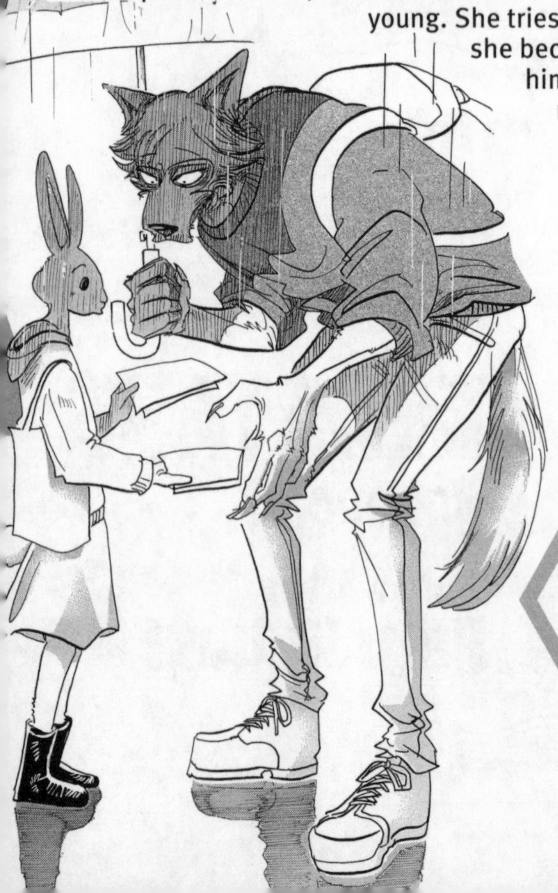

Legoshi

- ★Gray wolf ♂
- ★Former Cherryton Academy student
- ★Ate his friend Louis's leg to defeat Riz
- ★Lives alone at Beast Apartments

Louis

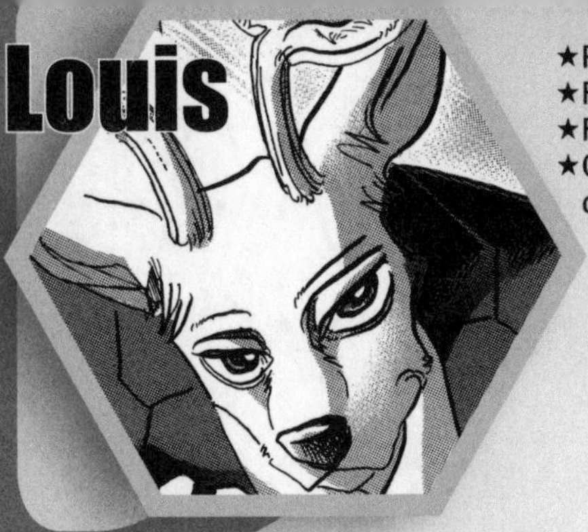

★Red deer ♂
★Former leader of the Drama Club actors pool
★Former leader of the Shishi-gumi lion gang
★Offered his leg to Legoshi so he could defeat Riz

Haru

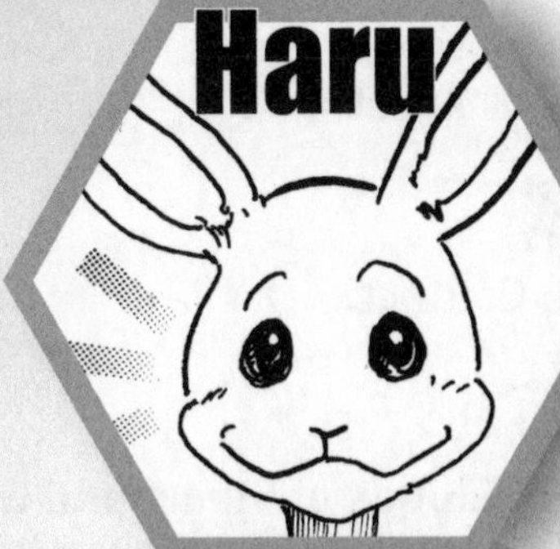

★Netherland dwarf rabbit ♀
★University student

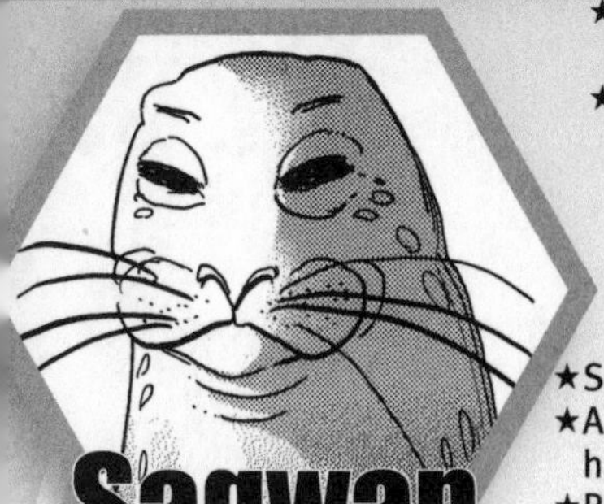

Sagwan

★Spotted seal ♂
★A half-marine, half-land animal
★Resident of Beast Apartments

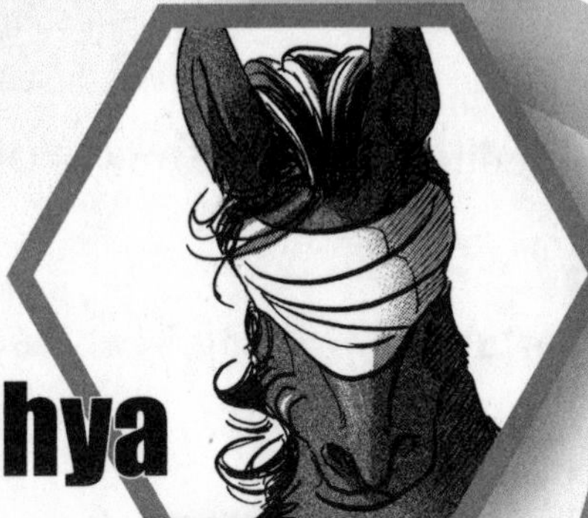

Yahya

★Horse ♂
★Current Beastar
★Powerful combatant

Gosha

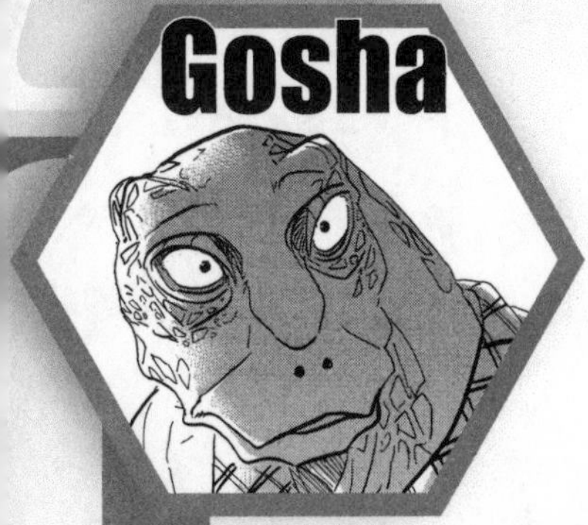

★Komodo dragon ♂
★Legoshi's grandfather
★Has a history with Beastar Yahya

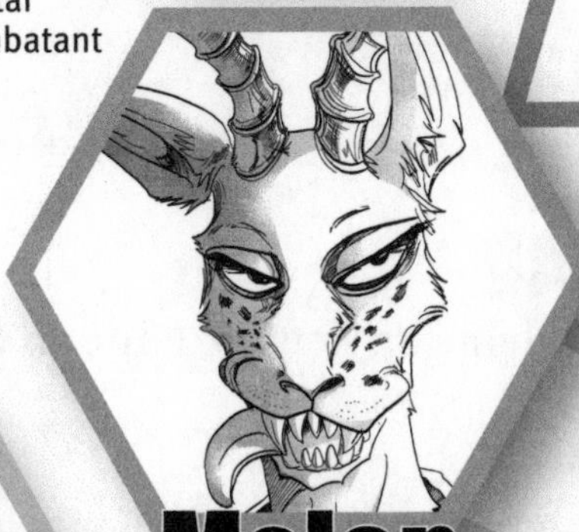

Melon

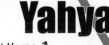

★Half-leopard, half-gazelle ♂
★Elephant poacher who sells tusks on the black market

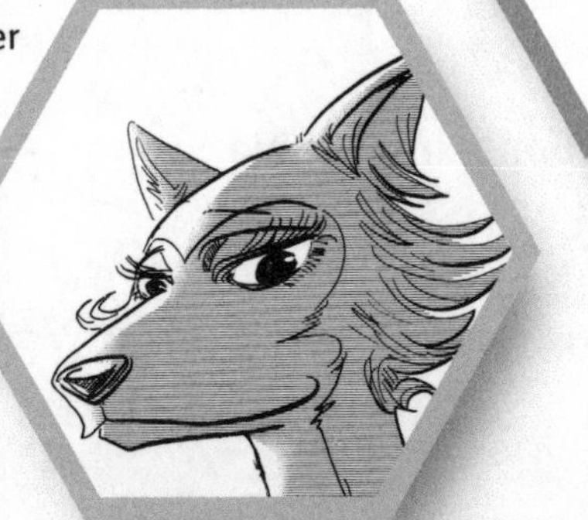

Leanno

★Legoshi's beautiful mother
★Gosha's daughter
★Why did she take her own life?

BEASTARS

Volume 16

CONTENTS

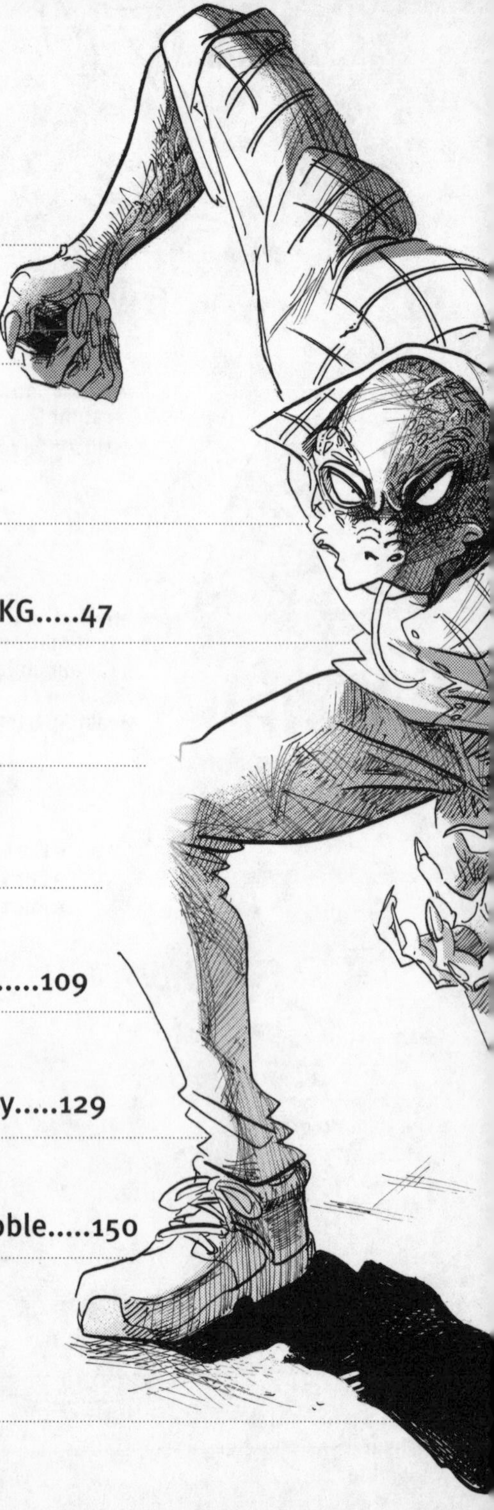

Chapter 134: Final Contact

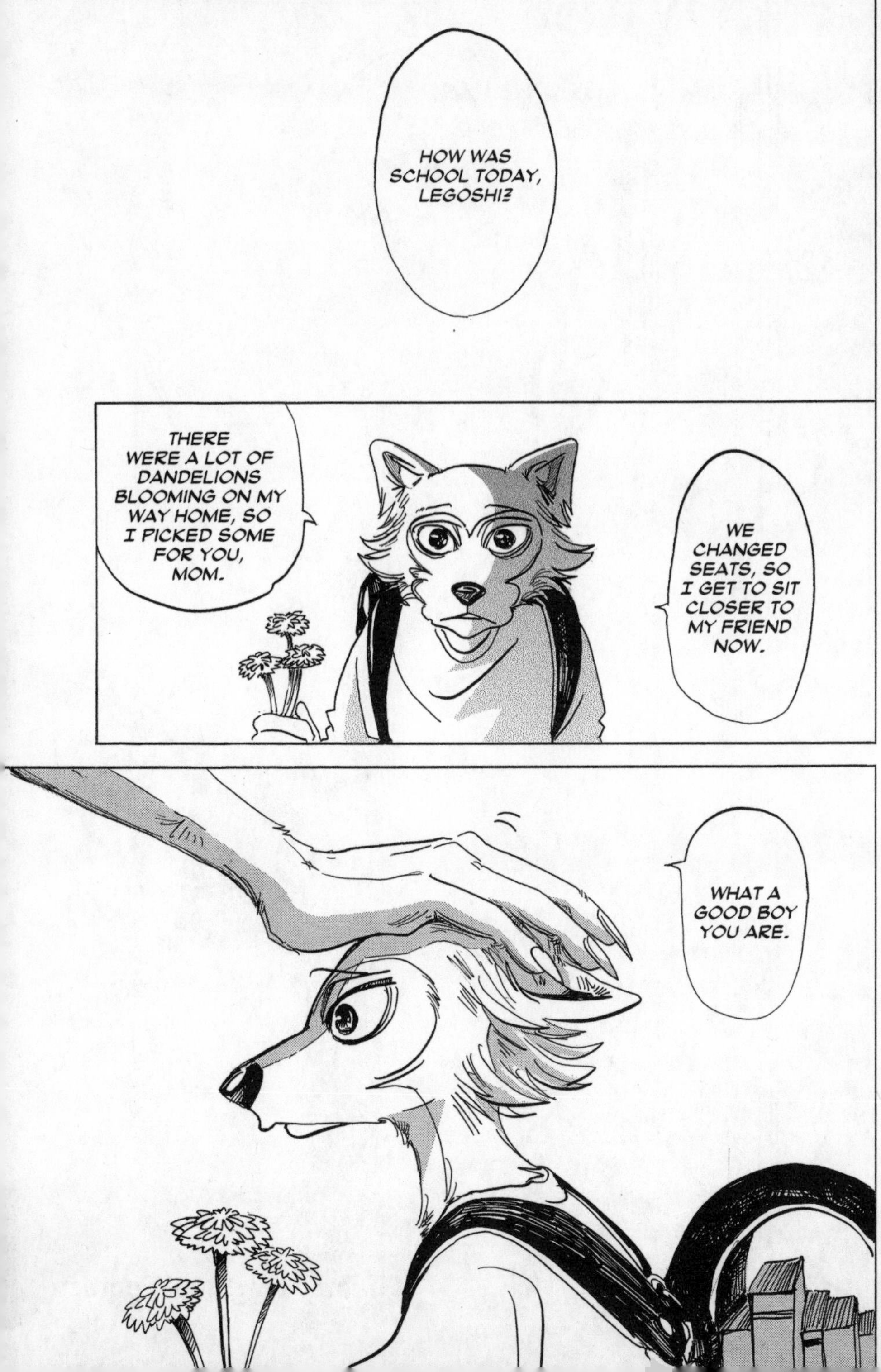
HOW WAS SCHOOL TODAY, LEGOSHI?
WE CHANGED SEATS, SO I GET TO SIT CLOSER TO MY FRIEND NOW.
THERE WERE A LOT OF DANDELIONS BLOOMING ON MY WAY HOME, SO I PICKED SOME FOR YOU, MOM.
WHAT A GOOD BOY YOU ARE.

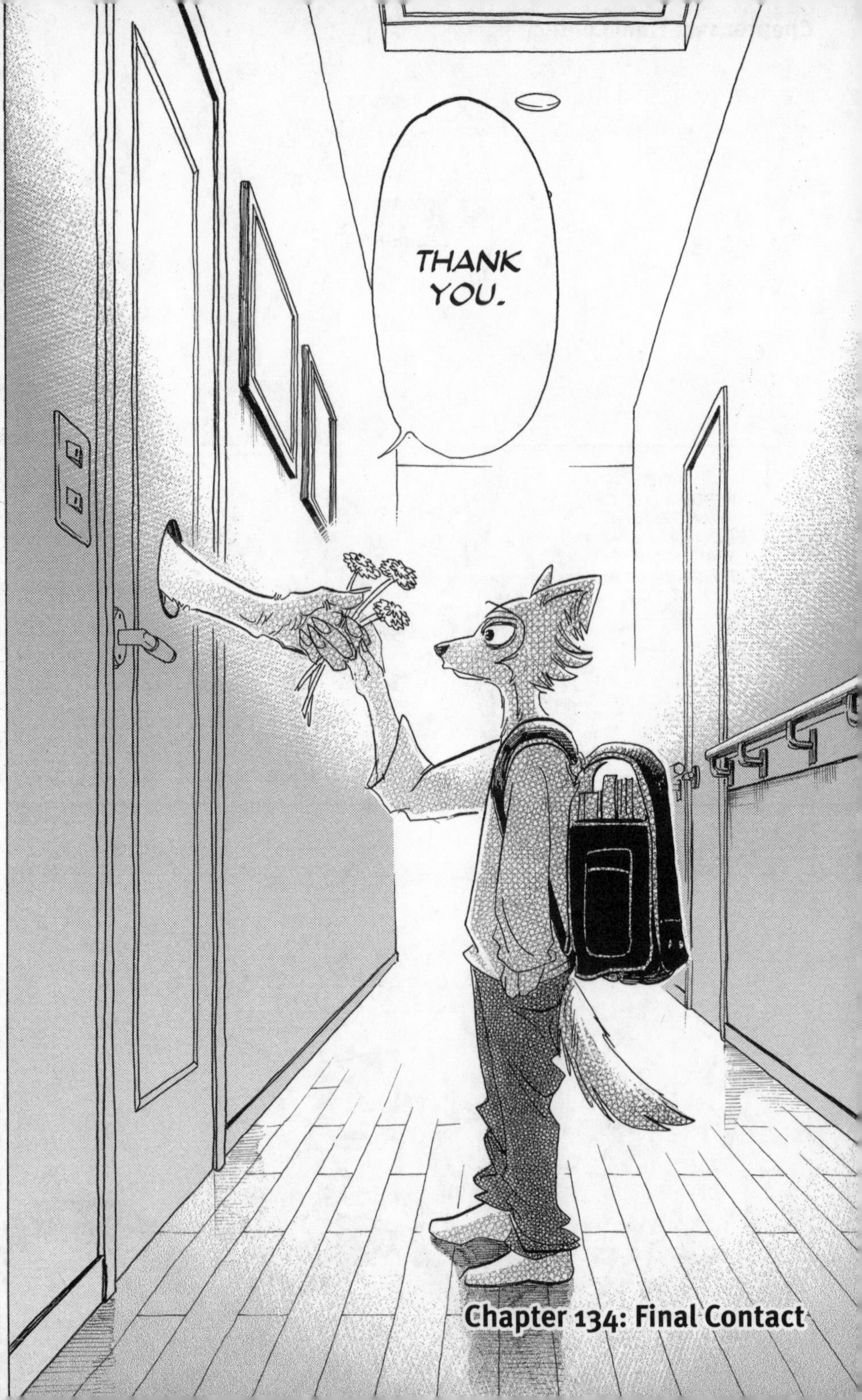
THANK YOU.

Chapter 134: Final Contact

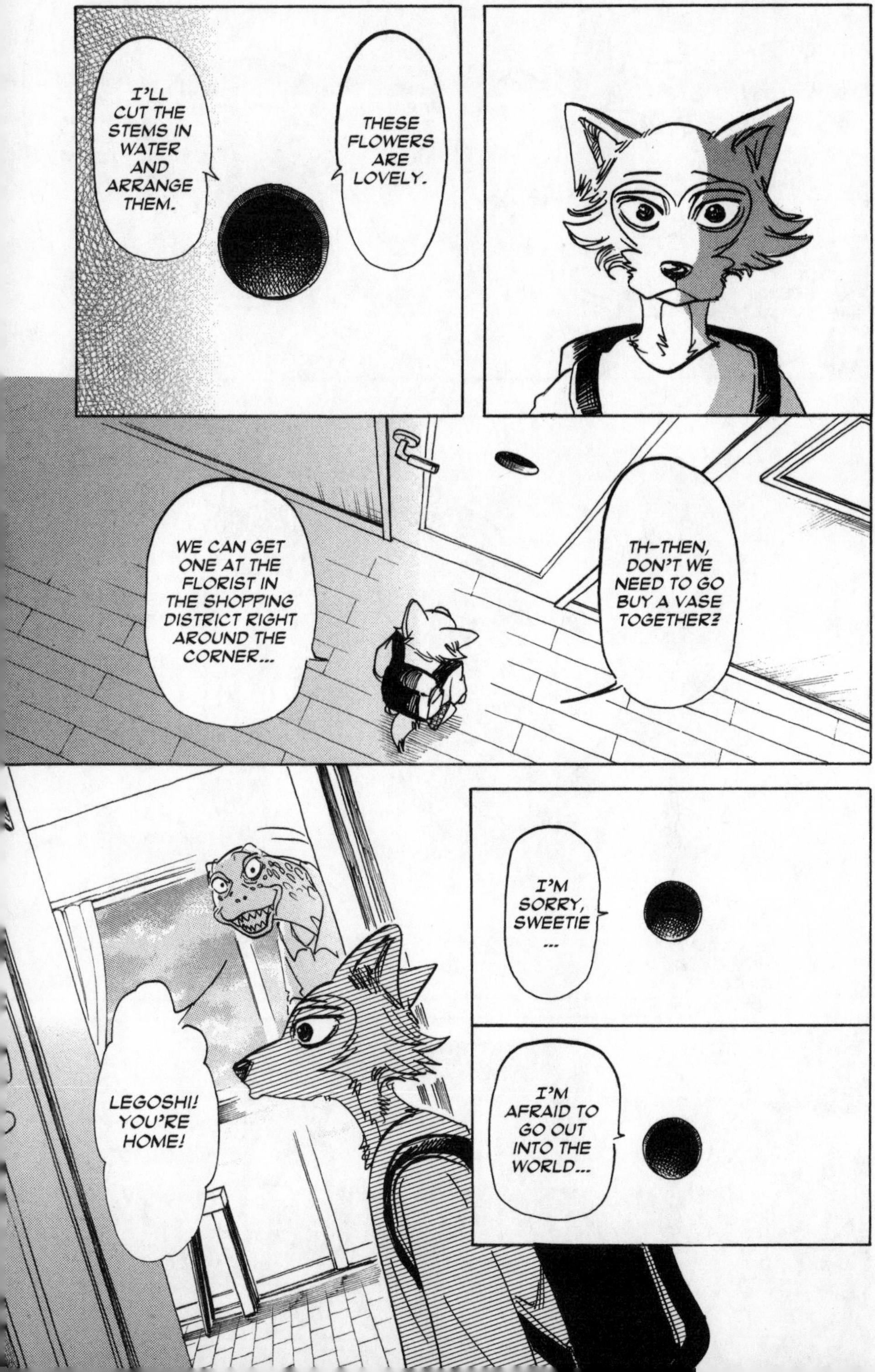
THESE FLOWERS ARE LOVELY.
I'LL CUT THE STEMS IN WATER AND ARRANGE THEM.
TH-THEN, DON'T WE NEED TO GO BUY A VASE TOGETHER?
WE CAN GET ONE AT THE FLORIST IN THE SHOPPING DISTRICT RIGHT AROUND THE CORNER...
I'M SORRY, SWEETIE ...
I'M AFRAID TO GO OUT INTO THE WORLD...
LEGOSHI! YOU'RE HOME!

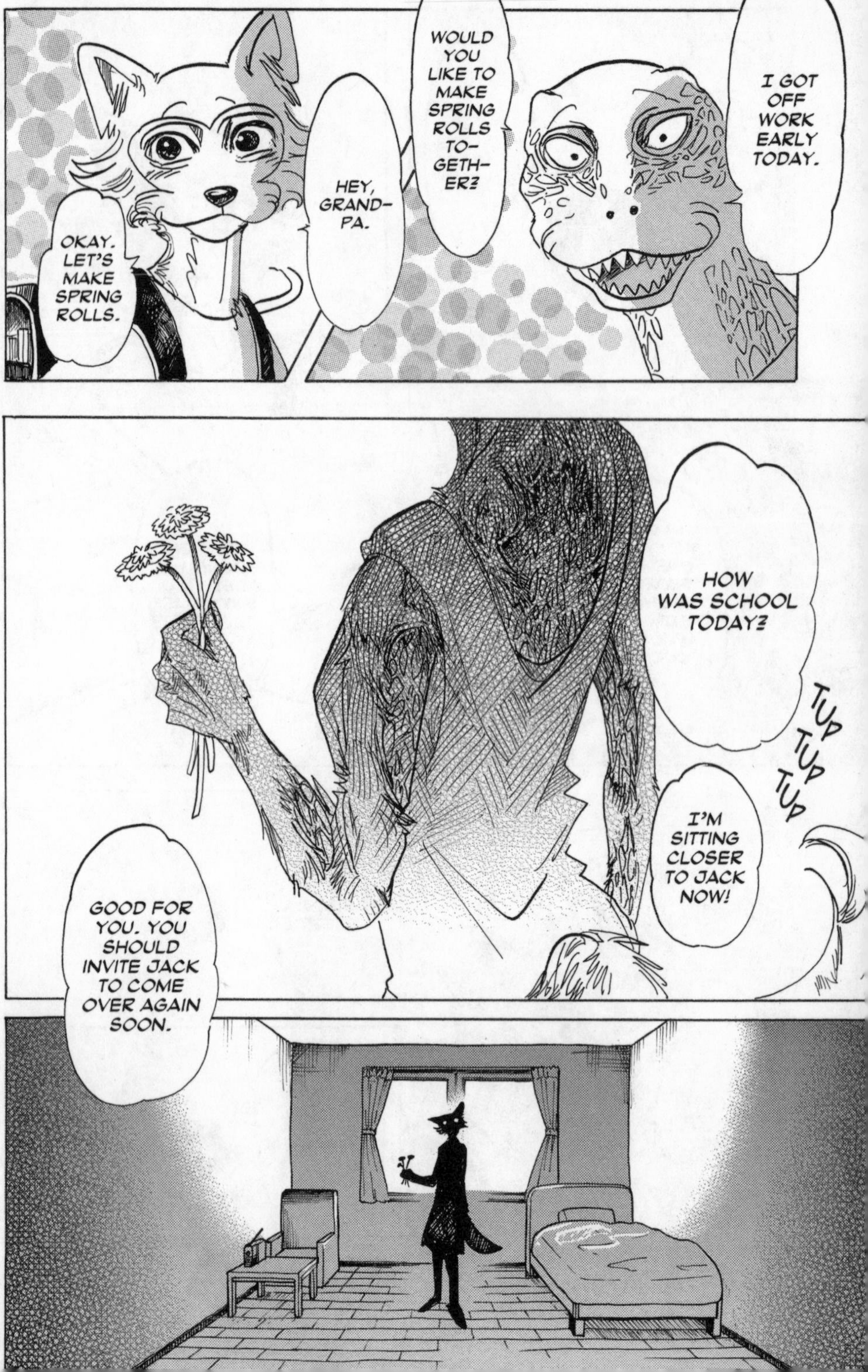
I GOT OFF WORK EARLY TODAY.
WOULD YOU LIKE TO MAKE SPRING ROLLS TO-GETH-ER?
HEY, GRAND-PA.
OKAY. LET'S MAKE SPRING ROLLS.
HOW WAS SCHOOL TODAY?
TUP TUP TUP
I'M SITTING CLOSER TO JACK NOW!
GOOD FOR YOU. YOU SHOULD INVITE JACK TO COME OVER AGAIN SOON.

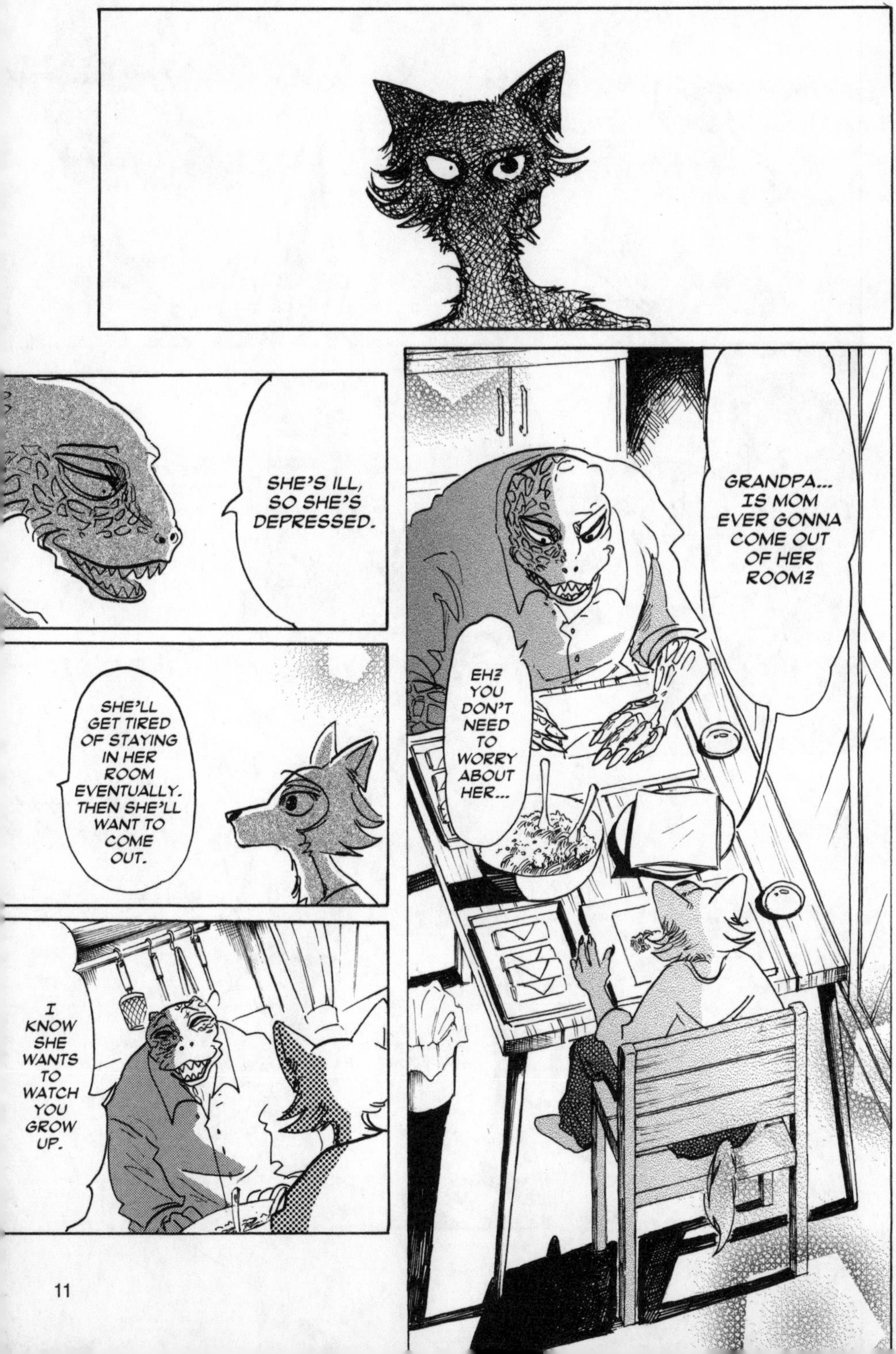
GRANDPA... IS MOM EVER GONNA COME OUT OF HER ROOM?
EH? YOU DON'T NEED TO WORRY ABOUT HER...
SHE'S ILL, SO SHE'S DEPRESSED.
SHE'LL GET TIRED OF STAYING IN HER ROOM EVENTUALLY. THEN SHE'LL WANT TO COME OUT.
I KNOW SHE WANTS TO WATCH YOU GROW UP.

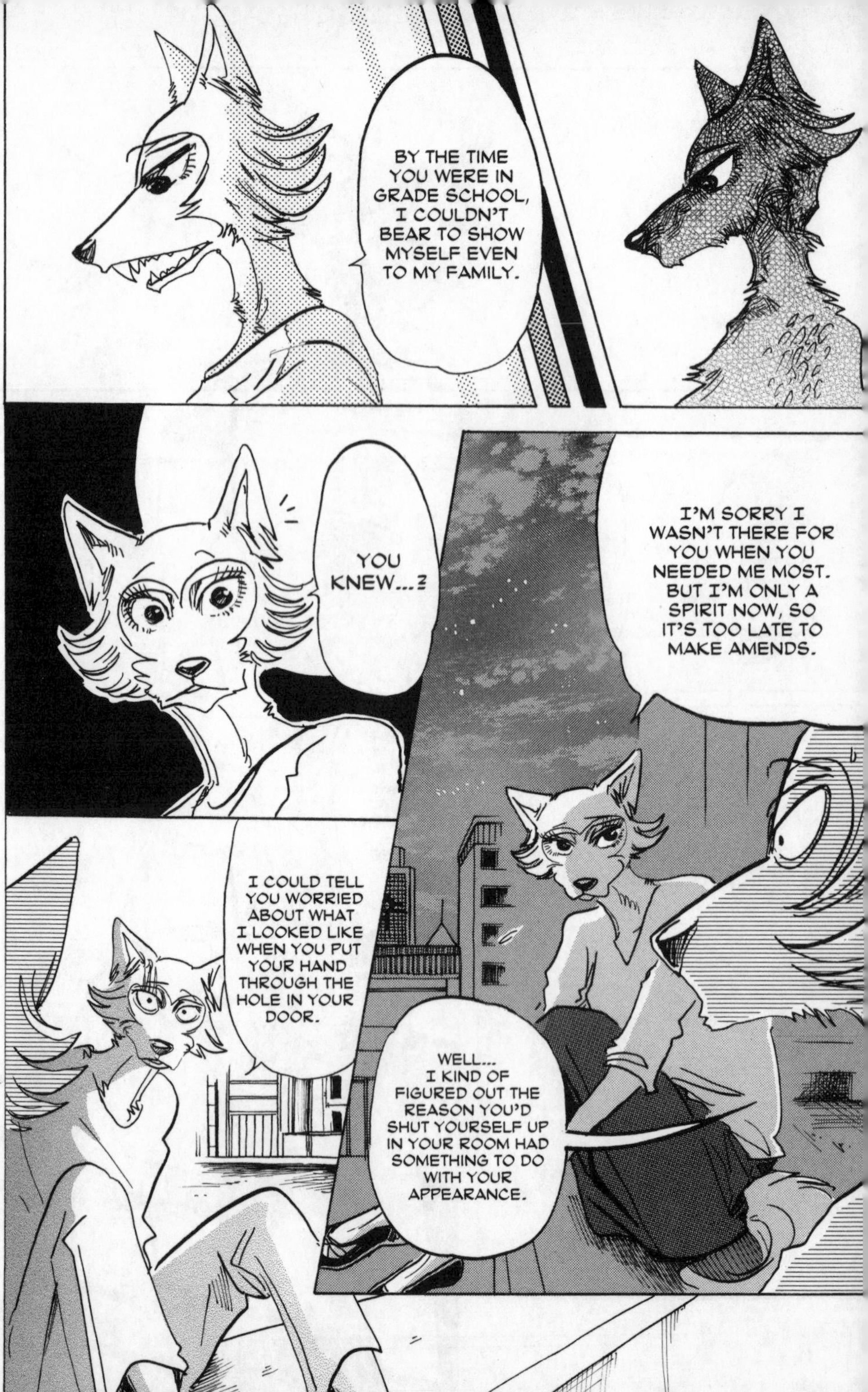
BY THE TIME YOU WERE IN GRADE SCHOOL, I COULDN'T BEAR TO SHOW MYSELF EVEN TO MY FAMILY.
I'M SORRY I WASN'T THERE FOR YOU WHEN YOU NEEDED ME MOST. BUT I'M ONLY A SPIRIT NOW, SO IT'S TOO LATE TO MAKE AMENDS.
WELL... I KIND OF FIGURED OUT THE REASON YOU'D SHUT YOURSELF UP IN YOUR ROOM HAD SOMETHING TO DO WITH YOUR APPEARANCE.
YOU KNEW...?
I COULD TELL YOU WORRIED ABOUT WHAT I LOOKED LIKE WHEN YOU PUT YOUR HAND THROUGH THE HOLE IN YOUR DOOR.

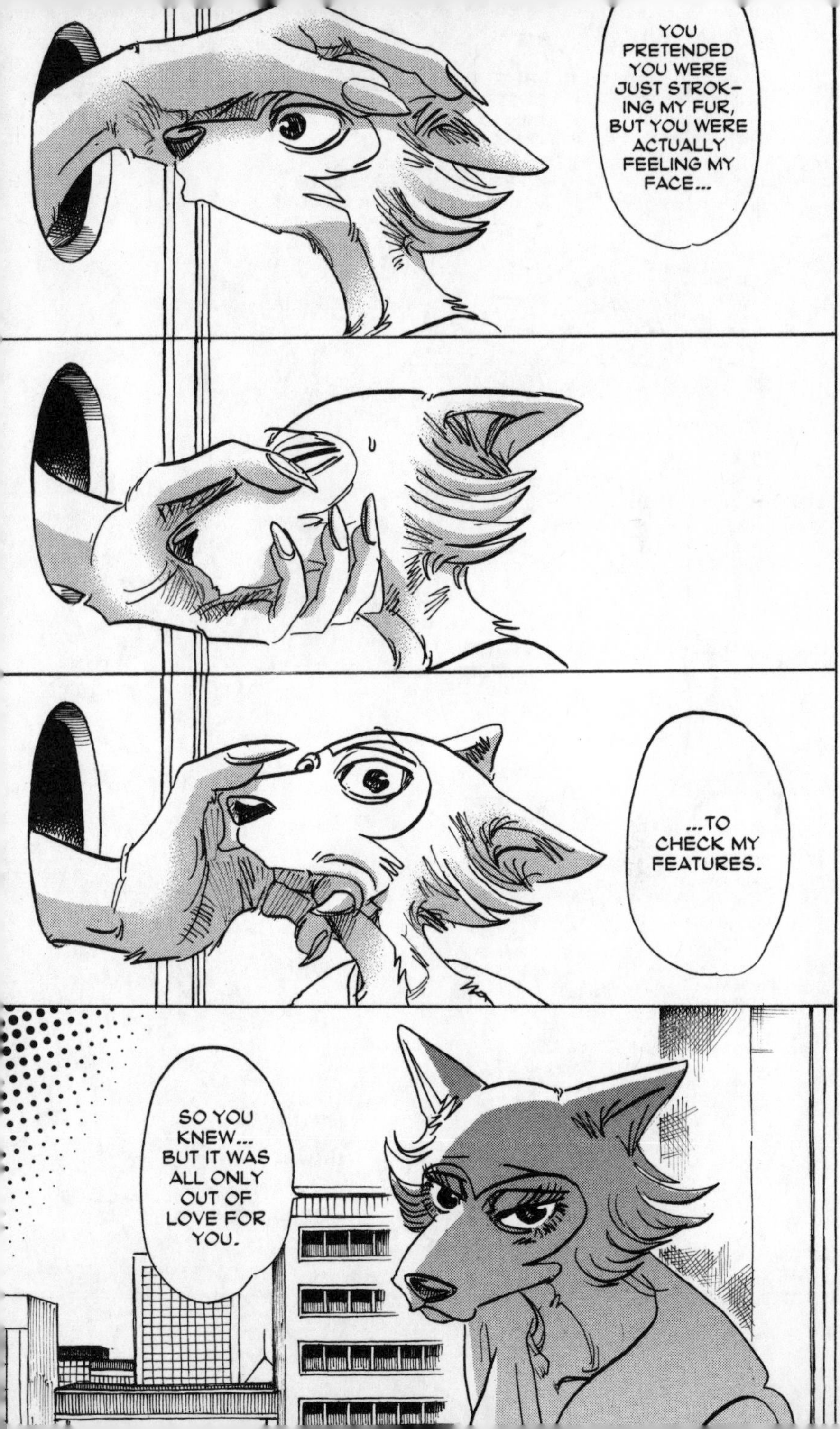
YOU PRETENDED YOU WERE JUST STROK-ING MY FUR, BUT YOU WERE ACTUALLY FEELING MY FACE...
...TO CHECK MY FEATURES.
SO YOU KNEW... BUT IT WAS ALL ONLY OUT OF LOVE FOR YOU.

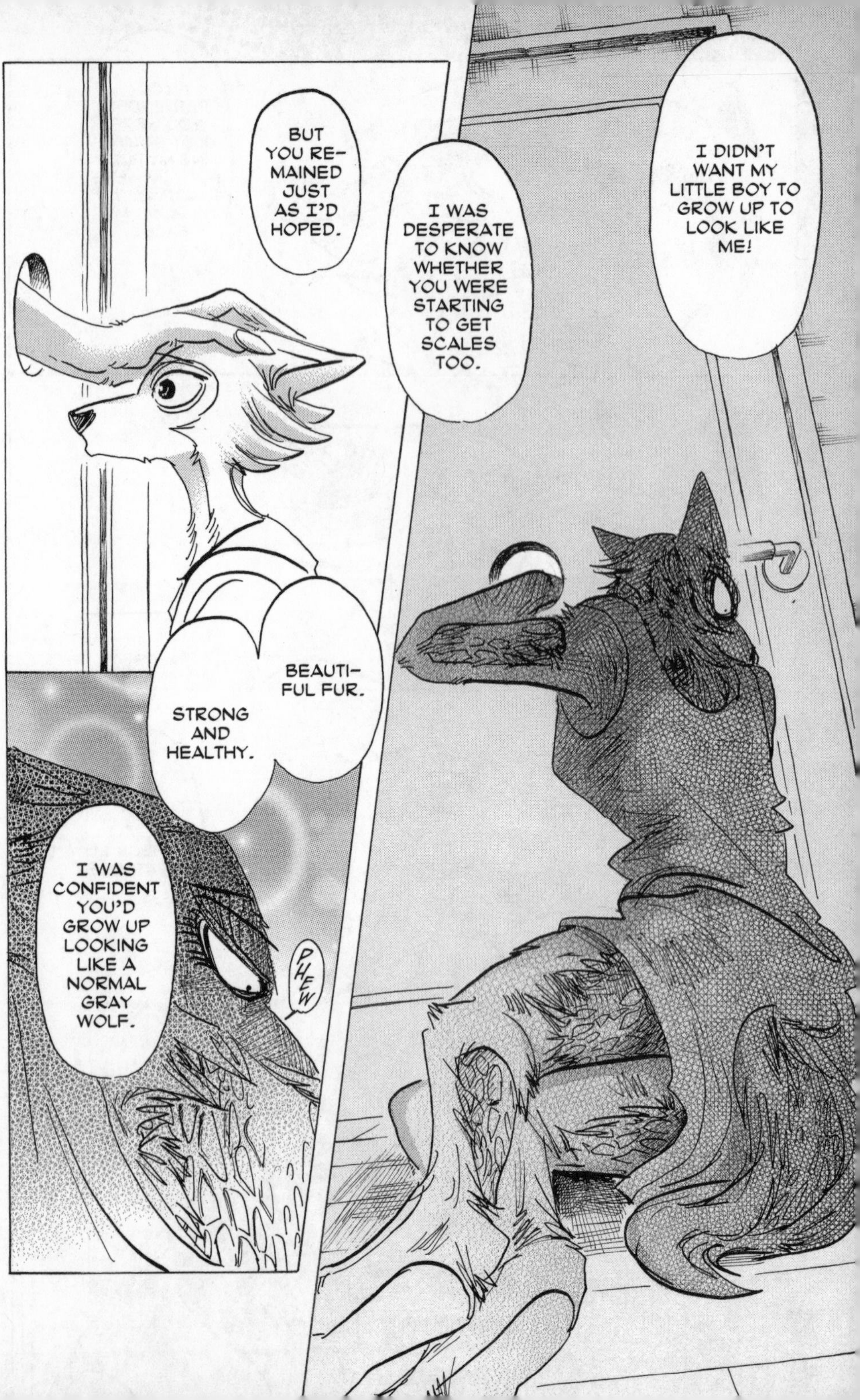
I DIDN'T WANT MY LITTLE BOY TO GROW UP TO LOOK LIKE ME!
I WAS DESPERATE TO KNOW WHETHER YOU WERE STARTING TO GET SCALES TOO.
BUT YOU RE-MAINED JUST AS I'D HOPED.
BEAUTI-FUL FUR.
STRONG AND HEALTHY.
I WAS CONFIDENT YOU'D GROW UP LOOKING LIKE A NORMAL GRAY WOLF.
PHEW

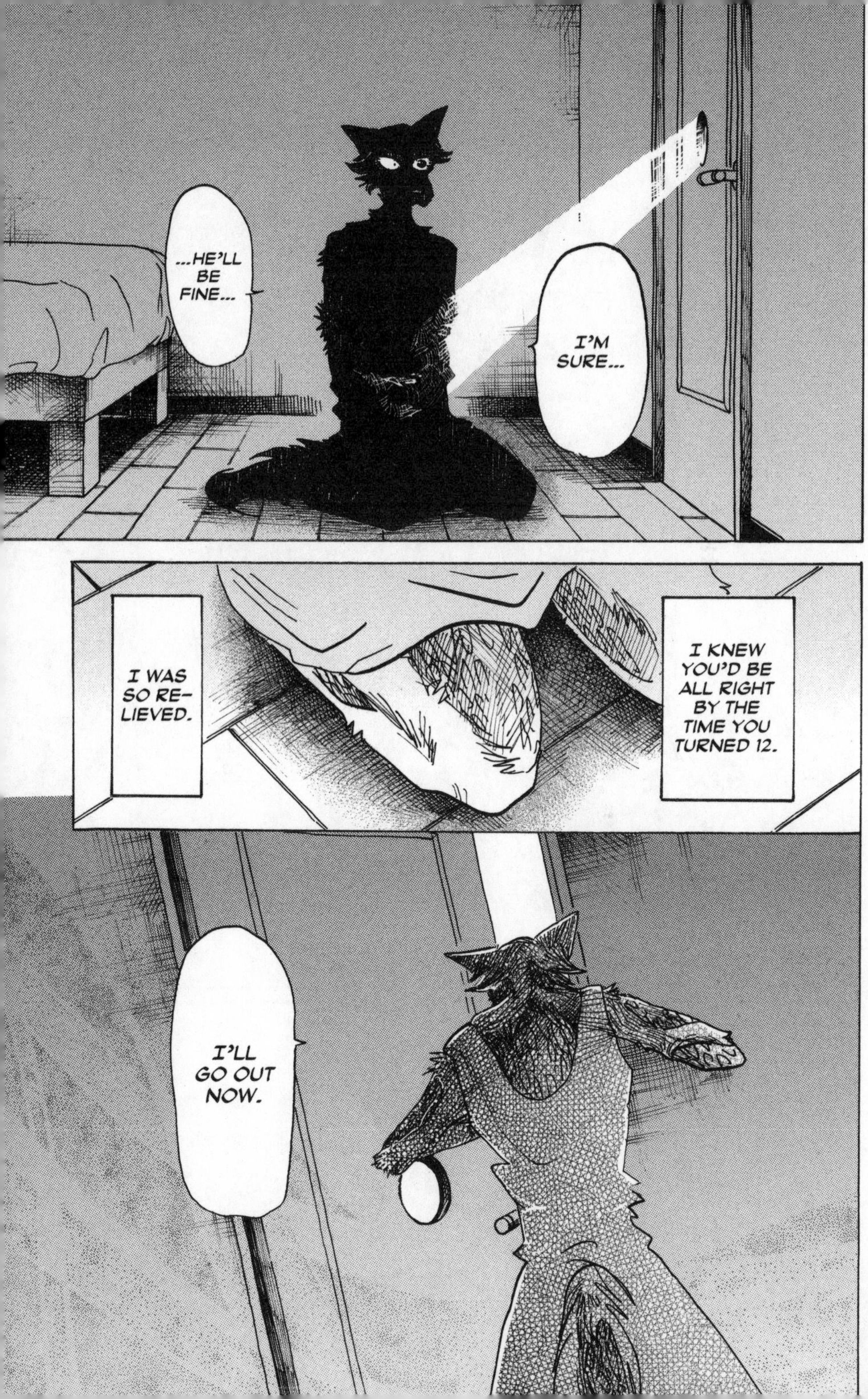
I'M SURE...
...HE'LL BE FINE...
I KNEW YOU'D BE ALL RIGHT BY THE TIME YOU TURNED 12.
I WAS SO RE-LIEVED.
I'LL GO OUT NOW.

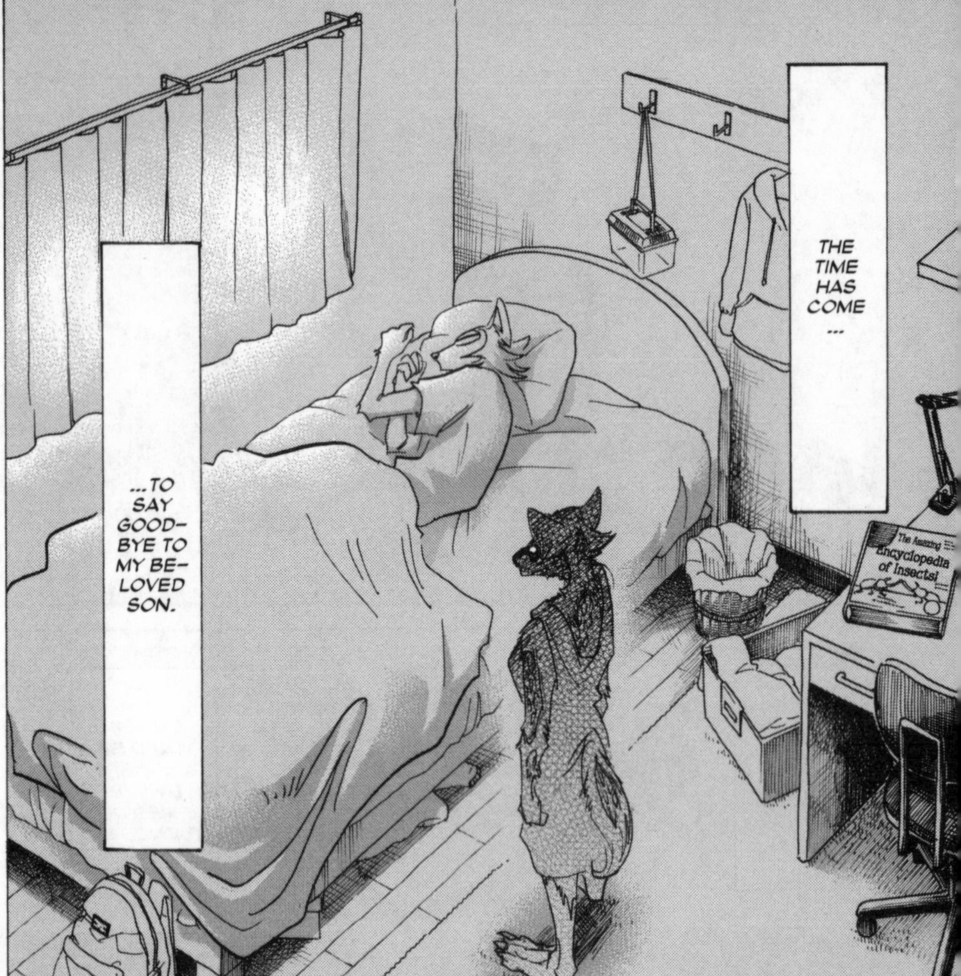
THE TIME HAS COME...
...TO SAY GOOD-BYE TO MY BE-LOVED SON.
The Amazing Encyclopedia of Insects!

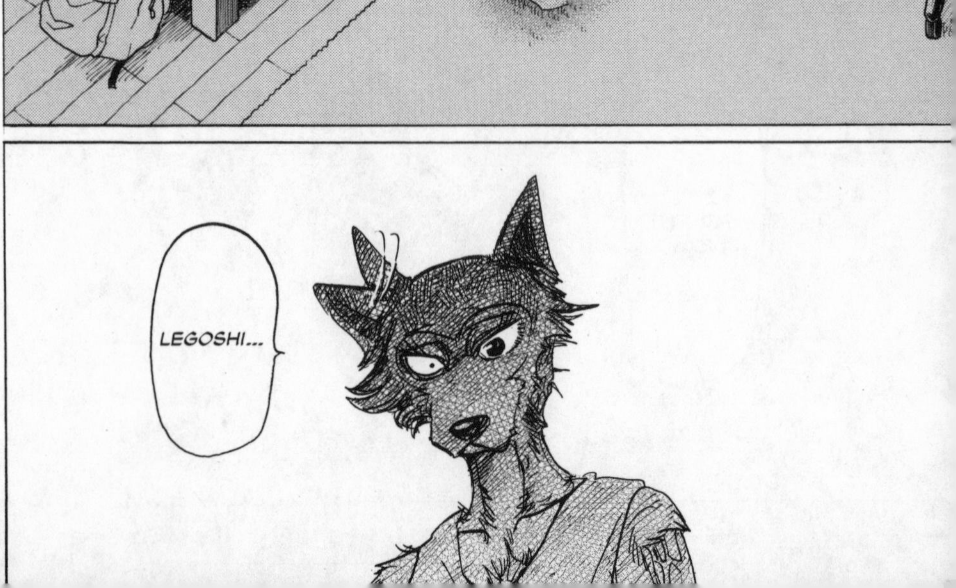
LEGOSHI...

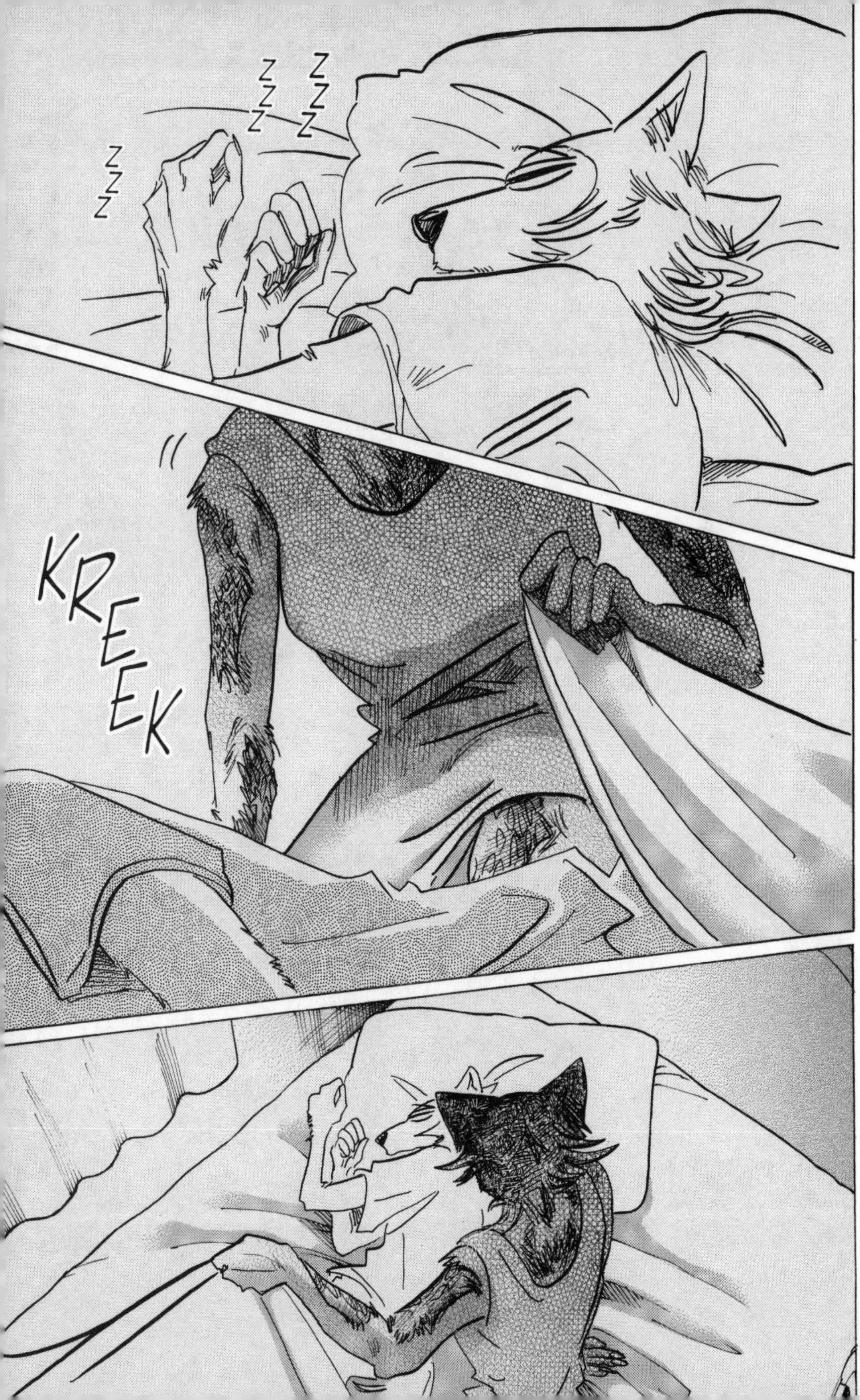
ZZZ
ZZZ
ZZZ
KREEEK

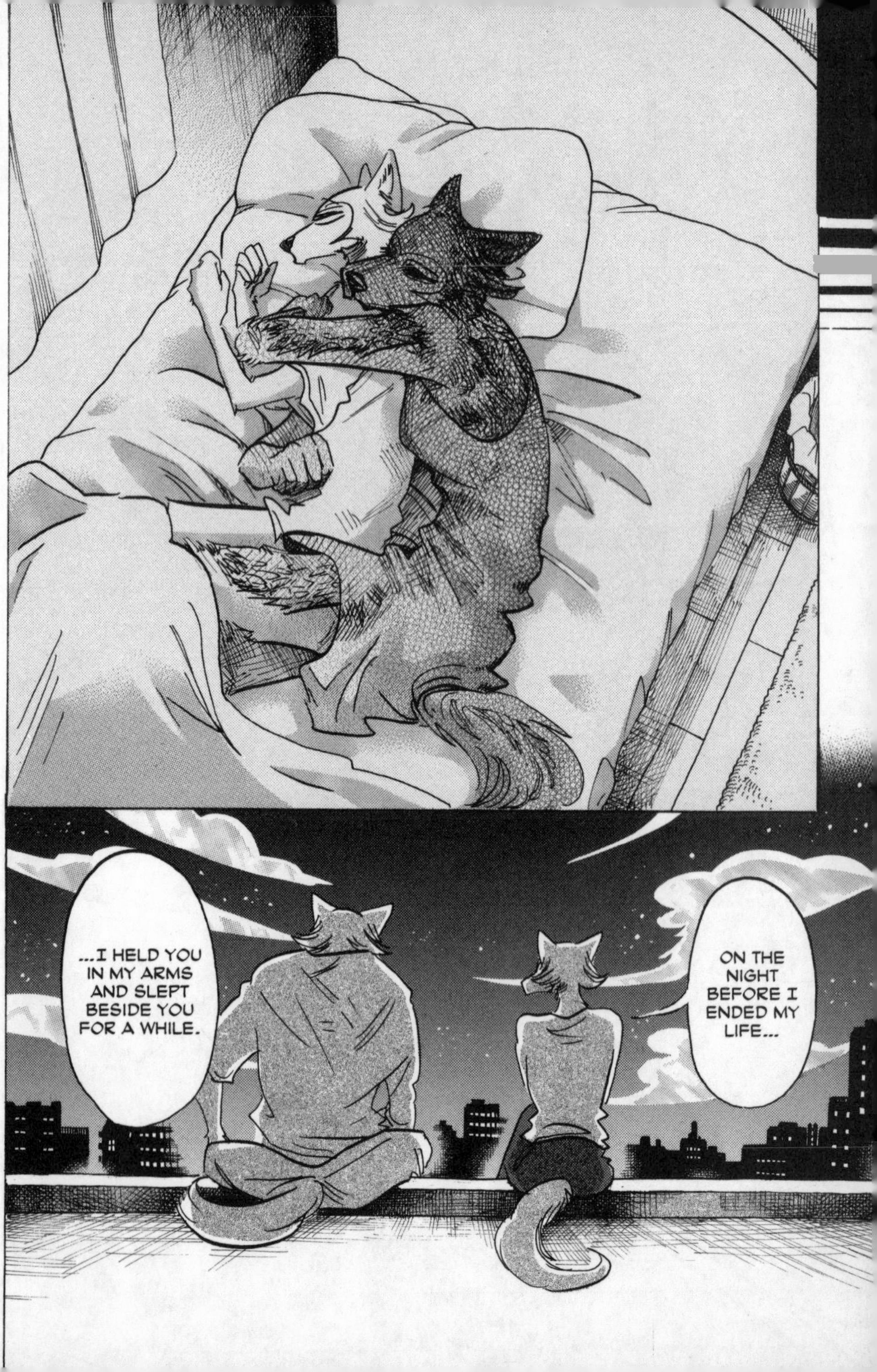
ON THE NIGHT BEFORE I ENDED MY LIFE...
...I HELD YOU IN MY ARMS AND SLEPT BESIDE YOU FOR A WHILE.

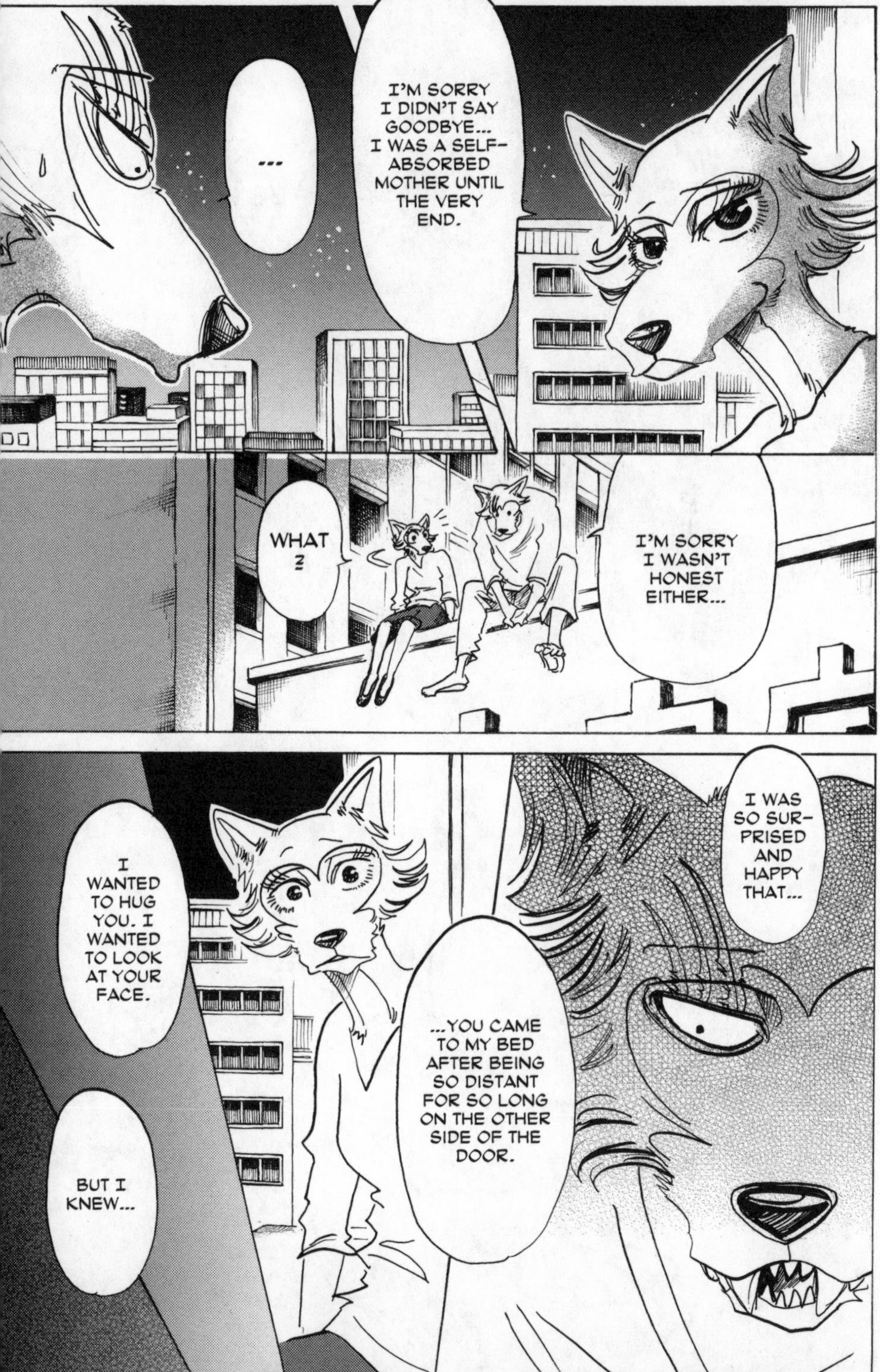
I'M SORRY I DIDN'T SAY GOODBYE... I WAS A SELF-ABSORBED MOTHER UNTIL THE VERY END.
...
I'M SORRY I WASN'T HONEST EITHER...
WHAT?
I WAS SO SUR-PRISED AND HAPPY THAT...
...YOU CAME TO MY BED AFTER BEING SO DISTANT FOR SO LONG ON THE OTHER SIDE OF THE DOOR.
I WANTED TO HUG YOU. I WANTED TO LOOK AT YOUR FACE.
BUT I KNEW...

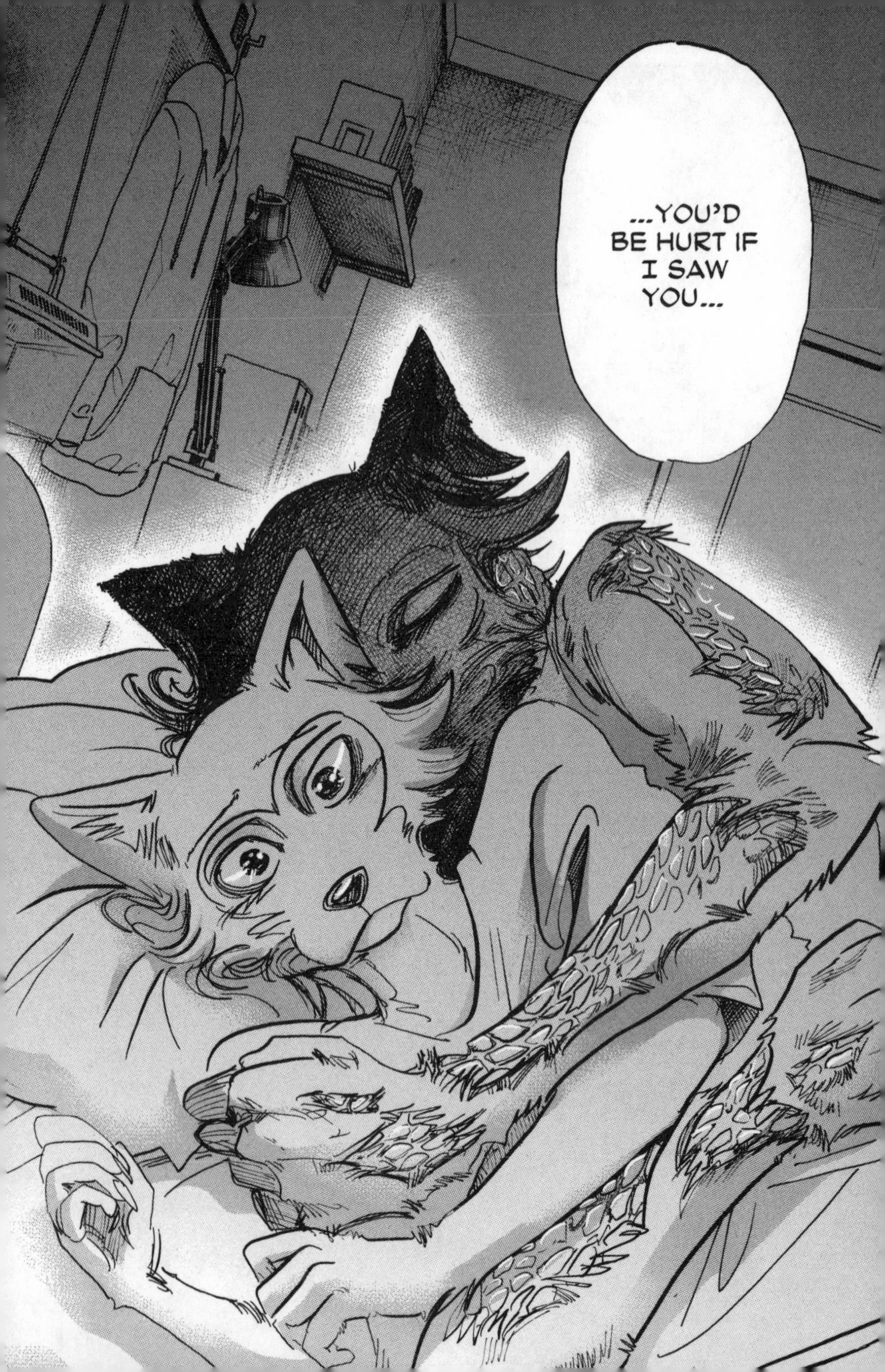
...YOU'D BE HURT IF I SAW YOU...

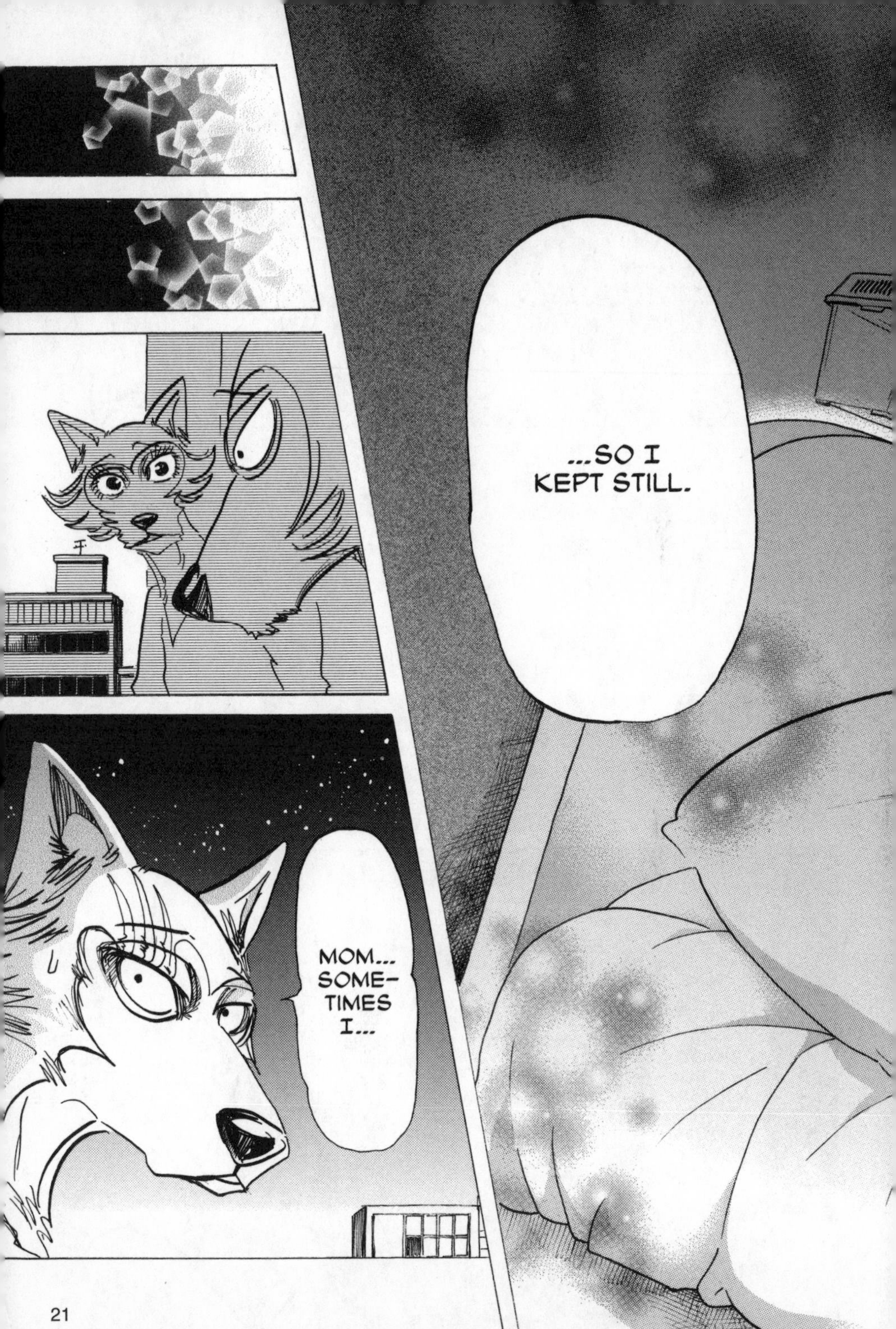
...SO I KEPT STILL.
MOM... SOME-TIMES I...

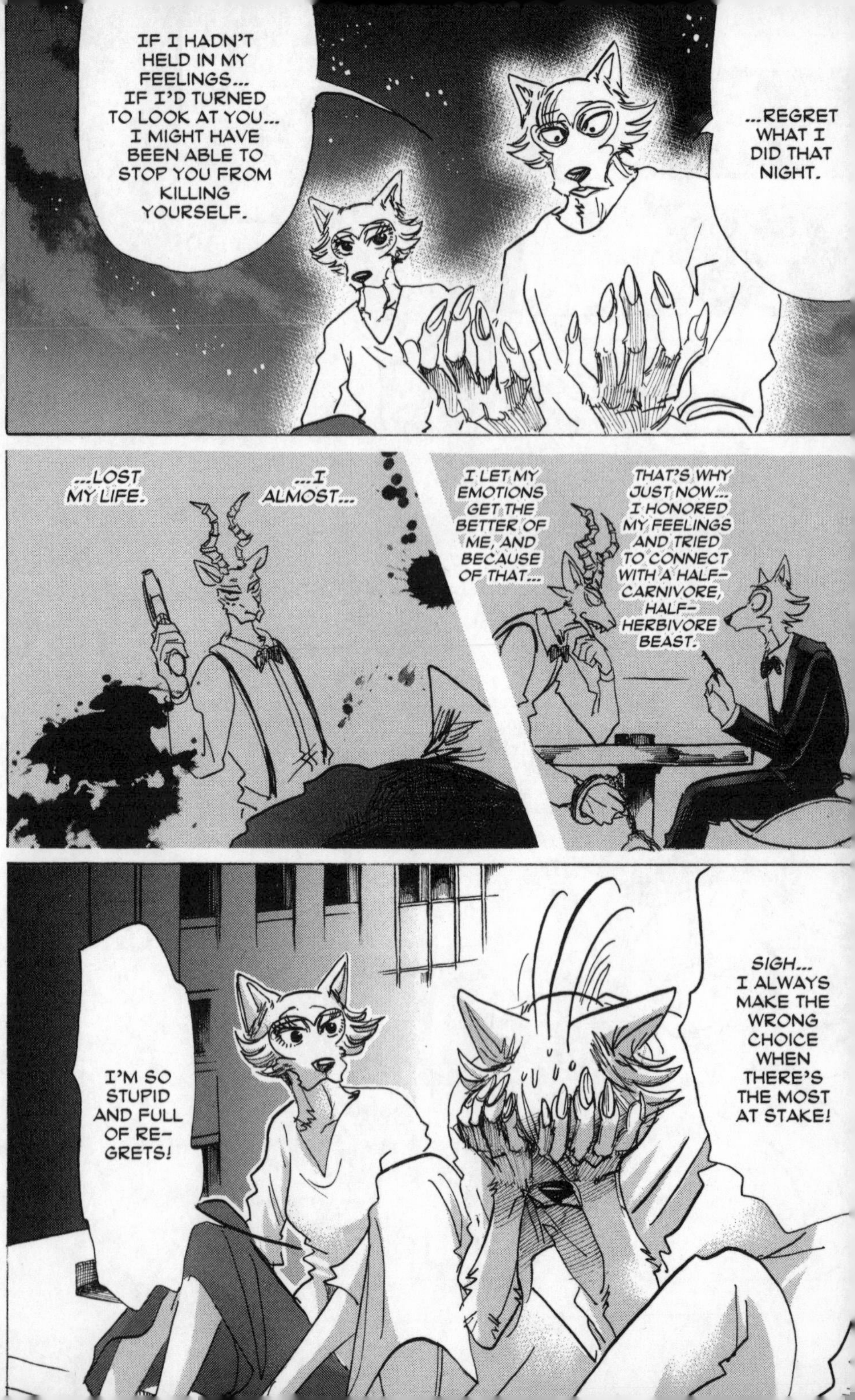
...REGRET WHAT I DID THAT NIGHT.
IF I HADN'T HELD IN MY FEELINGS... IF I'D TURNED TO LOOK AT YOU... I MIGHT HAVE BEEN ABLE TO STOP YOU FROM KILLING YOURSELF.
THAT'S WHY JUST NOW... I HONORED MY FEELINGS AND TRIED TO CONNECT WITH A HALF-CARNIVORE, HALF-HERBIVORE BEAST.
I LET MY EMOTIONS GET THE BETTER OF ME, AND BECAUSE OF THAT...
...I ALMOST...
...LOST MY LIFE.
SIGH... I ALWAYS MAKE THE WRONG CHOICE WHEN THERE'S THE MOST AT STAKE!
I'M SO STUPID AND FULL OF RE-GRETS!

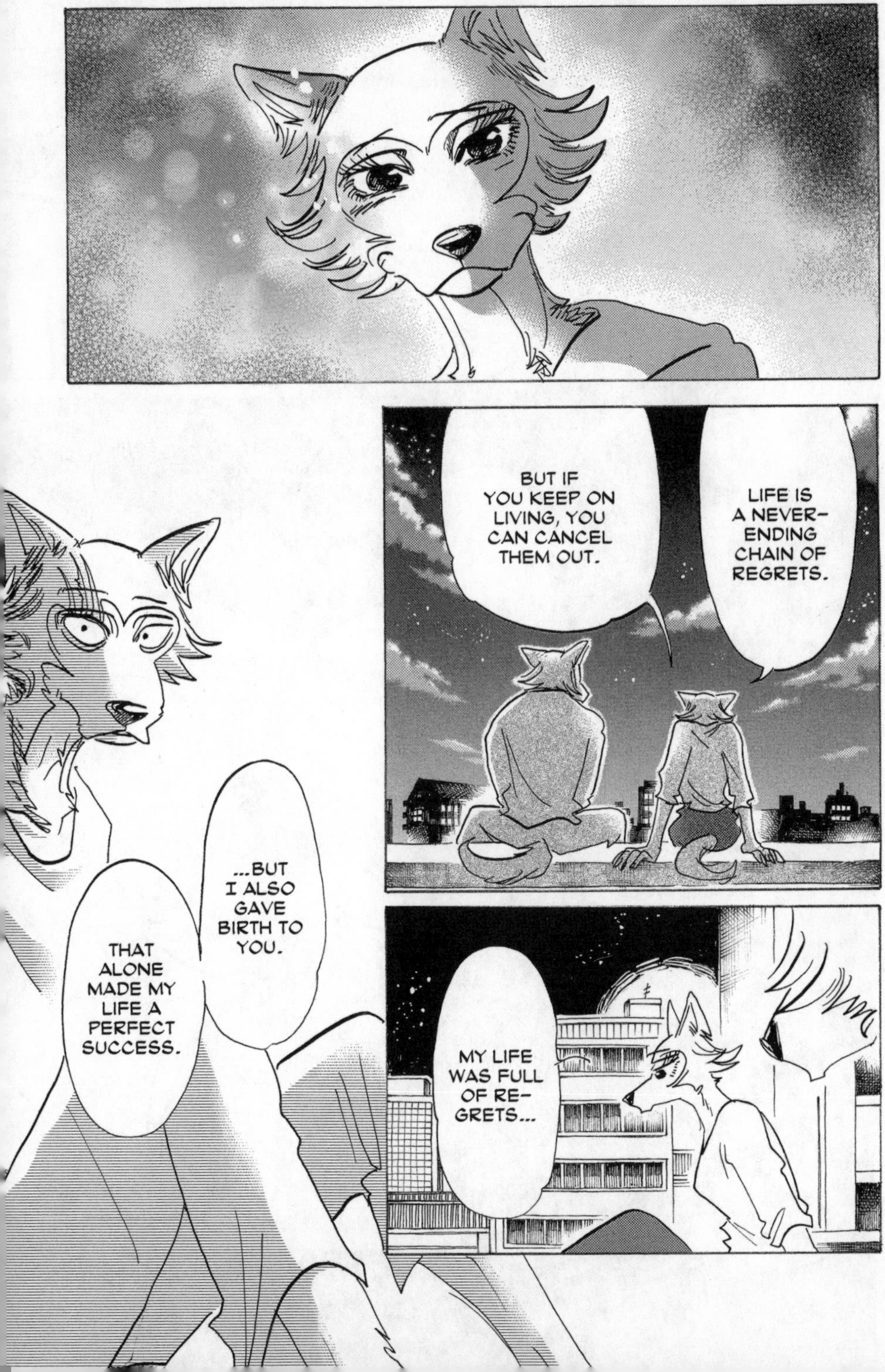
LIFE IS A NEVER-ENDING CHAIN OF REGRETS.
BUT IF YOU KEEP ON LIVING, YOU CAN CANCEL THEM OUT.
MY LIFE WAS FULL OF RE-GRETS...
...BUT I ALSO GAVE BIRTH TO YOU.
THAT ALONE MADE MY LIFE A PERFECT SUCCESS.

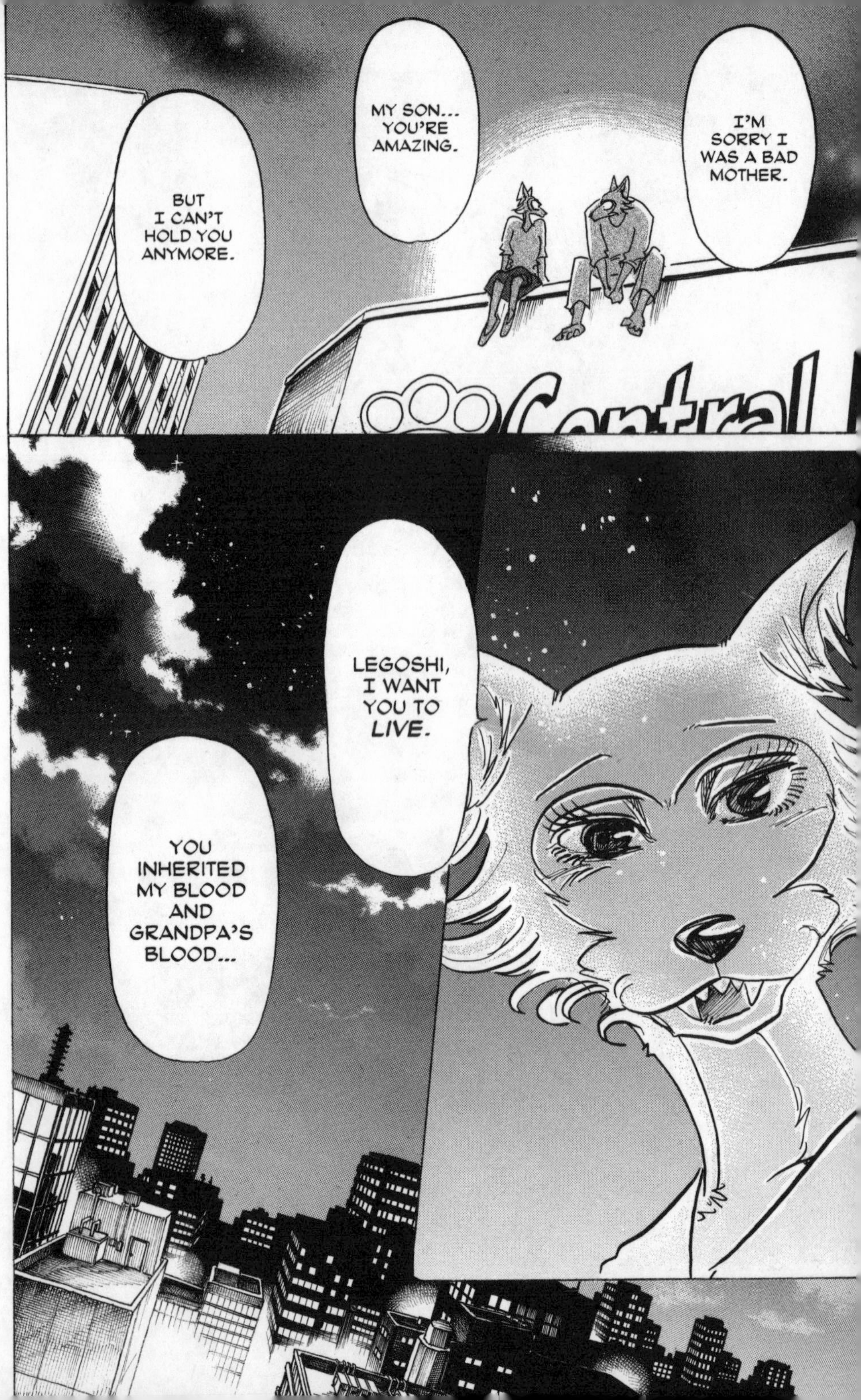
I'M SORRY I WAS A BAD MOTHER.
MY SON... YOU'RE AMAZING.
BUT I CAN'T HOLD YOU ANYMORE.
LEGOSHI, I WANT YOU TO *LIVE.*
YOU INHERITED MY BLOOD AND GRANDPA'S BLOOD...

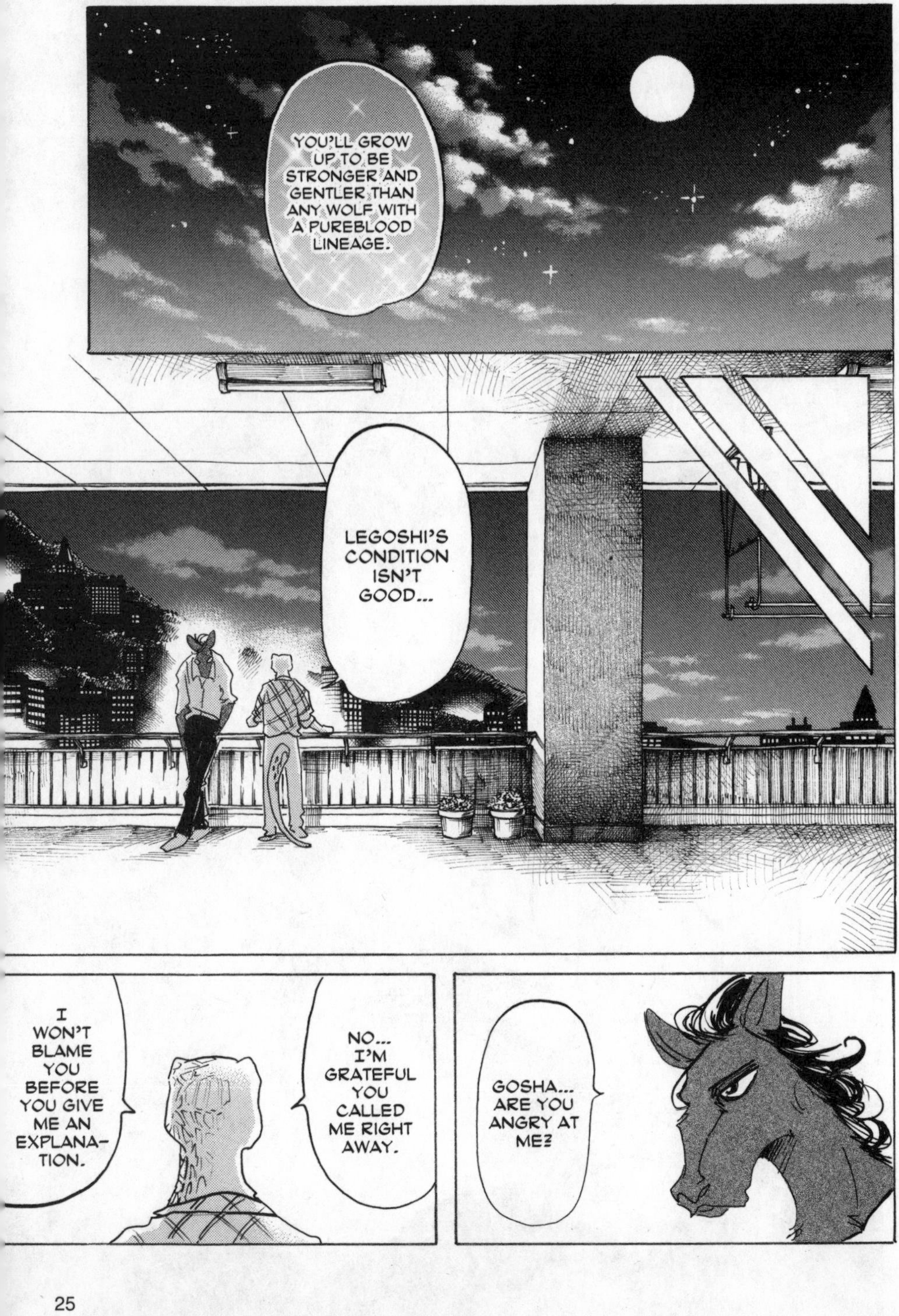
YOU'LL GROW UP TO BE STRONGER AND GENTLER THAN ANY WOLF WITH A PUREBLOOD LINEAGE.
LEGOSHI'S CONDITION ISN'T GOOD...
GOSHA... ARE YOU ANGRY AT ME?
NO... I'M GRATEFUL YOU CALLED ME RIGHT AWAY.
I WON'T BLAME YOU BEFORE YOU GIVE ME AN EXPLANA-TION.

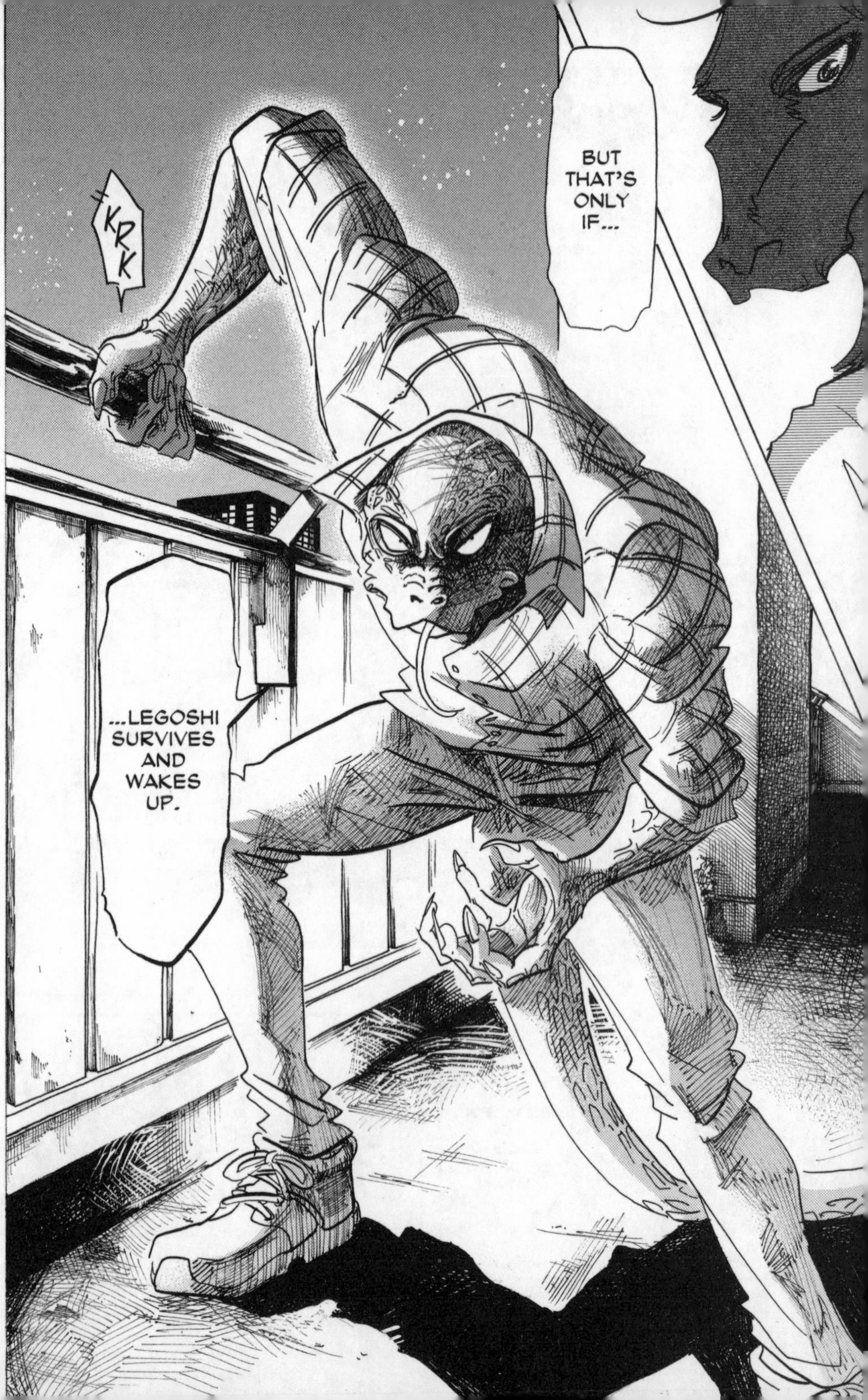
BUT THAT'S ONLY IF...
KRK
...LEGOSHI SURVIVES AND WAKES UP.

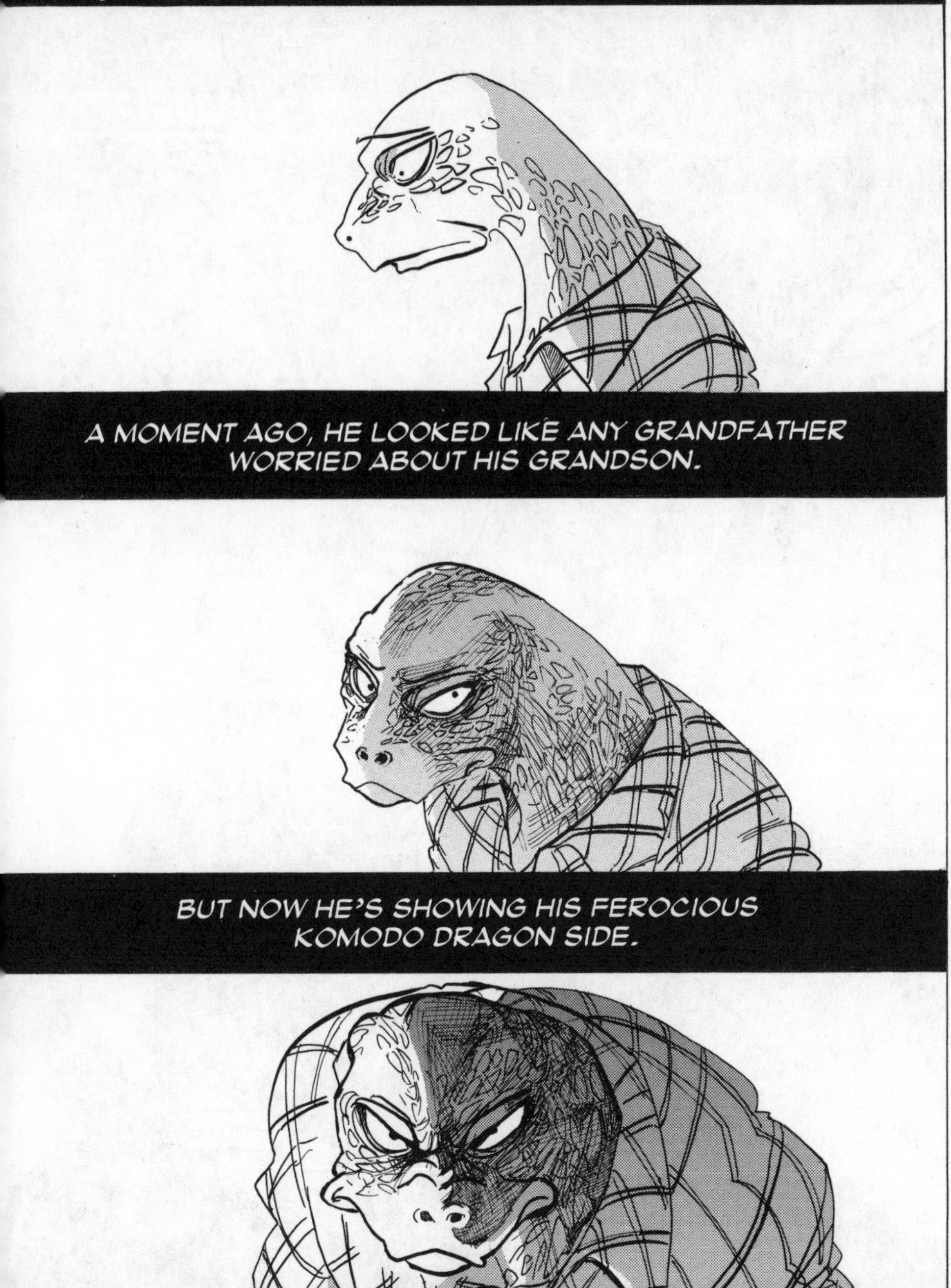
A MOMENT AGO, HE LOOKED LIKE ANY GRANDFATHER WORRIED ABOUT HIS GRANDSON.
BUT NOW HE'S SHOWING HIS FEROCIOUS KOMODO DRAGON SIDE.

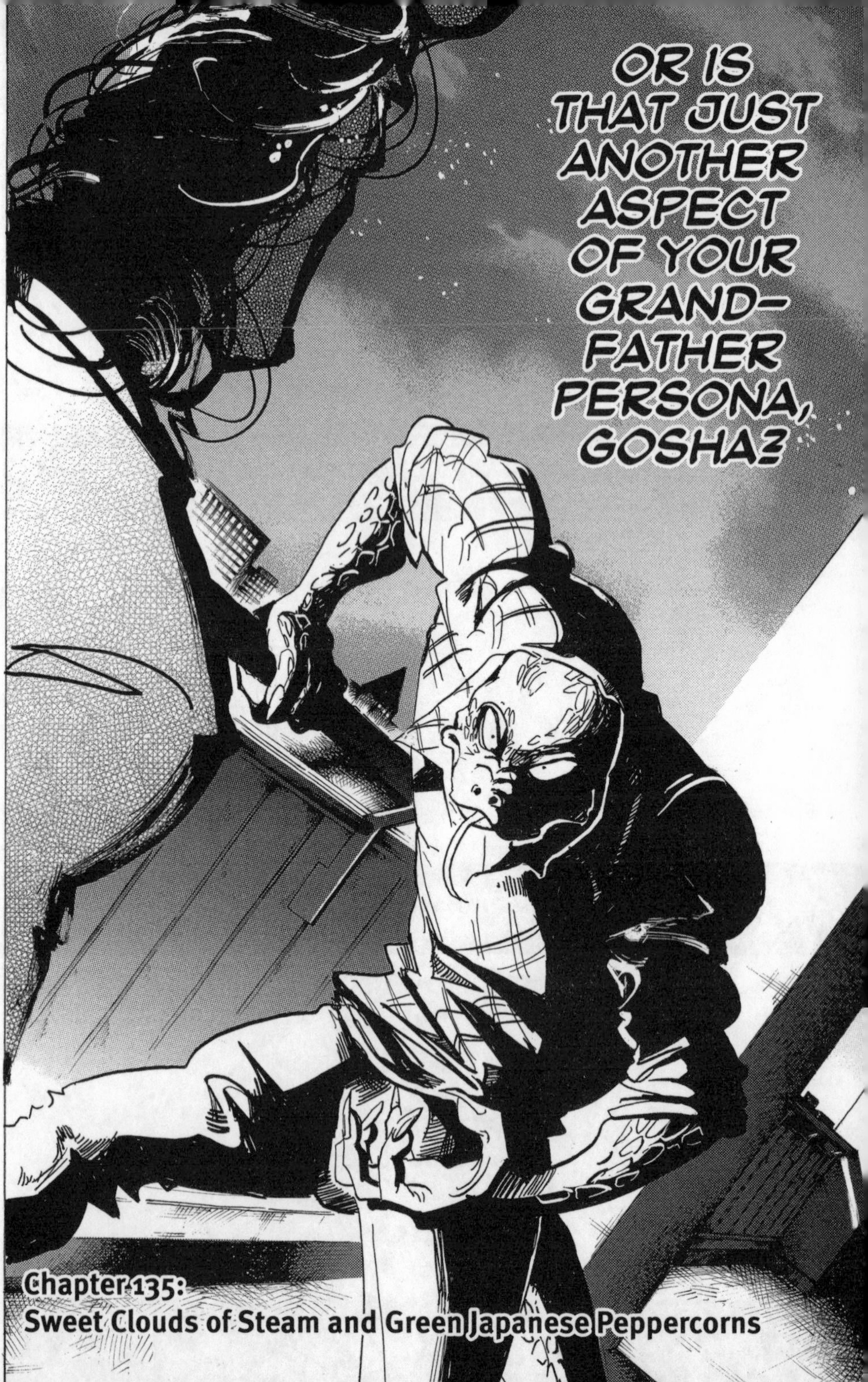
OR IS THAT JUST ANOTHER ASPECT OF YOUR GRAND-FATHER PERSONA, GOSHA?

Chapter 135: Sweet Clouds of Steam and Green Japanese Peppercorns

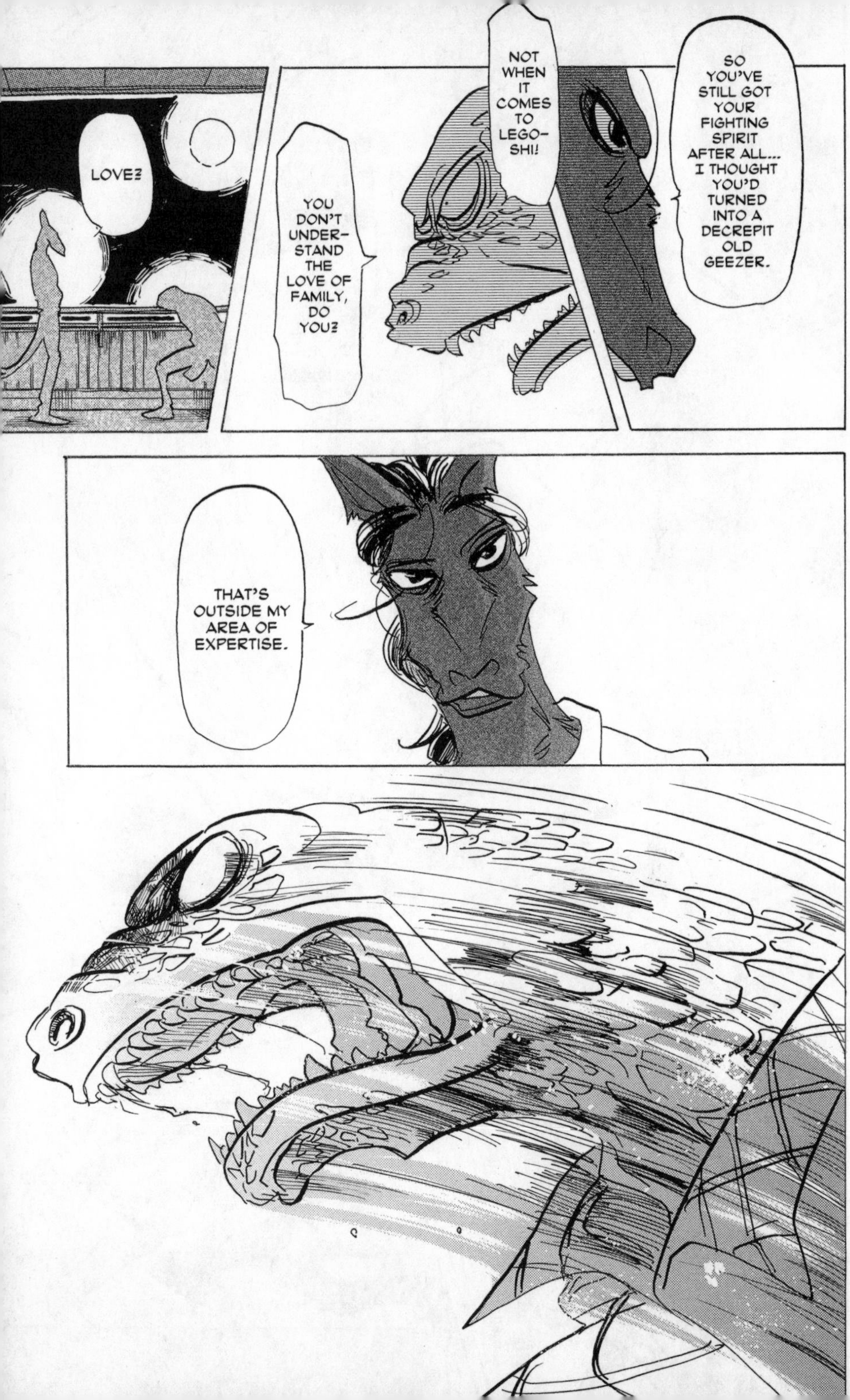
SO YOU'VE STILL GOT YOUR FIGHTING SPIRIT AFTER ALL... I THOUGHT YOU'D TURNED INTO A DECREPIT OLD GEEZER.
NOT WHEN IT COMES TO LEGO-SHI!
YOU DON'T UNDER-STAND THE LOVE OF FAMILY, DO YOU?
LOVE?
THAT'S OUTSIDE MY AREA OF EXPERTISE.

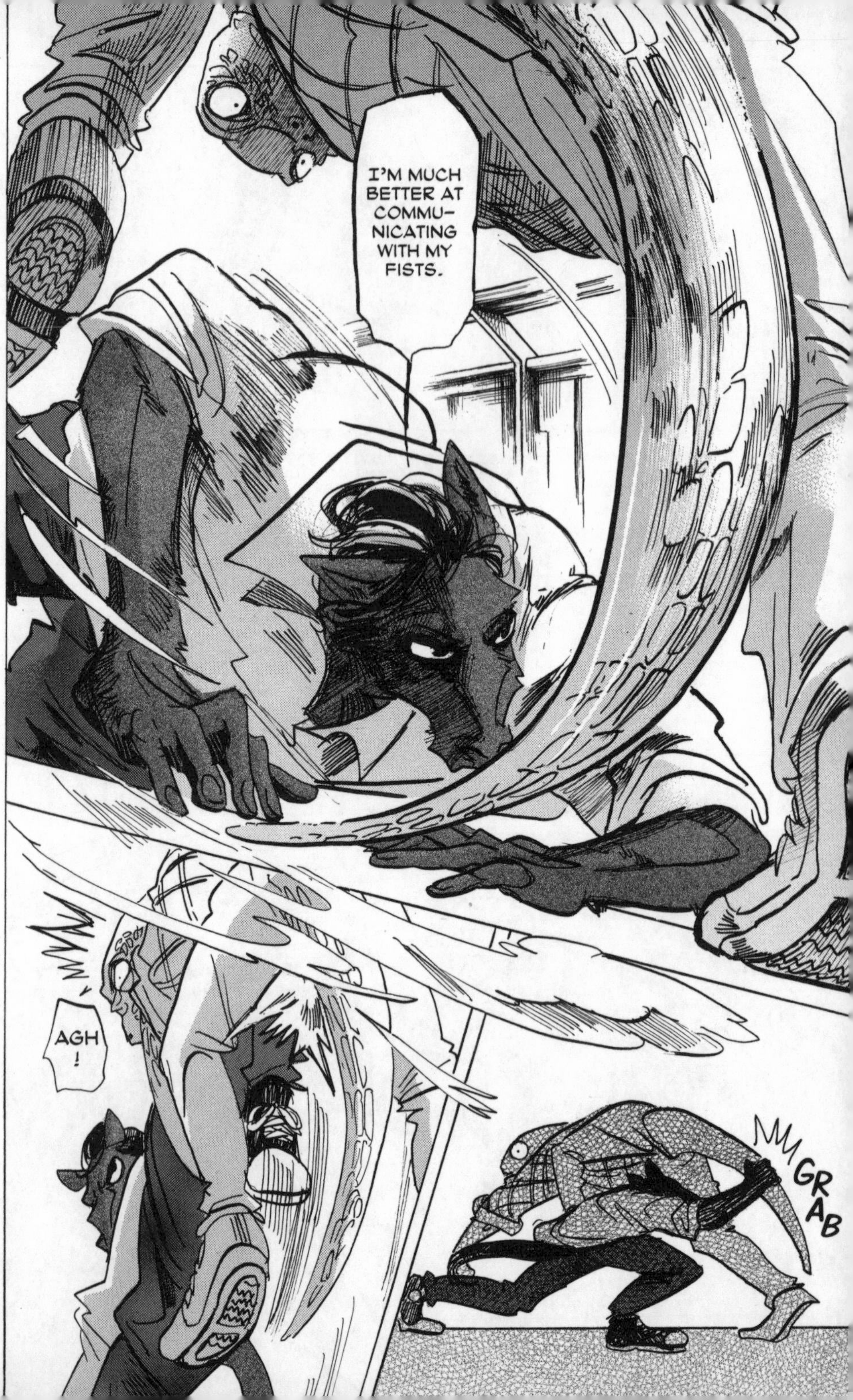
I'M MUCH BETTER AT COMMUNICATING WITH MY FISTS.
GRAB
AGH!

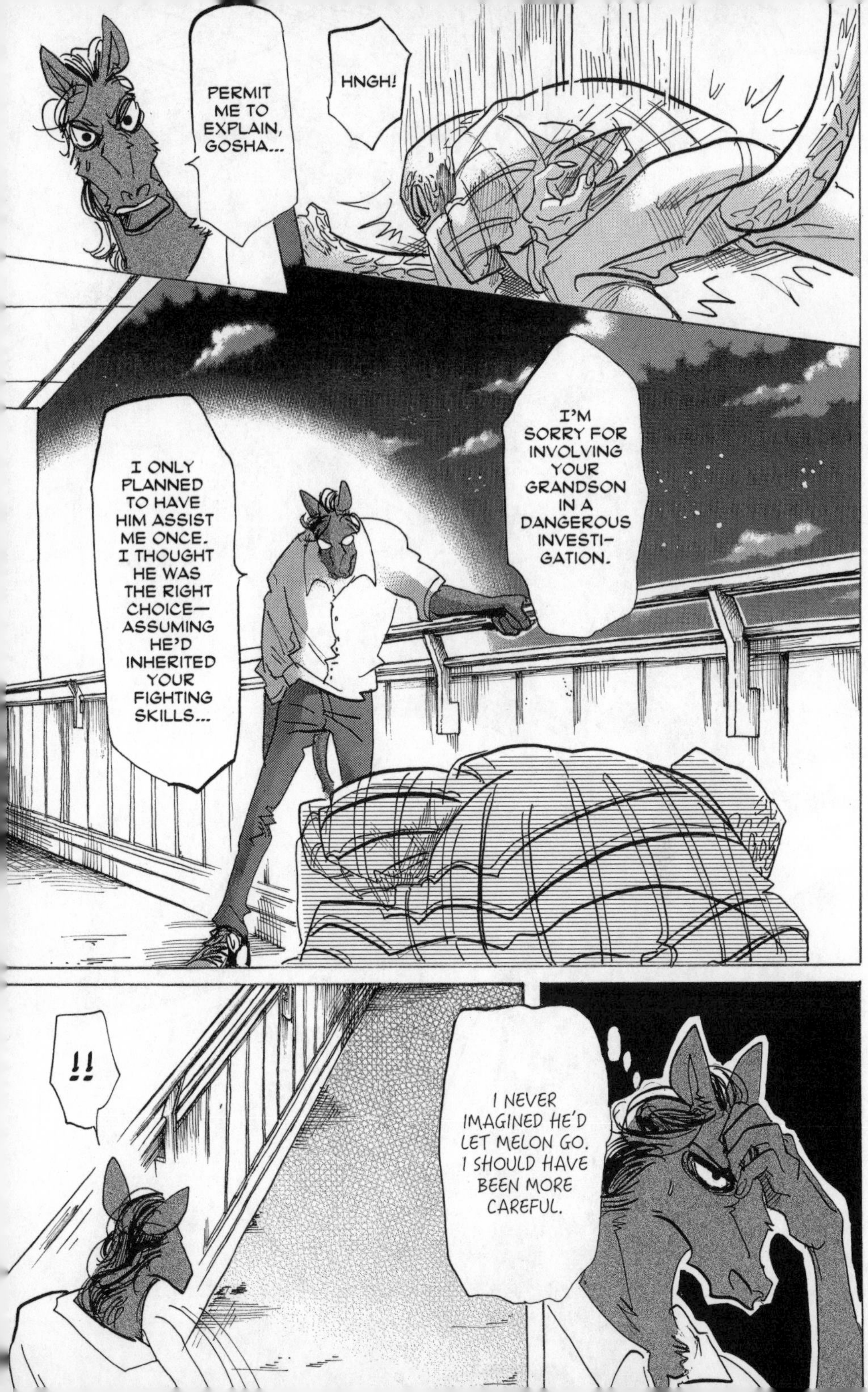
HNGH!
PERMIT ME TO EXPLAIN, GOSHA...
I'M SORRY FOR INVOLVING YOUR GRANDSON IN A DANGEROUS INVESTI-GATION.
I ONLY PLANNED TO HAVE HIM ASSIST ME ONCE. I THOUGHT HE WAS THE RIGHT CHOICE—ASSUMING HE'D INHERITED YOUR FIGHTING SKILLS...
I NEVER IMAGINED HE'D LET MELON GO. I SHOULD HAVE BEEN MORE CAREFUL.
!!

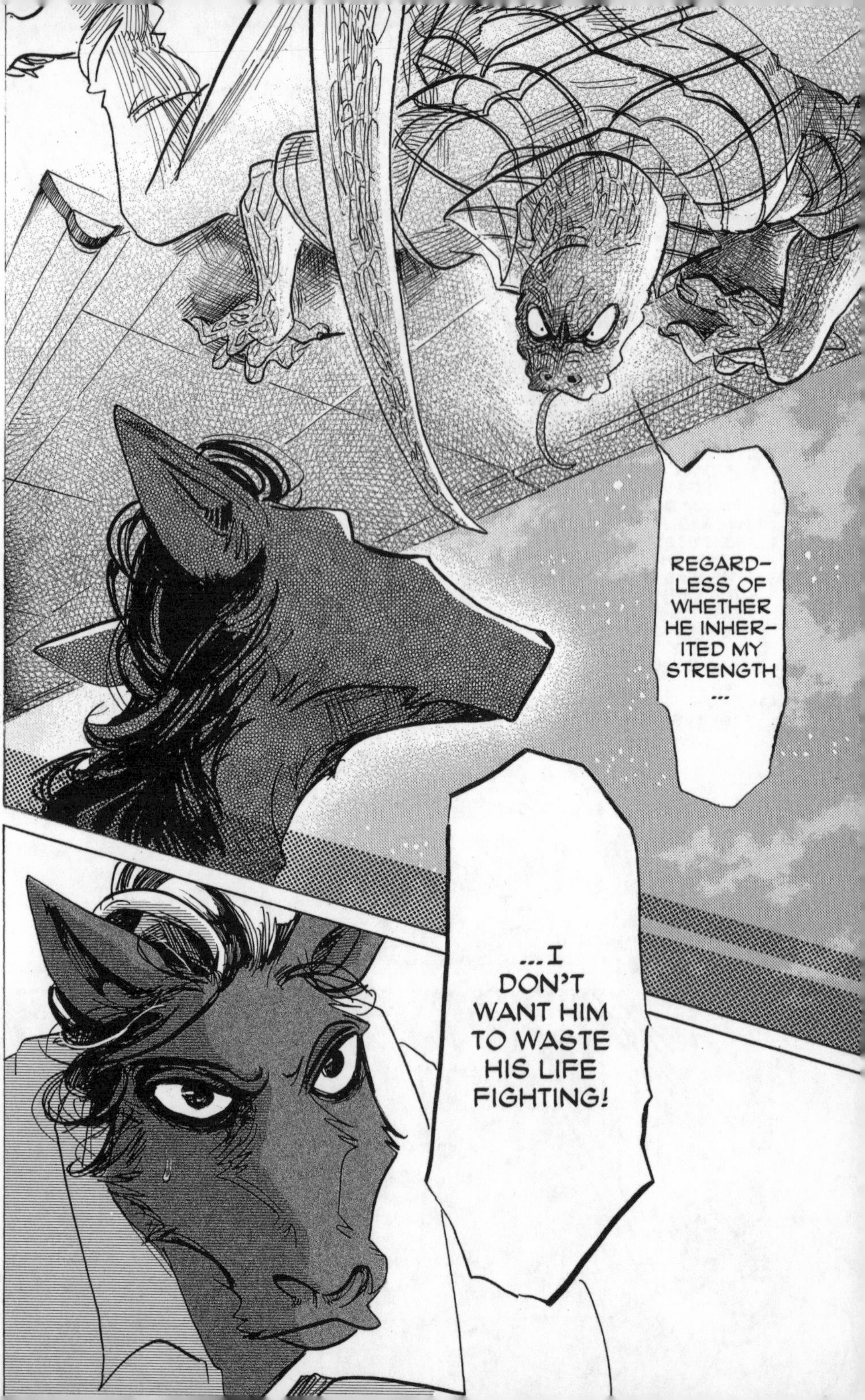
REGARDLESS OF WHETHER HE INHERITED MY STRENGTH ...
...I DON'T WANT HIM TO WASTE HIS LIFE FIGHTING!

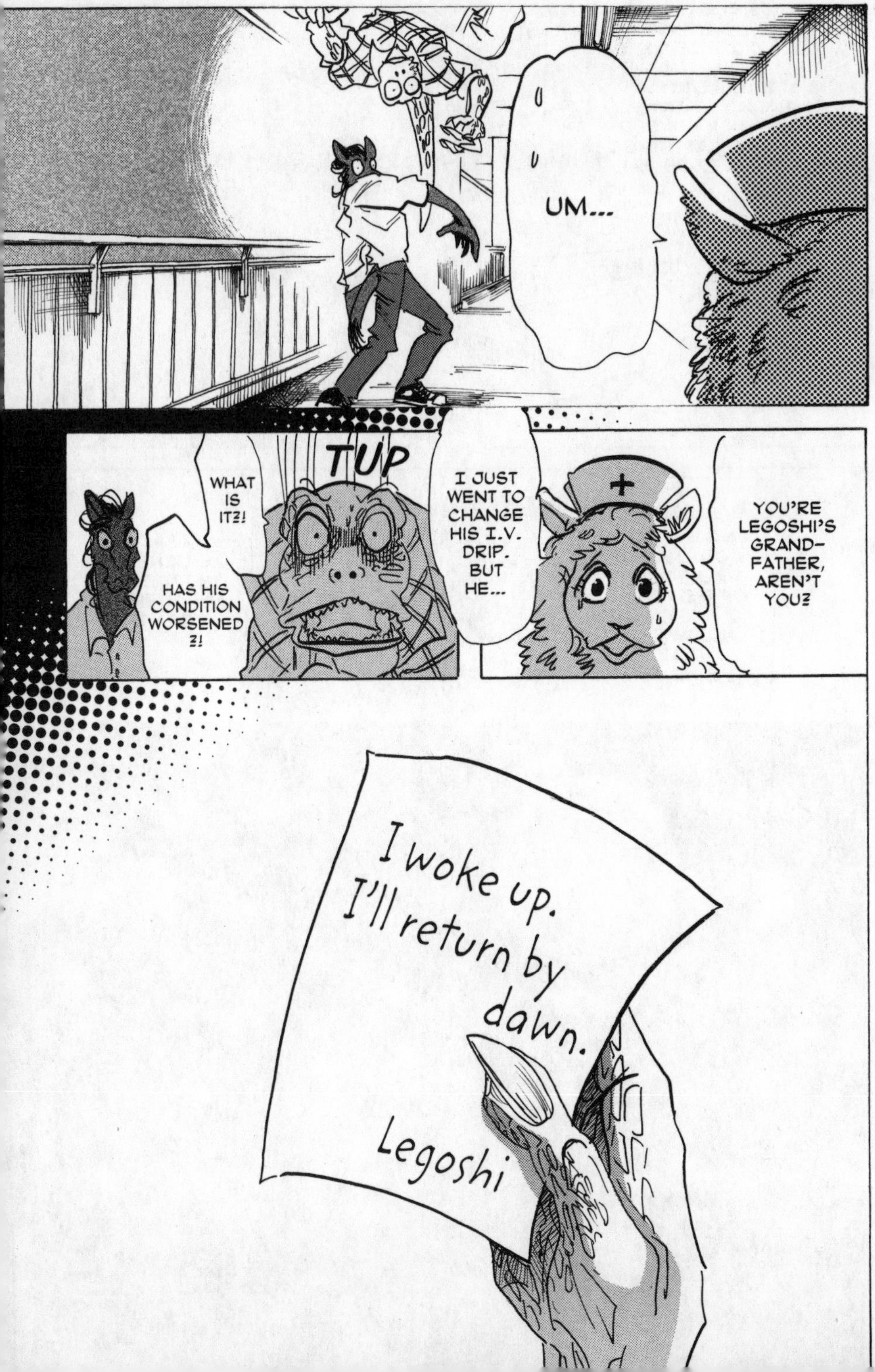
UM...
YOU'RE LEGOSHI'S GRAND-FATHER, AREN'T YOU?
I JUST WENT TO CHANGE HIS I.V. DRIP. BUT HE...
TUP
WHAT IS IT?!
HAS HIS CONDITION WORSENED?!
I woke up. I'll return by dawn.
Legoshi

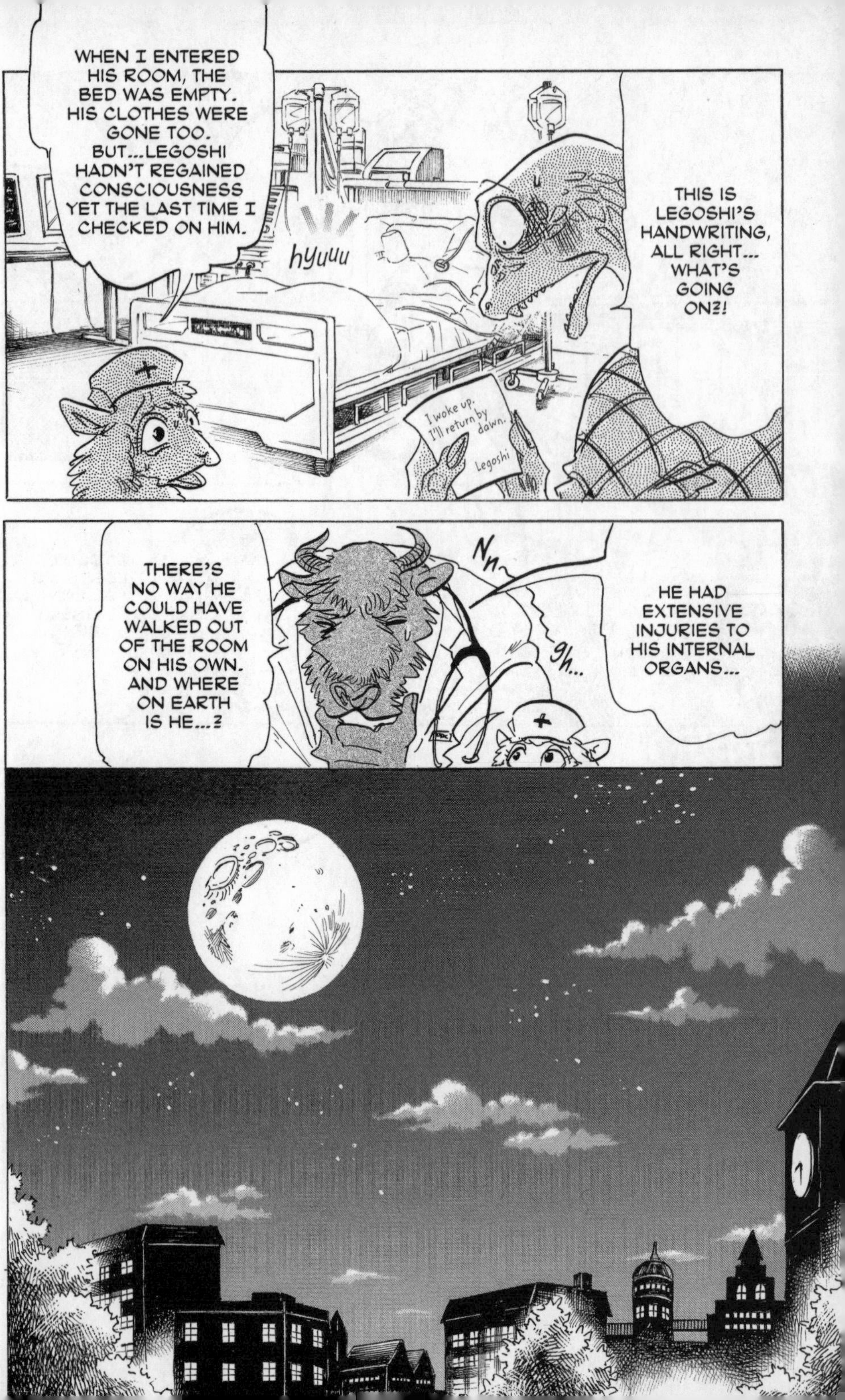
WHEN I ENTERED HIS ROOM, THE BED WAS EMPTY. HIS CLOTHES WERE GONE TOO. BUT...LEGOSHI HADN'T REGAINED CONSCIOUSNESS YET THE LAST TIME I CHECKED ON HIM.
THIS IS LEGOSHI'S HANDWRITING, ALL RIGHT... WHAT'S GOING ON?!
hyuuu
I woke up. I'll return by dawn. Legoshi
HE HAD EXTENSIVE INJURIES TO HIS INTERNAL ORGANS...
Nn
gh...
THERE'S NO WAY HE COULD HAVE WALKED OUT OF THE ROOM ON HIS OWN. AND WHERE ON EARTH IS HE...?

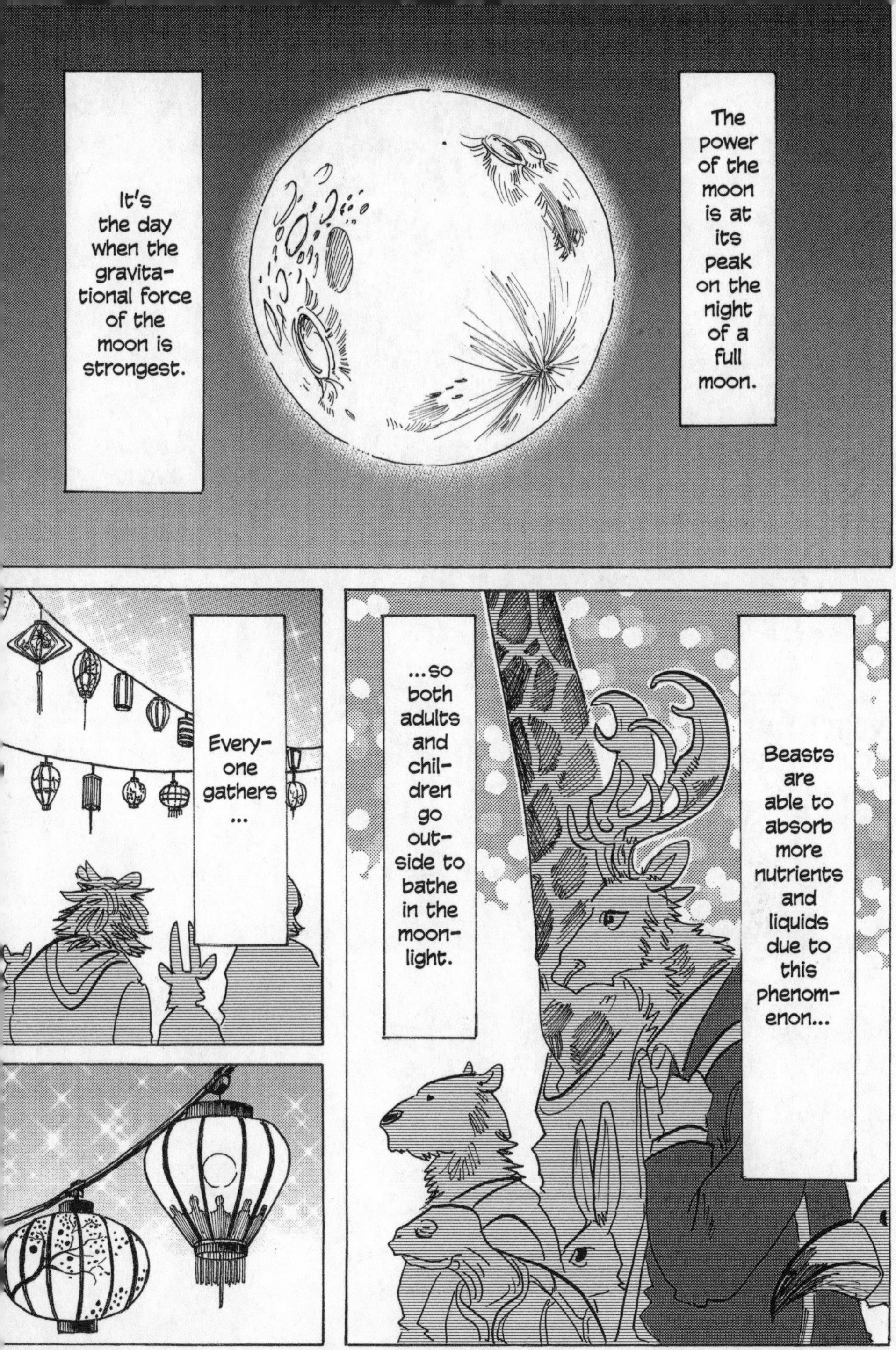

The power of the moon is at its peak on the night of a full moon.
It's the day when the gravitational force of the moon is strongest.
Beasts are able to absorb more nutrients and liquids due to this phenomenon...
...so both adults and children go outside to bathe in the moonlight.
Everyone gathers...

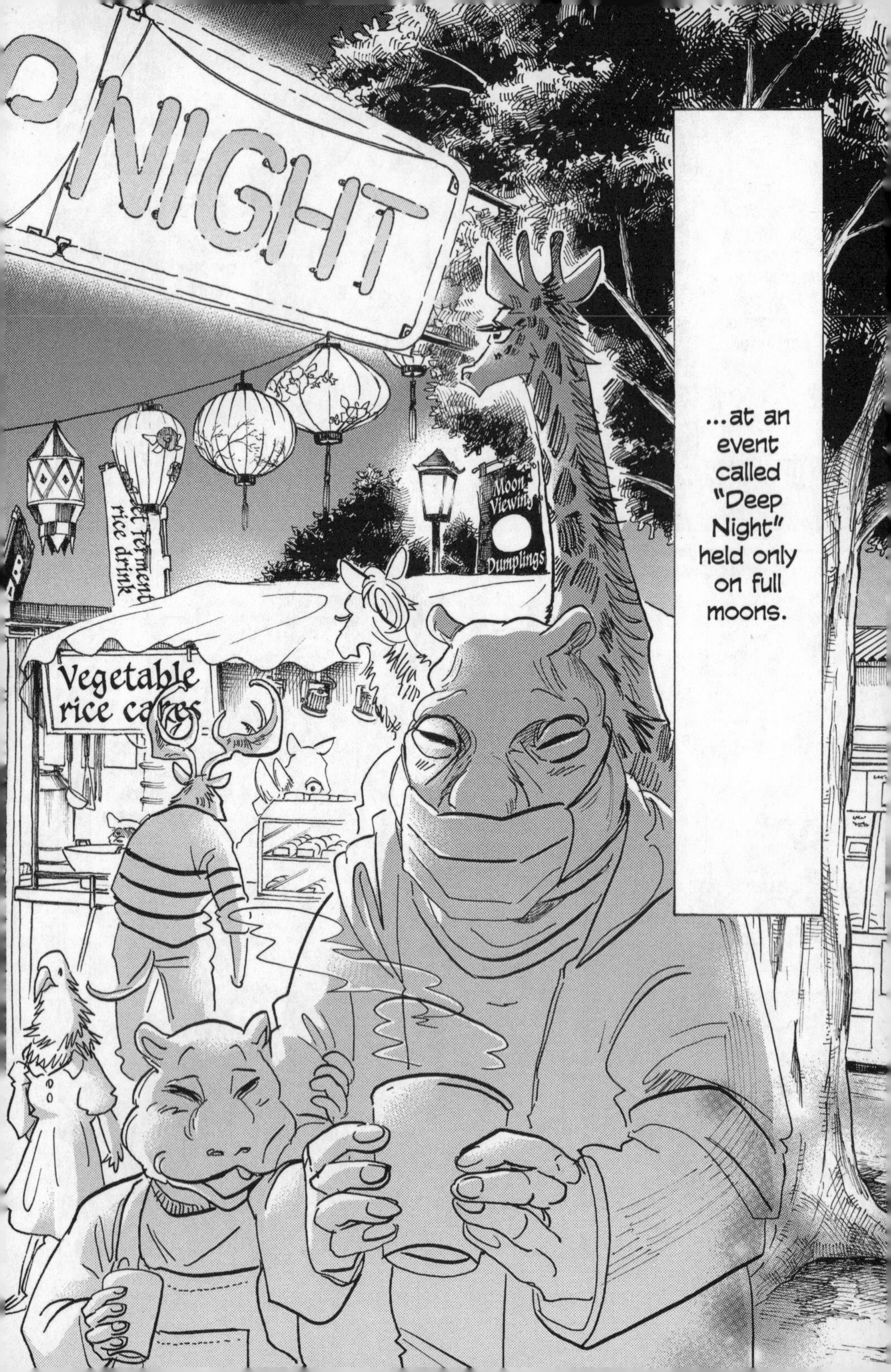
...at an event called "Deep Night" held only on full moons.
NIGHT
Moon Viewing Dumplings
rice drink
Vegetable rice cakes

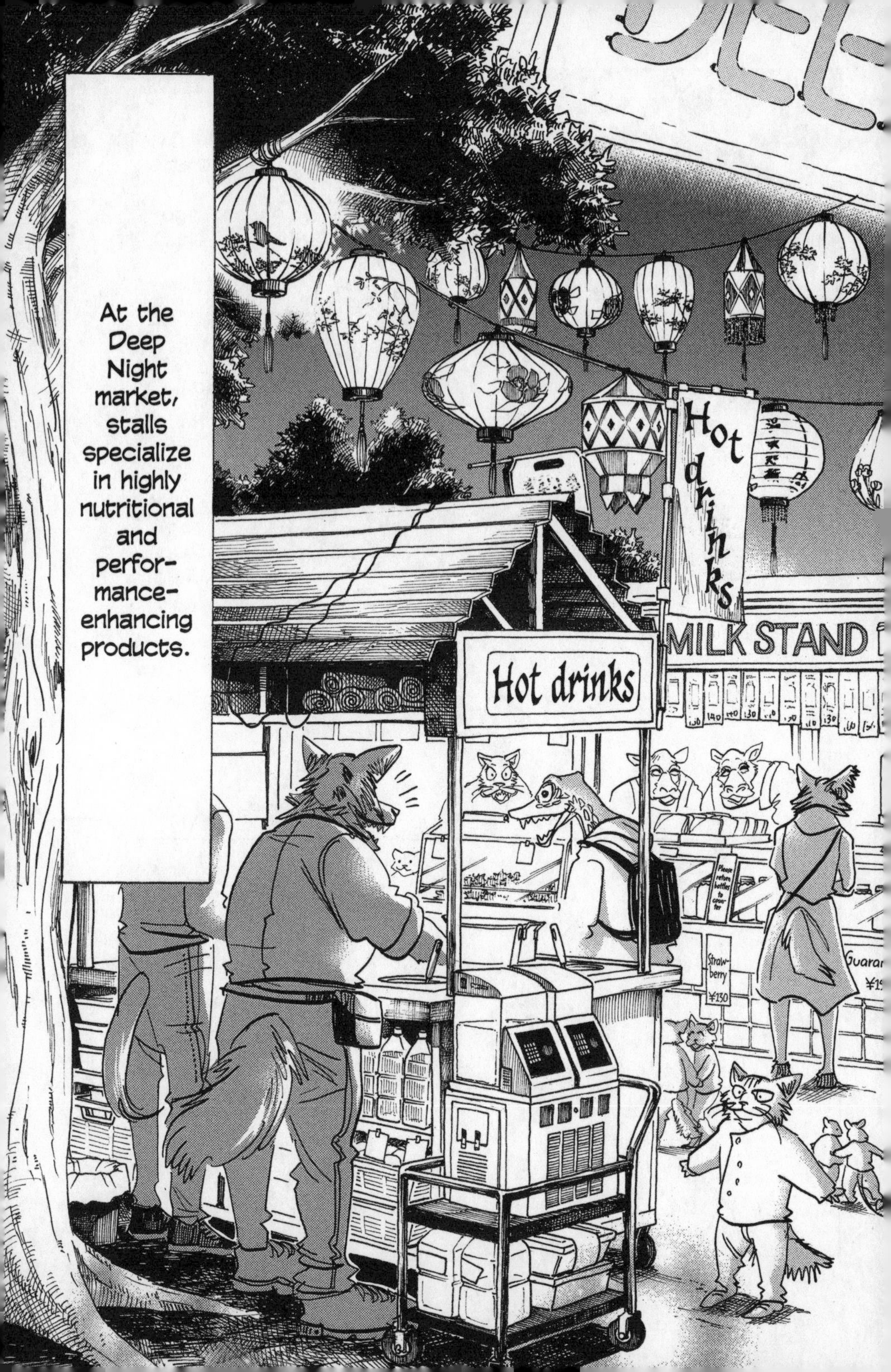
At the Deep Night market, stalls specialize in highly nutritional and performance-enhancing products.
Hot drinks
Hot drinks
MILK STAND
Strawberry ¥130

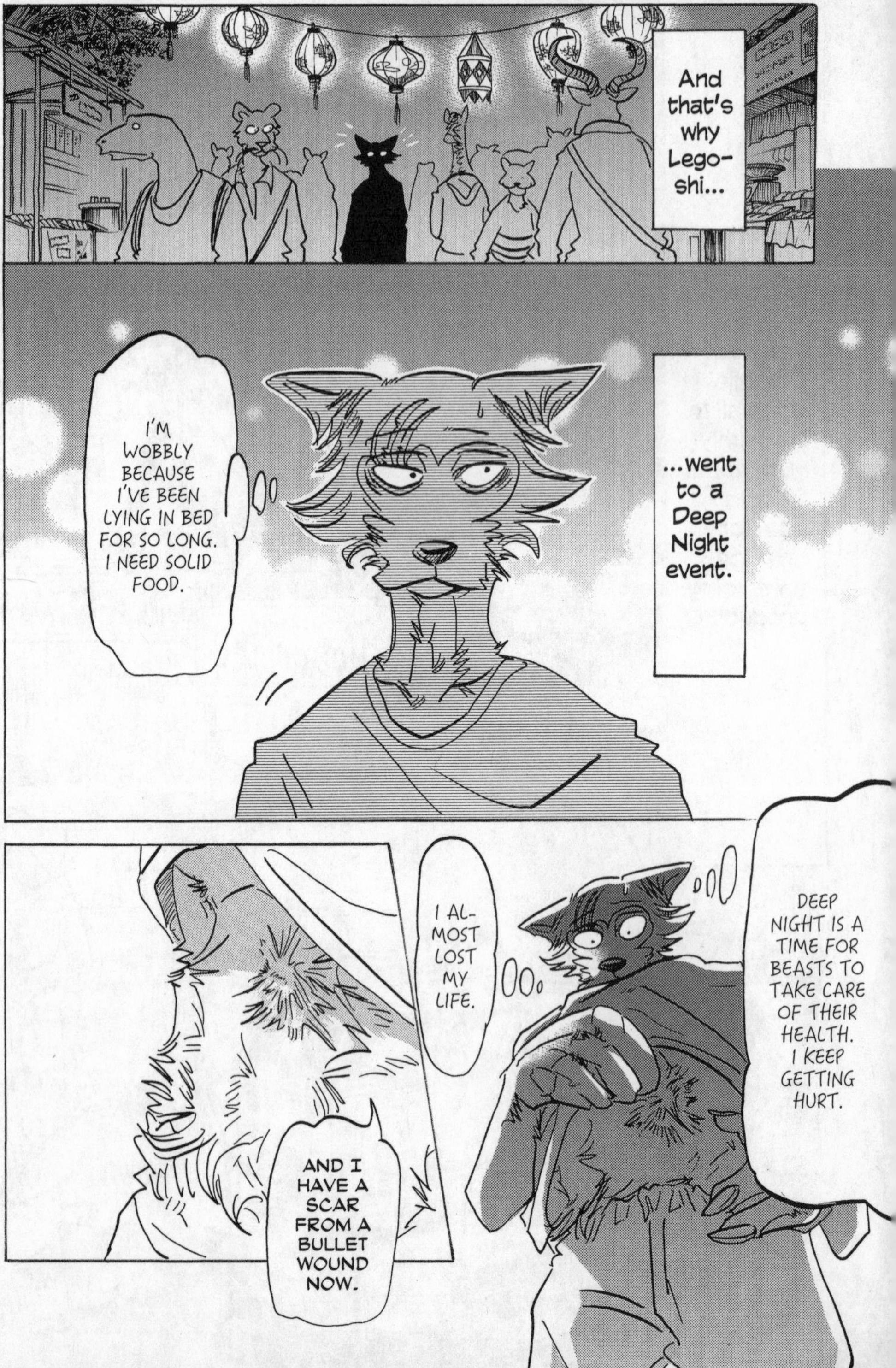
And that's why Lego-shi...
...went to a Deep Night event.
I'M WOBBLY BECAUSE I'VE BEEN LYING IN BED FOR SO LONG. I NEED SOLID FOOD.
DEEP NIGHT IS A TIME FOR BEASTS TO TAKE CARE OF THEIR HEALTH. I KEEP GETTING HURT.
I AL-MOST LOST MY LIFE.
AND I HAVE A SCAR FROM A BULLET WOUND NOW.

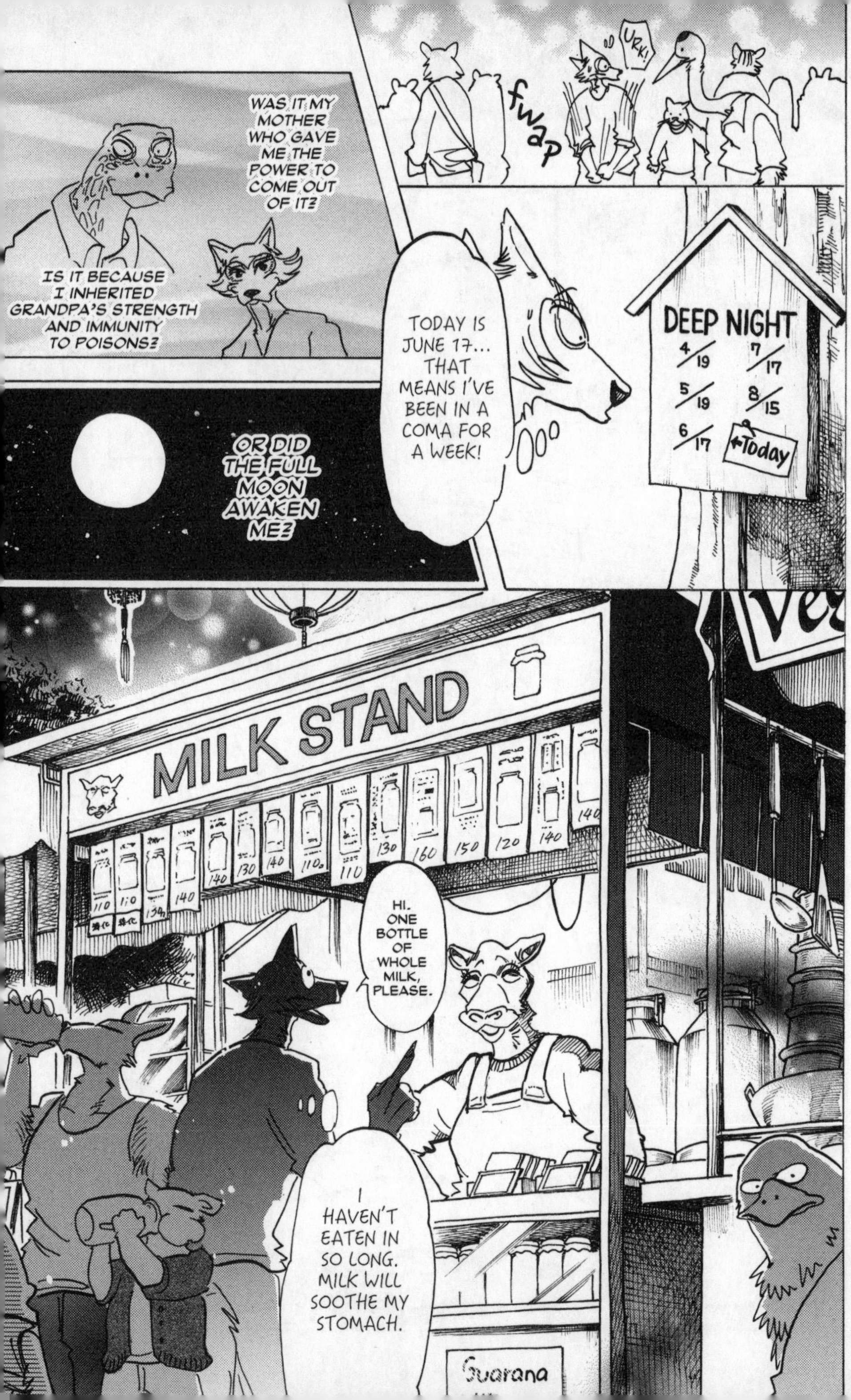
URK!
fwap
TODAY IS JUNE 17... THAT MEANS I'VE BEEN IN A COMA FOR A WEEK!
DEEP NIGHT
4/19
5/19
6/17
7/17
8/15
←Today
WAS IT MY MOTHER WHO GAVE ME THE POWER TO COME OUT OF IT?
IS IT BECAUSE I INHERITED GRANDPA'S STRENGTH AND IMMUNITY TO POISONS?
OR DID THE FULL MOON AWAKEN ME?
MILK STAND
HI. ONE BOTTLE OF WHOLE MILK, PLEASE.
I HAVEN'T EATEN IN SO LONG. MILK WILL SOOTHE MY STOMACH.
Guarana

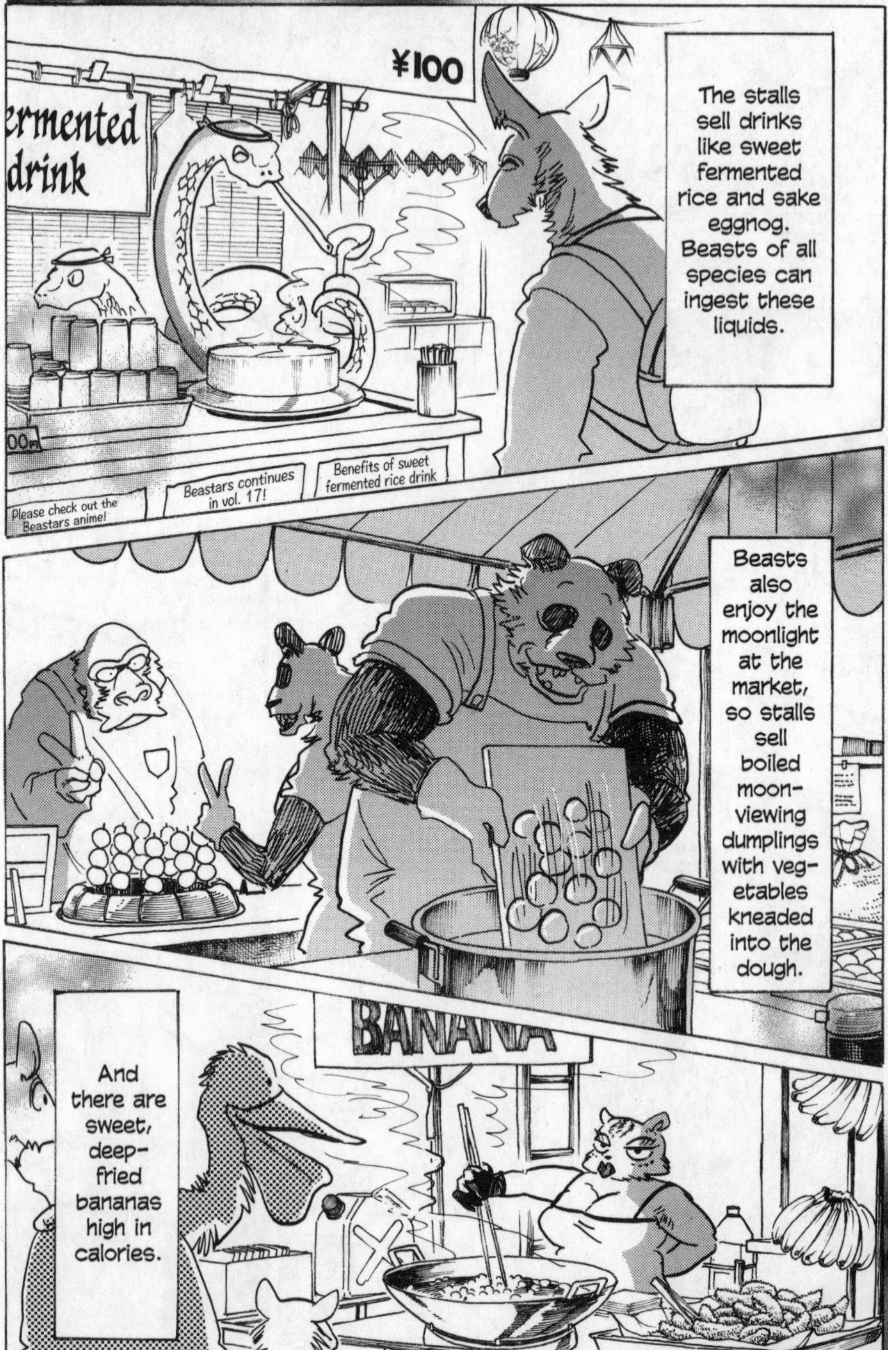

The stalls sell drinks like sweet fermented rice and sake eggnog. Beasts of all species can ingest these liquids.
¥100
ermented drink
Benefits of sweet fermented rice drink
Beastars continues in vol. 17!
Please check out the Beastars anime!
Beasts also enjoy the moonlight at the market, so stalls sell boiled moon-viewing dumplings with veg-etables kneaded into the dough.
BANANA
And there are sweet, deep-fried bananas high in calories.

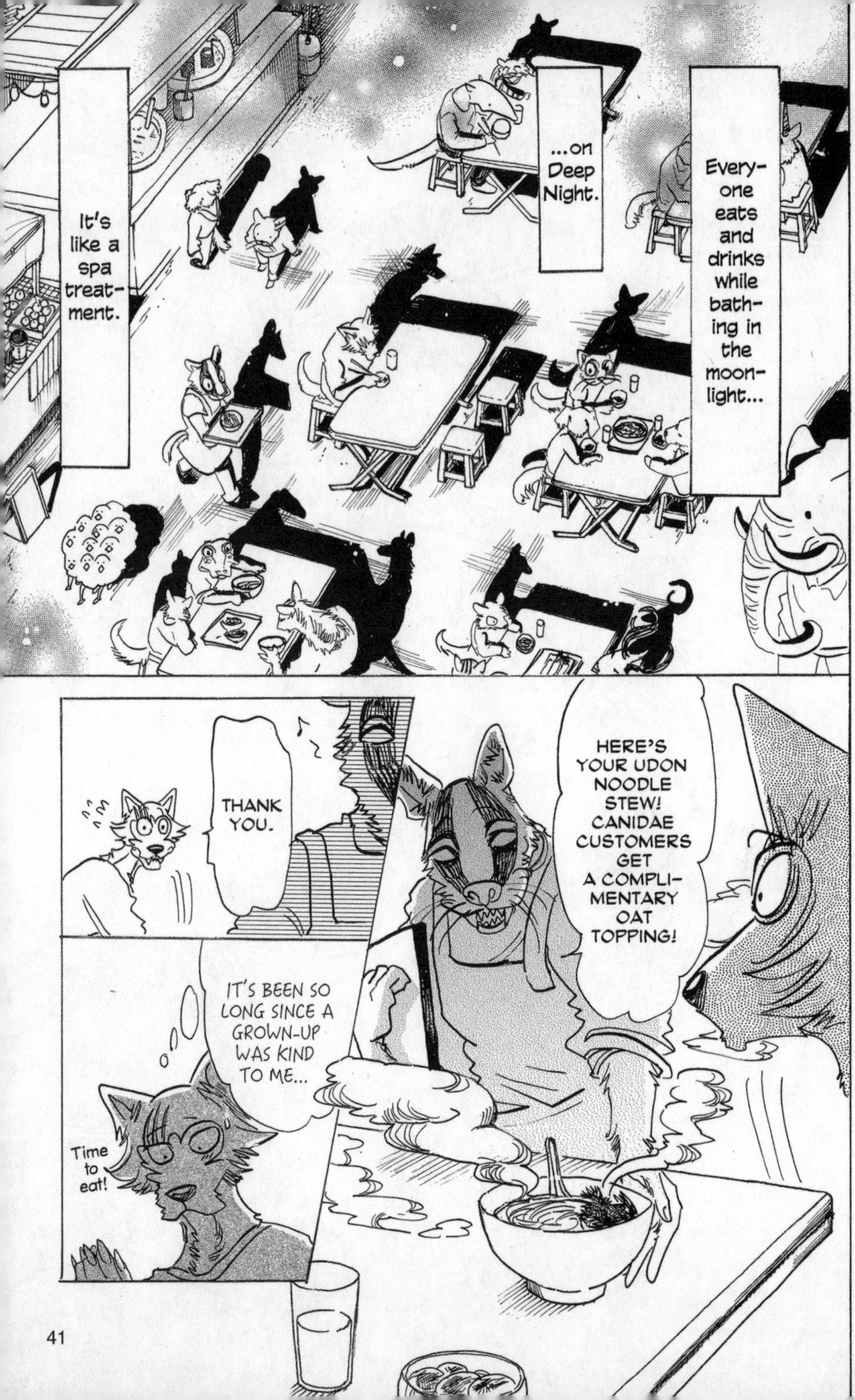
Every-one eats and drinks while bath-ing in the moon-light...
...on Deep Night.
It's like a spa treat-ment.
HERE'S YOUR UDON NOODLE STEW! CANIDAE CUSTOMERS GET A COMPLI-MENTARY OAT TOPPING!
THANK YOU.
IT'S BEEN SO LONG SINCE A GROWN-UP WAS KIND TO ME...
Time to eat!

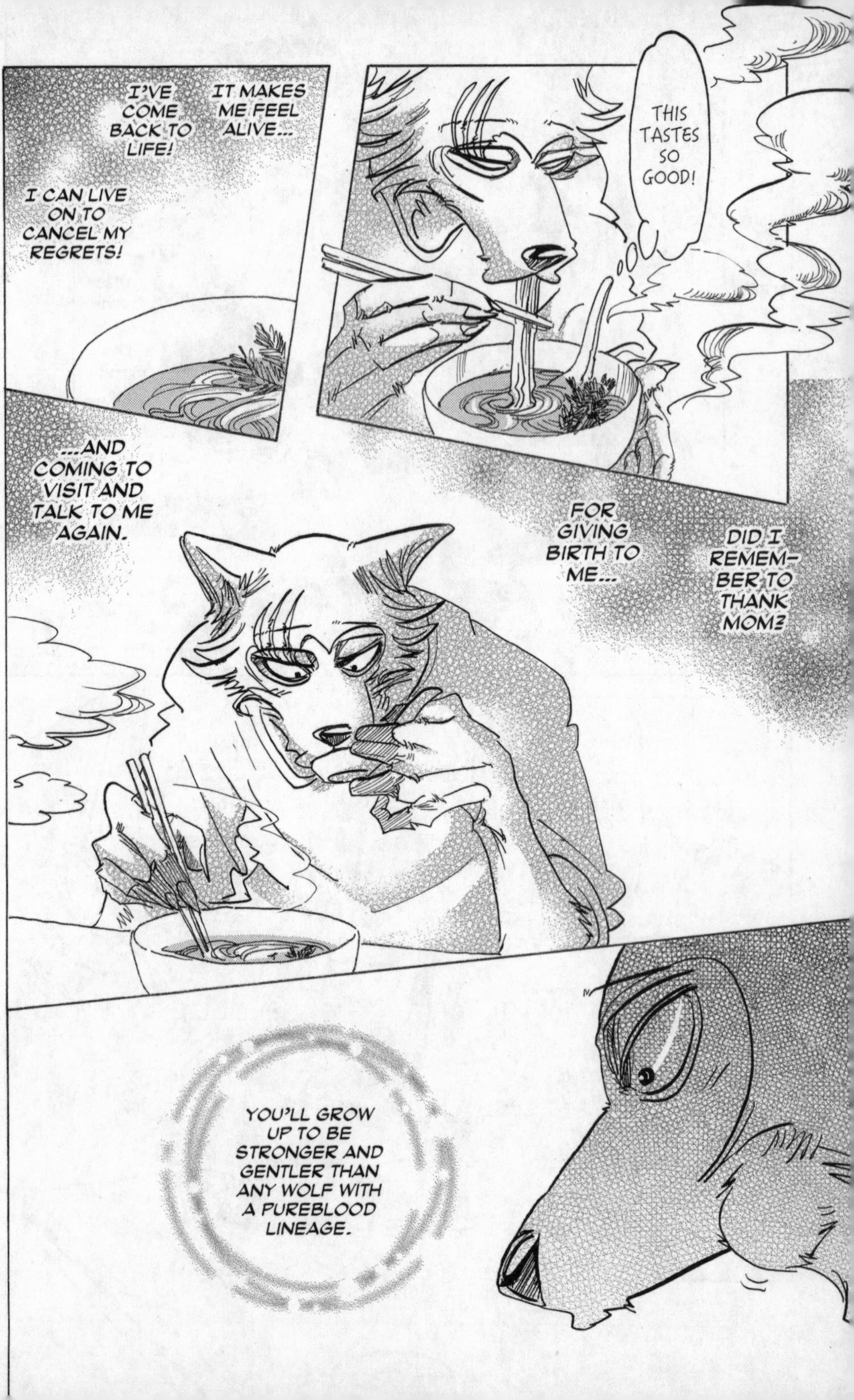
THIS TASTES SO GOOD!
IT MAKES ME FEEL ALIVE...
I'VE COME BACK TO LIFE!
I CAN LIVE ON TO CANCEL MY REGRETS!
DID I REMEMBER TO THANK MOM?
FOR GIVING BIRTH TO ME...
...AND COMING TO VISIT AND TALK TO ME AGAIN.
YOU'LL GROW UP TO BE STRONGER AND GENTLER THAN ANY WOLF WITH A PUREBLOOD LINEAGE.

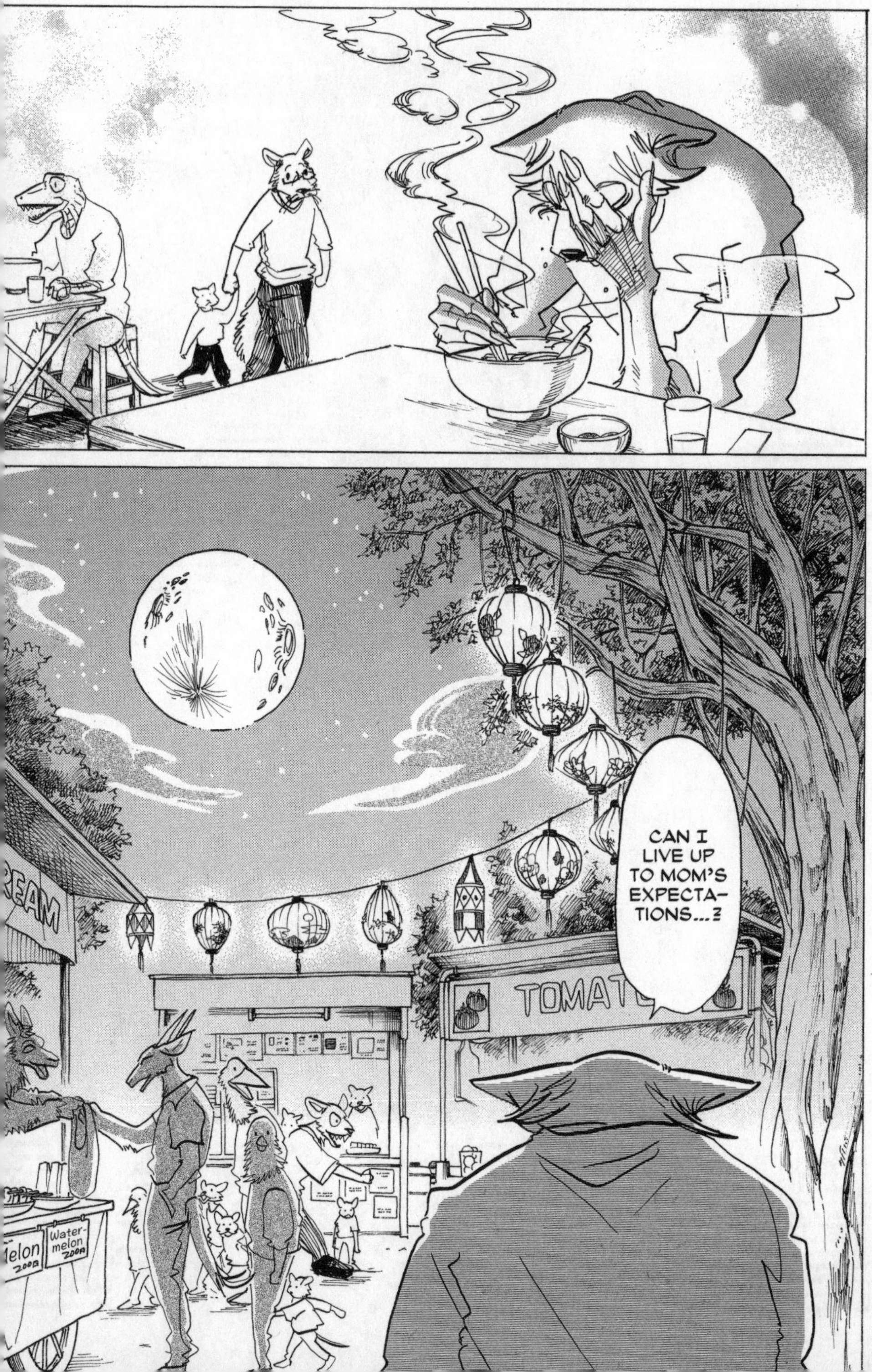
CAN I LIVE UP TO MOM'S EXPECTATIONS...?
Water-melon

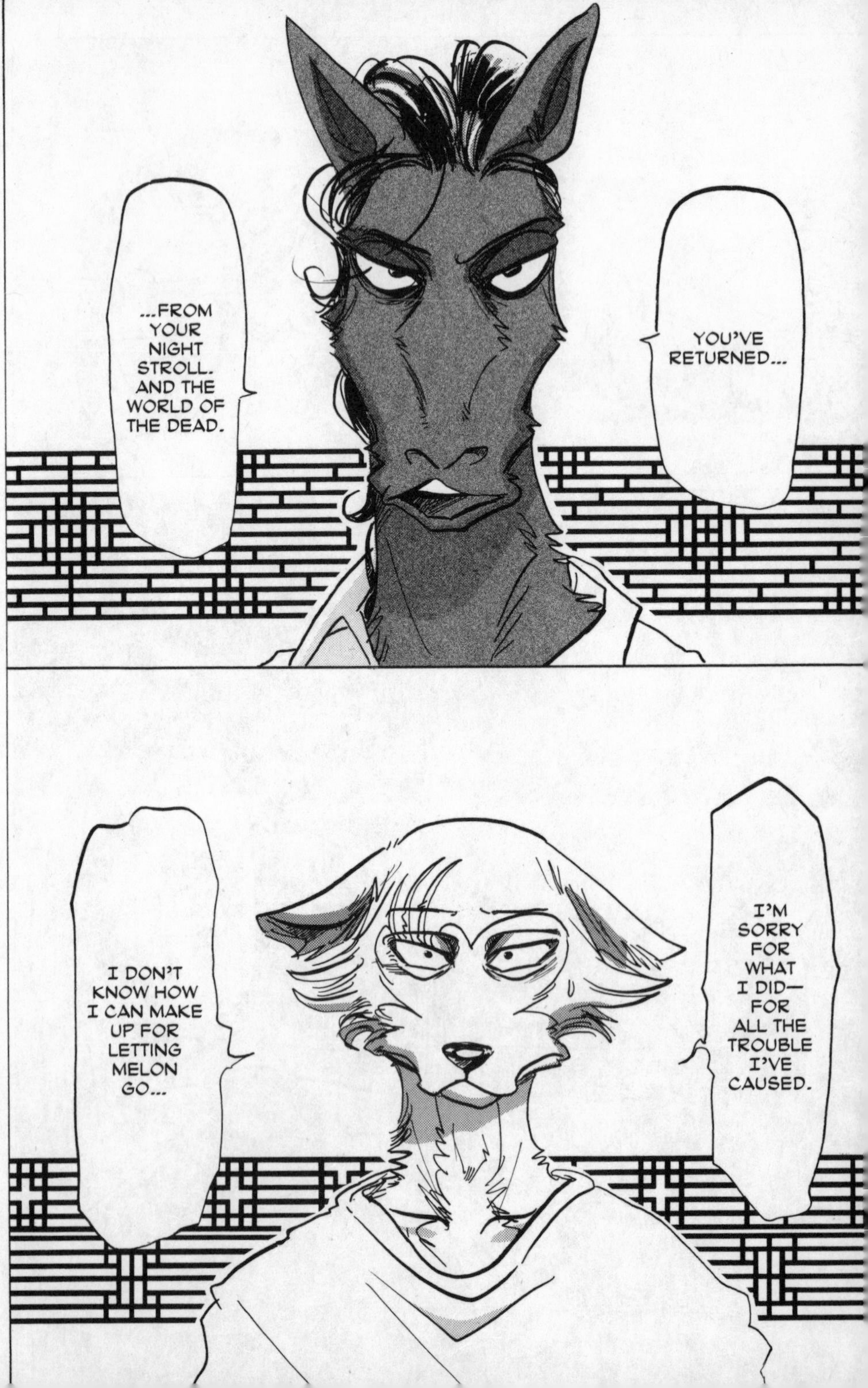
YOU'VE RETURNED...
...FROM YOUR NIGHT STROLL. AND THE WORLD OF THE DEAD.
I'M SORRY FOR WHAT I DID—FOR ALL THE TROUBLE I'VE CAUSED.
I DON'T KNOW HOW I CAN MAKE UP FOR LETTING MELON GO...

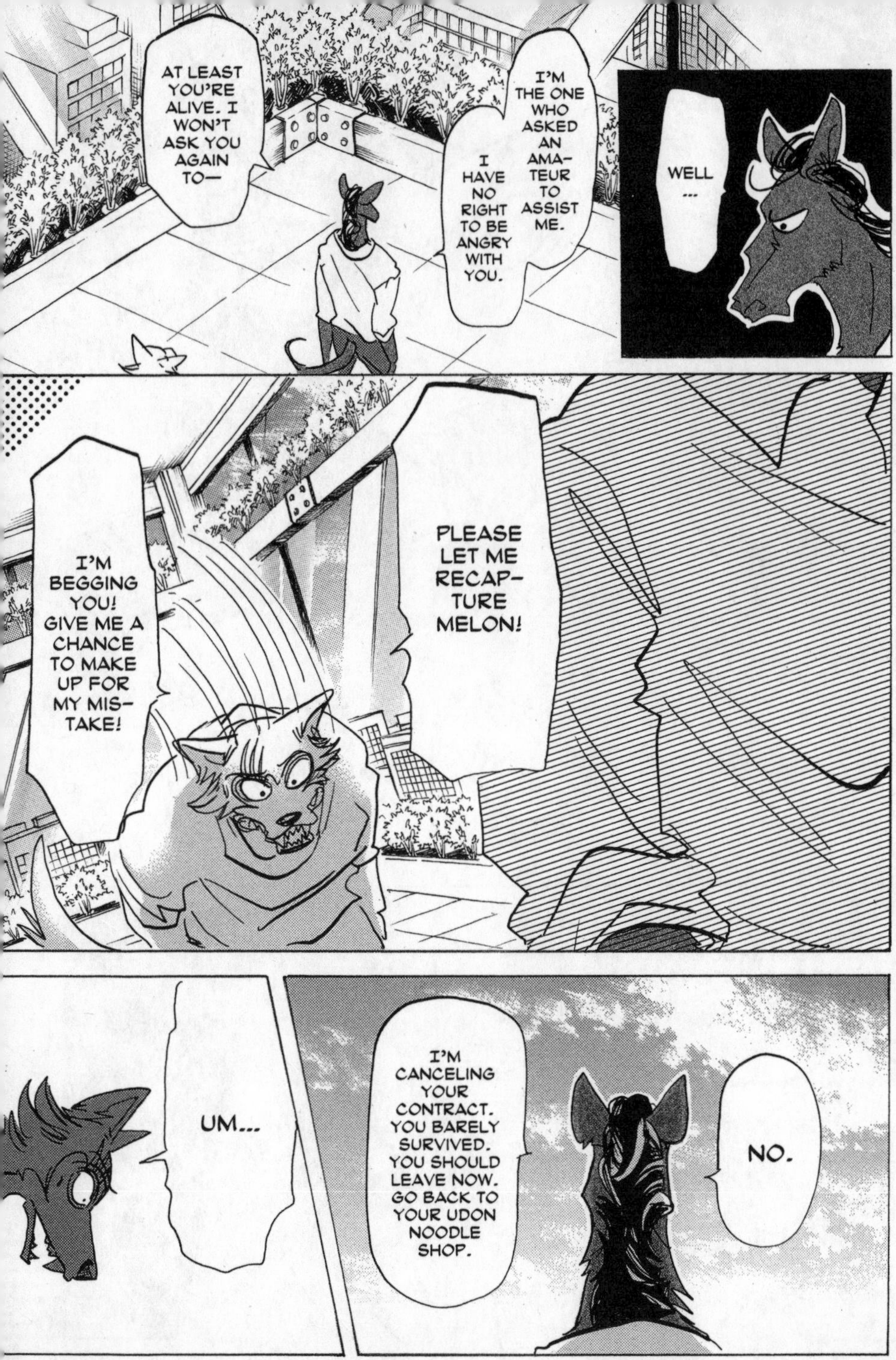
WELL ...
I'M THE ONE WHO ASKED AN AMATEUR TO ASSIST ME.
I HAVE NO RIGHT TO BE ANGRY WITH YOU.
AT LEAST YOU'RE ALIVE. I WON'T ASK YOU AGAIN TO—
PLEASE LET ME RECAPTURE MELON!
I'M BEGGING YOU! GIVE ME A CHANCE TO MAKE UP FOR MY MISTAKE!
NO.
I'M CANCELING YOUR CONTRACT. YOU BARELY SURVIVED. YOU SHOULD LEAVE NOW. GO BACK TO YOUR UDON NOODLE SHOP.
UM...

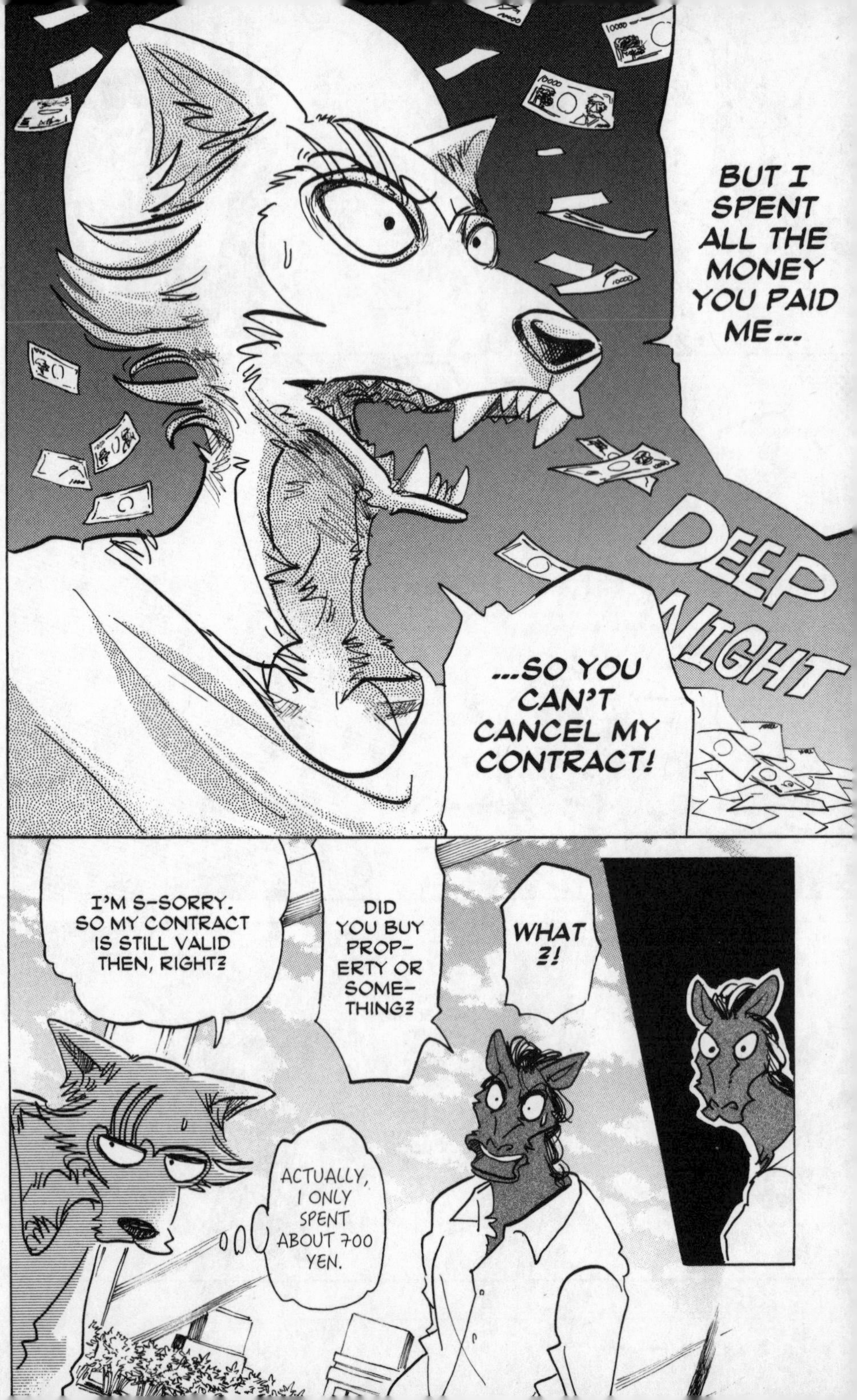
BUT I SPENT ALL THE MONEY YOU PAID ME...
DEEP NIGHT
...SO YOU CAN'T CANCEL MY CONTRACT!
WHAT?!
DID YOU BUY PROPERTY OR SOMETHING?
I'M S-SORRY. SO MY CONTRACT IS STILL VALID THEN, RIGHT?
ACTUALLY, I ONLY SPENT ABOUT 700 YEN.

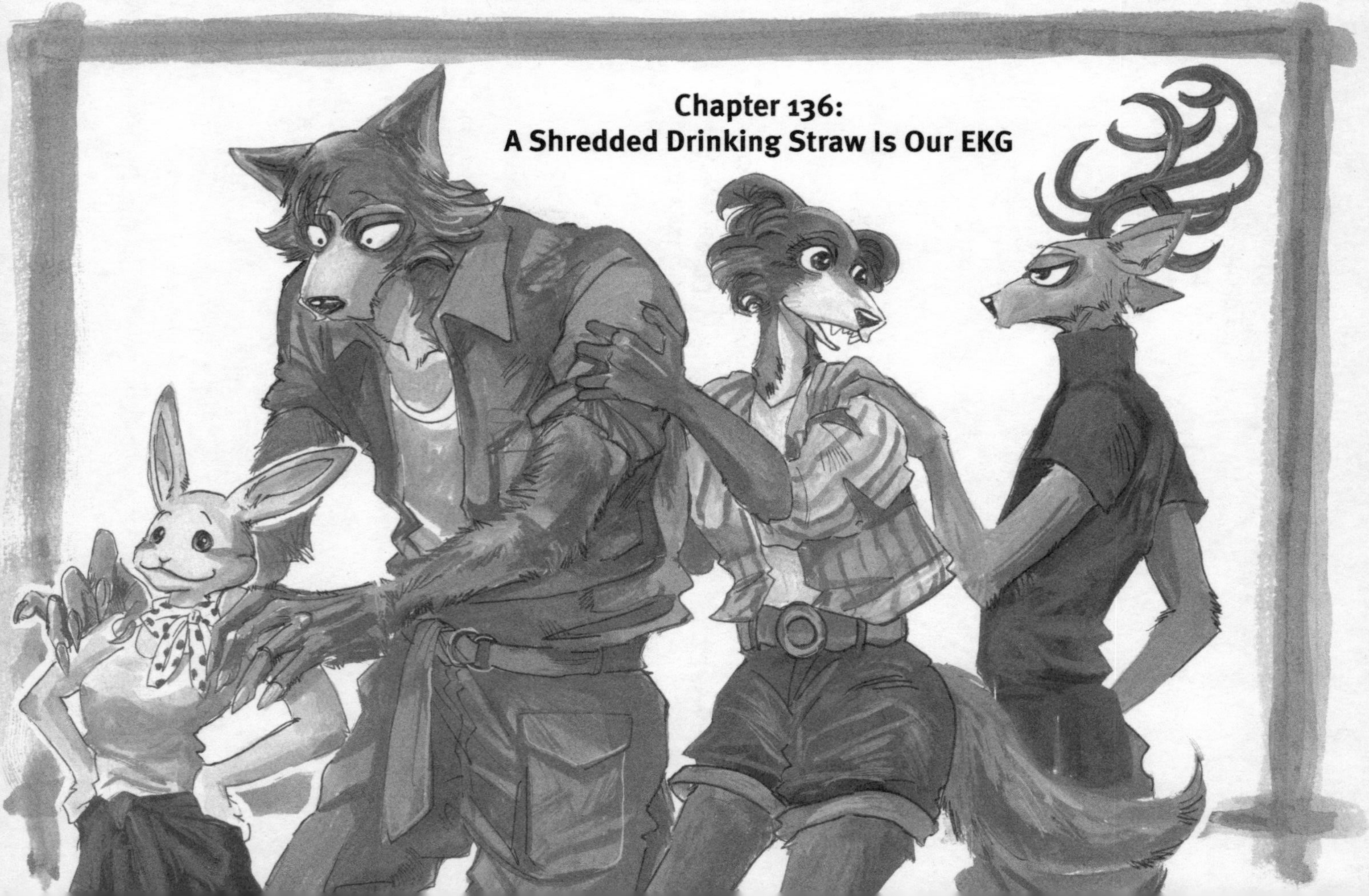
Chapter 136:
A Shredded Drinking Straw Is Our EKG

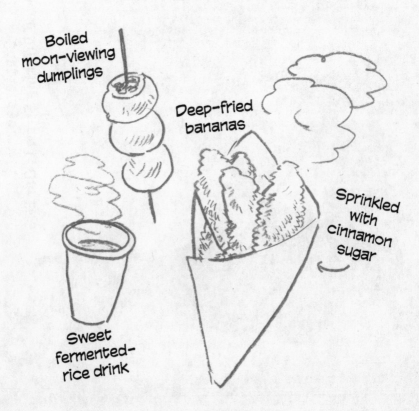

Boiled moon-viewing dumplings

Deep-fried bananas

Sprinkled with cinnamon sugar

Sweet fermented-rice drink

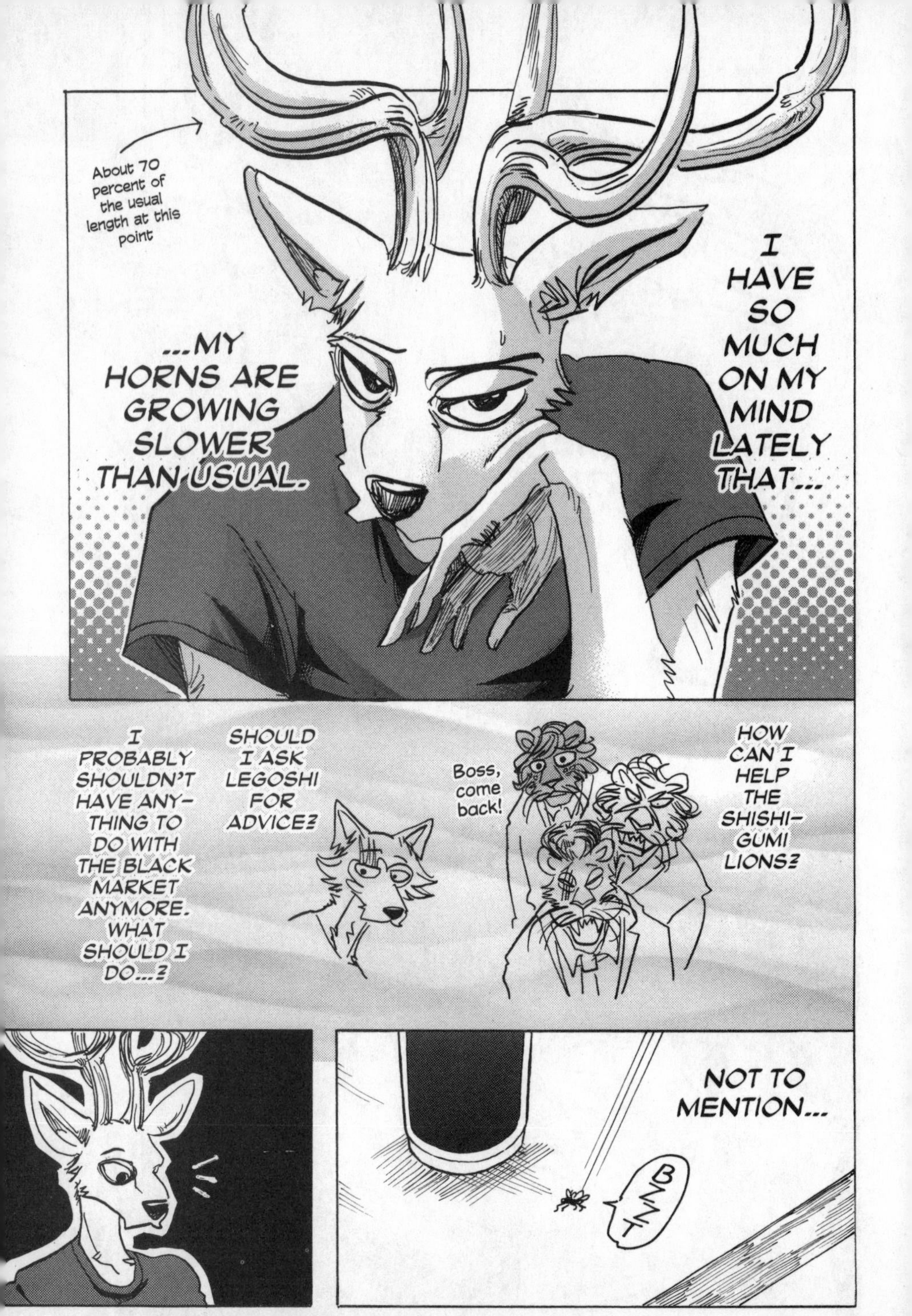
I HAVE SO MUCH ON MY MIND LATELY THAT...
...MY HORNS ARE GROWING SLOWER THAN USUAL.
About 70 percent of the usual length at this point
HOW CAN I HELP THE SHISHI-GUMI LIONS?
Boss, come back!
SHOULD I ASK LEGOSHI FOR ADVICE?
I PROBABLY SHOULDN'T HAVE ANYTHING TO DO WITH THE BLACK MARKET ANYMORE. WHAT SHOULD I DO...?
NOT TO MENTION...
BZZT

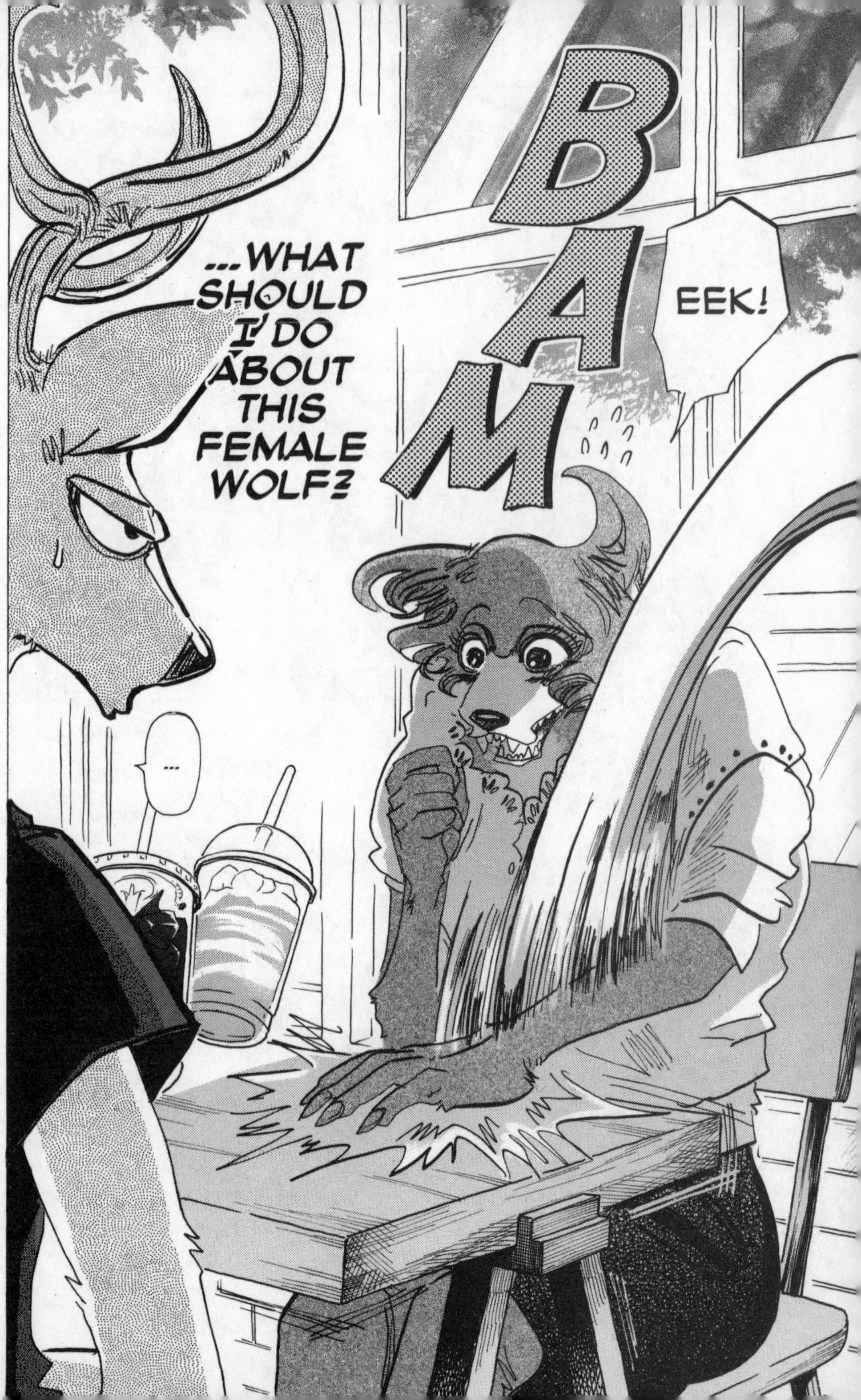
EEK!
BAM
...WHAT SHOULD I DO ABOUT THIS FEMALE WOLF?
...

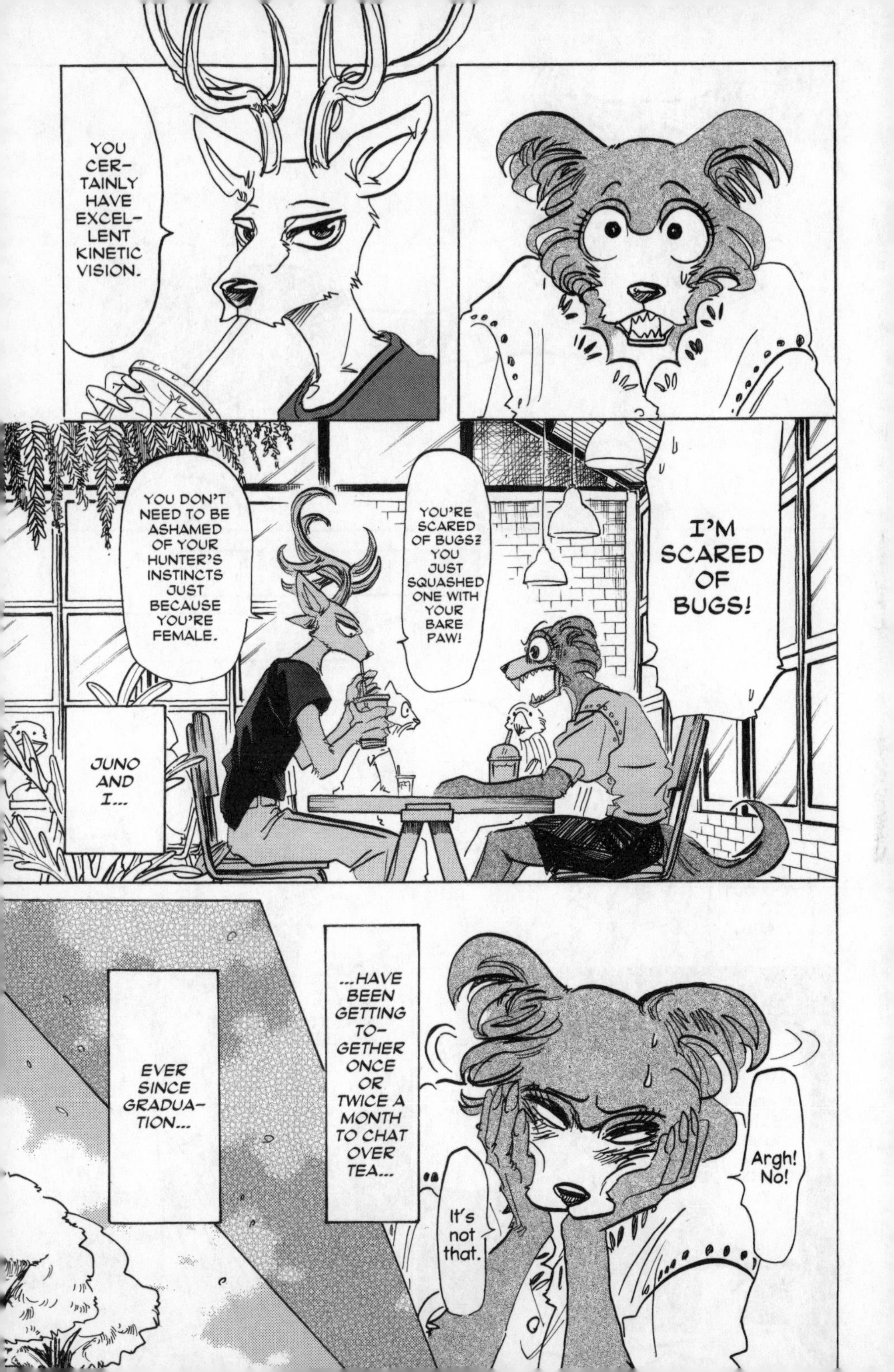
YOU CERTAINLY HAVE EXCELLENT KINETIC VISION.
I'M SCARED OF BUGS!
YOU'RE SCARED OF BUGS? YOU JUST SQUASHED ONE WITH YOUR BARE PAW!
YOU DON'T NEED TO BE ASHAMED OF YOUR HUNTER'S INSTINCTS JUST BECAUSE YOU'RE FEMALE.
JUNO AND I...
Argh! No!
It's not that.
...HAVE BEEN GETTING TOGETHER ONCE OR TWICE A MONTH TO CHAT OVER TEA...
EVER SINCE GRADUATION...

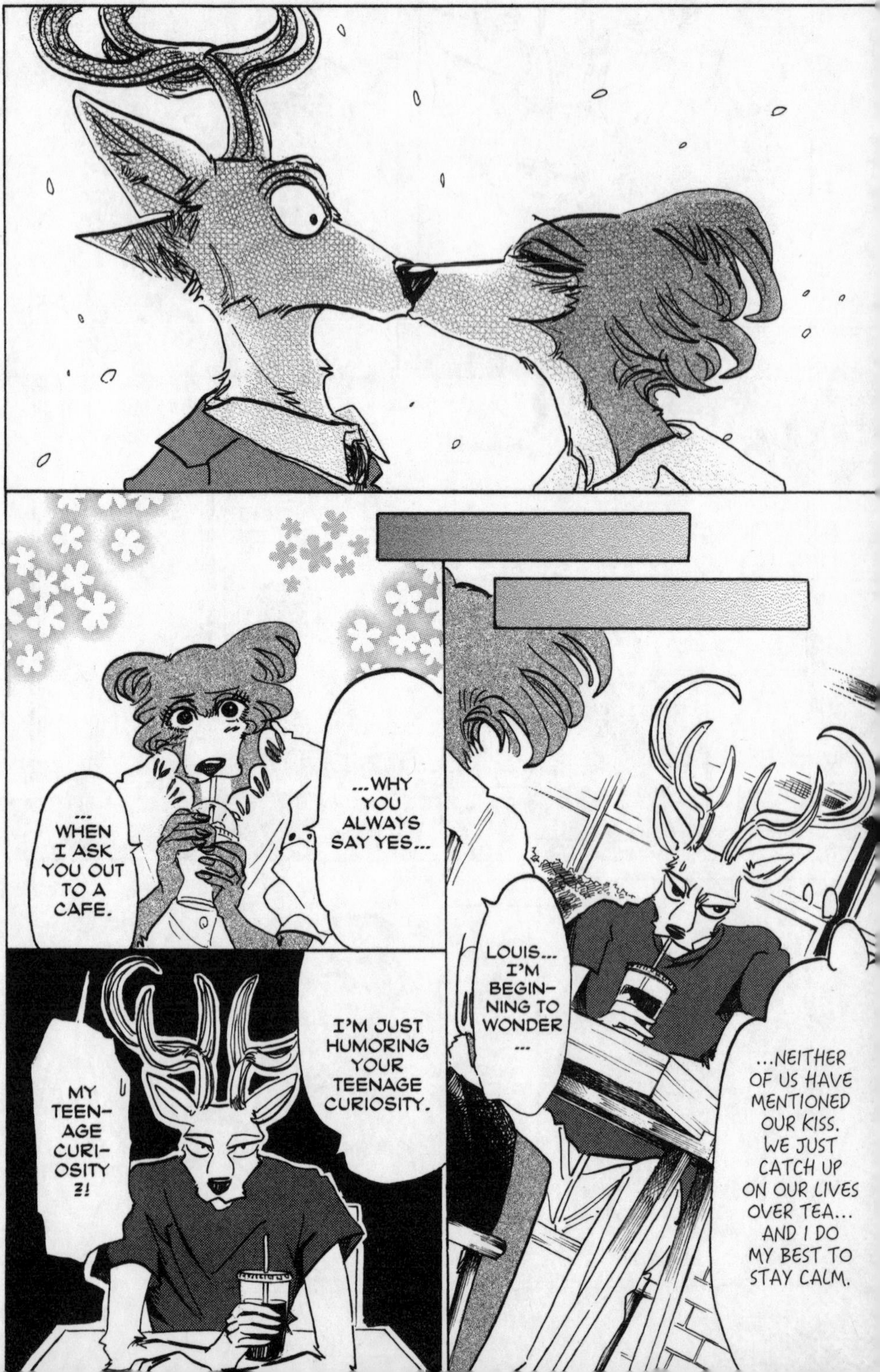

LOUIS... I'M BEGIN-NING TO WONDER...
...NEITHER OF US HAVE MENTIONED OUR KISS. WE JUST CATCH UP ON OUR LIVES OVER TEA... AND I DO MY BEST TO STAY CALM.
...WHY YOU ALWAYS SAY YES...
...WHEN I ASK YOU OUT TO A CAFE.
I'M JUST HUMORING YOUR TEENAGE CURIOSITY.
MY TEEN-AGE CURI-OSITY ?!

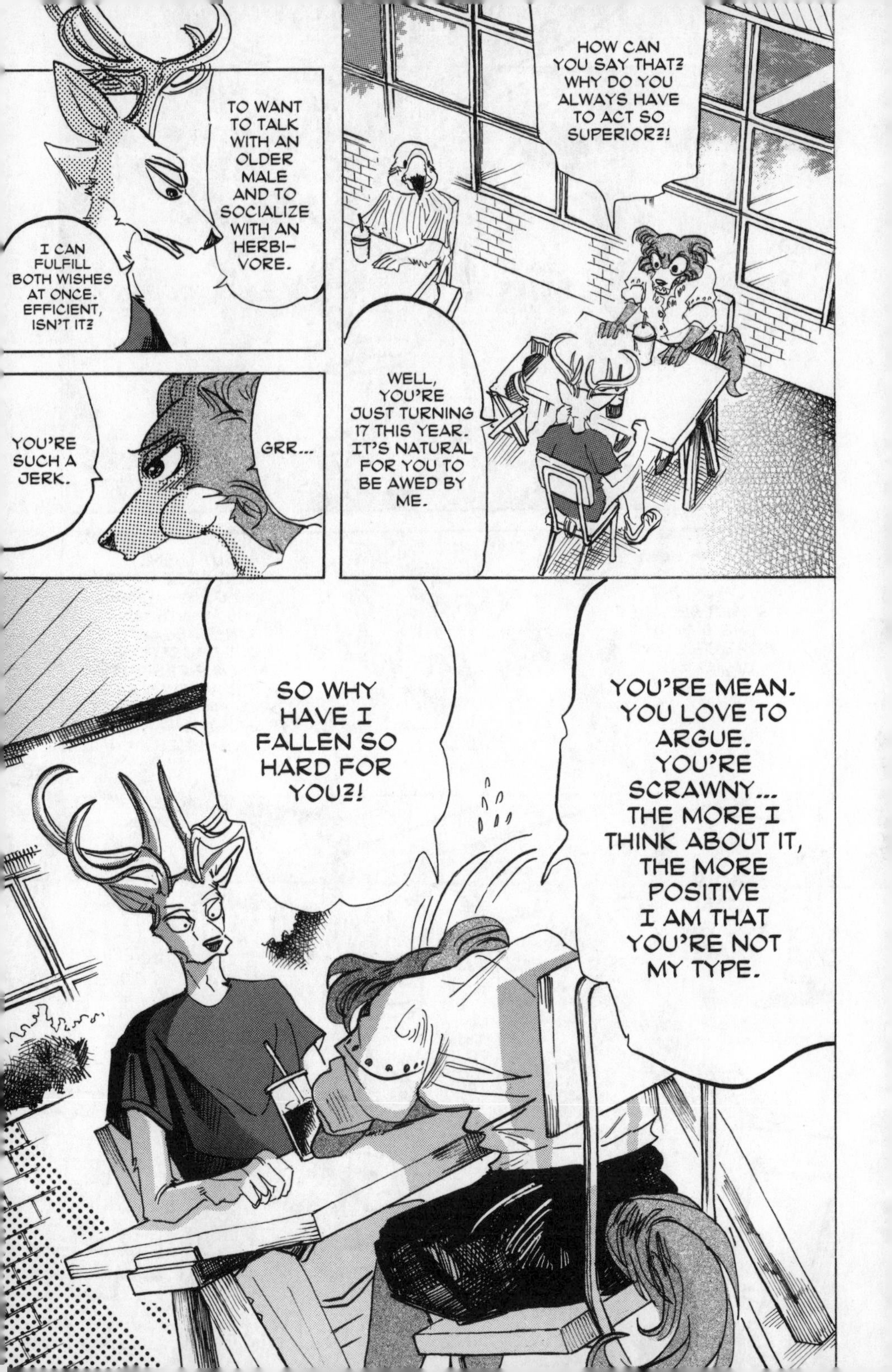
HOW CAN YOU SAY THAT? WHY DO YOU ALWAYS HAVE TO ACT SO SUPERIOR?!
WELL, YOU'RE JUST TURNING 17 THIS YEAR. IT'S NATURAL FOR YOU TO BE AWED BY ME.
TO WANT TO TALK WITH AN OLDER MALE AND TO SOCIALIZE WITH AN HERBI-VORE.
I CAN FULFILL BOTH WISHES AT ONCE. EFFICIENT, ISN'T IT?
GRR...
YOU'RE SUCH A JERK.
YOU'RE MEAN. YOU LOVE TO ARGUE. YOU'RE SCRAWNY... THE MORE I THINK ABOUT IT, THE MORE POSITIVE I AM THAT YOU'RE NOT MY TYPE.
SO WHY HAVE I FALLEN SO HARD FOR YOU?!

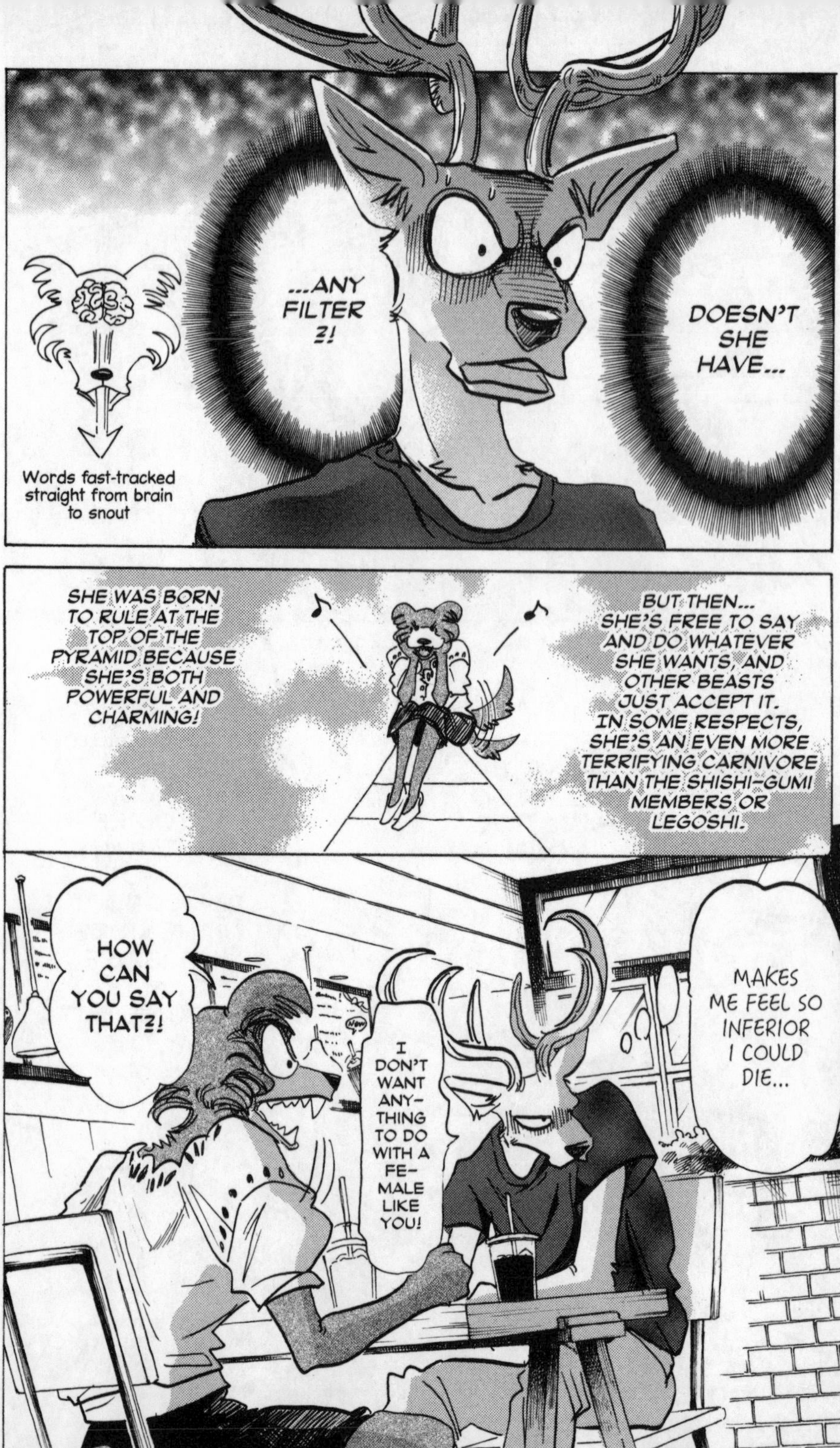
DOESN'T SHE HAVE...
...ANY FILTER?!
Words fast-tracked straight from brain to snout
BUT THEN... SHE'S FREE TO SAY AND DO WHATEVER SHE WANTS, AND OTHER BEASTS JUST ACCEPT IT. IN SOME RESPECTS, SHE'S AN EVEN MORE TERRIFYING CARNIVORE THAN THE SHISHI-GUMI MEMBERS OR LEGOSHI.
SHE WAS BORN TO RULE AT THE TOP OF THE PYRAMID BECAUSE SHE'S BOTH POWERFUL AND CHARMING!
MAKES ME FEEL SO INFERIOR I COULD DIE...
I DON'T WANT ANYTHING TO DO WITH A FEMALE LIKE YOU!
HOW CAN YOU SAY THAT?!

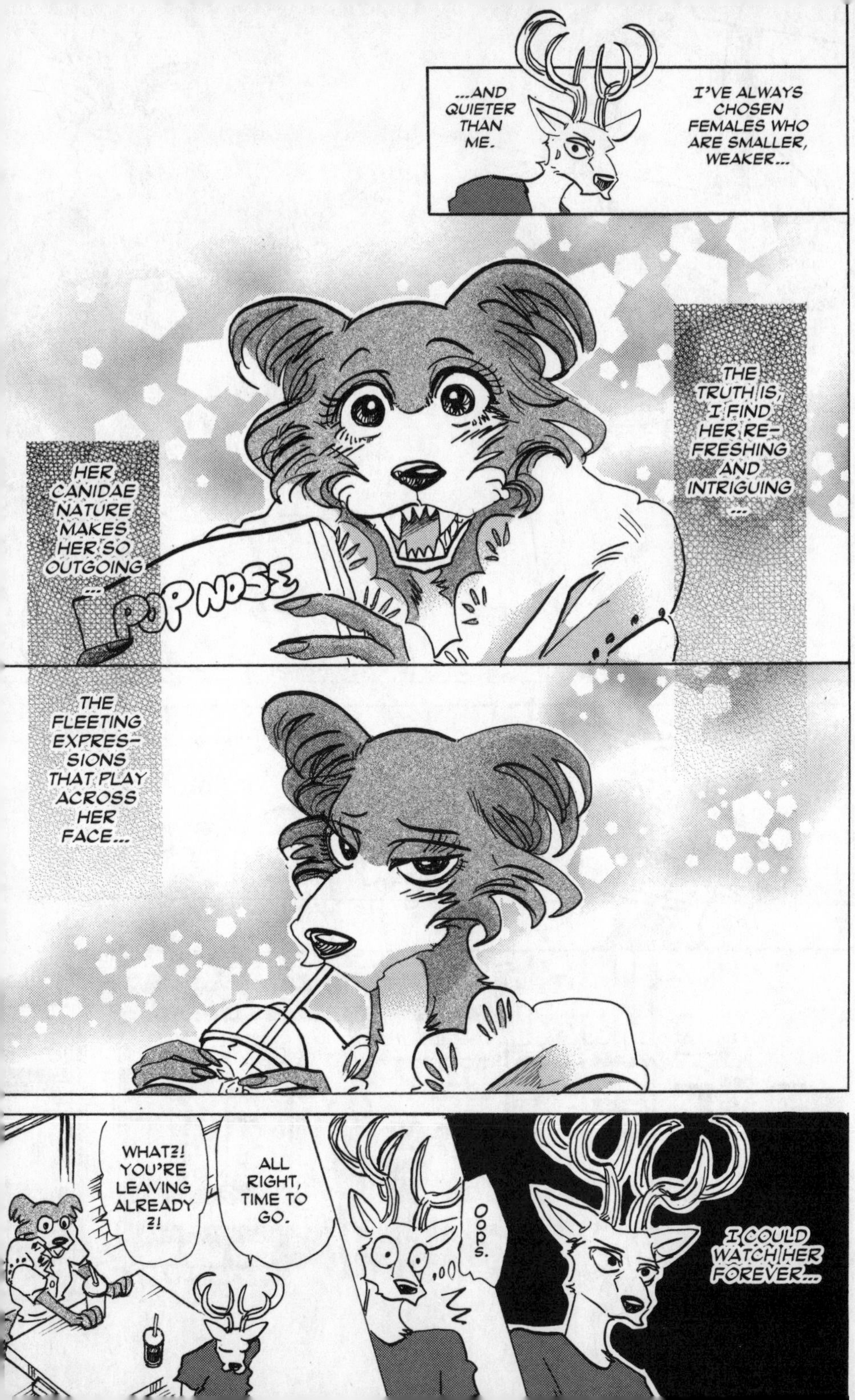
I'VE ALWAYS CHOSEN FEMALES WHO ARE SMALLER, WEAKER...
...AND QUIETER THAN ME.
THE TRUTH IS, I FIND HER RE-FRESHING AND INTRIGUING...
HER CANIDAE NATURE MAKES HER SO OUTGOING...
POP NOSE
THE FLEETING EXPRES-SIONS THAT PLAY ACROSS HER FACE...
I COULD WATCH HER FOREVER...
Oops.
ALL RIGHT, TIME TO GO.
WHAT?! YOU'RE LEAVING ALREADY?!

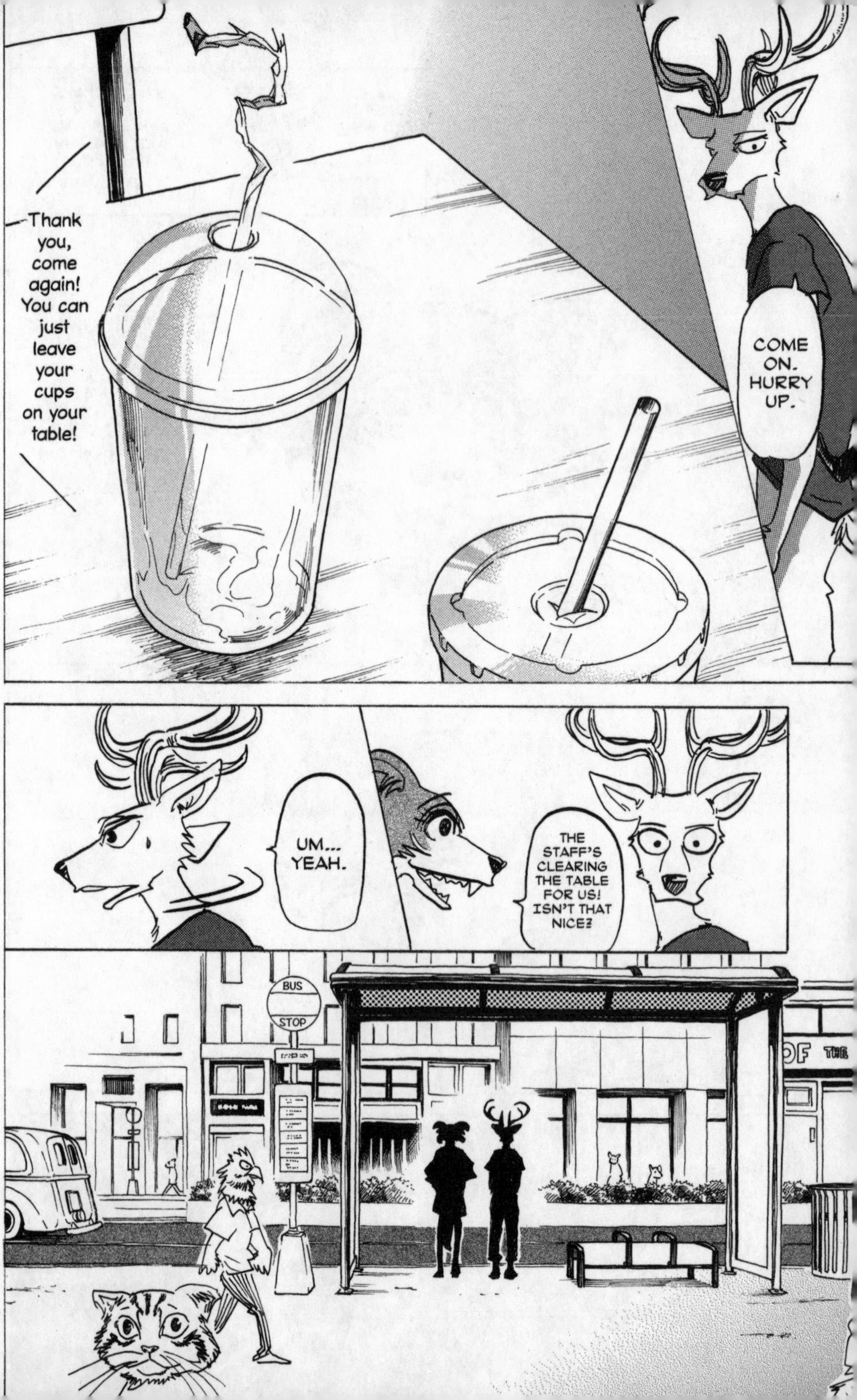
COME ON. HURRY UP.
Thank you, come again! You can just leave your cups on your table!
THE STAFF'S CLEARING THE TABLE FOR US! ISN'T THAT NICE?
UM... YEAH.
BUS
STOP

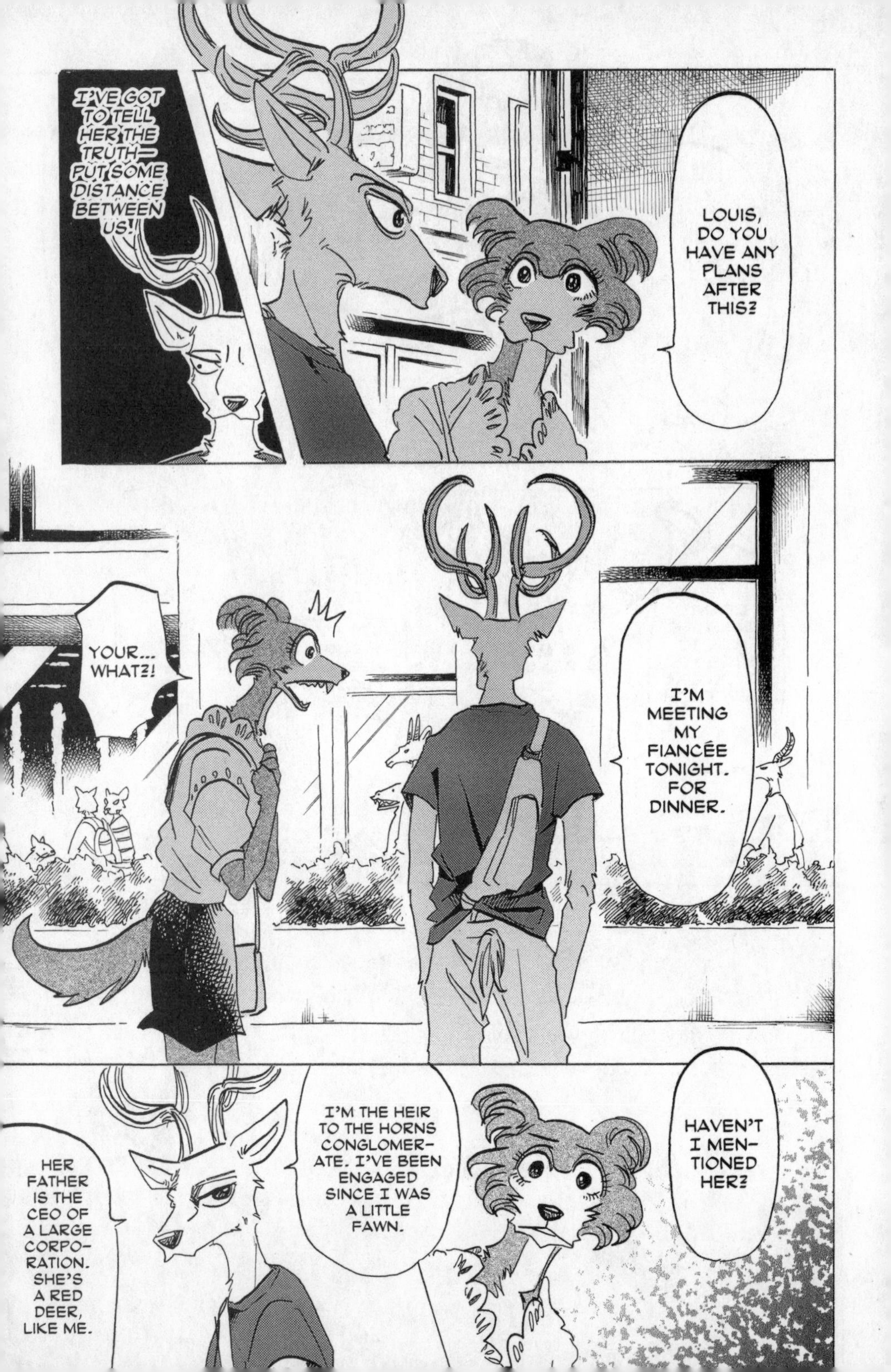
LOUIS, DO YOU HAVE ANY PLANS AFTER THIS?
I'VE GOT TO TELL HER THE TRUTH—PUT SOME DISTANCE BETWEEN US!
I'M MEETING MY FIANCÉE TONIGHT. FOR DINNER.
YOUR... WHAT?!
HAVEN'T I MENTIONED HER?
I'M THE HEIR TO THE HORNS CONGLOMERATE. I'VE BEEN ENGAGED SINCE I WAS A LITTLE FAWN.
HER FATHER IS THE CEO OF A LARGE CORPORATION. SHE'S A RED DEER, LIKE ME.

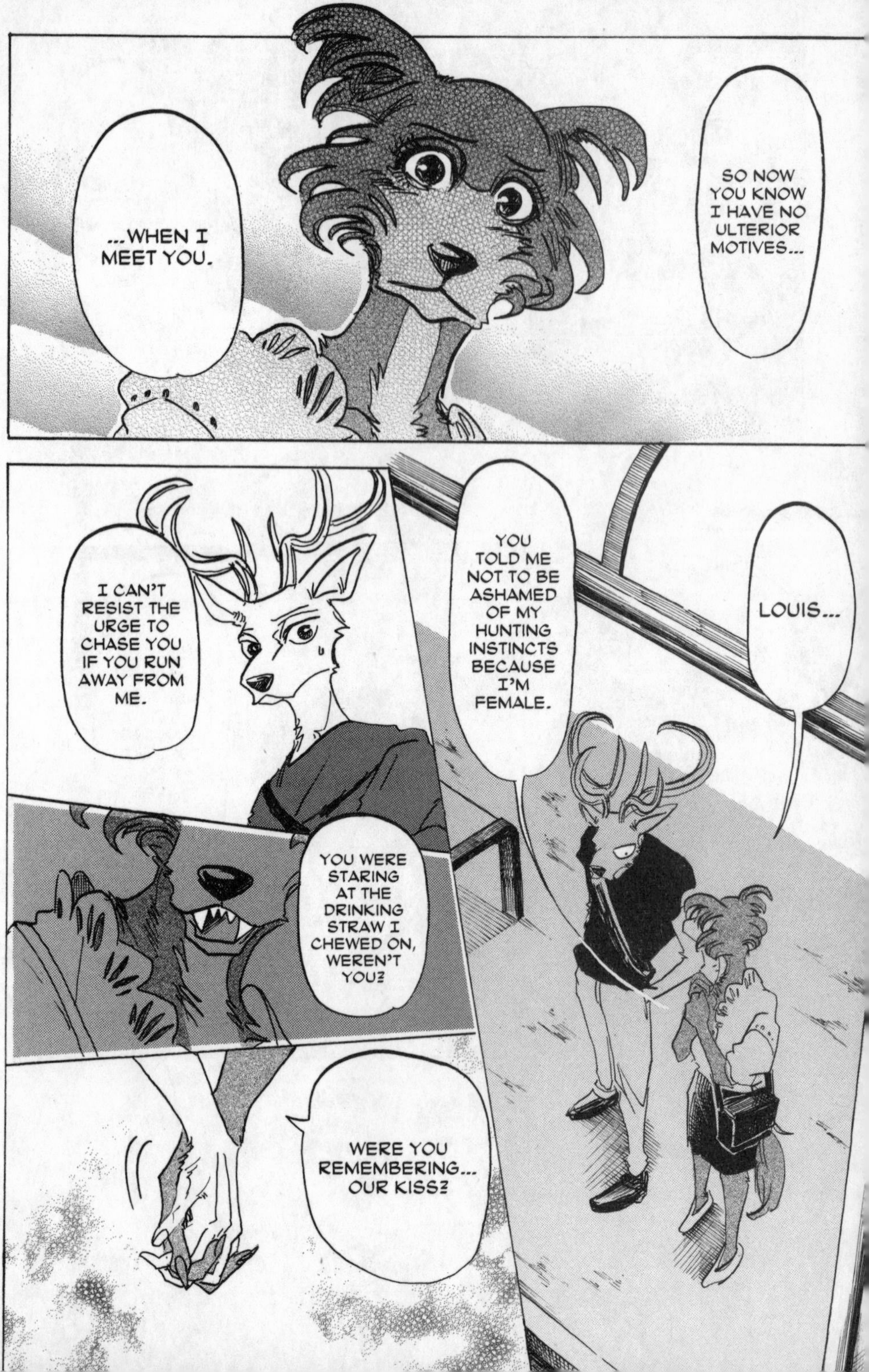
SO NOW YOU KNOW I HAVE NO ULTERIOR MOTIVES...
...WHEN I MEET YOU.
LOUIS...
YOU TOLD ME NOT TO BE ASHAMED OF MY HUNTING INSTINCTS BECAUSE I'M FEMALE.
I CAN'T RESIST THE URGE TO CHASE YOU IF YOU RUN AWAY FROM ME.
YOU WERE STARING AT THE DRINKING STRAW I CHEWED ON, WEREN'T YOU?
WERE YOU REMEMBERING... OUR KISS?

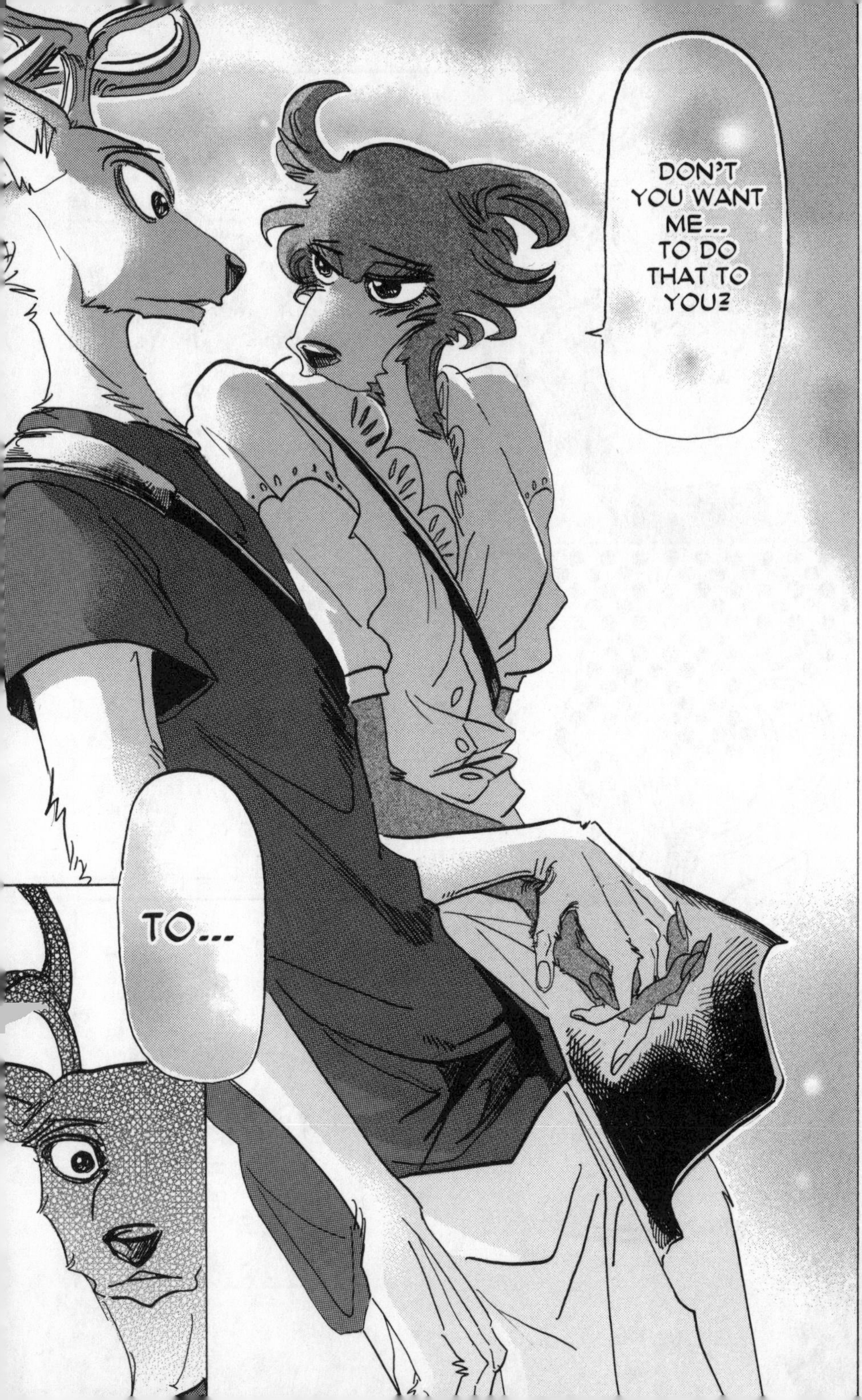
DON'T YOU WANT ME... TO DO THAT TO YOU?
TO...

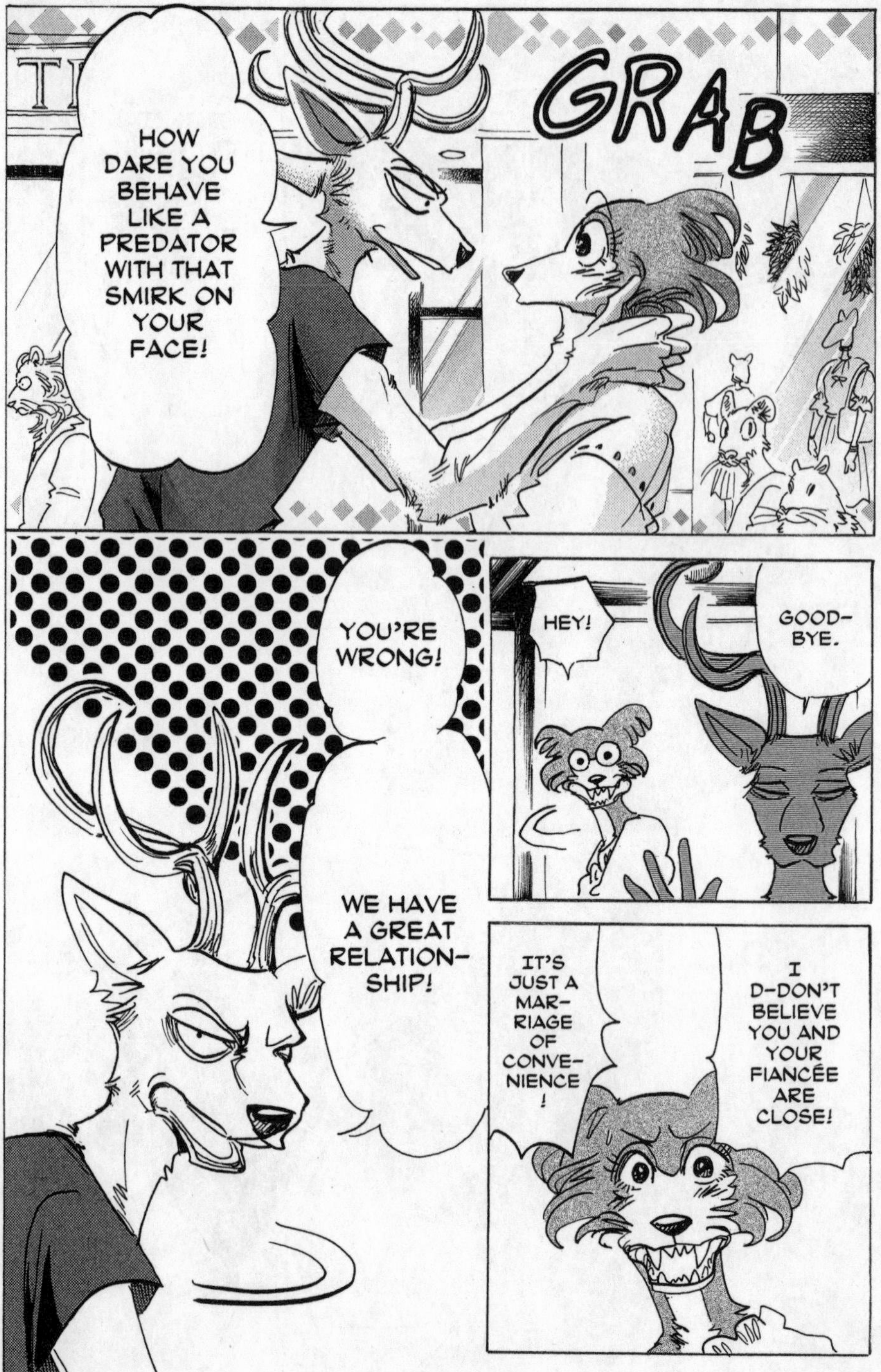
GRAB
HOW DARE YOU BEHAVE LIKE A PREDATOR WITH THAT SMIRK ON YOUR FACE!
GOOD-BYE.
HEY!
I D-DON'T BELIEVE YOU AND YOUR FIANCÉE ARE CLOSE!
IT'S JUST A MARRIAGE OF CONVENIENCE!
YOU'RE WRONG!
WE HAVE A GREAT RELATIONSHIP!

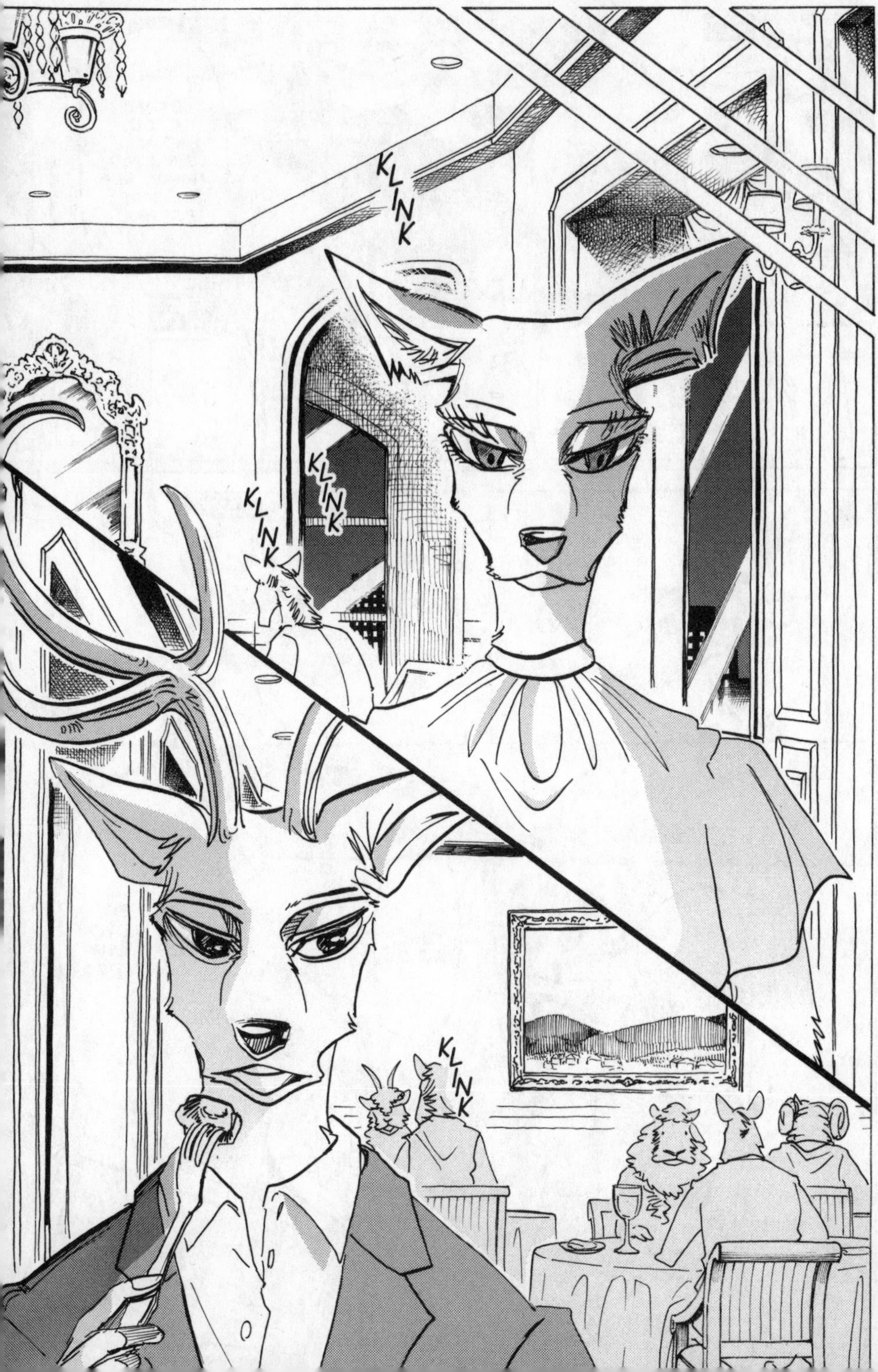
KLINK
KLINK
KLINK
KLINK

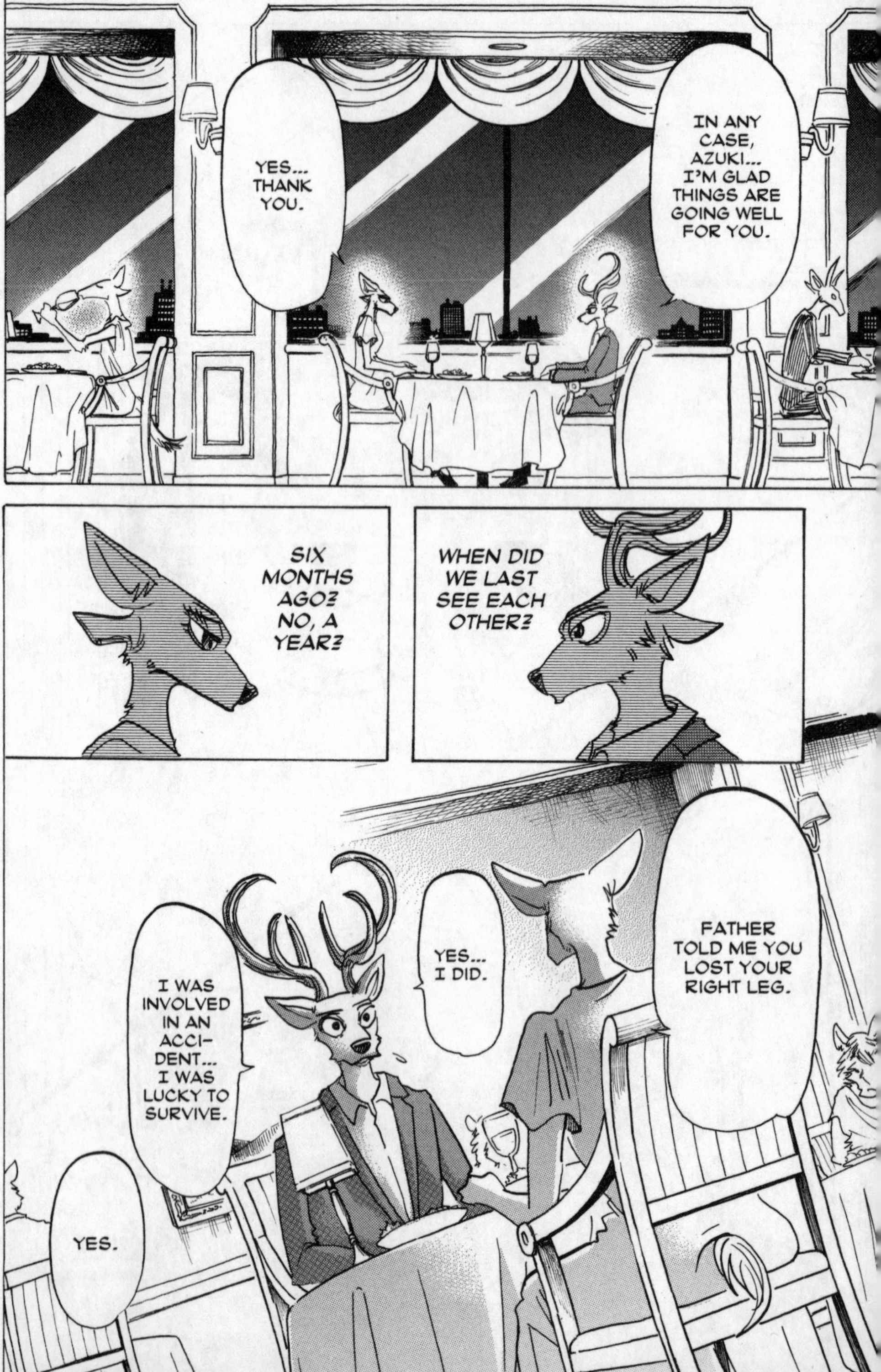
IN ANY CASE, AZUKI... I'M GLAD THINGS ARE GOING WELL FOR YOU.
YES... THANK YOU.
WHEN DID WE LAST SEE EACH OTHER?
SIX MONTHS AGO? NO, A YEAR?
FATHER TOLD ME YOU LOST YOUR RIGHT LEG.
YES... I DID.
I WAS INVOLVED IN AN ACCI-DENT... I WAS LUCKY TO SURVIVE.
YES.

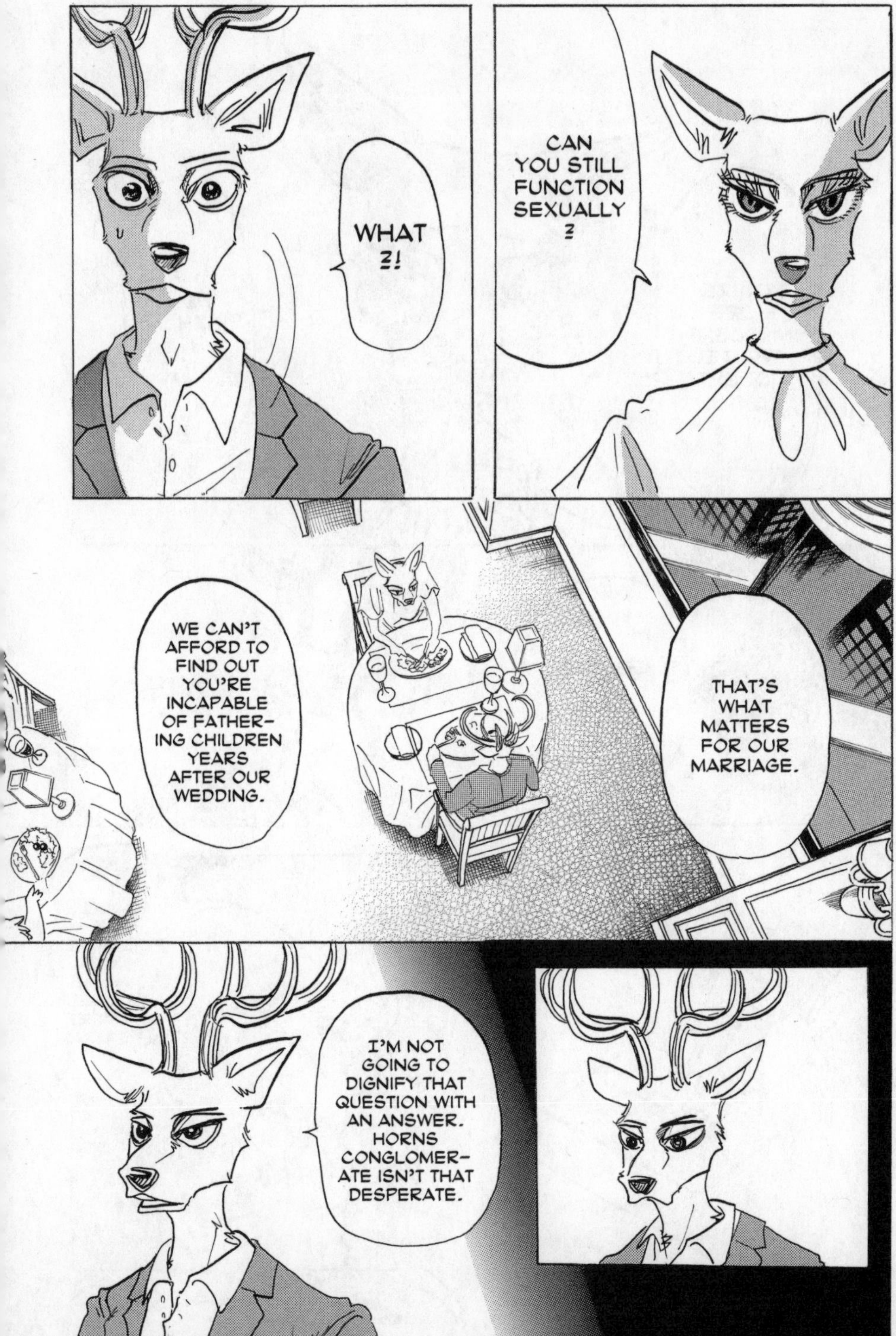
CAN YOU STILL FUNCTION SEXUALLY?
WHAT?!
THAT'S WHAT MATTERS FOR OUR MARRIAGE.
WE CAN'T AFFORD TO FIND OUT YOU'RE INCAPABLE OF FATHERING CHILDREN YEARS AFTER OUR WEDDING.
I'M NOT GOING TO DIGNIFY THAT QUESTION WITH AN ANSWER. HORNS CONGLOMERATE ISN'T THAT DESPERATE.

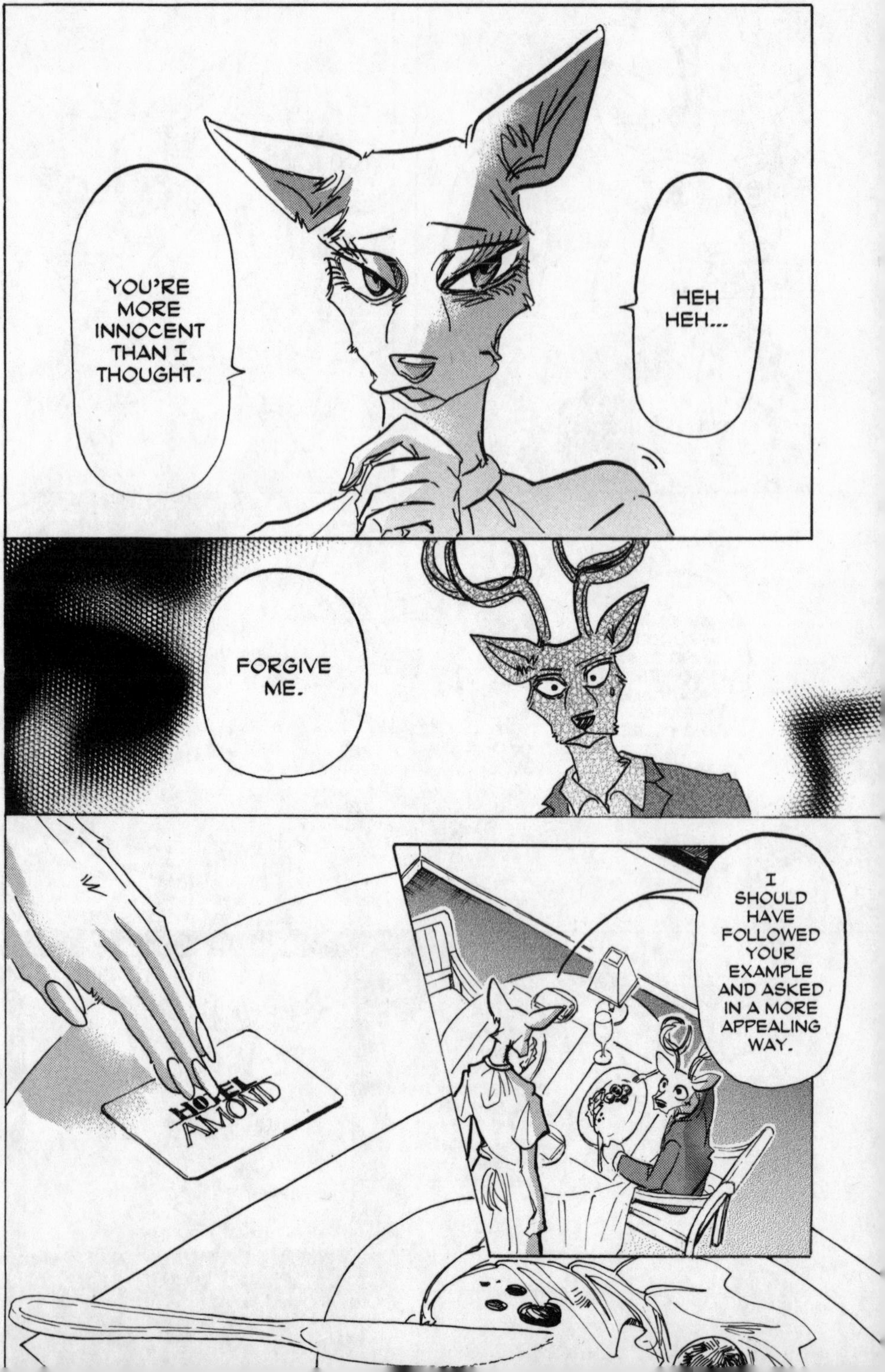
HEH HEH...
YOU'RE MORE INNOCENT THAN I THOUGHT.
FORGIVE ME.
I SHOULD HAVE FOLLOWED YOUR EXAMPLE AND ASKED IN A MORE APPEALING WAY.
HOTEL AMOND

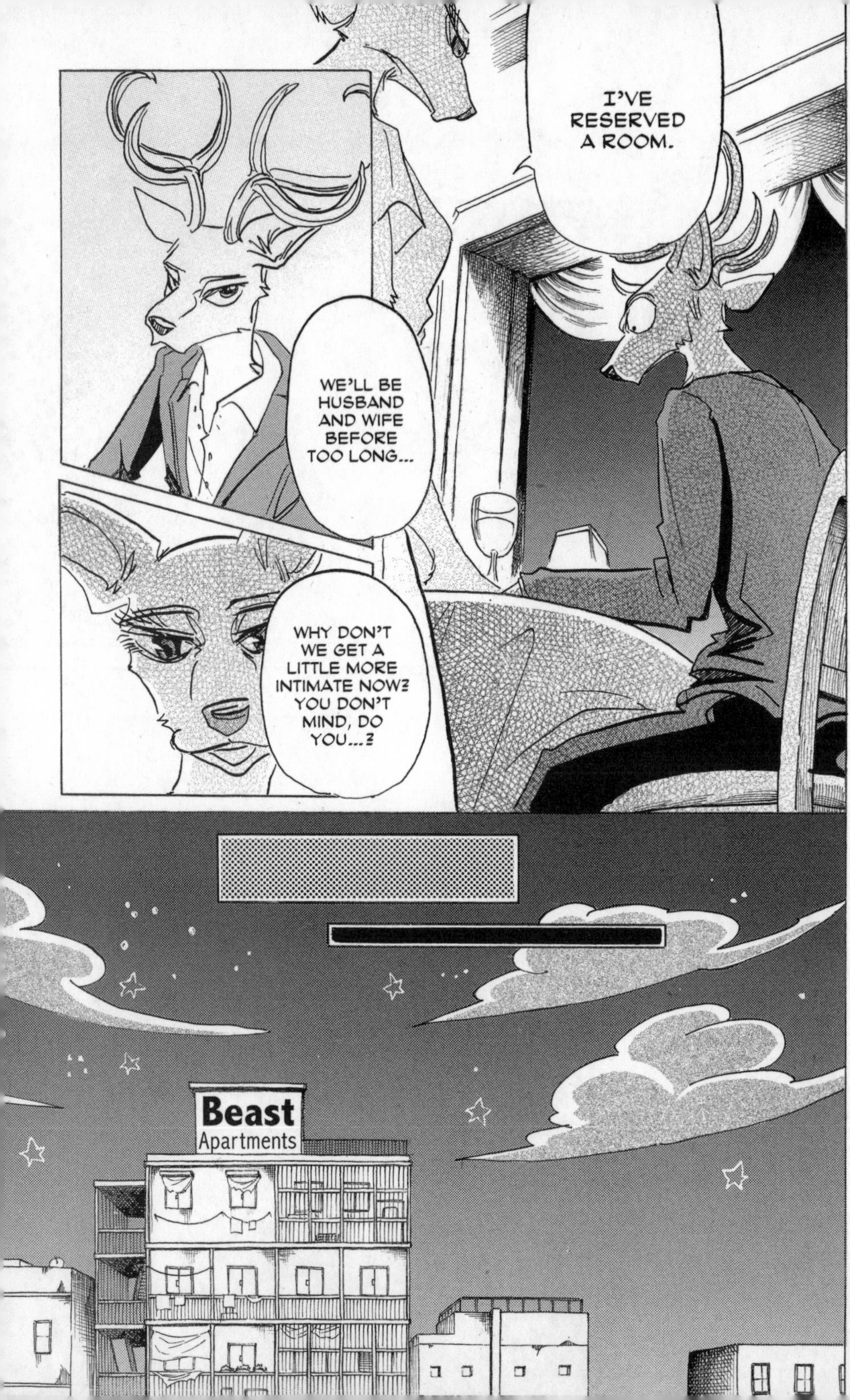
I'VE RESERVED A ROOM.
WE'LL BE HUSBAND AND WIFE BEFORE TOO LONG...
WHY DON'T WE GET A LITTLE MORE INTIMATE NOW? YOU DON'T MIND, DO YOU...?
Beast Apartments

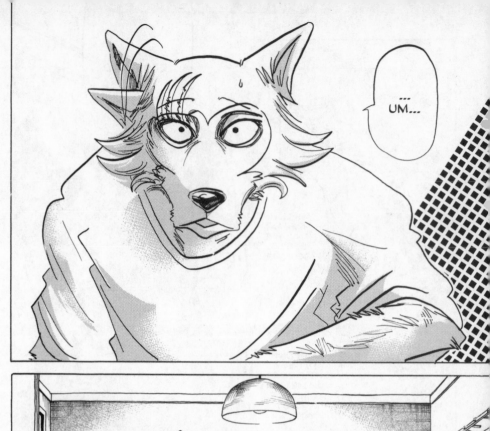

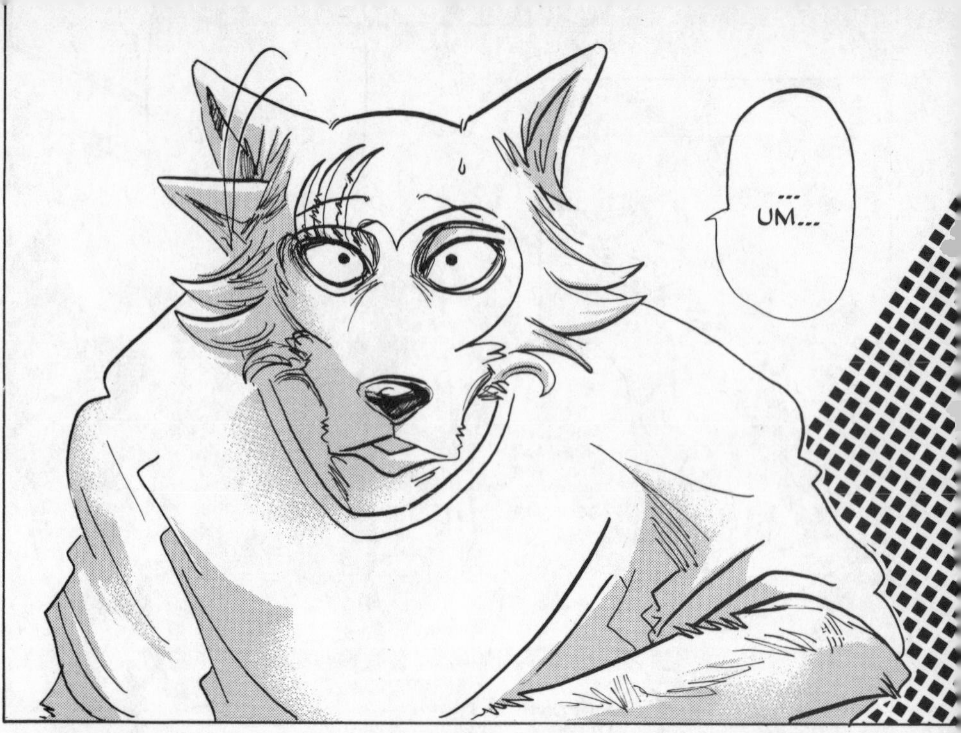
... UM...

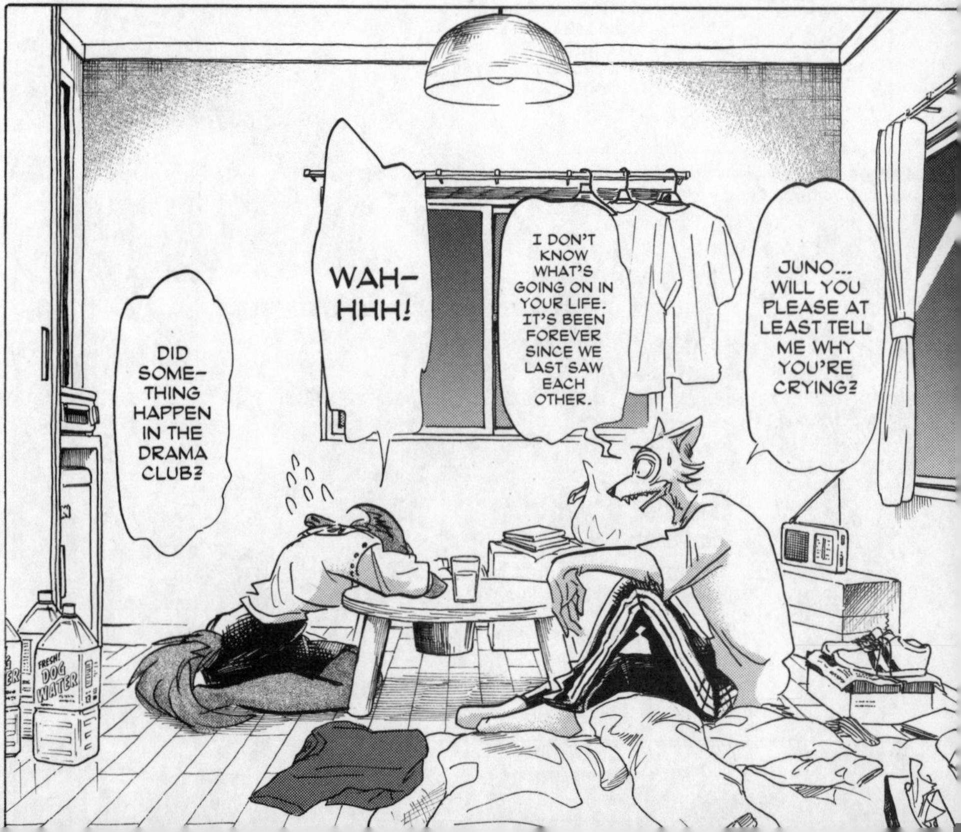
JUNO... WILL YOU PLEASE AT LEAST TELL ME WHY YOU'RE CRYING?
I DON'T KNOW WHAT'S GOING ON IN YOUR LIFE. IT'S BEEN FOREVER SINCE WE LAST SAW EACH OTHER.
WAH-HHH!
DID SOME-THING HAPPEN IN THE DRAMA CLUB?
FRESH! DOG WATER

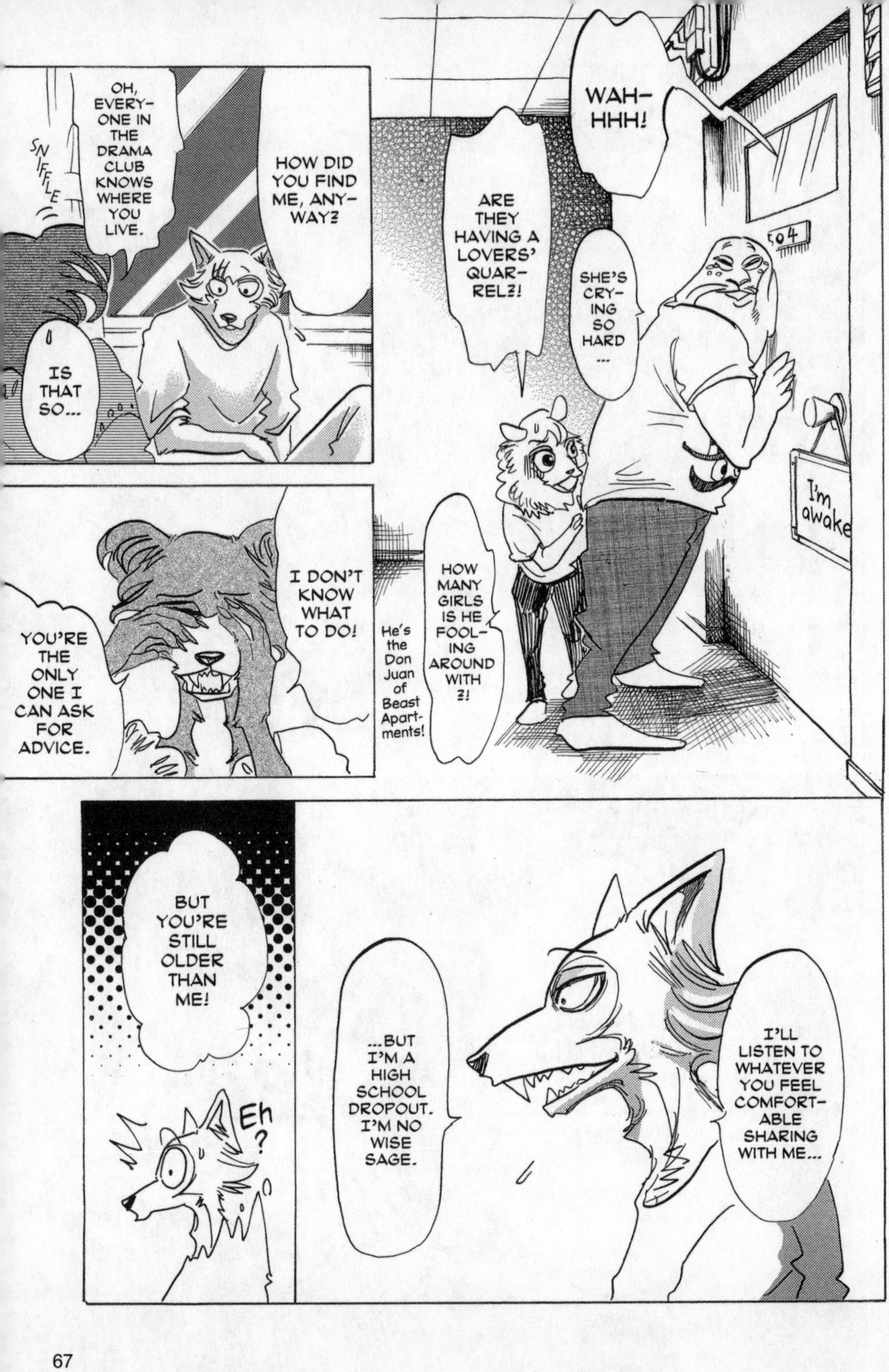
WAH-HHH!
ARE THEY HAVING A LOVERS' QUARREL?!
SHE'S CRYING SO HARD...
HOW MANY GIRLS IS HE FOOLING AROUND WITH?!
He's the Don Juan of Beast Apartments!
I'm awake
HOW DID YOU FIND ME, ANYWAY?
OH, EVERYONE IN THE DRAMA CLUB KNOWS WHERE YOU LIVE.
SNIFFLE
IS THAT SO...
I DON'T KNOW WHAT TO DO!
YOU'RE THE ONLY ONE I CAN ASK FOR ADVICE.
I'LL LISTEN TO WHATEVER YOU FEEL COMFORTABLE SHARING WITH ME...
...BUT I'M A HIGH SCHOOL DROPOUT. I'M NO WISE SAGE.
BUT YOU'RE STILL OLDER THAN ME!
Eh?

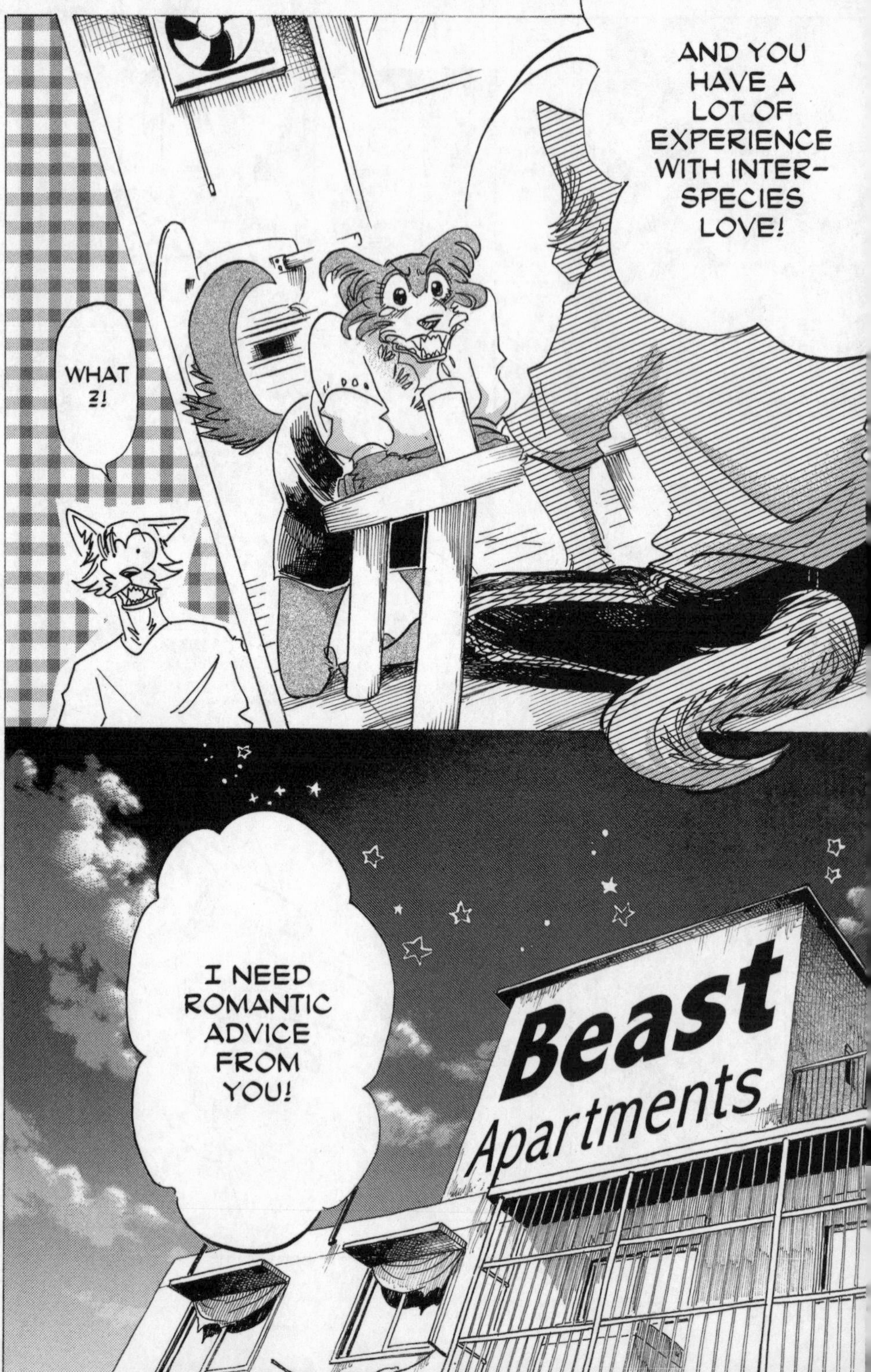
AND YOU HAVE A LOT OF EXPERIENCE WITH INTER-SPECIES LOVE!
WHAT?!
I NEED ROMANTIC ADVICE FROM YOU!
Beast Apartments

Chapter 137: Departure from Shangri-La

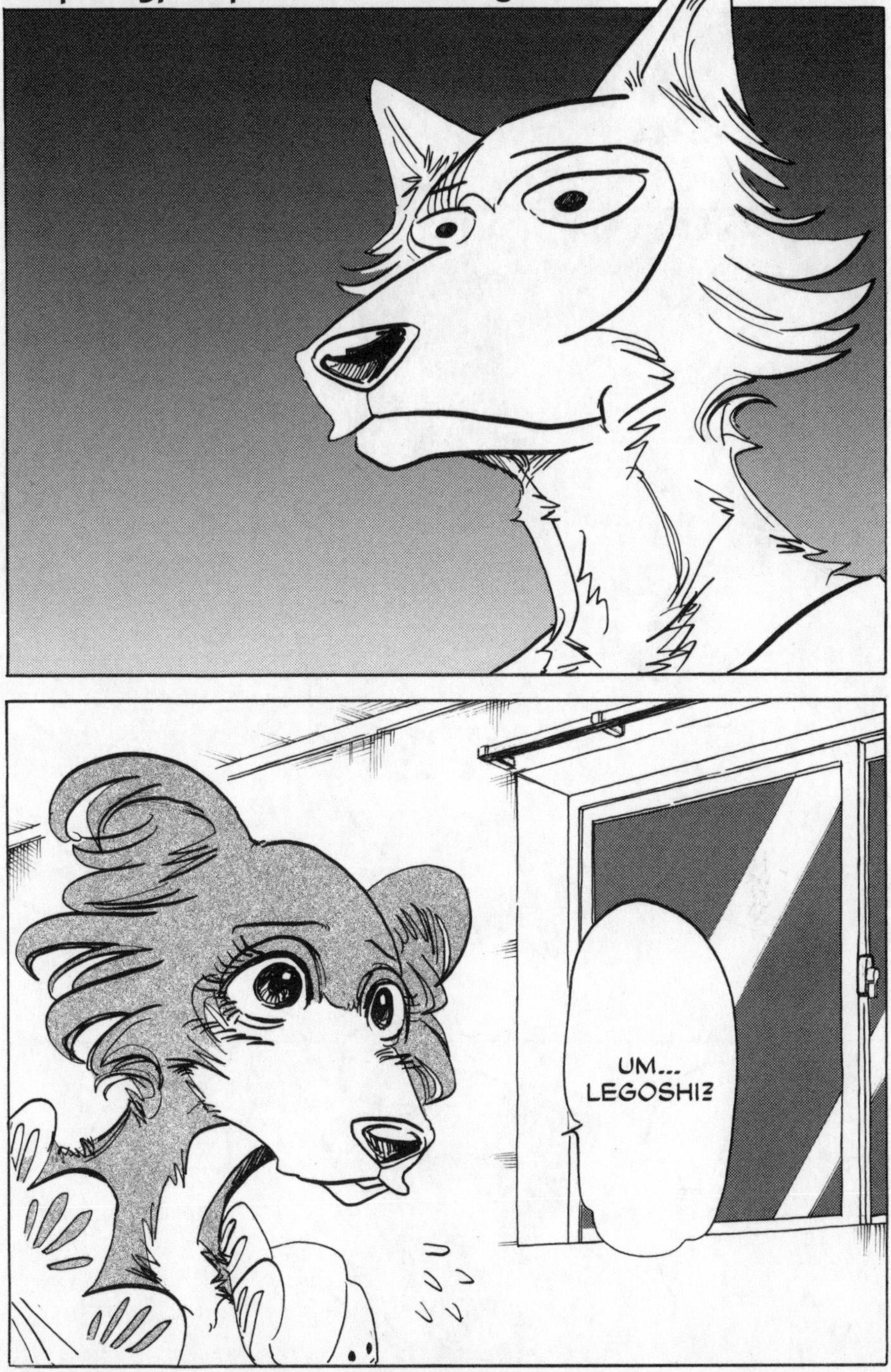
UM...
LEGOSHI?

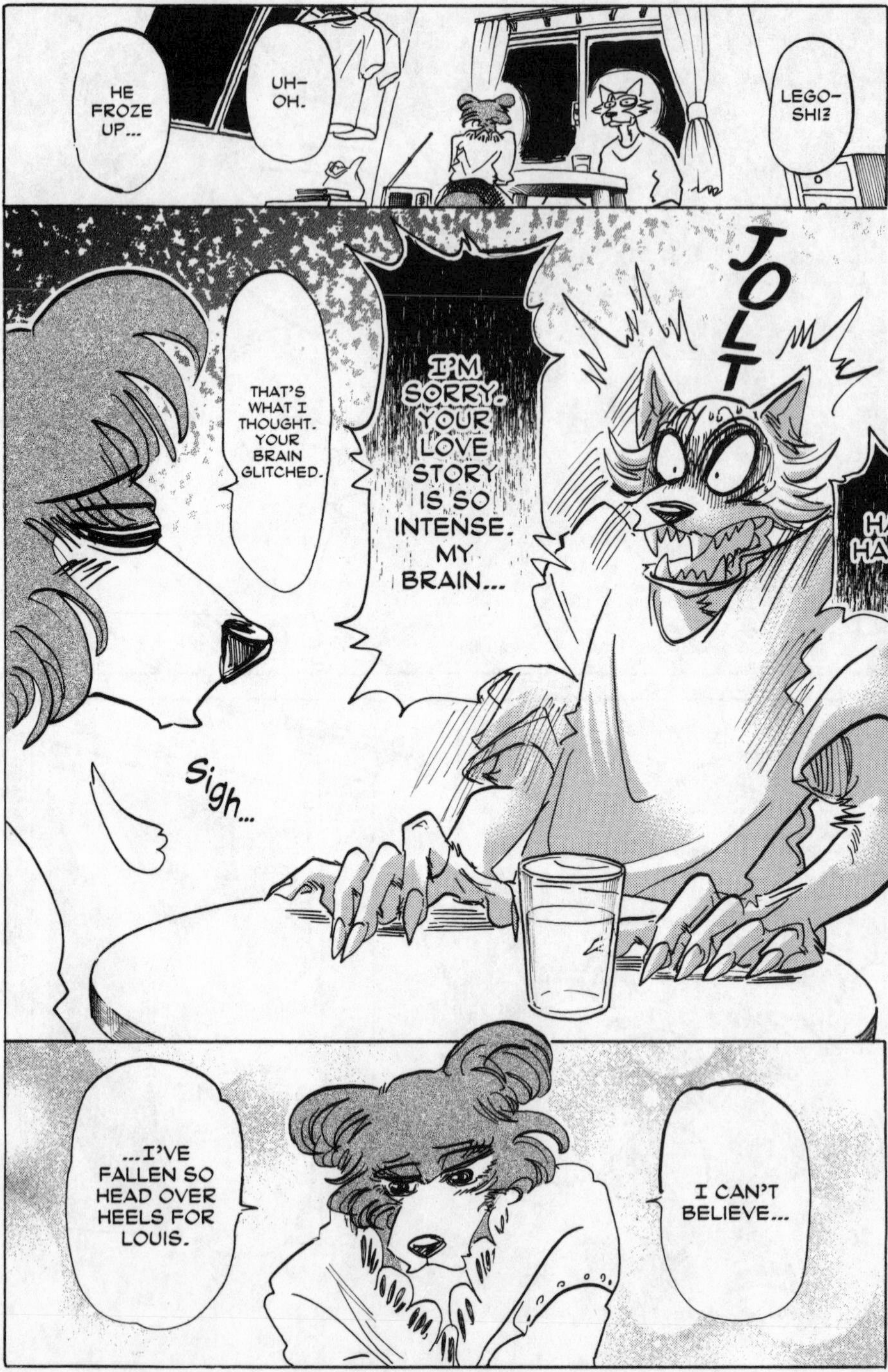
LEGO-SHI?
UH-OH.
HE FROZE UP...
JOLT
HA HA...
I'M SORRY. YOUR LOVE STORY IS SO INTENSE. MY BRAIN...
THAT'S WHAT I THOUGHT. YOUR BRAIN GLITCHED.
Sigh...
I CAN'T BELIEVE...
...I'VE FALLEN SO HEAD OVER HEELS FOR LOUIS.

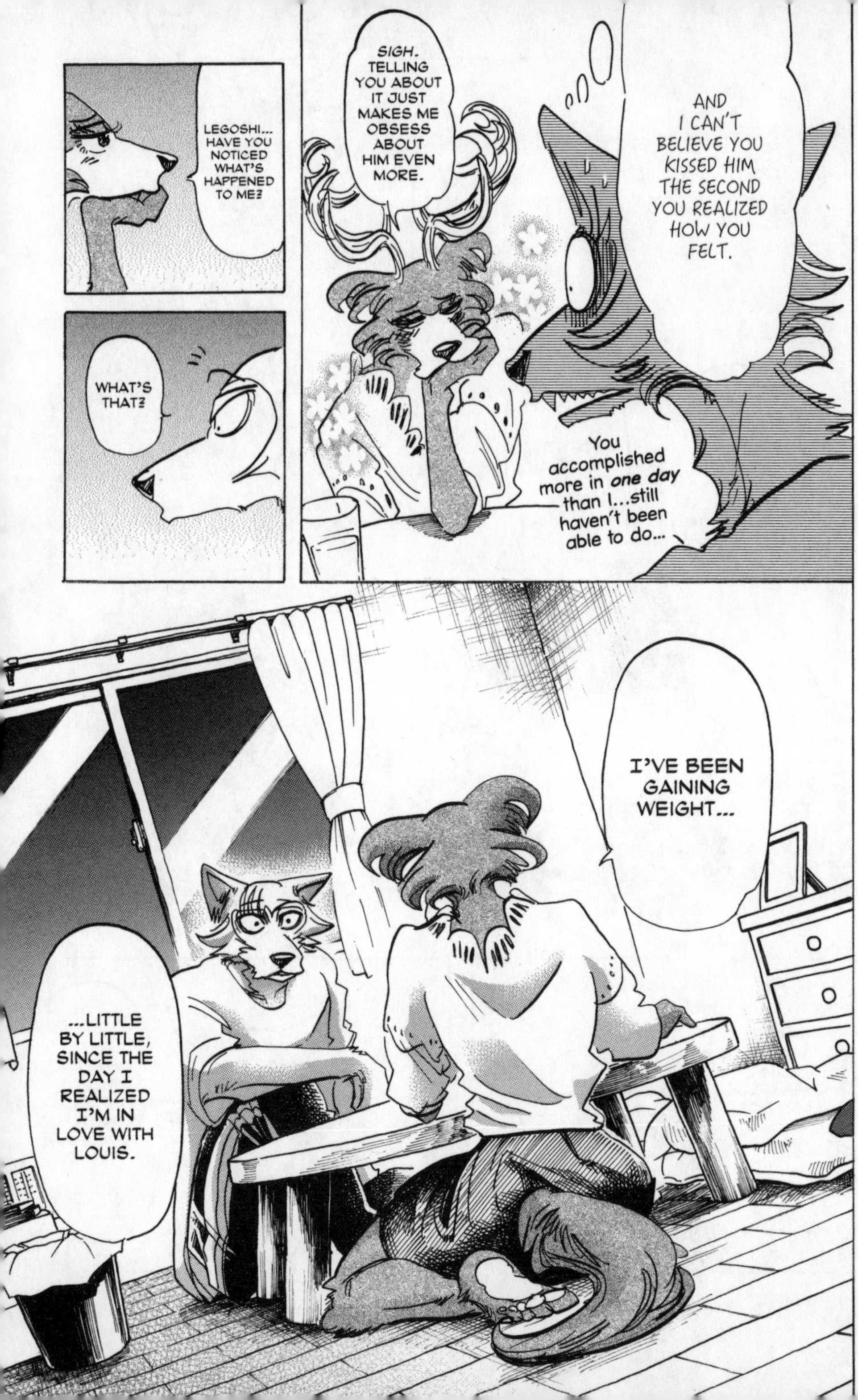

SIGH. TELLING YOU ABOUT IT JUST MAKES ME OBSESS ABOUT HIM EVEN MORE.
AND I CAN'T BELIEVE YOU KISSED HIM THE SECOND YOU REALIZED HOW YOU FELT.
You accomplished more in *one day* than I...still haven't been able to do...
LEGOSHI... HAVE YOU NOTICED WHAT'S HAPPENED TO ME?
WHAT'S THAT?
I'VE BEEN GAINING WEIGHT...
...LITTLE BY LITTLE, SINCE THE DAY I REALIZED I'M IN LOVE WITH LOUIS.

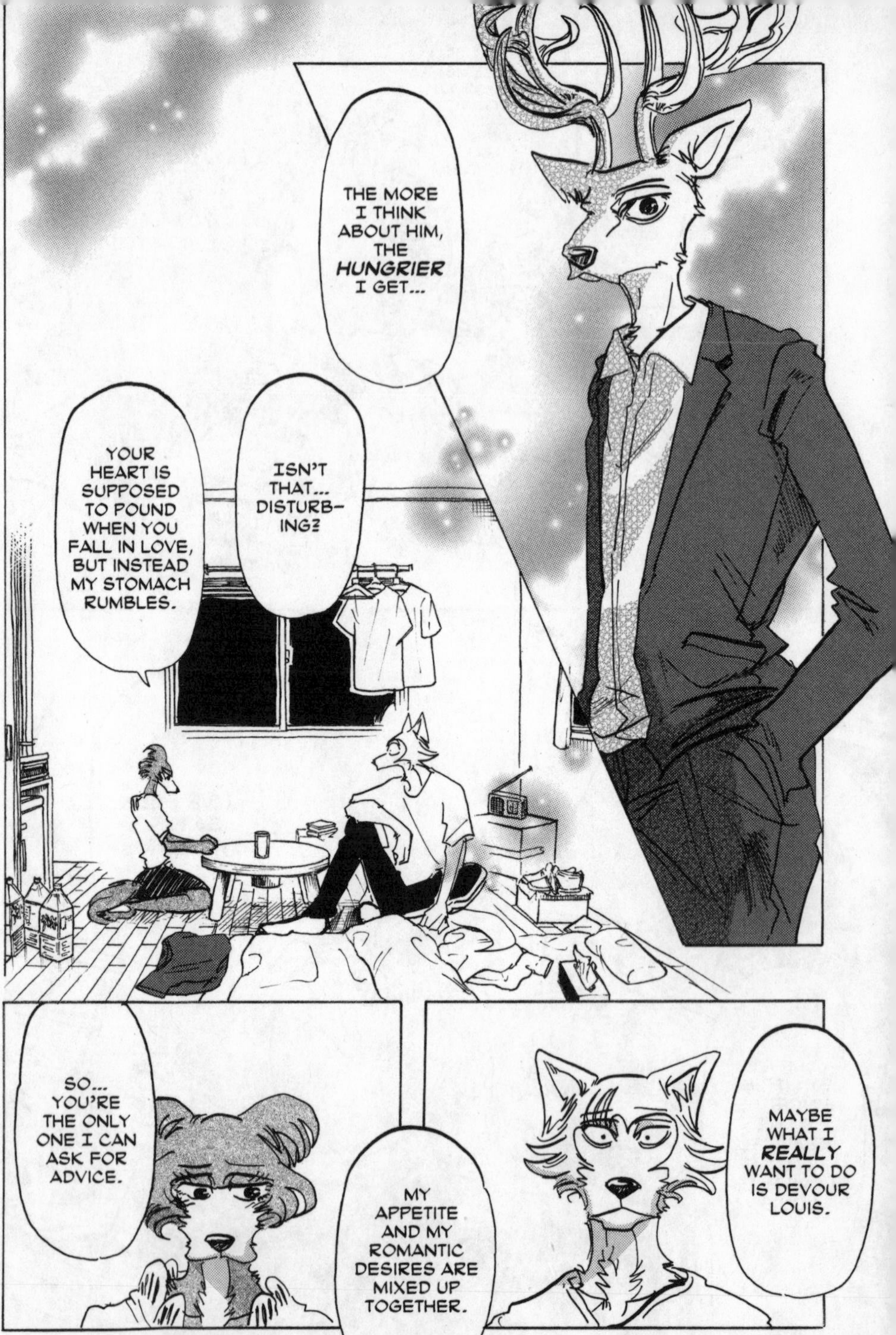
THE MORE I THINK ABOUT HIM, THE ***HUNGRIER*** I GET...
ISN'T THAT... DISTURBING?
YOUR HEART IS SUPPOSED TO POUND WHEN YOU FALL IN LOVE, BUT INSTEAD MY STOMACH RUMBLES.
MAYBE WHAT I ***REALLY*** WANT TO DO IS DEVOUR LOUIS.
MY APPETITE AND MY ROMANTIC DESIRES ARE MIXED UP TOGETHER.
SO... YOU'RE THE ONLY ONE I CAN ASK FOR ADVICE.

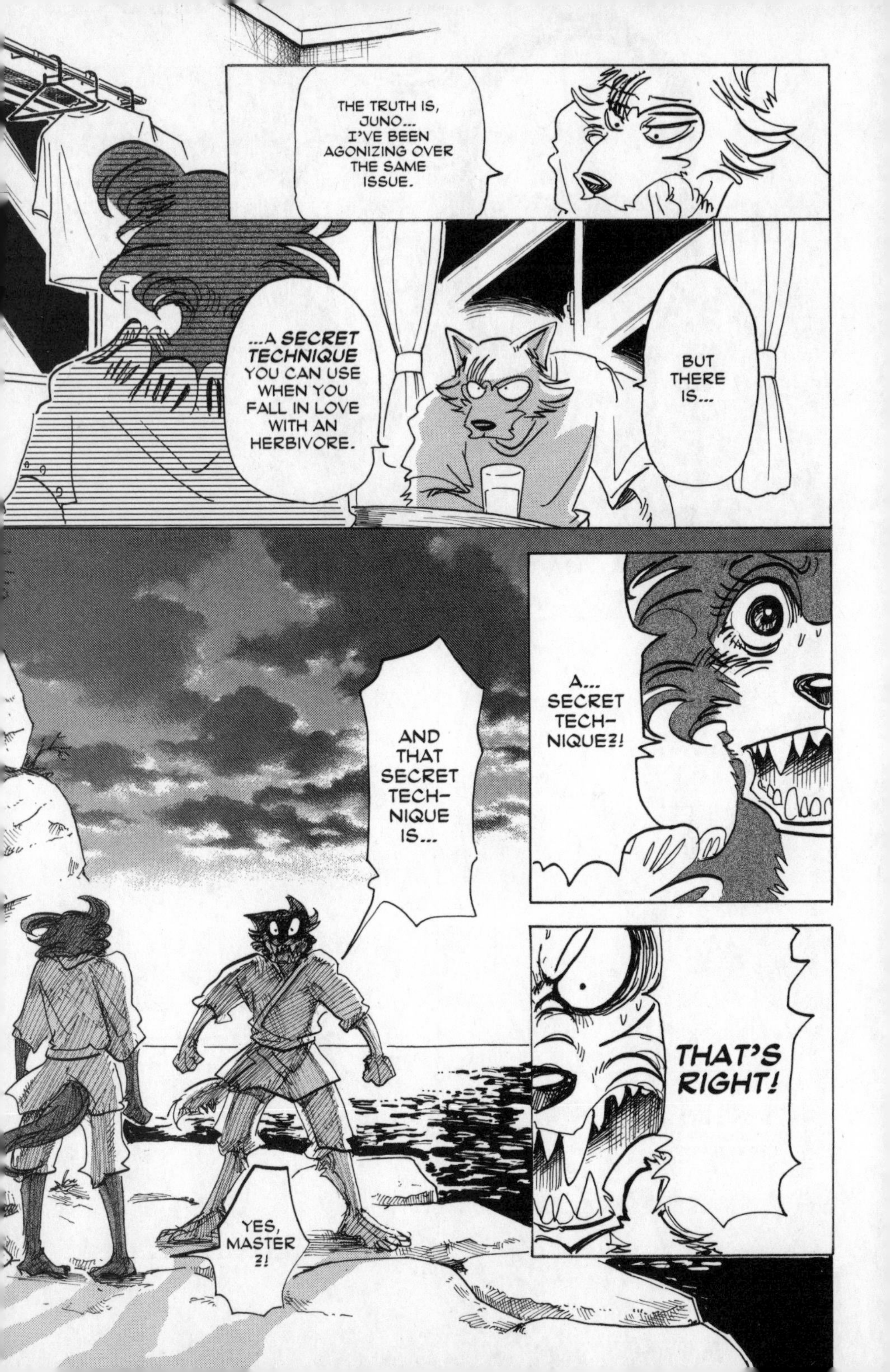
THE TRUTH IS, JUNO... I'VE BEEN AGONIZING OVER THE SAME ISSUE.
BUT THERE IS...
...A SECRET TECHNIQUE YOU CAN USE WHEN YOU FALL IN LOVE WITH AN HERBIVORE.
A... SECRET TECH-NIQUE?!
THAT'S RIGHT!
AND THAT SECRET TECH-NIQUE IS...
YES, MASTER?!

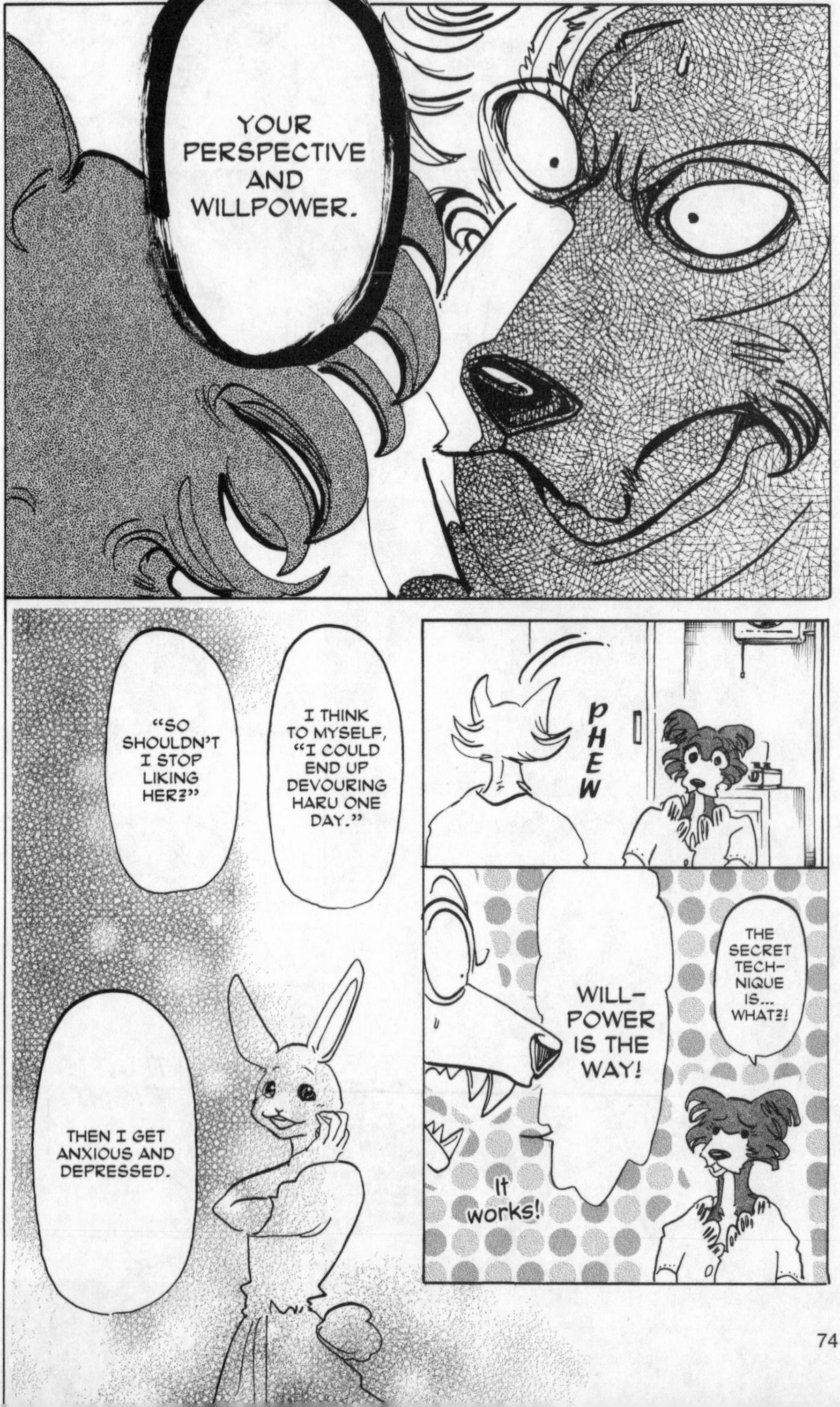
YOUR PERSPECTIVE AND WILLPOWER.
PHEW
THE SECRET TECH-NIQUE IS... WHAT?!
WILL-POWER IS THE WAY!
It works!
I THINK TO MYSELF, "I COULD END UP DEVOURING HARU ONE DAY."
"SO SHOULDN'T I STOP LIKING HER?"
THEN I GET ANXIOUS AND DEPRESSED.

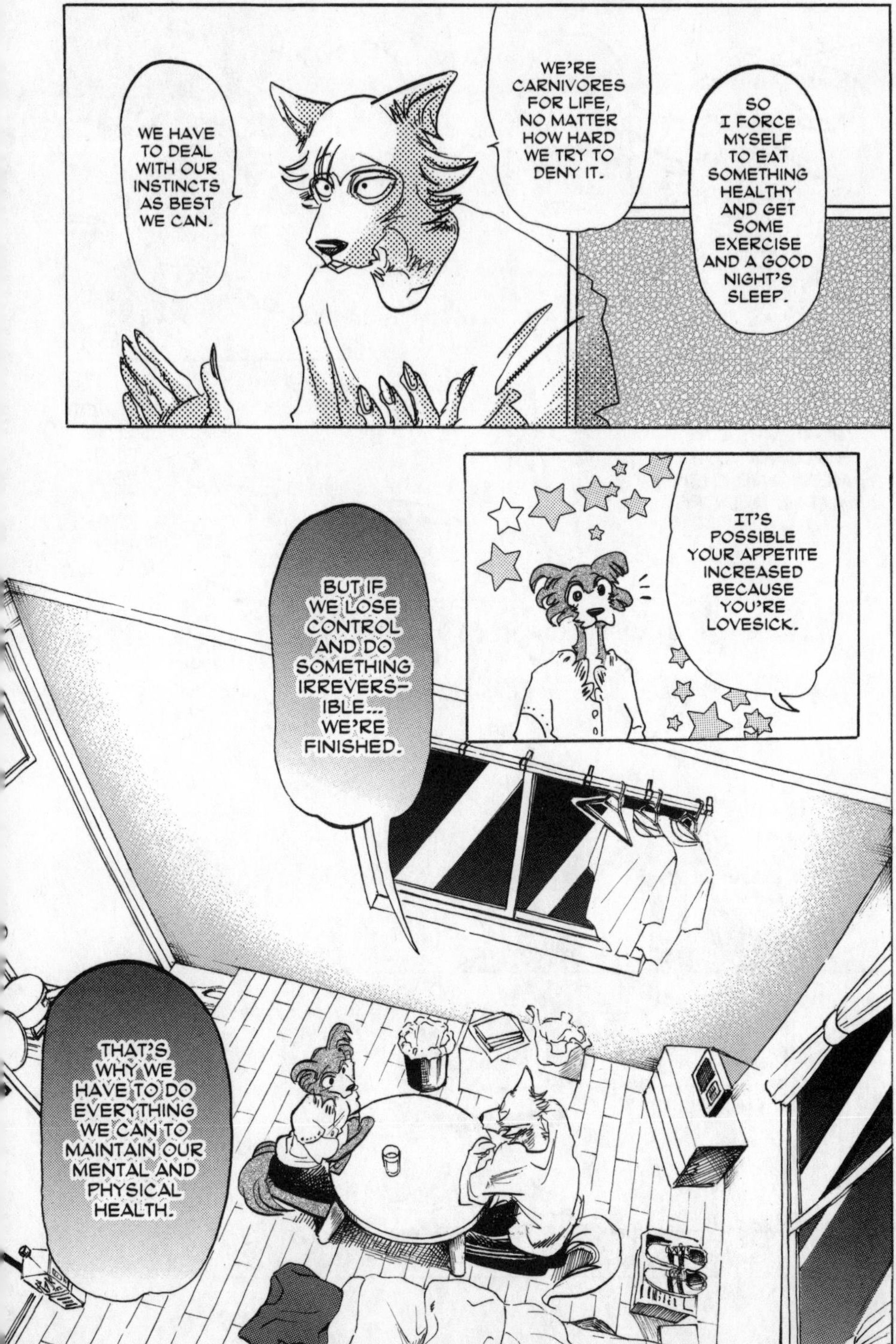
SO I FORCE MYSELF TO EAT SOMETHING HEALTHY AND GET SOME EXERCISE AND A GOOD NIGHT'S SLEEP.
WE'RE CARNIVORES FOR LIFE, NO MATTER HOW HARD WE TRY TO DENY IT.
WE HAVE TO DEAL WITH OUR INSTINCTS AS BEST WE CAN.
IT'S POSSIBLE YOUR APPETITE INCREASED BECAUSE YOU'RE LOVESICK.
BUT IF WE LOSE CONTROL AND DO SOMETHING IRREVERS-IBLE... WE'RE FINISHED.
THAT'S WHY WE HAVE TO DO EVERYTHING WE CAN TO MAINTAIN OUR MENTAL AND PHYSICAL HEALTH.

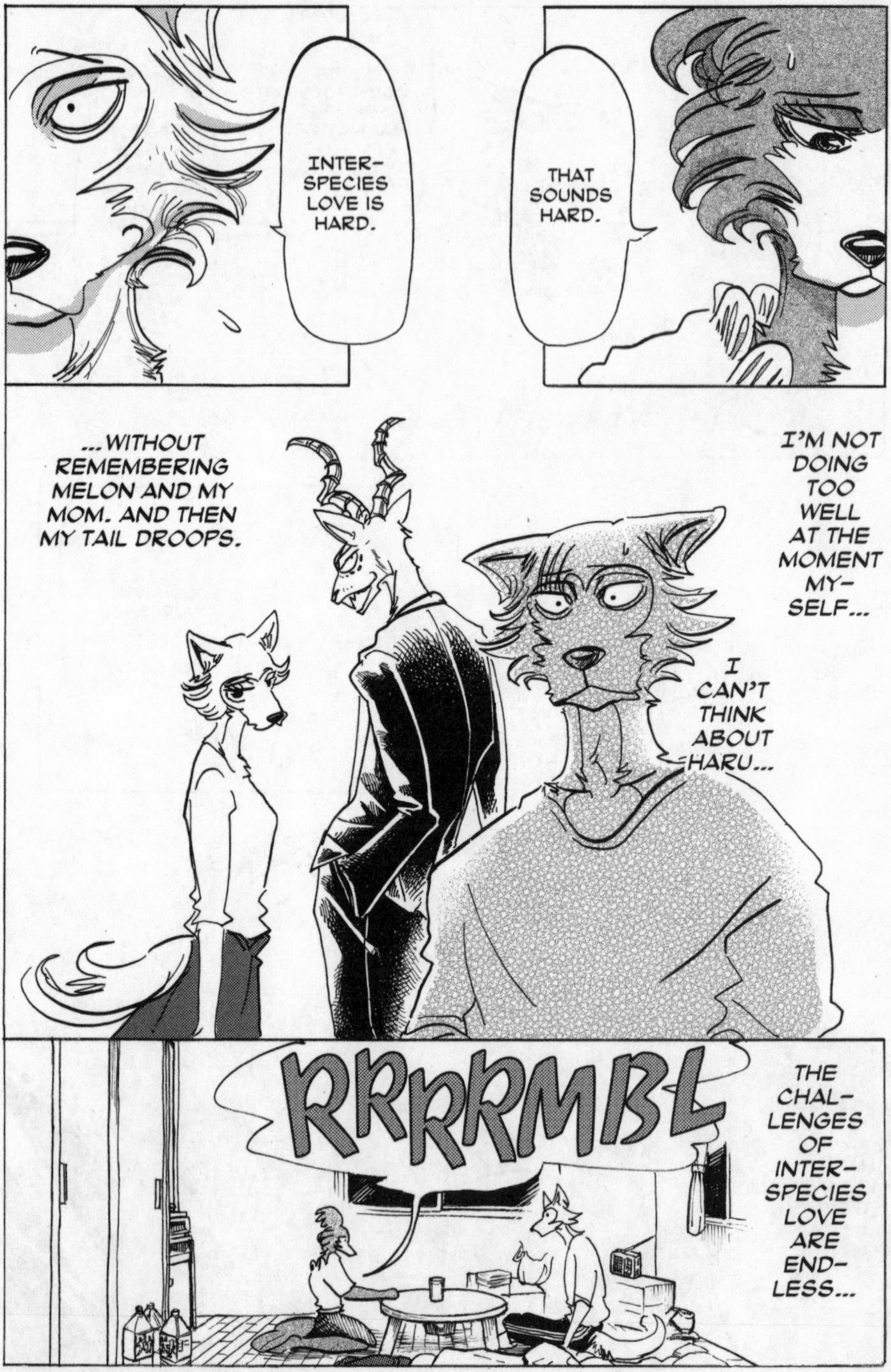
THAT SOUNDS HARD.
INTER-SPECIES LOVE IS HARD.
I'M NOT DOING TOO WELL AT THE MOMENT MYSELF...
I CAN'T THINK ABOUT HARU...
...WITHOUT REMEMBERING MELON AND MY MOM. AND THEN MY TAIL DROOPS.
THE CHAL-LENGES OF INTER-SPECIES LOVE ARE END-LESS...
RRRRMBL

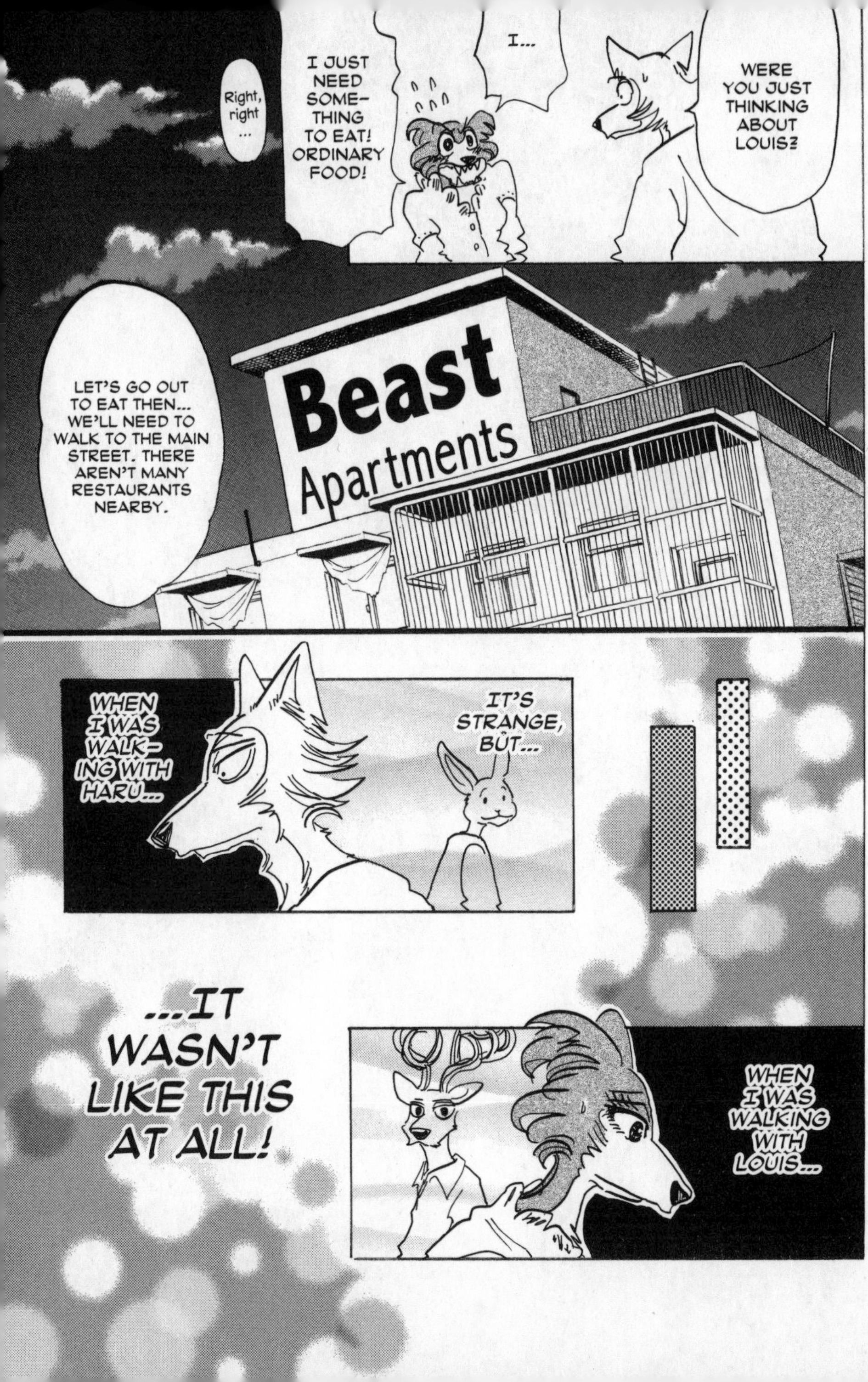
WERE YOU JUST THINKING ABOUT LOUIS?
I...
I JUST NEED SOME-THING TO EAT! ORDINARY FOOD!
Right, right...
Beast Apartments
LET'S GO OUT TO EAT THEN... WE'LL NEED TO WALK TO THE MAIN STREET. THERE AREN'T MANY RESTAURANTS NEARBY.
IT'S STRANGE, BUT...
WHEN I WAS WALK-ING WITH HARU...
WHEN I WAS WALKING WITH LOUIS...
...IT WASN'T LIKE THIS AT ALL!

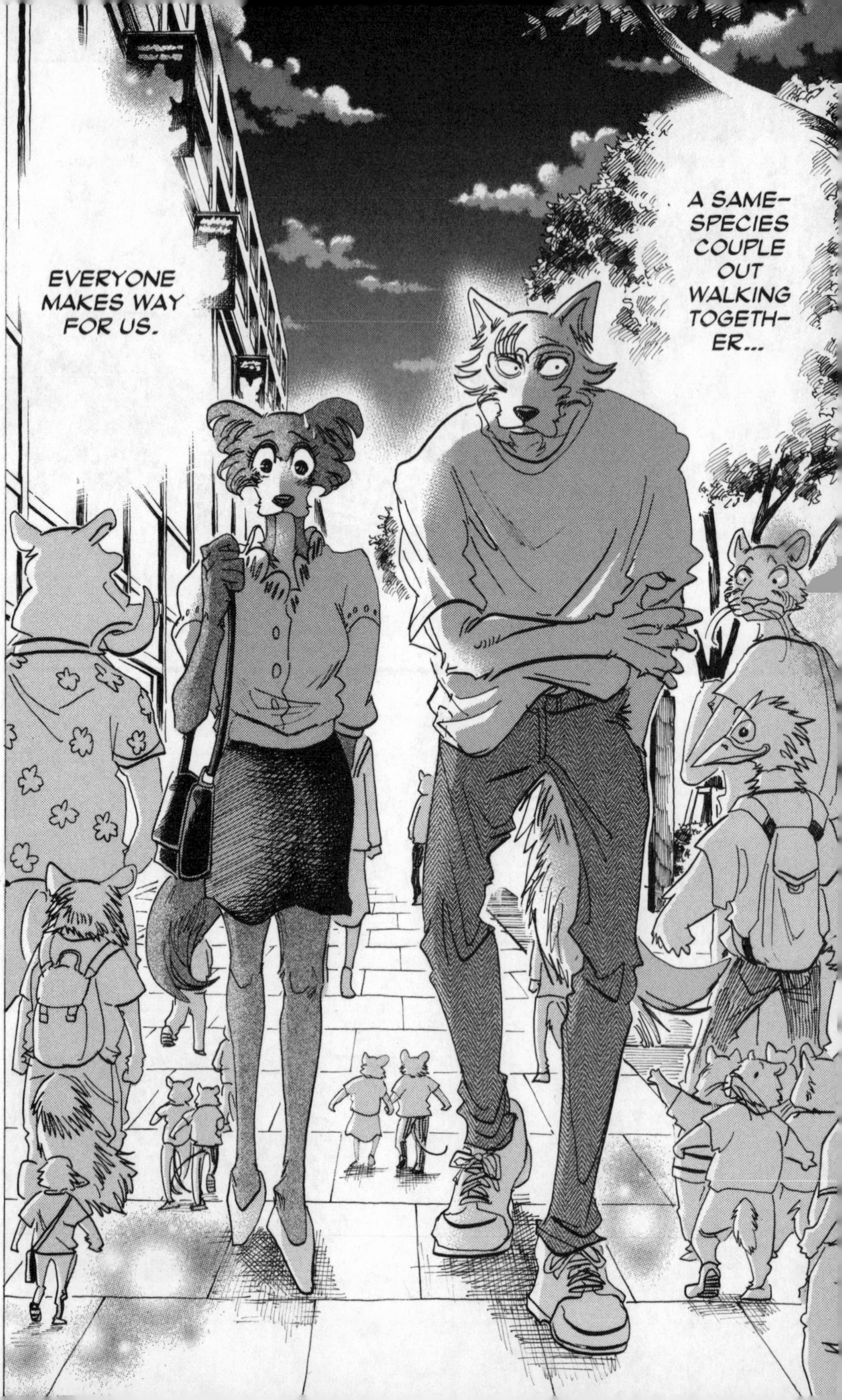
A SAME-SPECIES COUPLE OUT WALKING TOGETHER...
EVERYONE MAKES WAY FOR US.

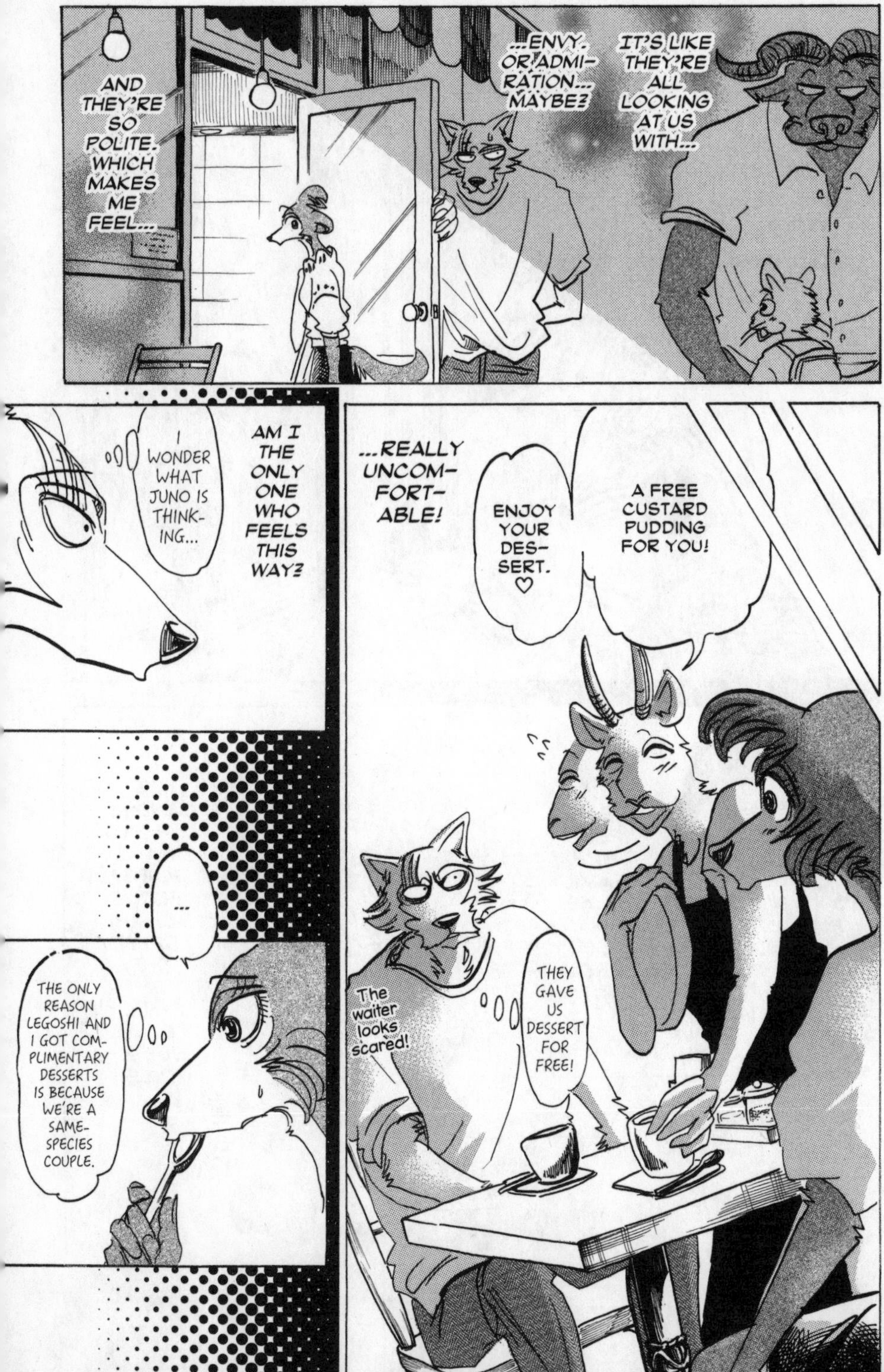
IT'S LIKE THEY'RE ALL LOOKING AT US WITH...
...ENVY. OR ADMIRATION... MAYBE?
AND THEY'RE SO POLITE. WHICH MAKES ME FEEL...
A FREE CUSTARD PUDDING FOR YOU!
ENJOY YOUR DESSERT. ♡
...REALLY UNCOMFORTABLE!
THEY GAVE US DESSERT FOR FREE!
The waiter looks scared!
AM I THE ONLY ONE WHO FEELS THIS WAY?
I WONDER WHAT JUNO IS THINKING...
...
THE ONLY REASON LEGOSHI AND I GOT COMPLIMENTARY DESSERTS IS BECAUSE WE'RE A SAME-SPECIES COUPLE.

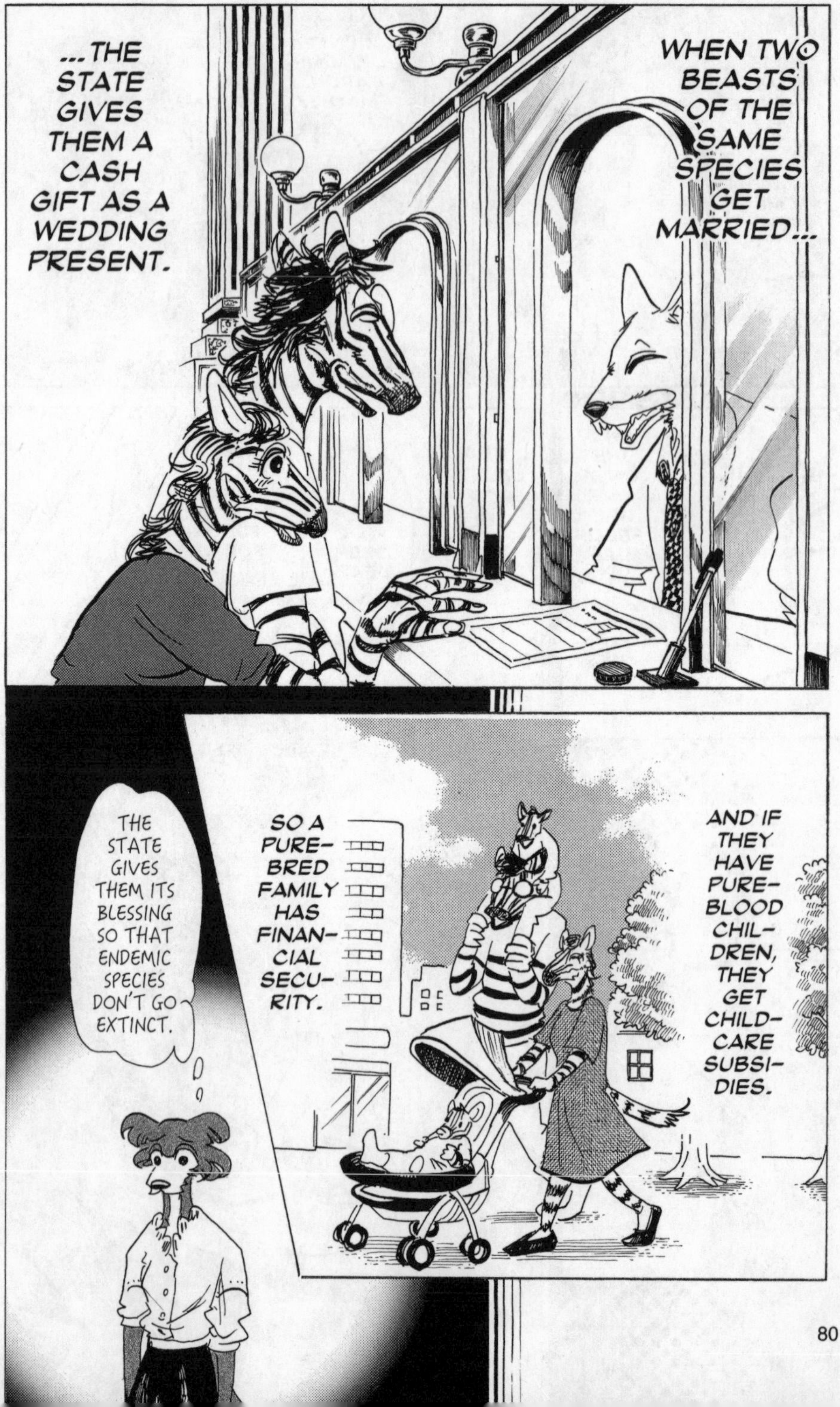
WHEN TWO BEASTS OF THE SAME SPECIES GET MARRIED...
...THE STATE GIVES THEM A CASH GIFT AS A WEDDING PRESENT.
AND IF THEY HAVE PURE-BLOOD CHIL-DREN, THEY GET CHILD-CARE SUBSI-DIES.
SO A PURE-BRED FAMILY HAS FINAN-CIAL SECU-RITY.
THE STATE GIVES THEM ITS BLESSING SO THAT ENDEMIC SPECIES DON'T GO EXTINCT.

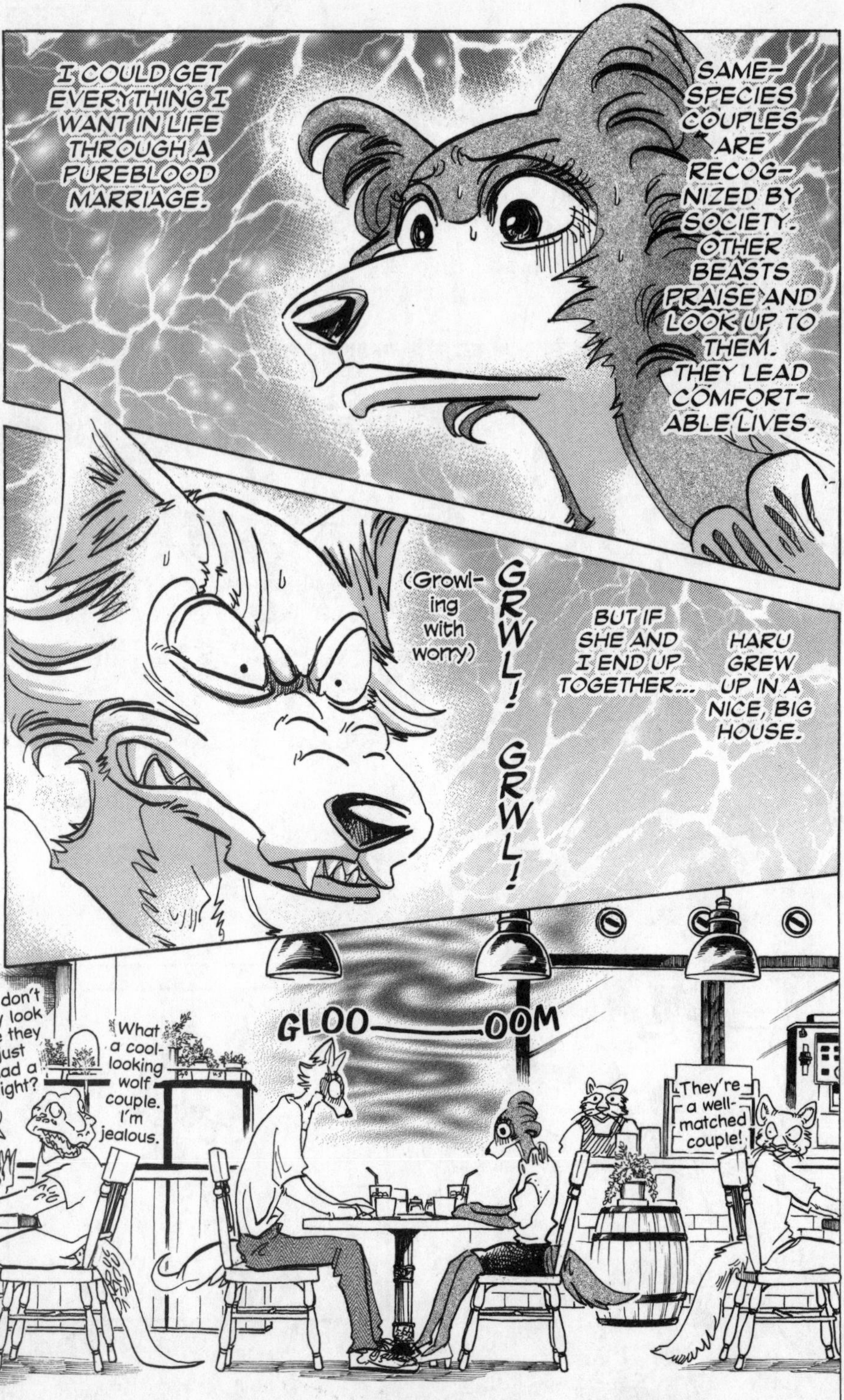
SAME-SPECIES COUPLES ARE RECOGNIZED BY SOCIETY. OTHER BEASTS PRAISE AND LOOK UP TO THEM. THEY LEAD COMFORTABLE LIVES.
I COULD GET EVERYTHING I WANT IN LIFE THROUGH A PUREBLOOD MARRIAGE.
HARU GREW UP IN A NICE, BIG HOUSE.
BUT IF SHE AND I END UP TOGETHER...
GRWL! GRWL!
(Growling with worry)
They're a well-matched couple!
GLOO——OOM
What a cool-looking wolf couple. I'm jealous.
But don't they look like they just had a fight?

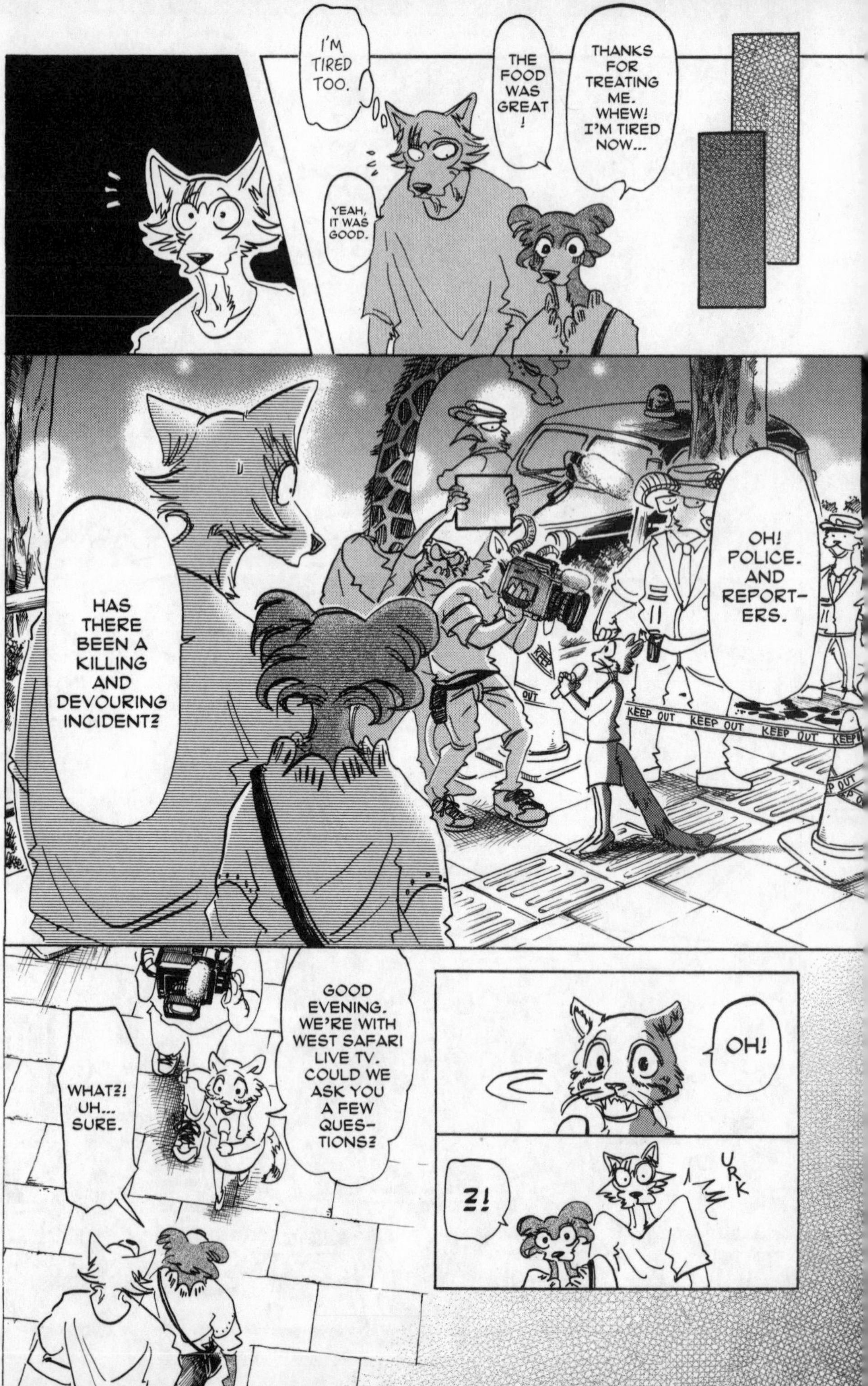
THANKS FOR TREATING ME. WHEW! I'M TIRED NOW...
THE FOOD WAS GREAT!
I'M TIRED TOO.
YEAH, IT WAS GOOD.
OH! POLICE. AND REPORTERS.
KEEP OUT KEEP OUT KEEP OUT
HAS THERE BEEN A KILLING AND DEVOURING INCIDENT?
OH!
?!
URK
GOOD EVENING. WE'RE WITH WEST SAFARI LIVE TV. COULD WE ASK YOU A FEW QUESTIONS?
WHAT?! UH... SURE.

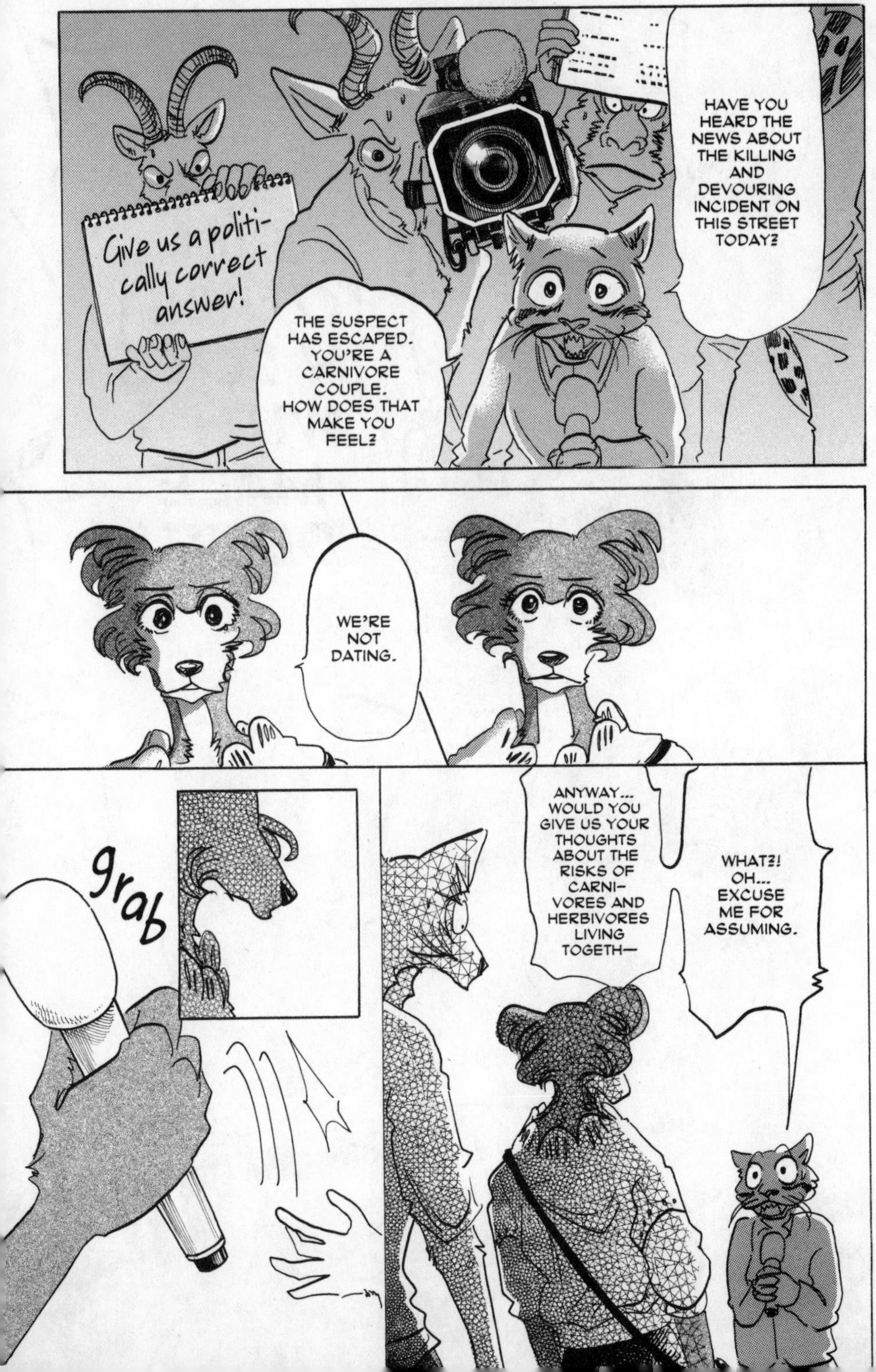
HAVE YOU HEARD THE NEWS ABOUT THE KILLING AND DEVOURING INCIDENT ON THIS STREET TODAY?
THE SUSPECT HAS ESCAPED. YOU'RE A CARNIVORE COUPLE. HOW DOES THAT MAKE YOU FEEL?
Give us a politi-cally correct answer!
WE'RE NOT DATING.
WHAT?! OH... EXCUSE ME FOR ASSUMING.
ANYWAY... WOULD YOU GIVE US YOUR THOUGHTS ABOUT THE RISKS OF CARNI-VORES AND HERBIVORES LIVING TOGETH—
grab

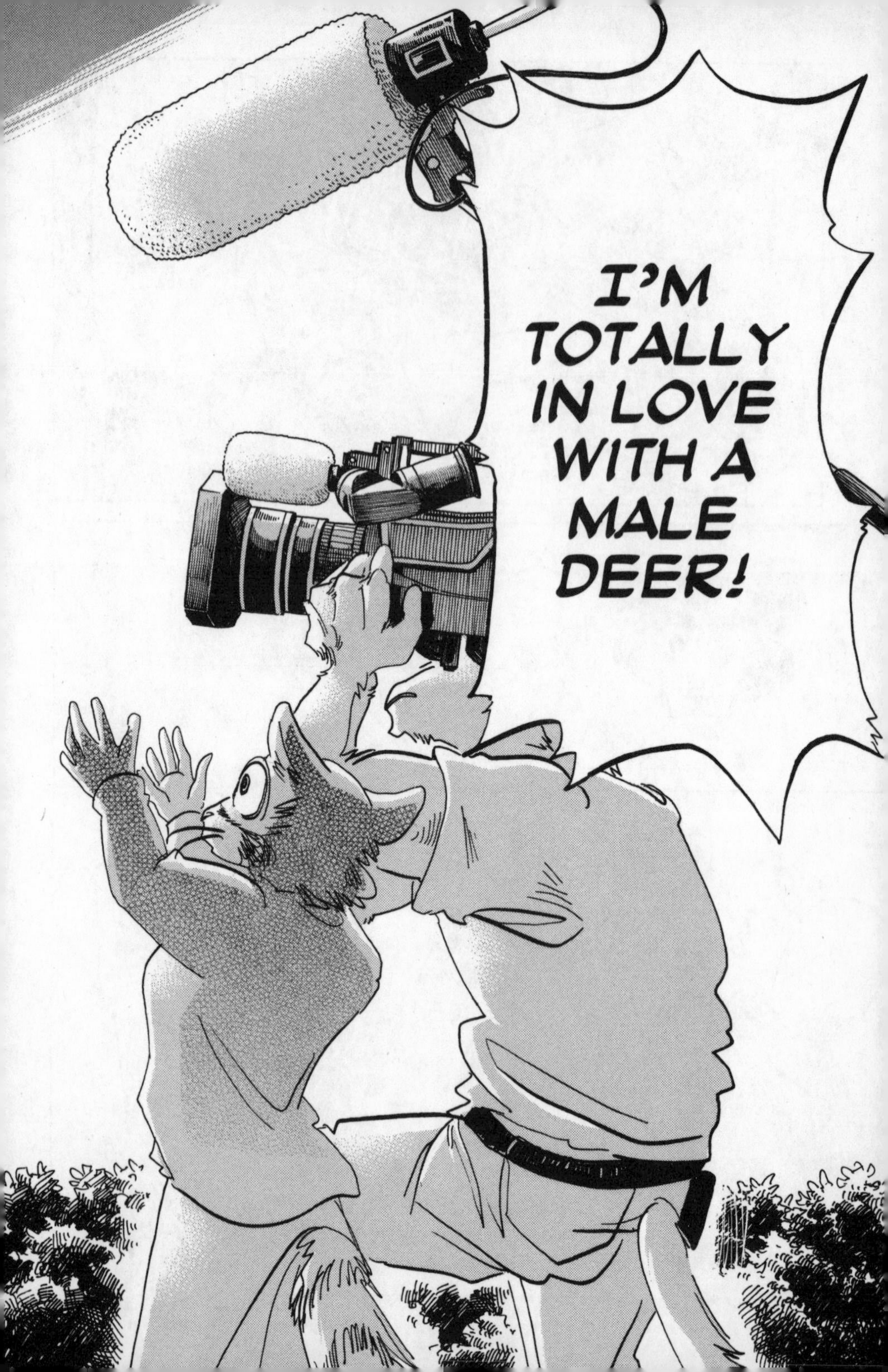
I'M TOTALLY IN LOVE WITH A MALE DEER!

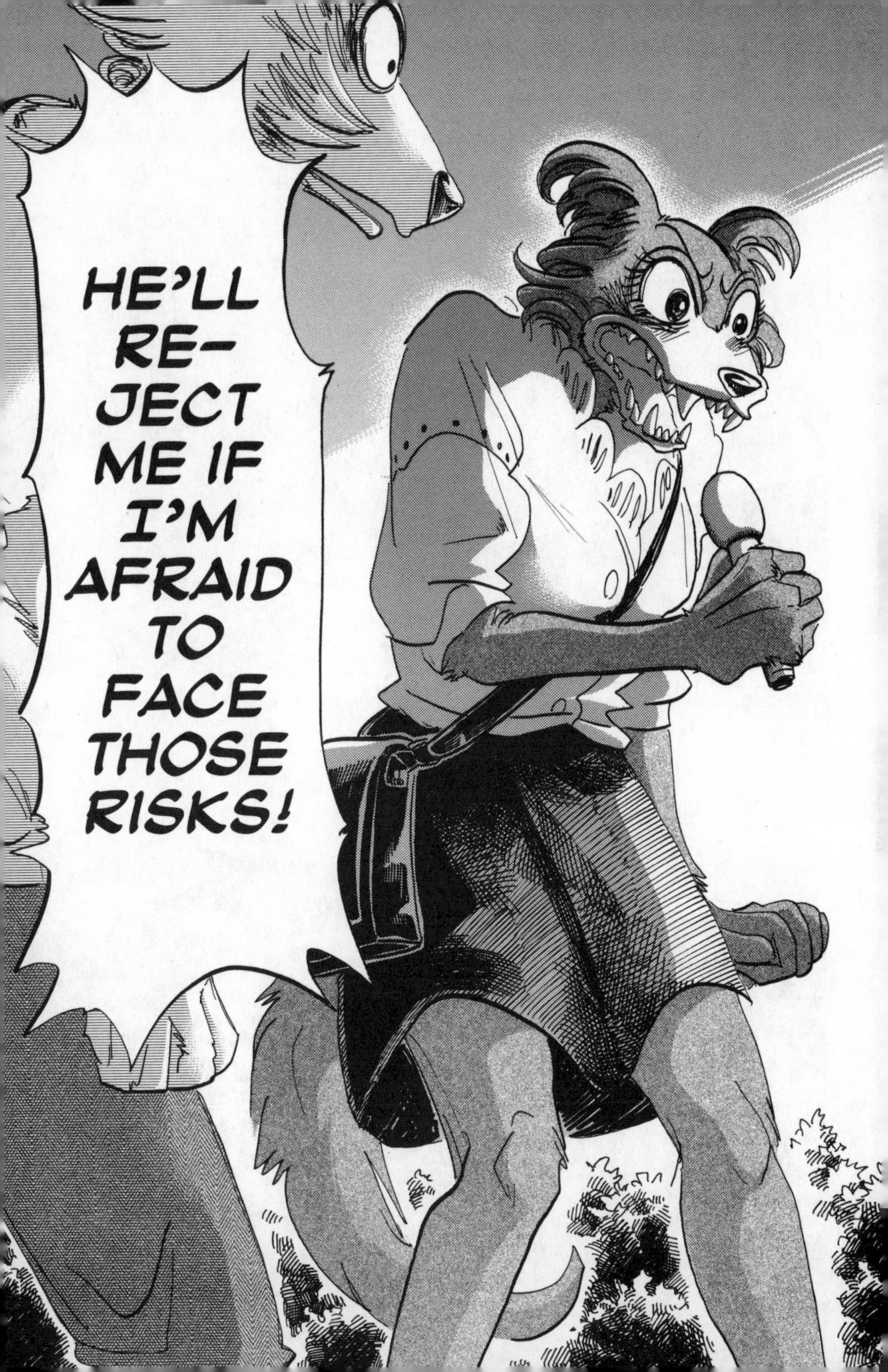
HE'LL RE-JECT ME IF I'M AFRAID TO FACE THOSE RISKS!

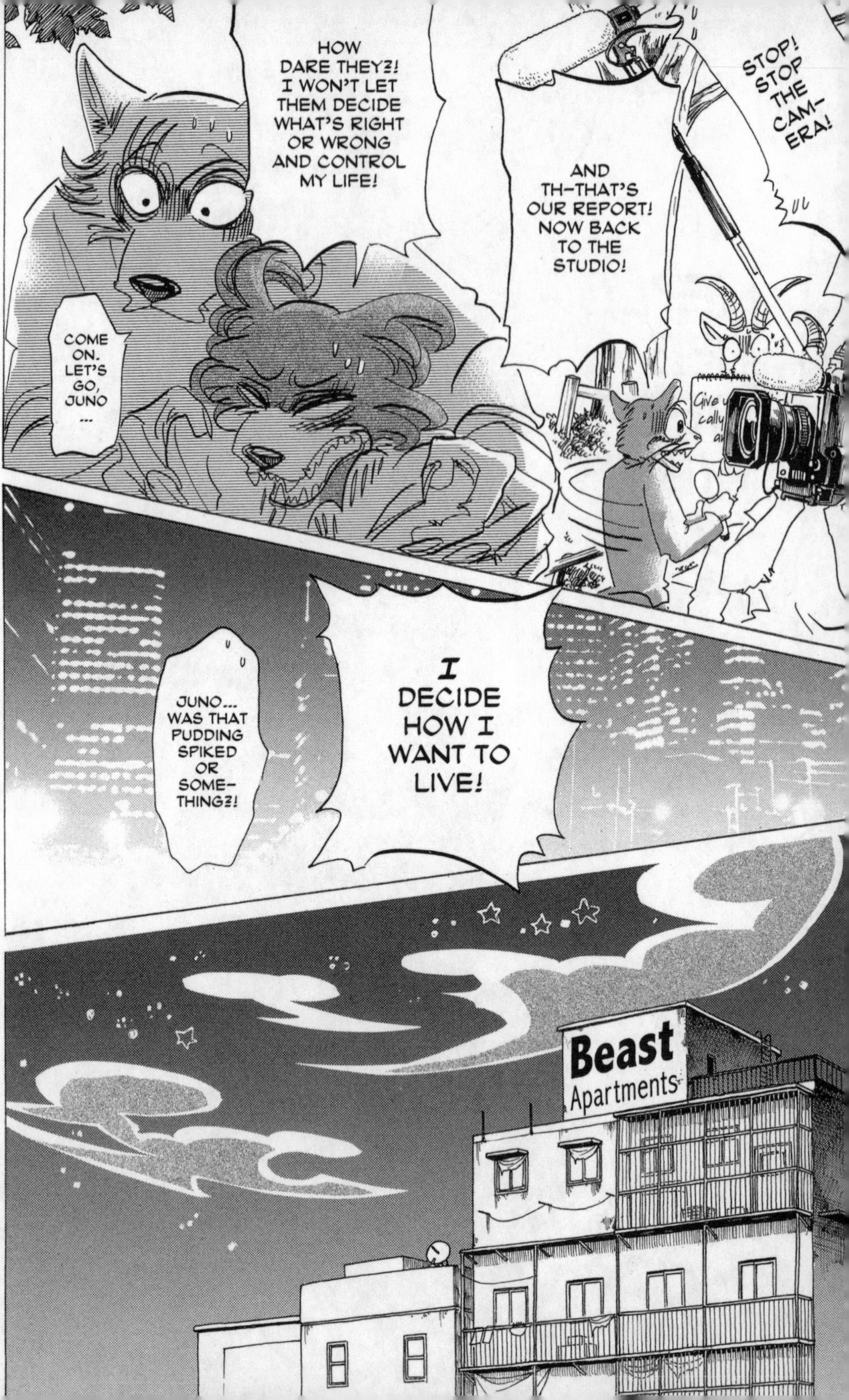
STOP! STOP THE CAM-ERA!
AND TH-THAT'S OUR REPORT! NOW BACK TO THE STUDIO!
HOW DARE THEY?! I WON'T LET THEM DECIDE WHAT'S RIGHT OR WRONG AND CONTROL MY LIFE!
COME ON. LET'S GO, JUNO ...
I DECIDE HOW I WANT TO LIVE!
JUNO... WAS THAT PUDDING SPIKED OR SOME-THING?!
Beast
Apartments

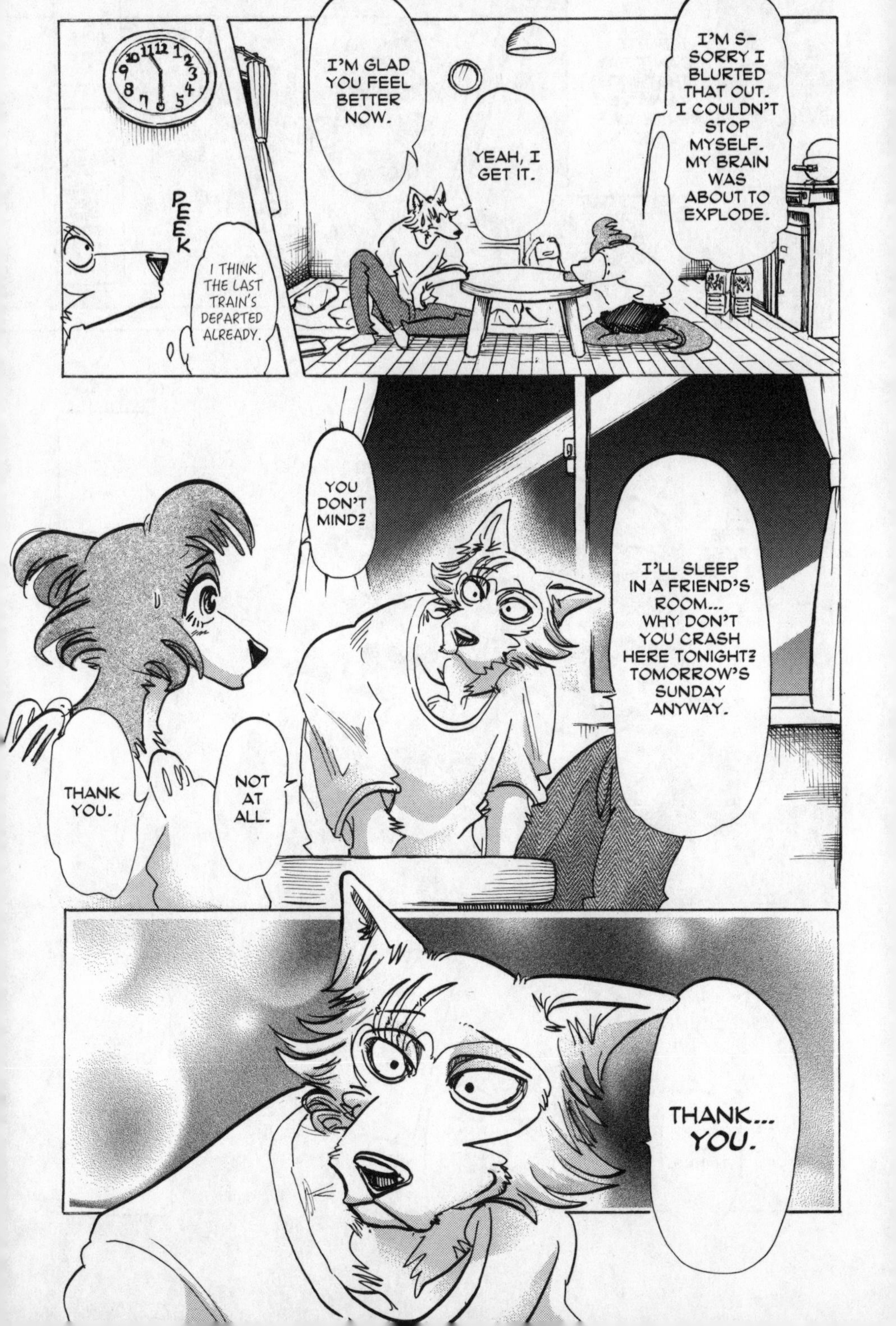
I'M S-SORRY I BLURTED THAT OUT. I COULDN'T STOP MYSELF. MY BRAIN WAS ABOUT TO EXPLODE.
YEAH, I GET IT.
I'M GLAD YOU FEEL BETTER NOW.
PEEK
I THINK THE LAST TRAIN'S DEPARTED ALREADY.
I'LL SLEEP IN A FRIEND'S ROOM... WHY DON'T YOU CRASH HERE TONIGHT? TOMORROW'S SUNDAY ANYWAY.
YOU DON'T MIND?
NOT AT ALL.
THANK YOU.
THANK... YOU.

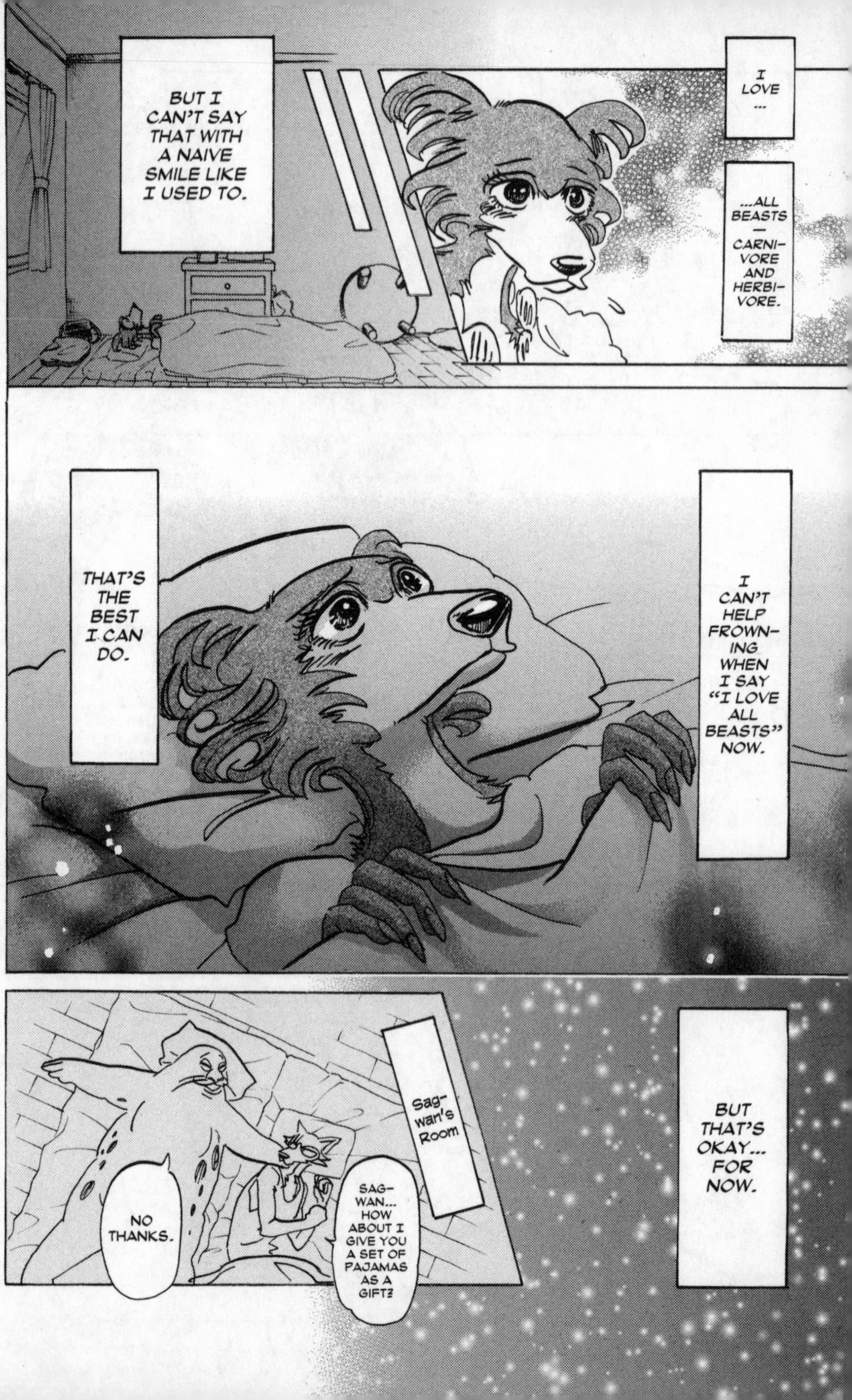
I LOVE...
...ALL BEASTS — CARNIVORE AND HERBIVORE.
BUT I CAN'T SAY THAT WITH A NAIVE SMILE LIKE I USED TO.
I CAN'T HELP FROWNING WHEN I SAY "I LOVE ALL BEASTS" NOW.
THAT'S THE BEST I CAN DO.
BUT THAT'S OKAY... FOR NOW.
Sagwan's Room
SAGWAN... HOW ABOUT I GIVE YOU A SET OF PAJAMAS AS A GIFT?
NO THANKS.

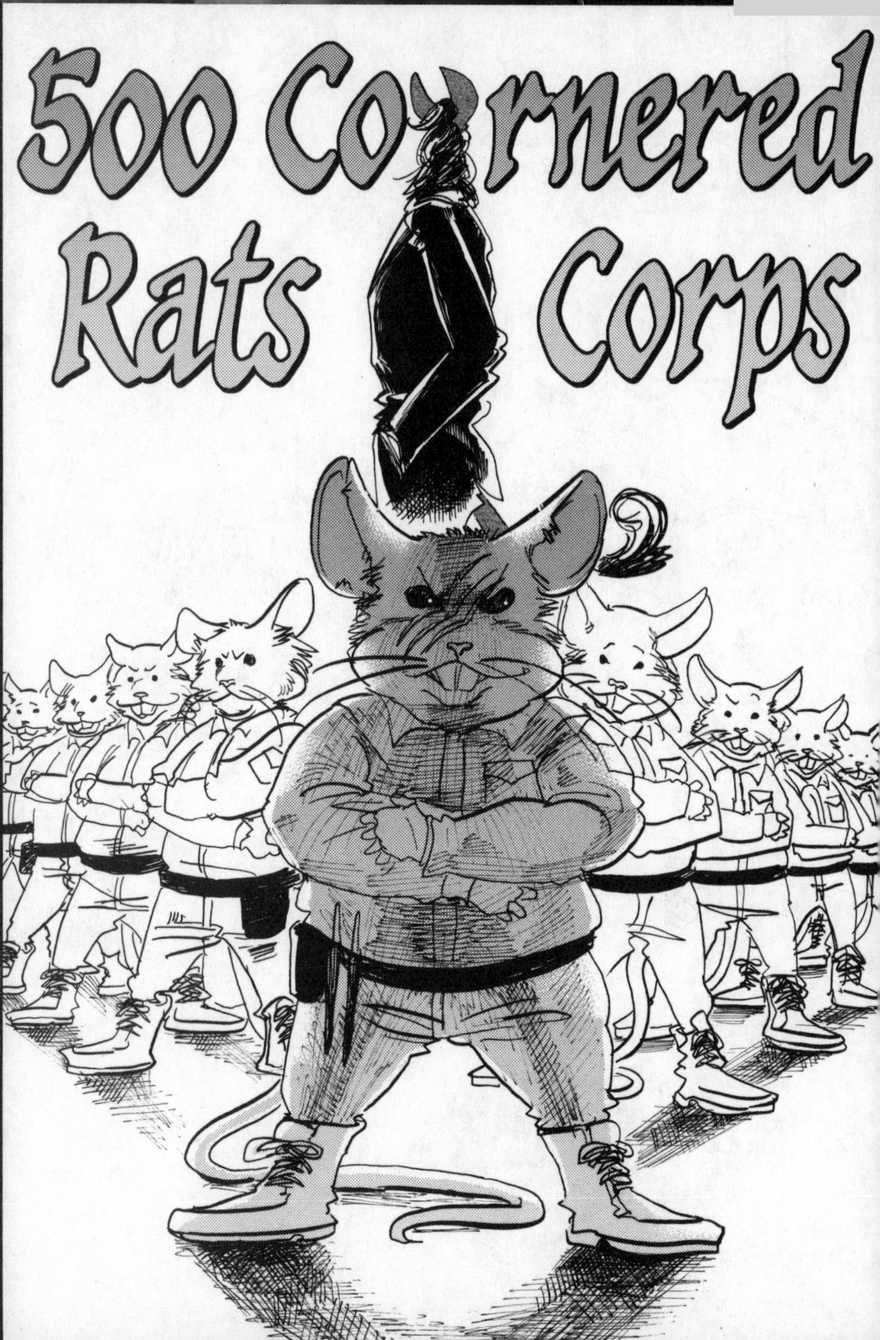
500 Cornered Rats Corps

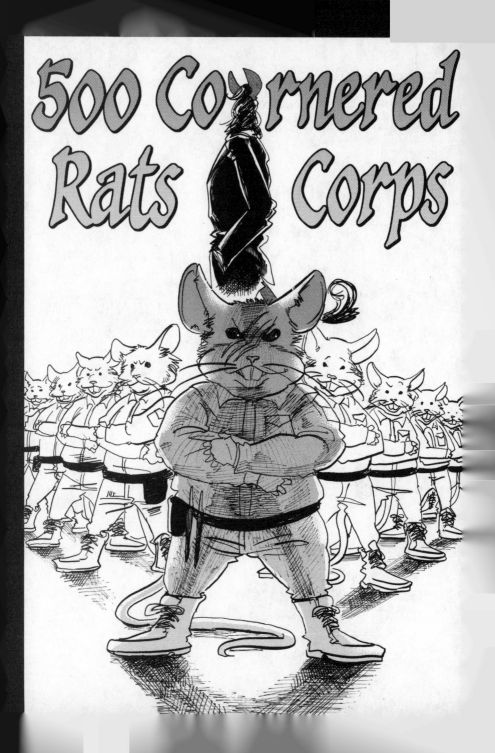

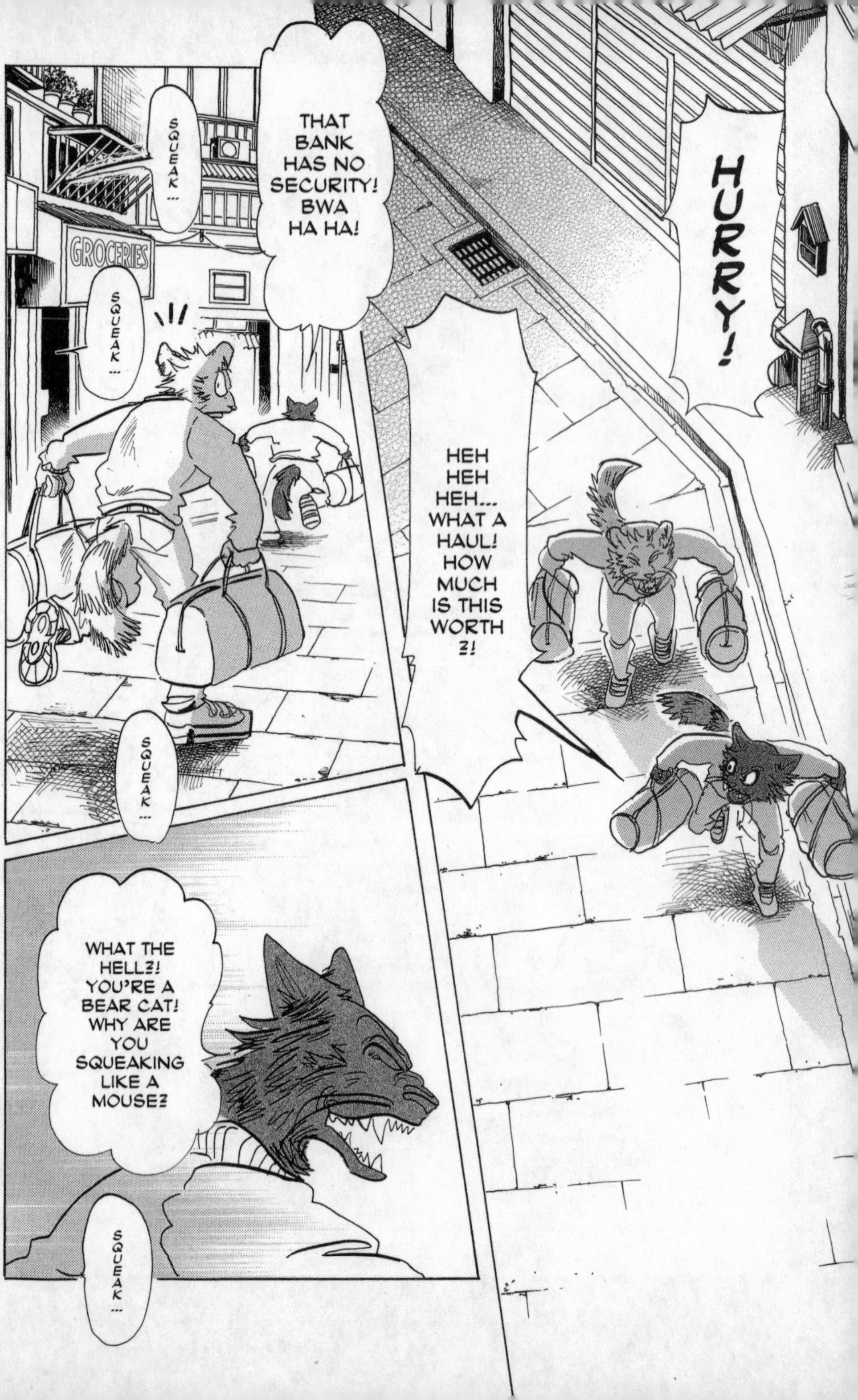
HURRY!
HEH HEH HEH... WHAT A HAUL! HOW MUCH IS THIS WORTH?!
THAT BANK HAS NO SECURITY! BWA HA HA!
SQUEAK...
SQUEAK...
SQUEAK...
WHAT THE HELL?! YOU'RE A BEAR CAT! WHY ARE YOU SQUEAKING LIKE A MOUSE?
SQUEAK...

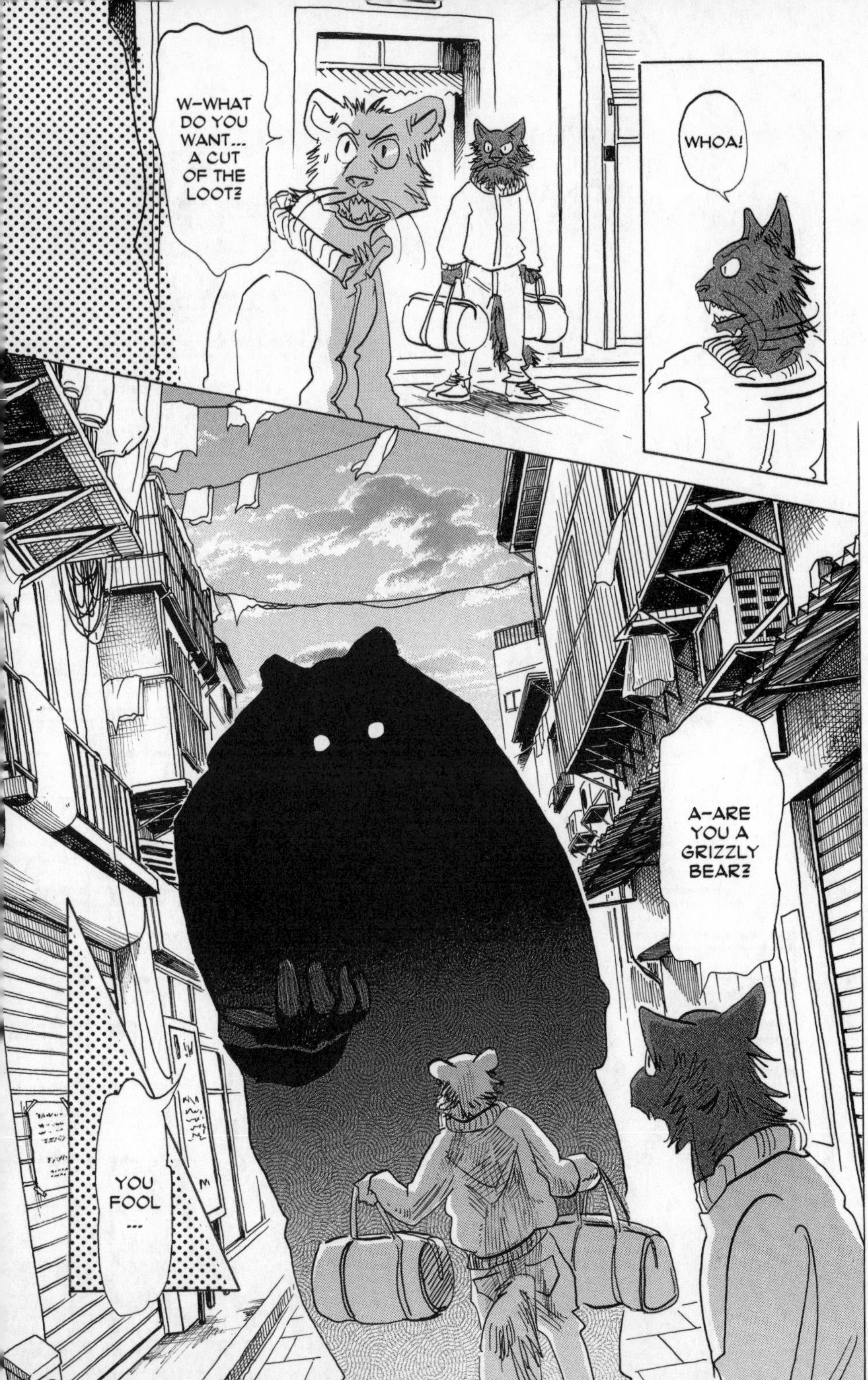
WHOA!
W-WHAT DO YOU WANT... A CUT OF THE LOOT?
A-ARE YOU A GRIZZLY BEAR?
YOU FOOL...

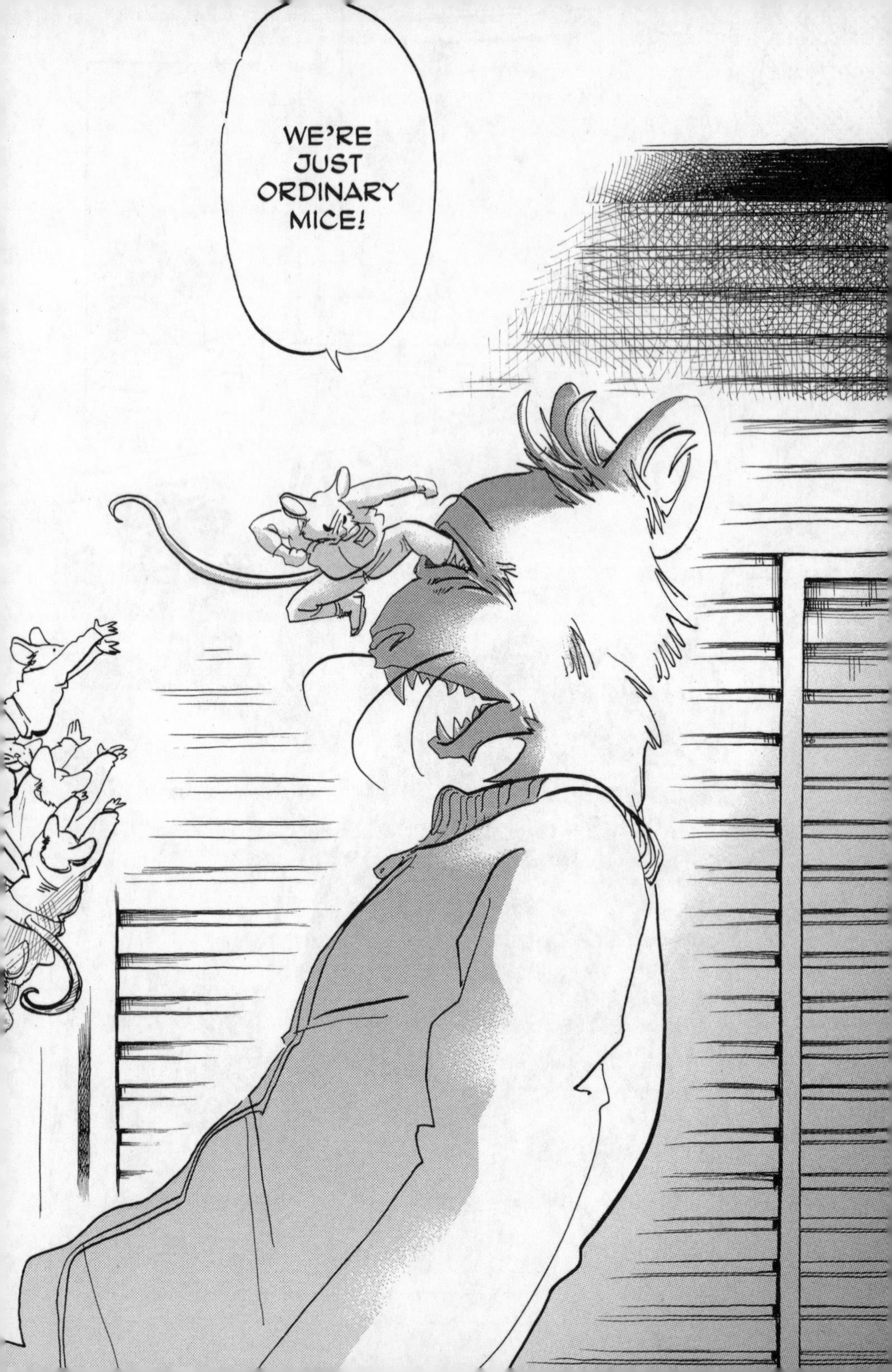
WE'RE JUST ORDINARY MICE!

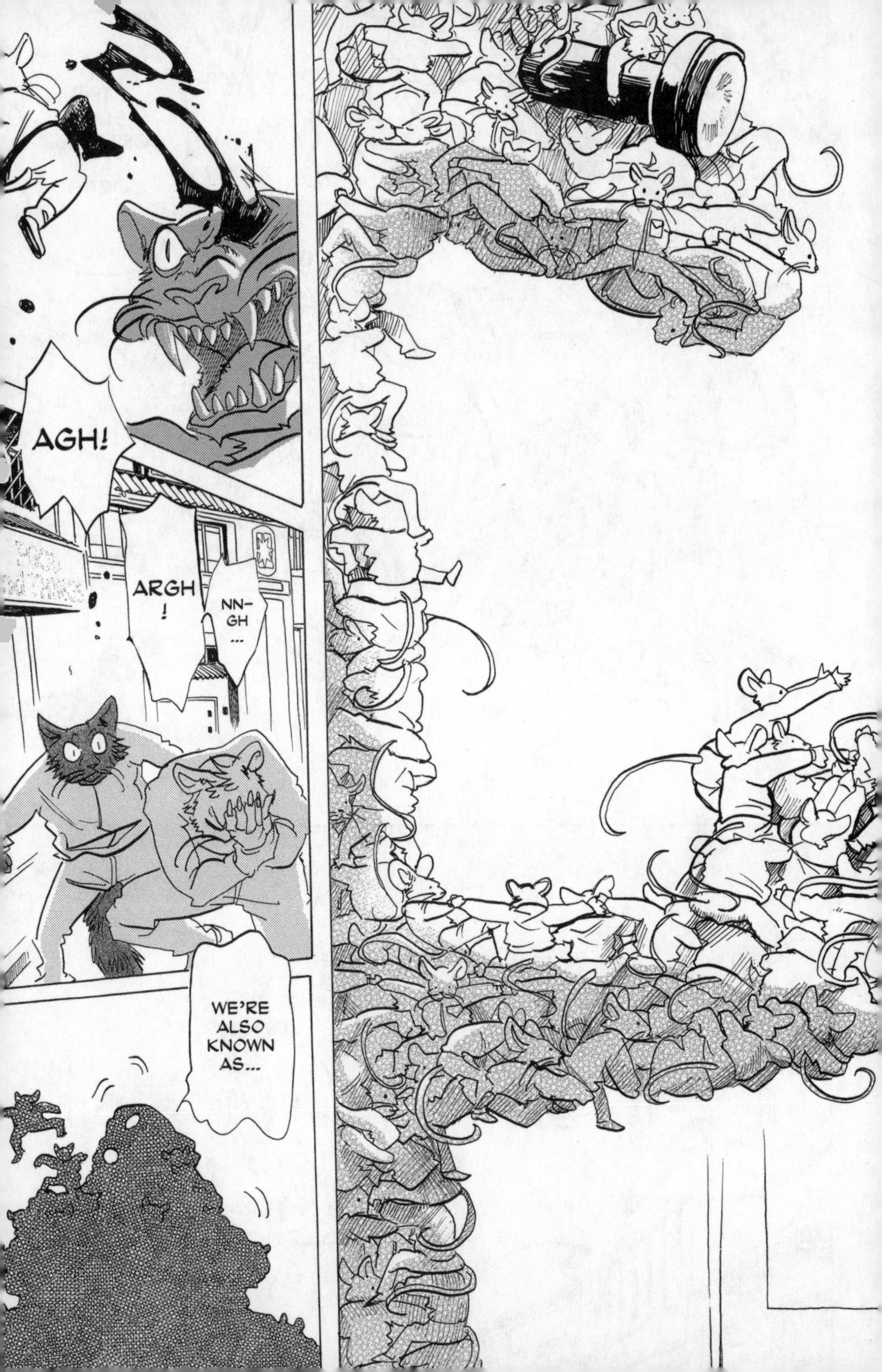
AGH!
NN-GH...
ARGH!
WE'RE ALSO KNOWN AS...

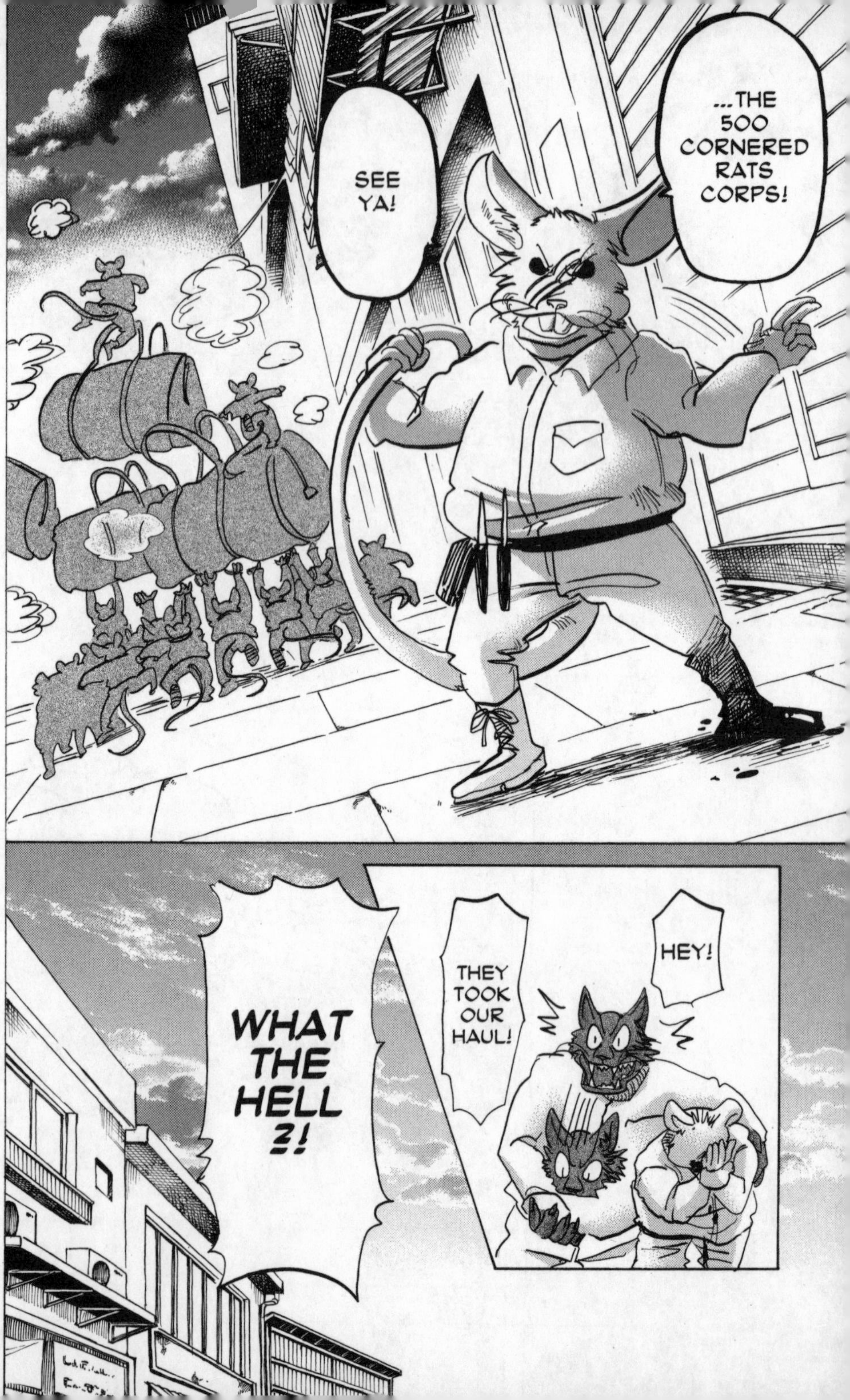
...THE 500 CORNERED RATS CORPS!
SEE YA!
HEY!
THEY TOOK OUR HAUL!
WHAT THE HELL ?!

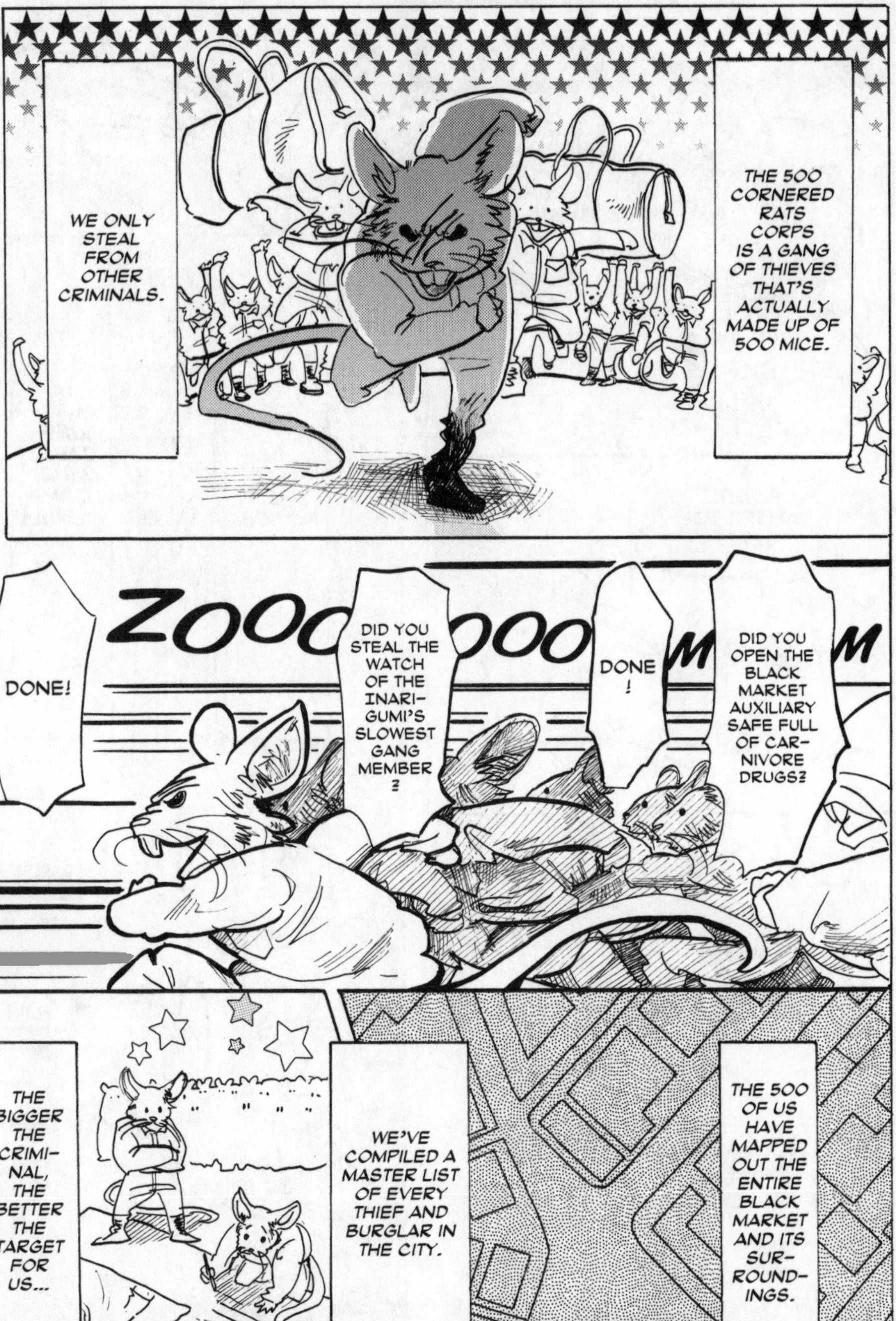

THE 500 CORNERED RATS CORPS IS A GANG OF THIEVES THAT'S ACTUALLY MADE UP OF 500 MICE.
WE ONLY STEAL FROM OTHER CRIMINALS.
DID YOU OPEN THE BLACK MARKET AUXILIARY SAFE FULL OF CARNIVORE DRUGS?
DONE!
DID YOU STEAL THE WATCH OF THE INARI-GUMI'S SLOWEST GANG MEMBER?
DONE!
THE 500 OF US HAVE MAPPED OUT THE ENTIRE BLACK MARKET AND ITS SURROUNDINGS.
WE'VE COMPILED A MASTER LIST OF EVERY THIEF AND BURGLAR IN THE CITY.
THE BIGGER THE CRIMINAL, THE BETTER THE TARGET FOR US...

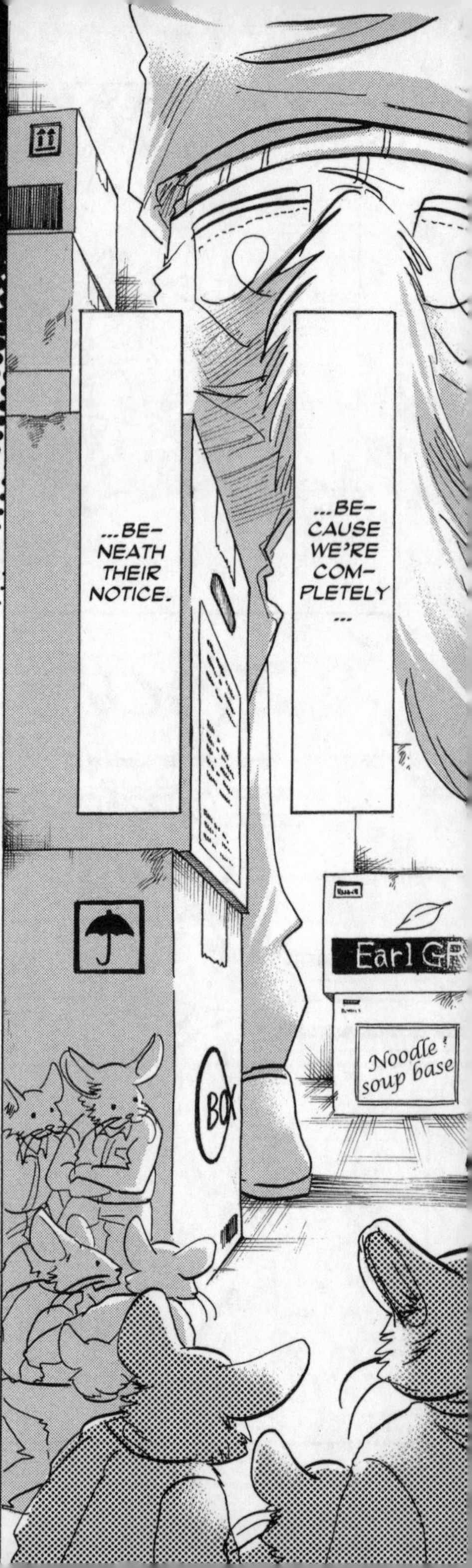
...BE-
CAUSE
WE'RE
COM-
PLETELY
...
...BE-
NEATH
THEIR
NOTICE.
BOX
Earl Gr
Noodle soup base

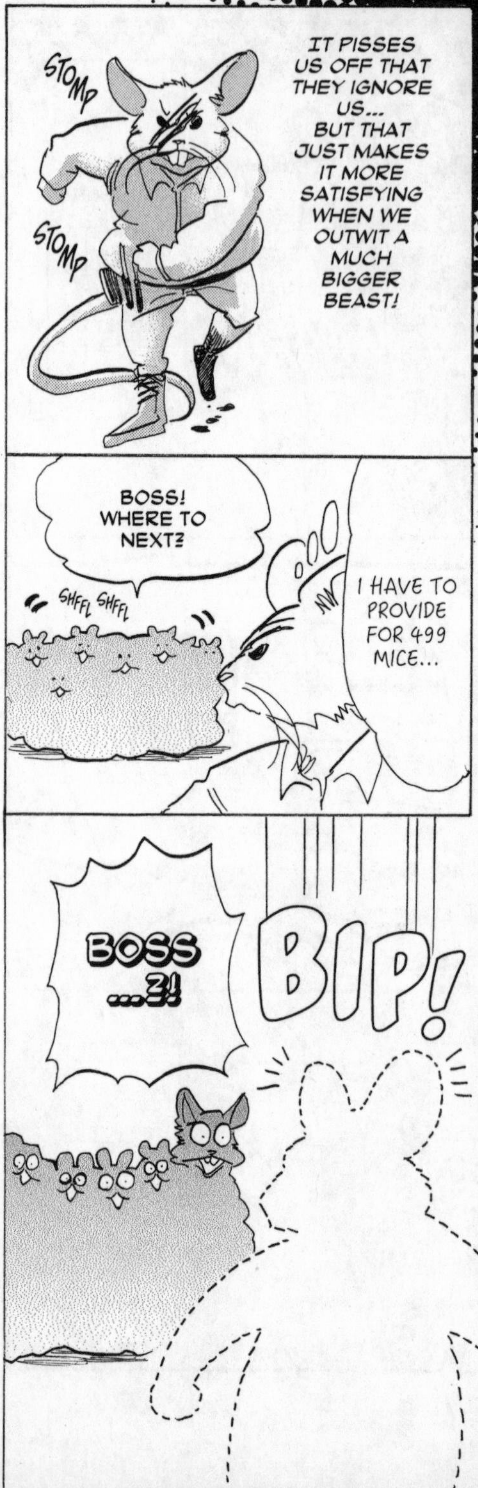
IT PISSES US OFF THAT THEY IGNORE US... BUT THAT JUST MAKES IT MORE SATISFYING WHEN WE OUTWIT A MUCH BIGGER BEAST!
STOMP
STOMP
I HAVE TO PROVIDE FOR 499 MICE...
BOSS! WHERE TO NEXT?
SHFFL SHFFL
BIP!
BOSS ...?!

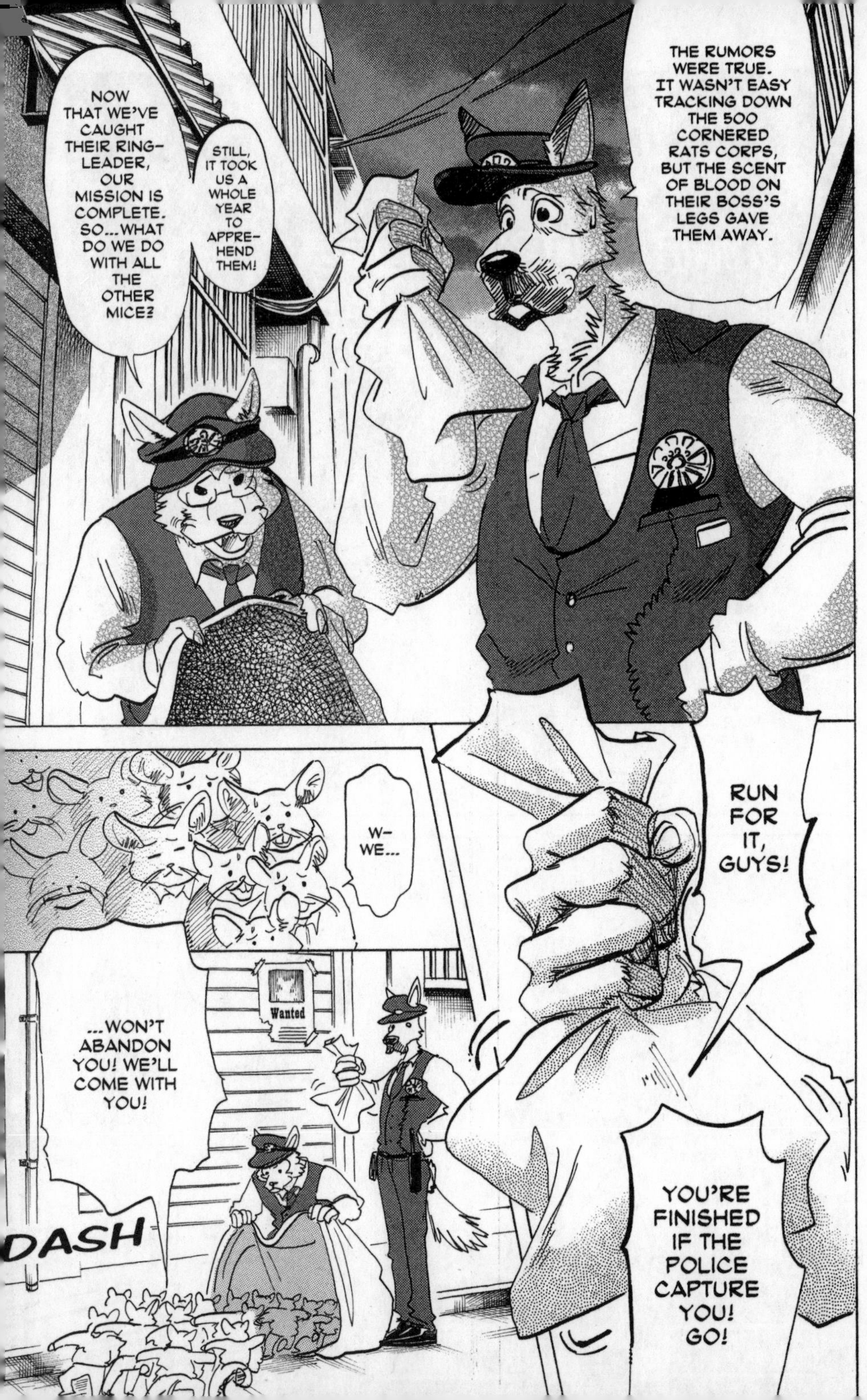
THE RUMORS WERE TRUE. IT WASN'T EASY TRACKING DOWN THE 500 CORNERED RATS CORPS, BUT THE SCENT OF BLOOD ON THEIR BOSS'S LEGS GAVE THEM AWAY.
STILL, IT TOOK US A WHOLE YEAR TO APPREHEND THEM!
NOW THAT WE'VE CAUGHT THEIR RINGLEADER, OUR MISSION IS COMPLETE. SO...WHAT DO WE DO WITH ALL THE OTHER MICE?
RUN FOR IT, GUYS!
YOU'RE FINISHED IF THE POLICE CAPTURE YOU! GO!
W-WE...
Wanted
...WON'T ABANDON YOU! WE'LL COME WITH YOU!
DASH

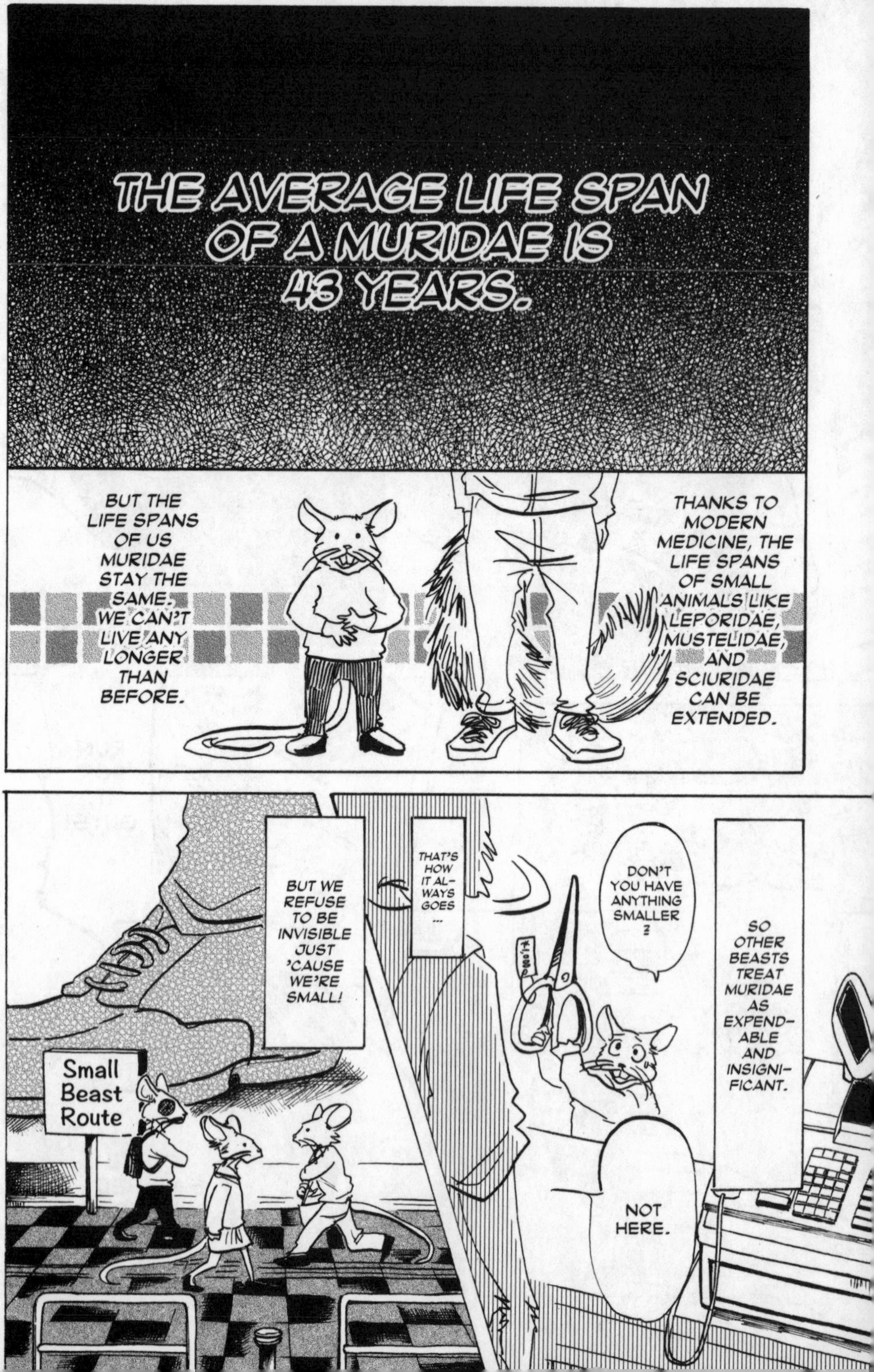
THE AVERAGE LIFE SPAN OF A MURIDAE IS 43 YEARS.
THANKS TO MODERN MEDICINE, THE LIFE SPANS OF SMALL ANIMALS LIKE LEPORIDAE, MUSTELIDAE, AND SCIURIDAE CAN BE EXTENDED.
BUT THE LIFE SPANS OF US MURIDAE STAY THE SAME. WE CAN'T LIVE ANY LONGER THAN BEFORE.
SO OTHER BEASTS TREAT MURIDAE AS EXPEND-ABLE AND INSIGNI-FICANT.
DON'T YOU HAVE ANYTHING SMALLER?
NOT HERE.
THAT'S HOW IT AL-WAYS GOES...
BUT WE REFUSE TO BE INVISIBLE JUST 'CAUSE WE'RE SMALL!
Small Beast Route

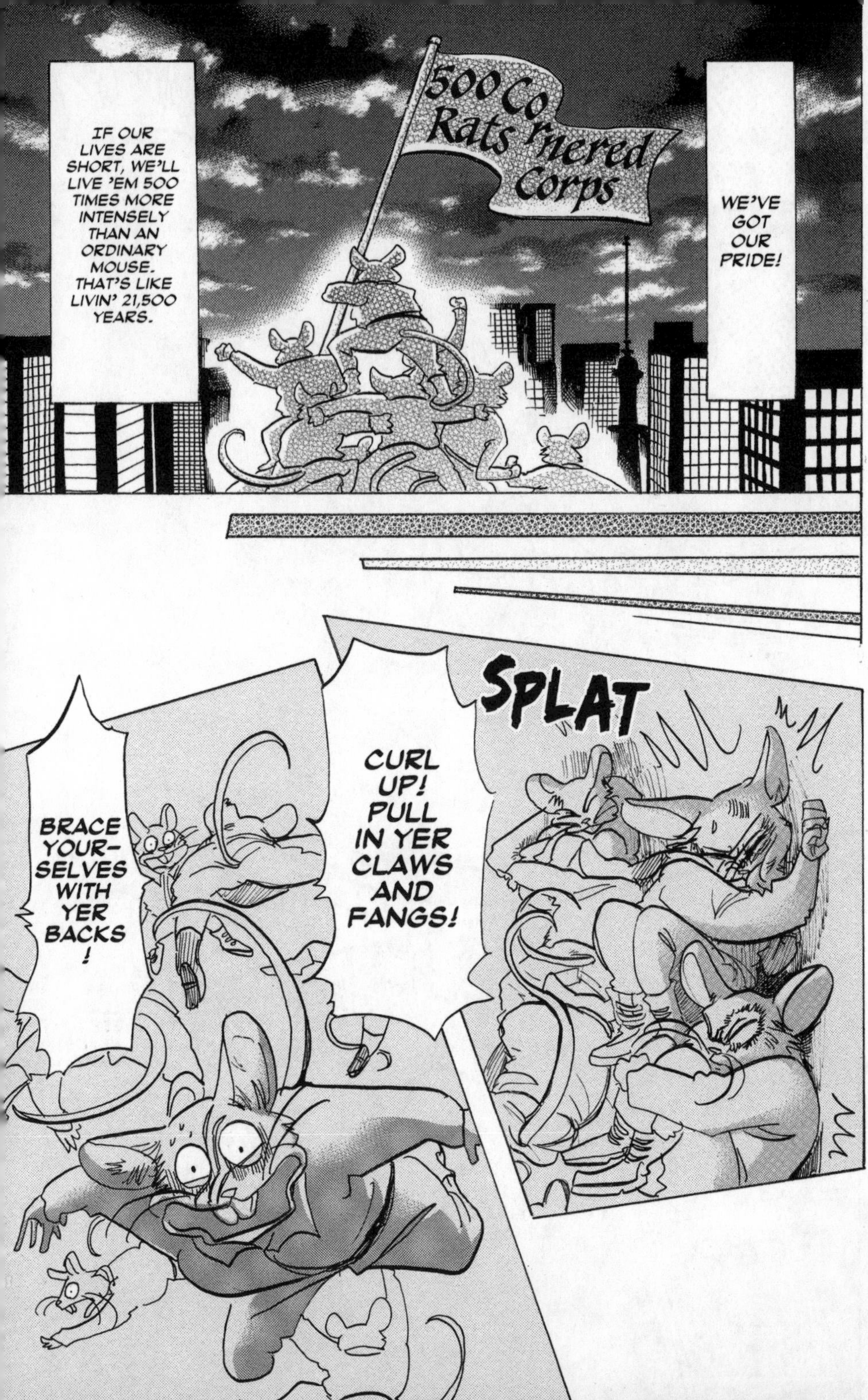
500 Cornered Rats Corps
WE'VE GOT OUR PRIDE!
IF OUR LIVES ARE SHORT, WE'LL LIVE 'EM 500 TIMES MORE INTENSELY THAN AN ORDINARY MOUSE. THAT'S LIKE LIVIN' 21,500 YEARS.
SPLAT
CURL UP! PULL IN YER CLAWS AND FANGS!
BRACE YOURSELVES WITH YER BACKS!

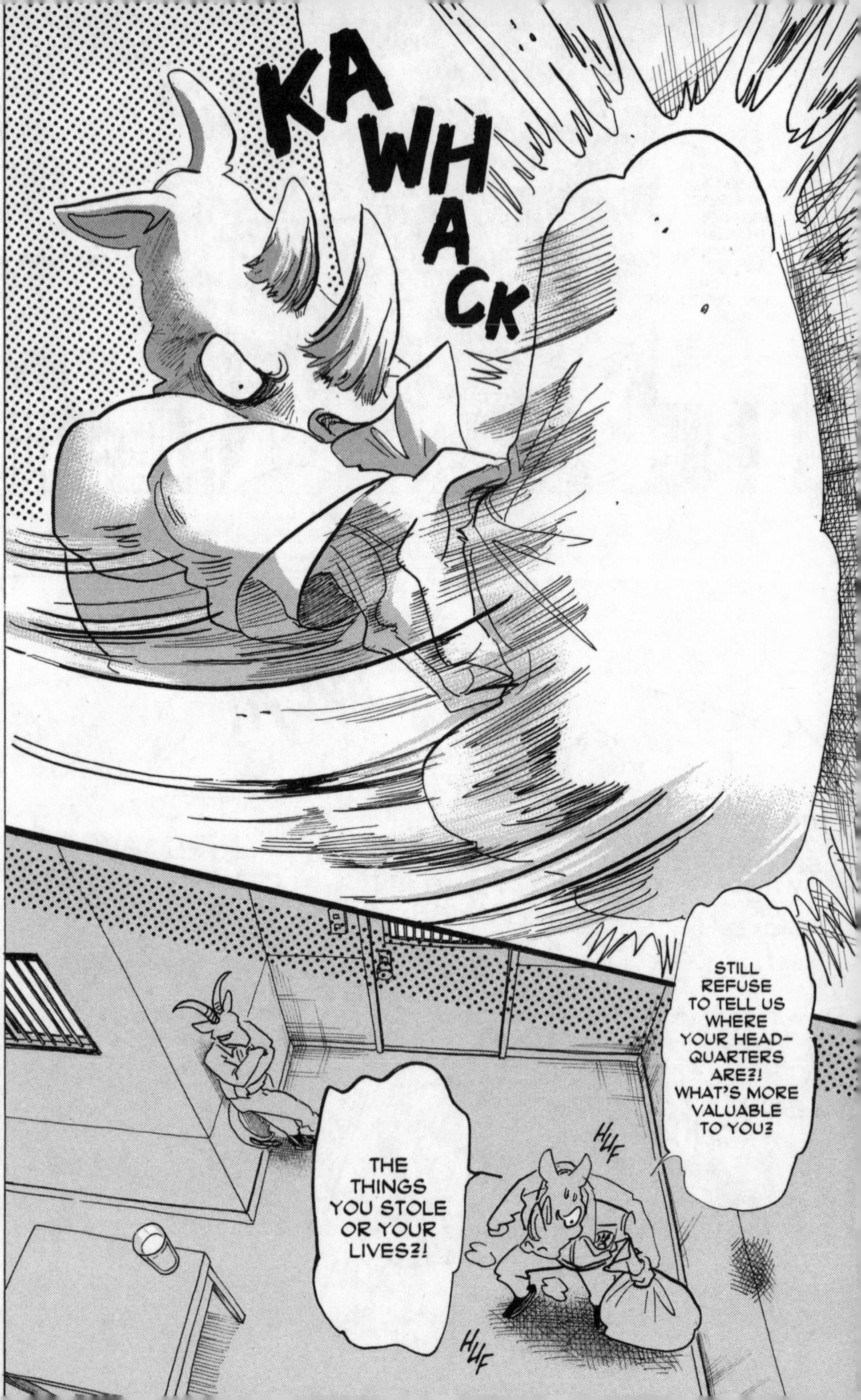
KA WH A CK
STILL REFUSE TO TELL US WHERE YOUR HEAD-QUARTERS ARE?! WHAT'S MORE VALUABLE TO YOU?
HUF
THE THINGS YOU STOLE OR YOUR LIVES?!
HUF

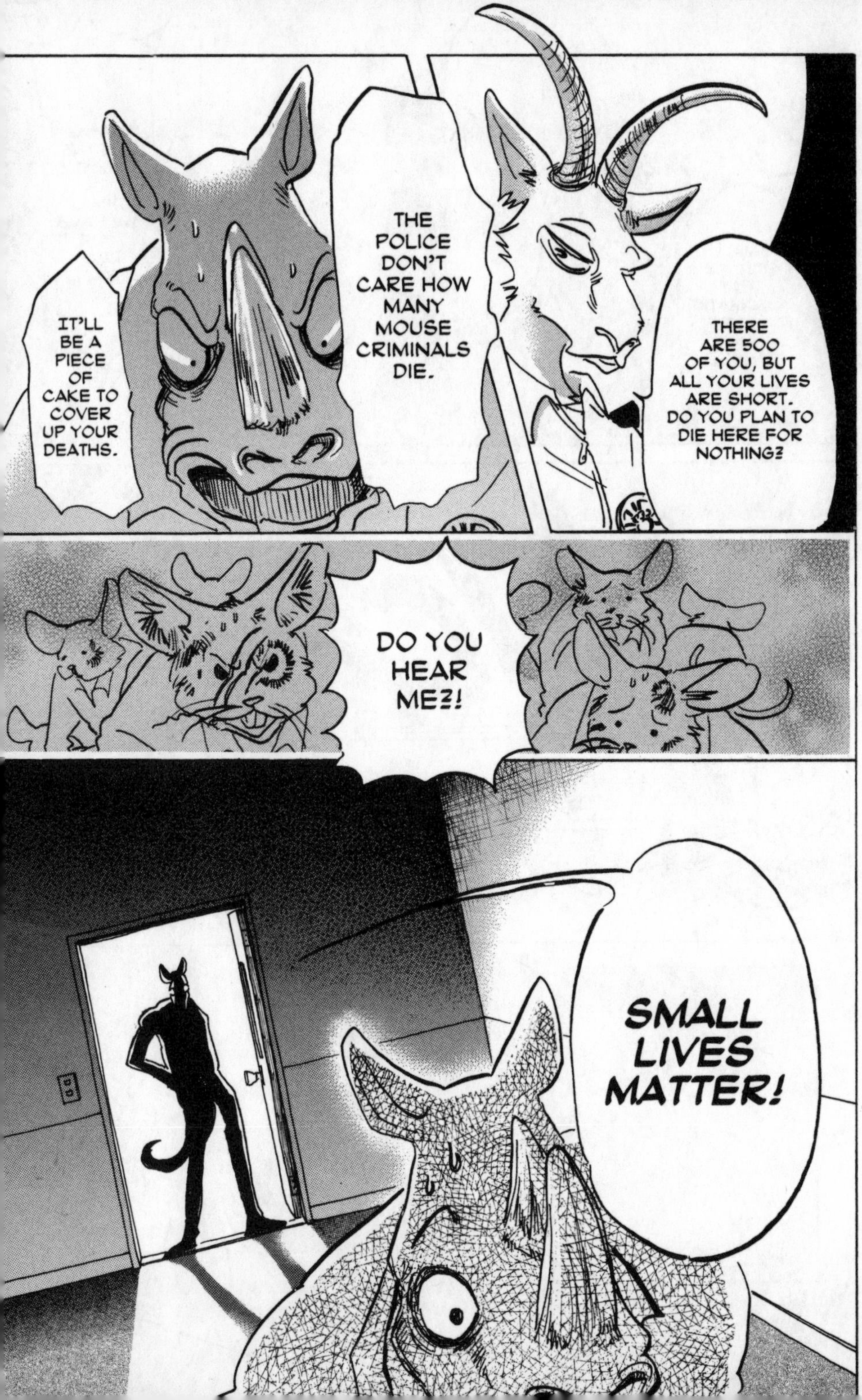
THERE ARE 500 OF YOU, BUT ALL YOUR LIVES ARE SHORT. DO YOU PLAN TO DIE HERE FOR NOTHING?
THE POLICE DON'T CARE HOW MANY MOUSE CRIMINALS DIE.
IT'LL BE A PIECE OF CAKE TO COVER UP YOUR DEATHS.
DO YOU HEAR ME?!
SMALL LIVES MATTER!

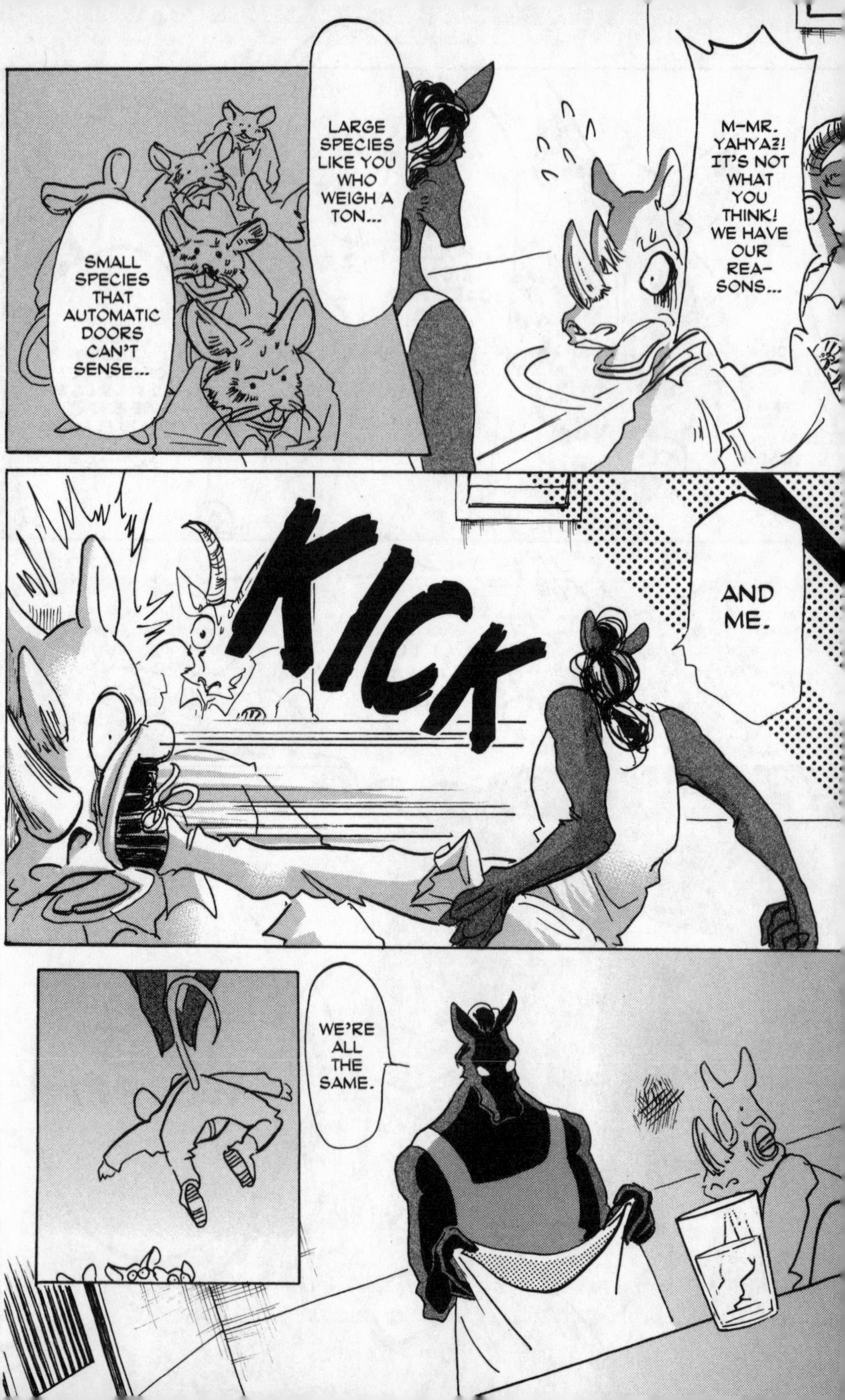
M-MR. YAHYA?! IT'S NOT WHAT YOU THINK! WE HAVE OUR REA-SONS...
LARGE SPECIES LIKE YOU WHO WEIGH A TON...
SMALL SPECIES THAT AUTOMATIC DOORS CAN'T SENSE...
AND ME.
KICK
WE'RE ALL THE SAME.

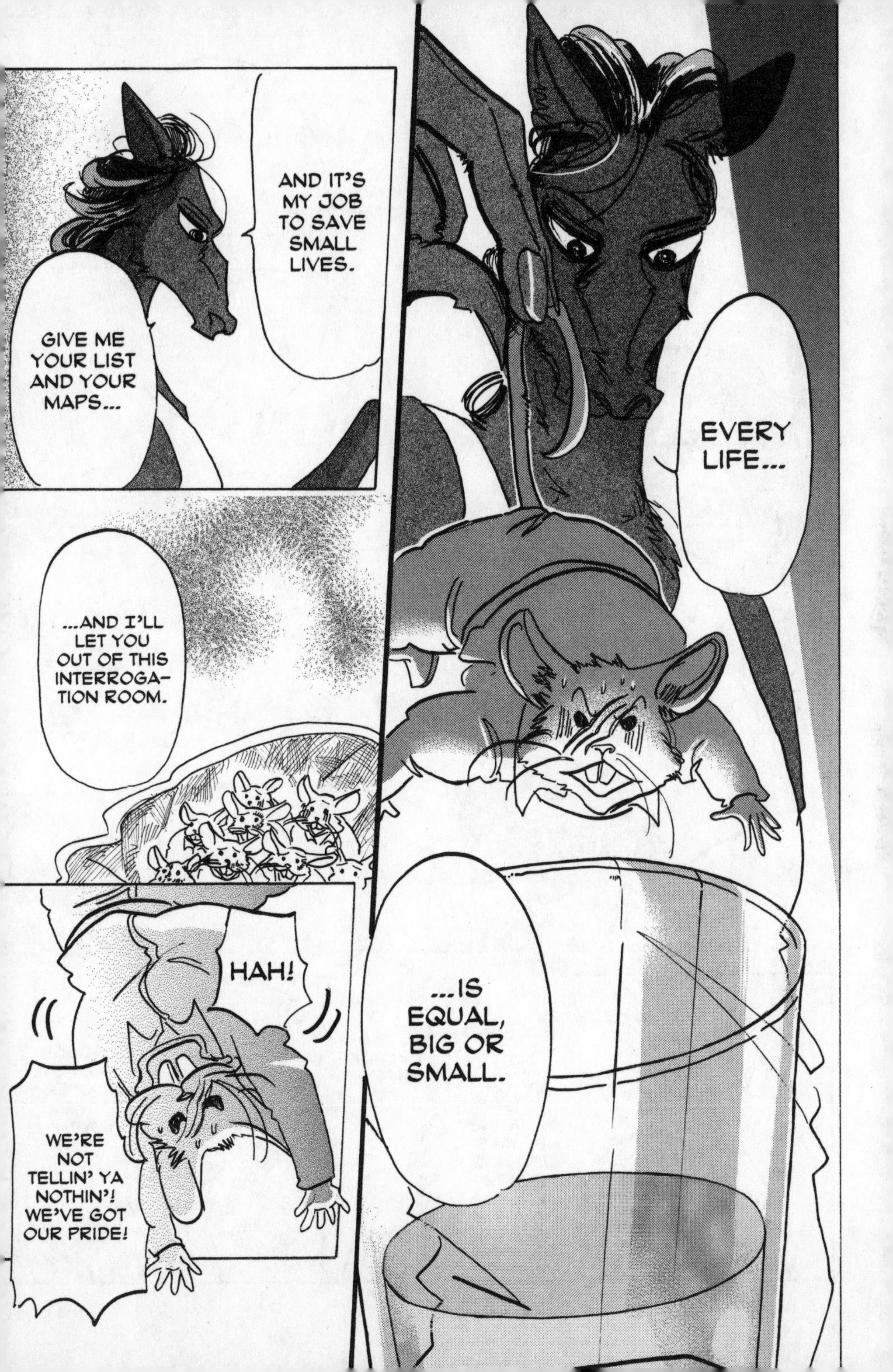
EVERY LIFE...
...IS EQUAL, BIG OR SMALL.
AND IT'S MY JOB TO SAVE SMALL LIVES.
GIVE ME YOUR LIST AND YOUR MAPS...
...AND I'LL LET YOU OUT OF THIS INTERROGATION ROOM.
HAH!
WE'RE NOT TELLIN' YA NOTHIN'! WE'VE GOT OUR PRIDE!

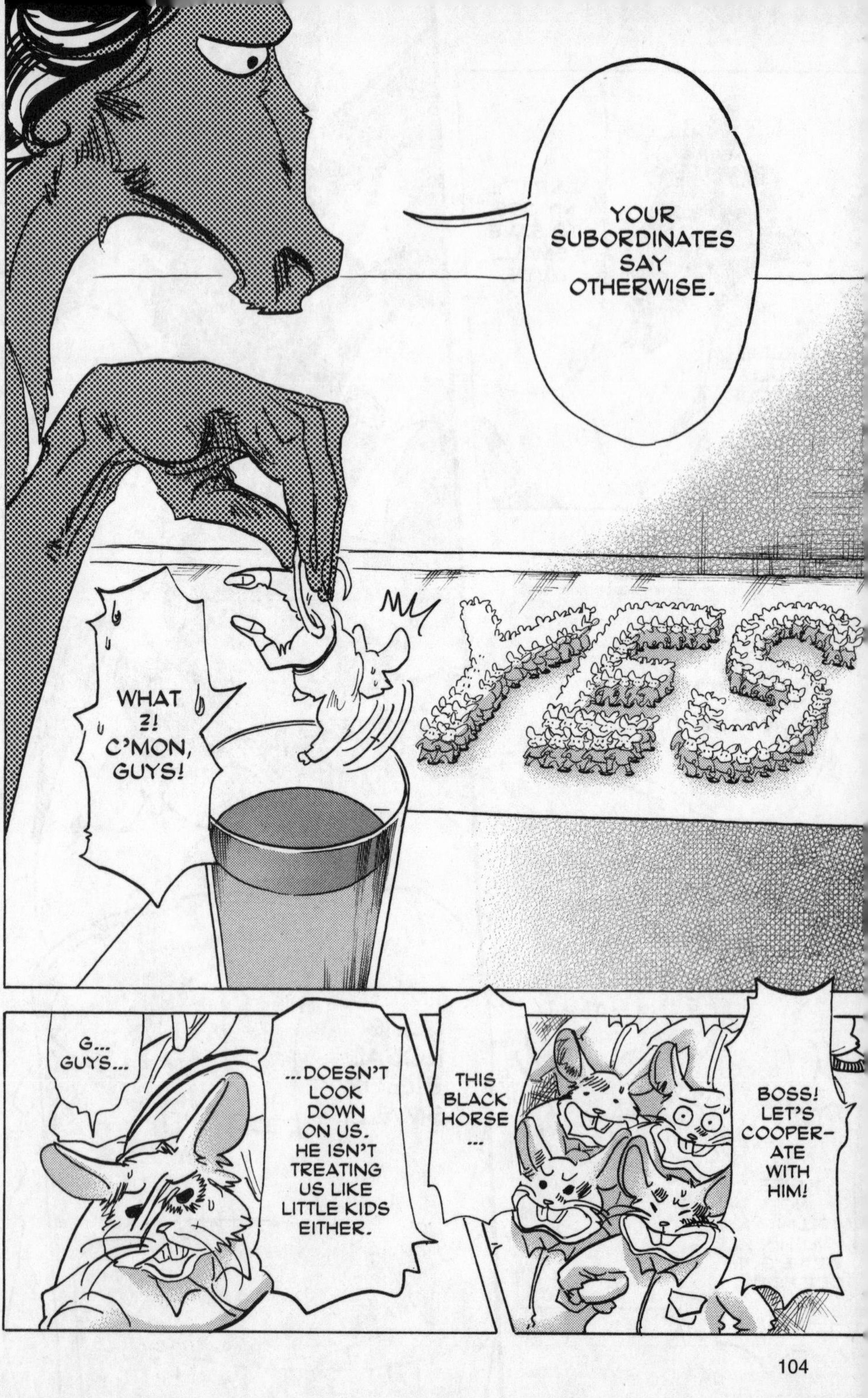
YOUR SUBORDINATES SAY OTHERWISE.
YES
WHAT?! C'MON, GUYS!
BOSS! LET'S COOPER-ATE WITH HIM!
THIS BLACK HORSE...
...DOESN'T LOOK DOWN ON US. HE ISN'T TREATING US LIKE LITTLE KIDS EITHER.
G... GUYS...

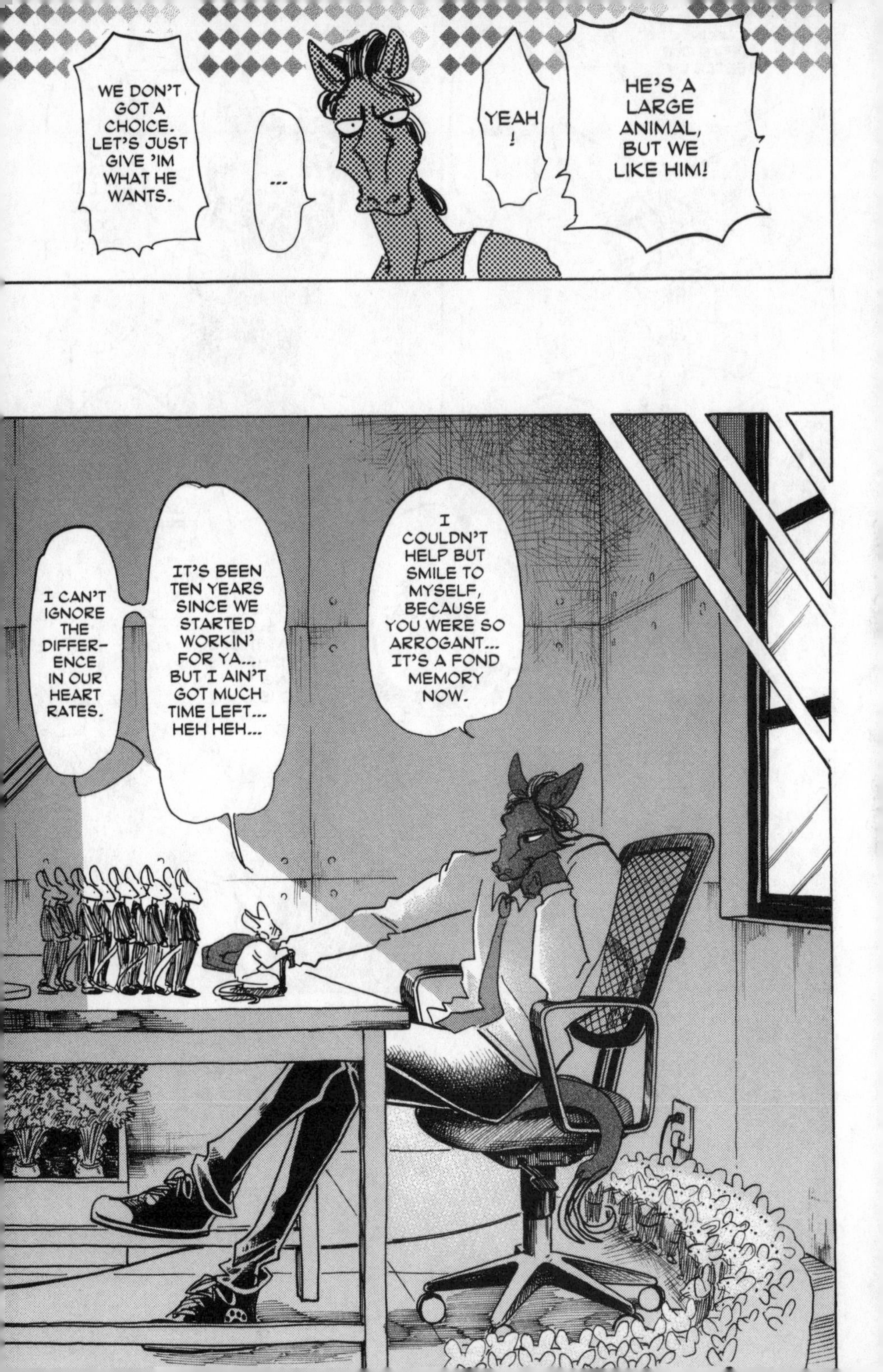
HE'S A LARGE ANIMAL, BUT WE LIKE HIM!
YEAH!
...
WE DON'T GOT A CHOICE. LET'S JUST GIVE 'IM WHAT HE WANTS.
I COULDN'T HELP BUT SMILE TO MYSELF, BECAUSE YOU WERE SO ARROGANT... IT'S A FOND MEMORY NOW.
IT'S BEEN TEN YEARS SINCE WE STARTED WORKIN' FOR YA... BUT I AIN'T GOT MUCH TIME LEFT... HEH HEH...
I CAN'T IGNORE THE DIFFER-ENCE IN OUR HEART RATES.

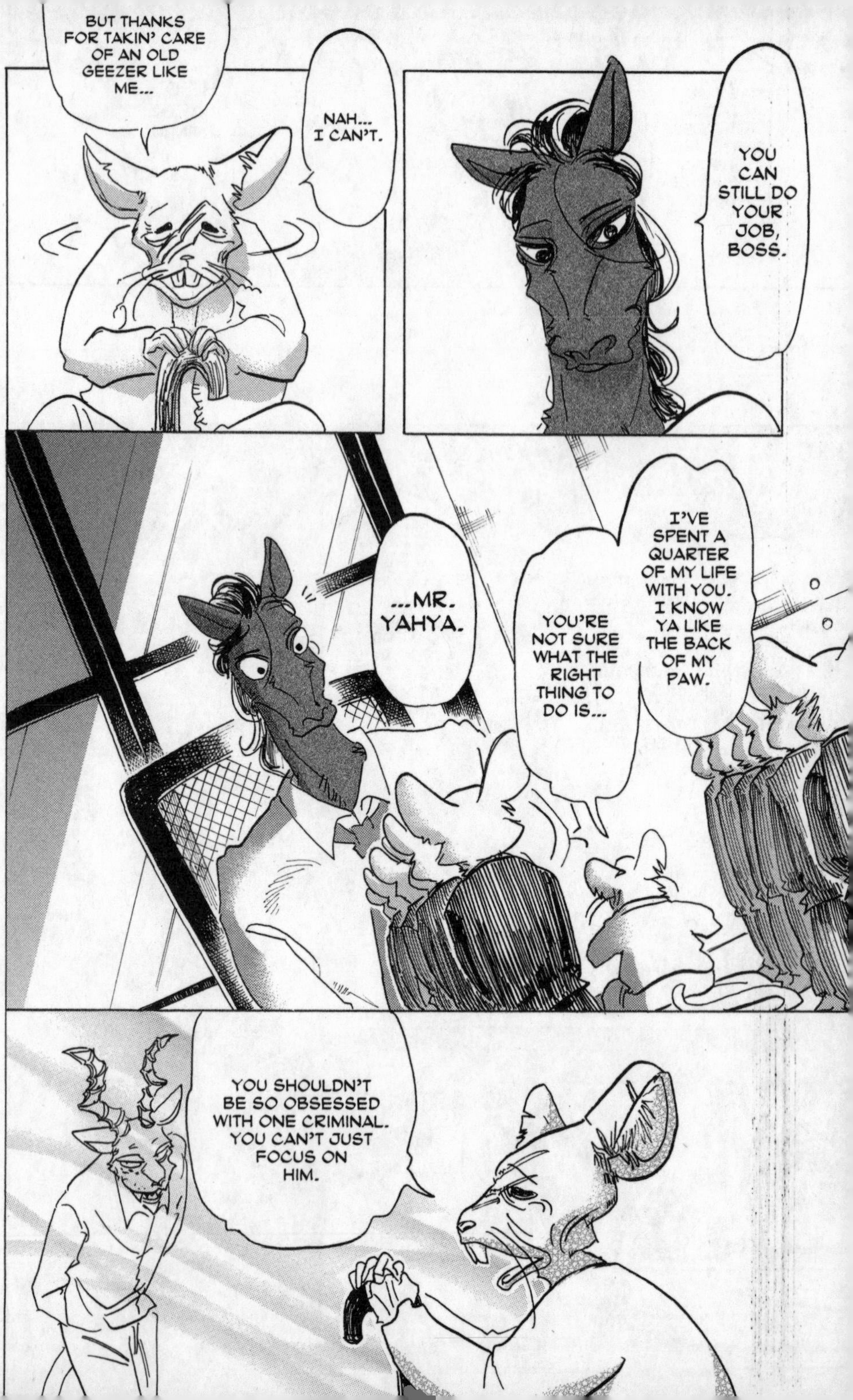
YOU CAN STILL DO YOUR JOB, BOSS.
NAH... I CAN'T.
BUT THANKS FOR TAKIN' CARE OF AN OLD GEEZER LIKE ME...
I'VE SPENT A QUARTER OF MY LIFE WITH YOU. I KNOW YA LIKE THE BACK OF MY PAW.
YOU'RE NOT SURE WHAT THE RIGHT THING TO DO IS...
...MR. YAHYA.
YOU SHOULDN'T BE SO OBSESSED WITH ONE CRIMINAL. YOU CAN'T JUST FOCUS ON HIM.

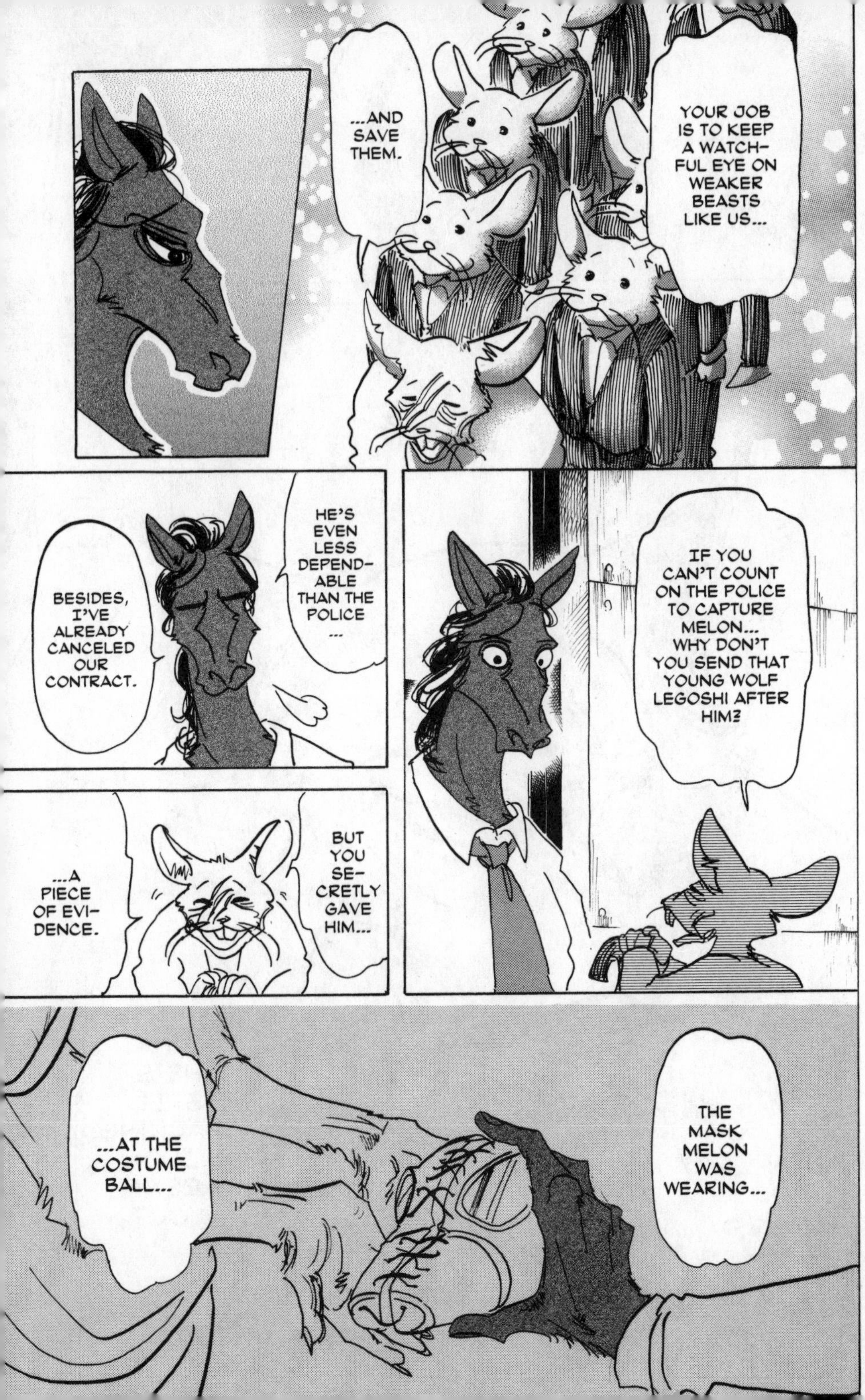
YOUR JOB IS TO KEEP A WATCHFUL EYE ON WEAKER BEASTS LIKE US...
...AND SAVE THEM.
IF YOU CAN'T COUNT ON THE POLICE TO CAPTURE MELON... WHY DON'T YOU SEND THAT YOUNG WOLF LEGOSHI AFTER HIM?
HE'S EVEN LESS DEPENDABLE THAN THE POLICE...
BESIDES, I'VE ALREADY CANCELED OUR CONTRACT.
BUT YOU SECRETLY GAVE HIM...
...A PIECE OF EVIDENCE.
THE MASK MELON WAS WEARING...
...AT THE COSTUME BALL...

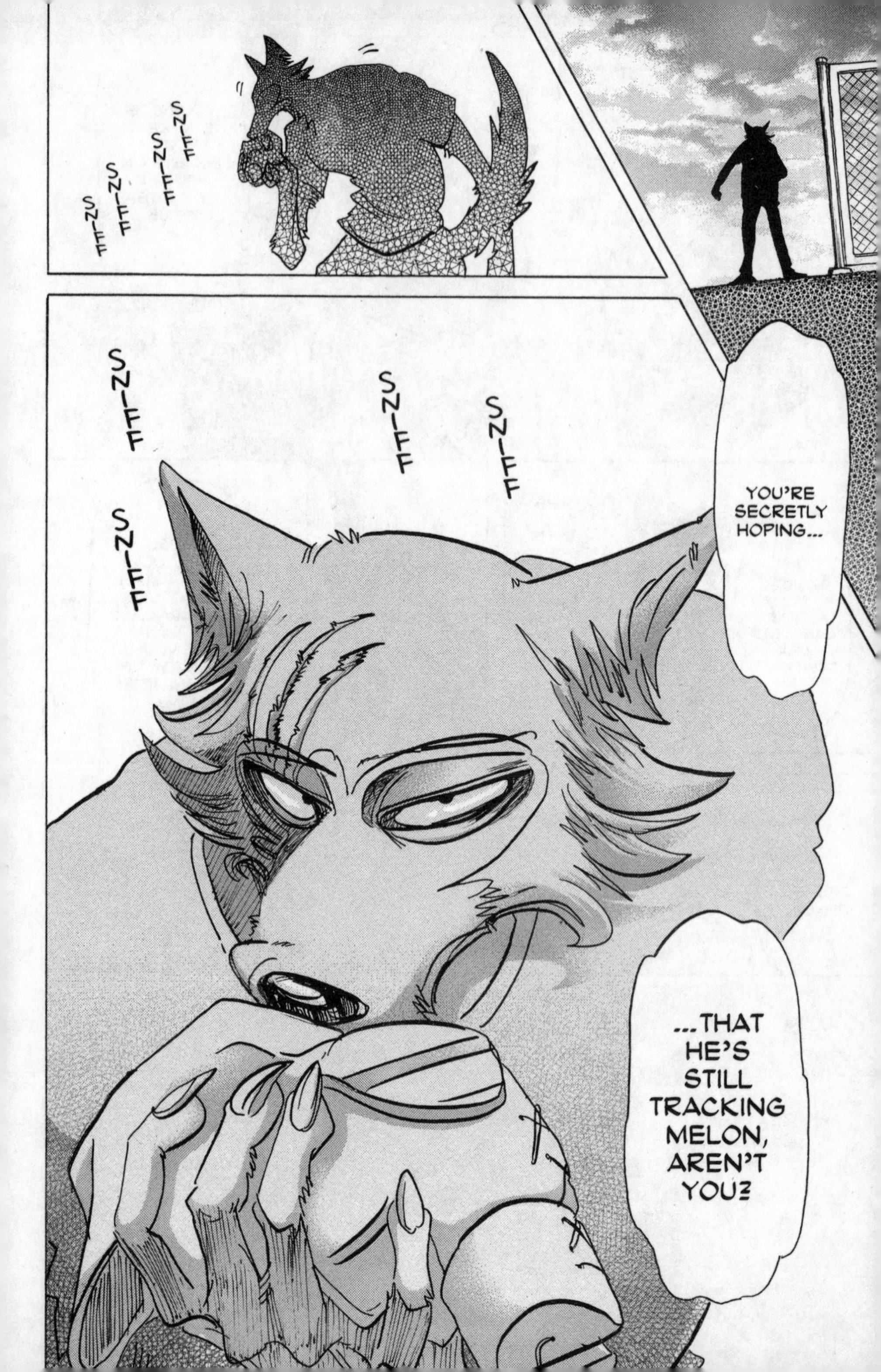
SNIFF
SNIFF
SNIFF
SNIFF
YOU'RE SECRETLY HOPING...
SNIFF
SNIFF
SNIFF
SNIFF
...THAT HE'S STILL TRACKING MELON, AREN'T YOU?

Chapter 139: The Crimson Sky, Plowing the Field

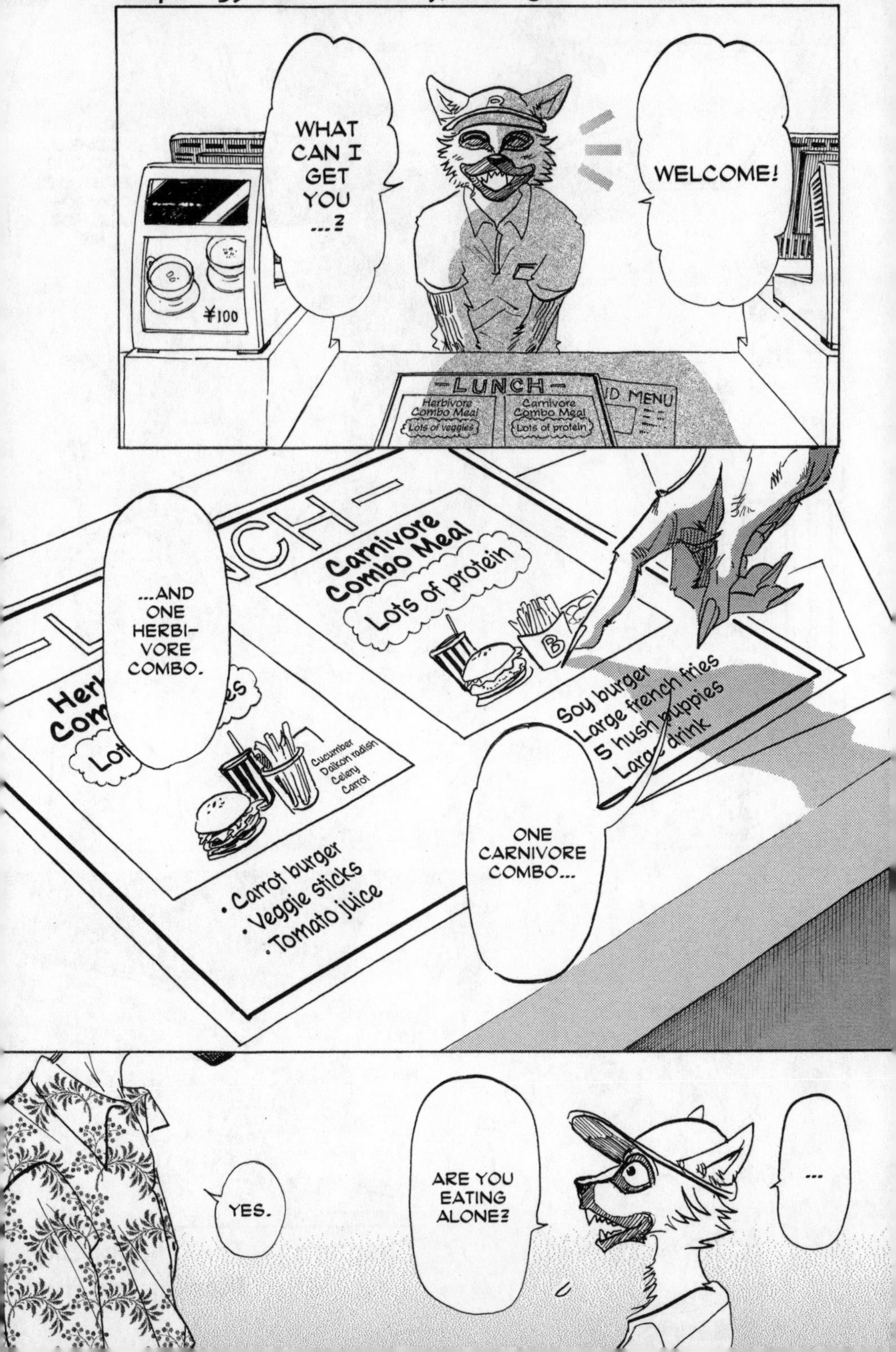
WELCOME!
WHAT CAN I GET YOU ...?
¥100
-LUNCH-
Herbivore Combo Meal
Lots of veggies
Carnivore Combo Meal
Lots of protein
ONE CARNIVORE COMBO...
...AND ONE HERBI-VORE COMBO.
Carnivore Combo Meal
Lots of protein
Soy burger
Large french fries
5 hush puppies
Large drink
Cucumber
Daikon radish
Celery
Carrot
• Carrot burger
• Veggie sticks
• Tomato juice
...
ARE YOU EATING ALONE?
YES.

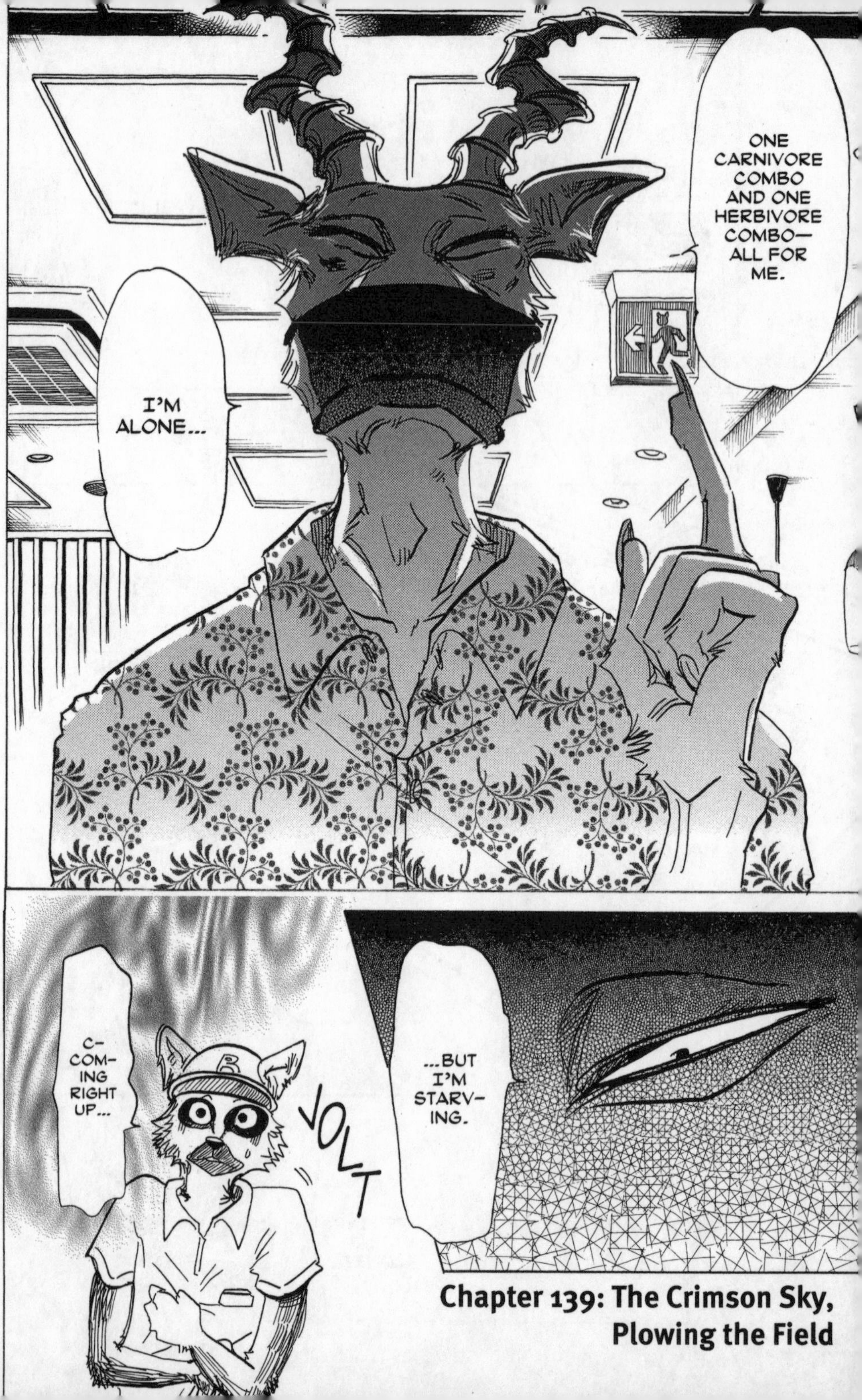
ONE CARNIVORE COMBO AND ONE HERBIVORE COMBO—ALL FOR ME.
I'M ALONE...
...BUT I'M STARV-ING.
JOLT
C-COM-ING RIGHT UP...

Chapter 139: The Crimson Sky, Plowing the Field

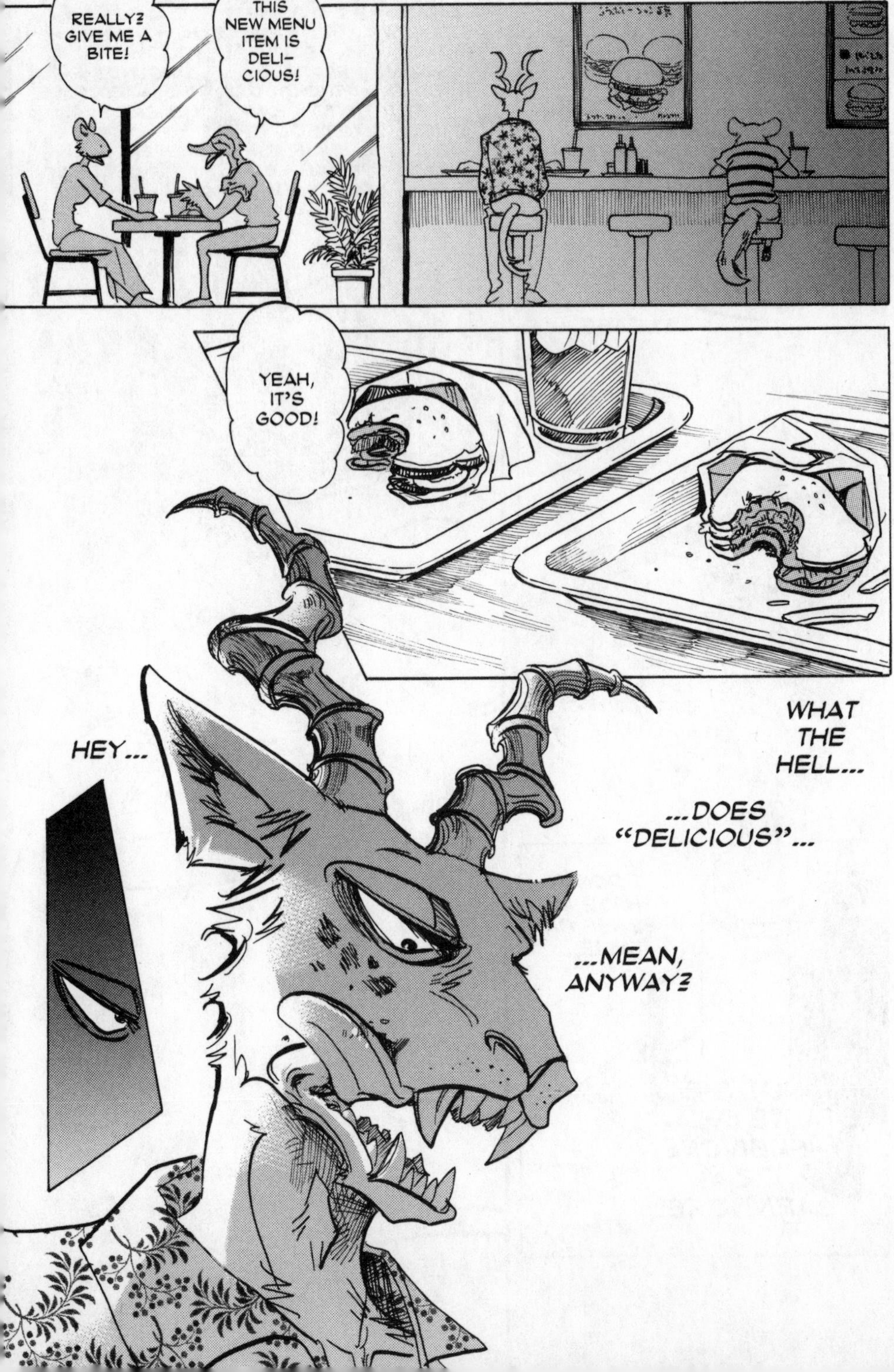
THIS NEW MENU ITEM IS DELICIOUS!
REALLY? GIVE ME A BITE!
YEAH, IT'S GOOD!
HEY...
WHAT THE HELL...
...DOES "DELICIOUS"...
...MEAN, ANYWAY?

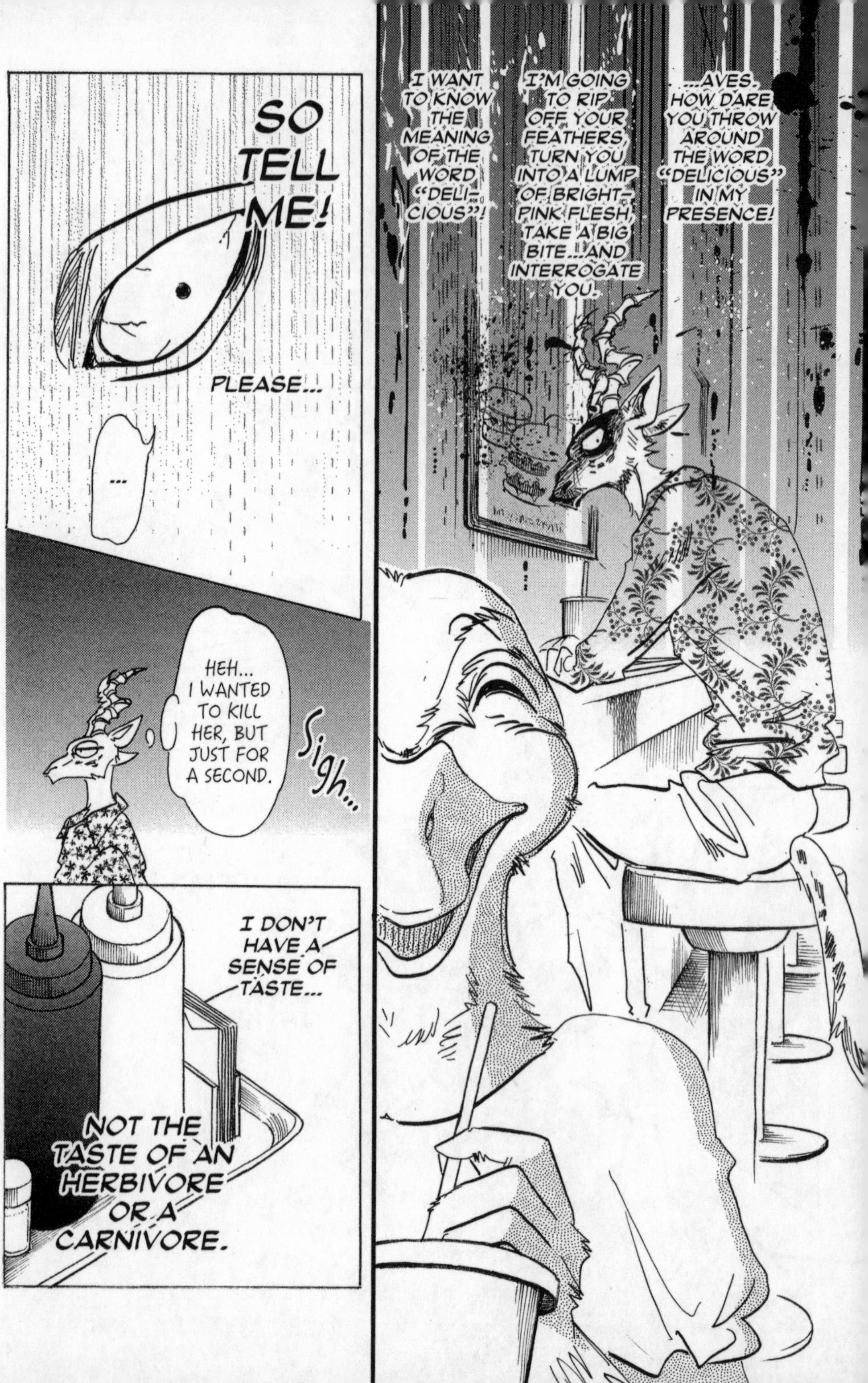
...AVES. HOW DARE YOU THROW AROUND THE WORD "DELICIOUS" IN MY PRESENCE!
I'M GOING TO RIP OFF YOUR FEATHERS, TURN YOU INTO A LUMP OF BRIGHT-PINK FLESH, TAKE A BIG BITE... AND INTERROGATE YOU.
I WANT TO KNOW THE MEANING OF THE WORD "DELI-CIOUS"!
SO TELL ME!
PLEASE...
...
HEH... I WANTED TO KILL HER, BUT JUST FOR A SECOND.
Sigh...
I DON'T HAVE A SENSE OF TASTE...
NOT THE TASTE OF AN HERBIVORE OR A CARNIVORE.

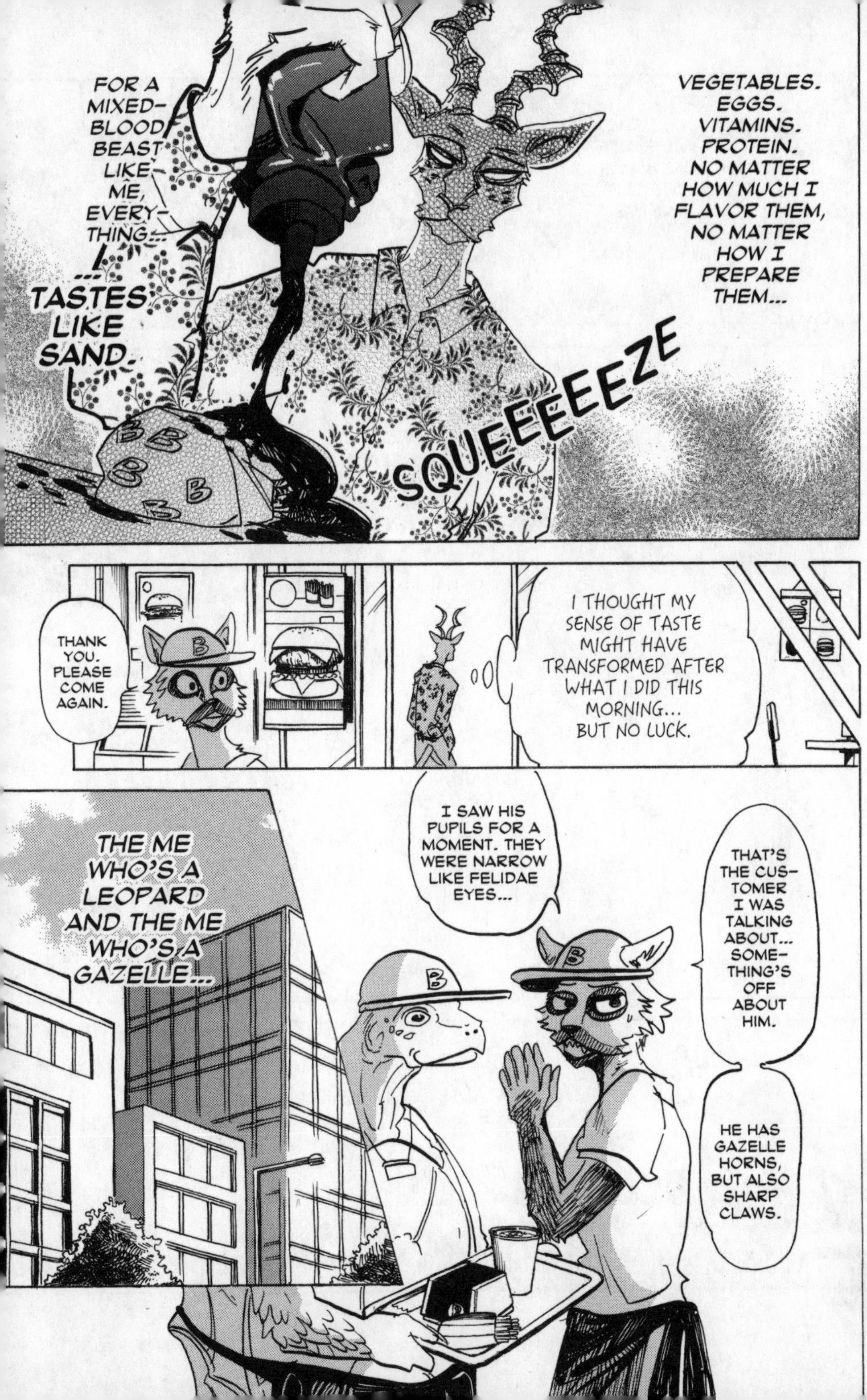
VEGETABLES. EGGS. VITAMINS. PROTEIN. NO MATTER HOW MUCH I FLAVOR THEM, NO MATTER HOW I PREPARE THEM...
FOR A MIXED-BLOOD BEAST LIKE ME, EVERYTHING...
...TASTES LIKE SAND.
SQUEEEEEZE
I THOUGHT MY SENSE OF TASTE MIGHT HAVE TRANSFORMED AFTER WHAT I DID THIS MORNING... BUT NO LUCK.
THANK YOU. PLEASE COME AGAIN.
THAT'S THE CUSTOMER I WAS TALKING ABOUT... SOMETHING'S OFF ABOUT HIM.
I SAW HIS PUPILS FOR A MOMENT. THEY WERE NARROW LIKE FELIDAE EYES...
HE HAS GAZELLE HORNS, BUT ALSO SHARP CLAWS.
THE ME WHO'S A LEOPARD AND THE ME WHO'S A GAZELLE...

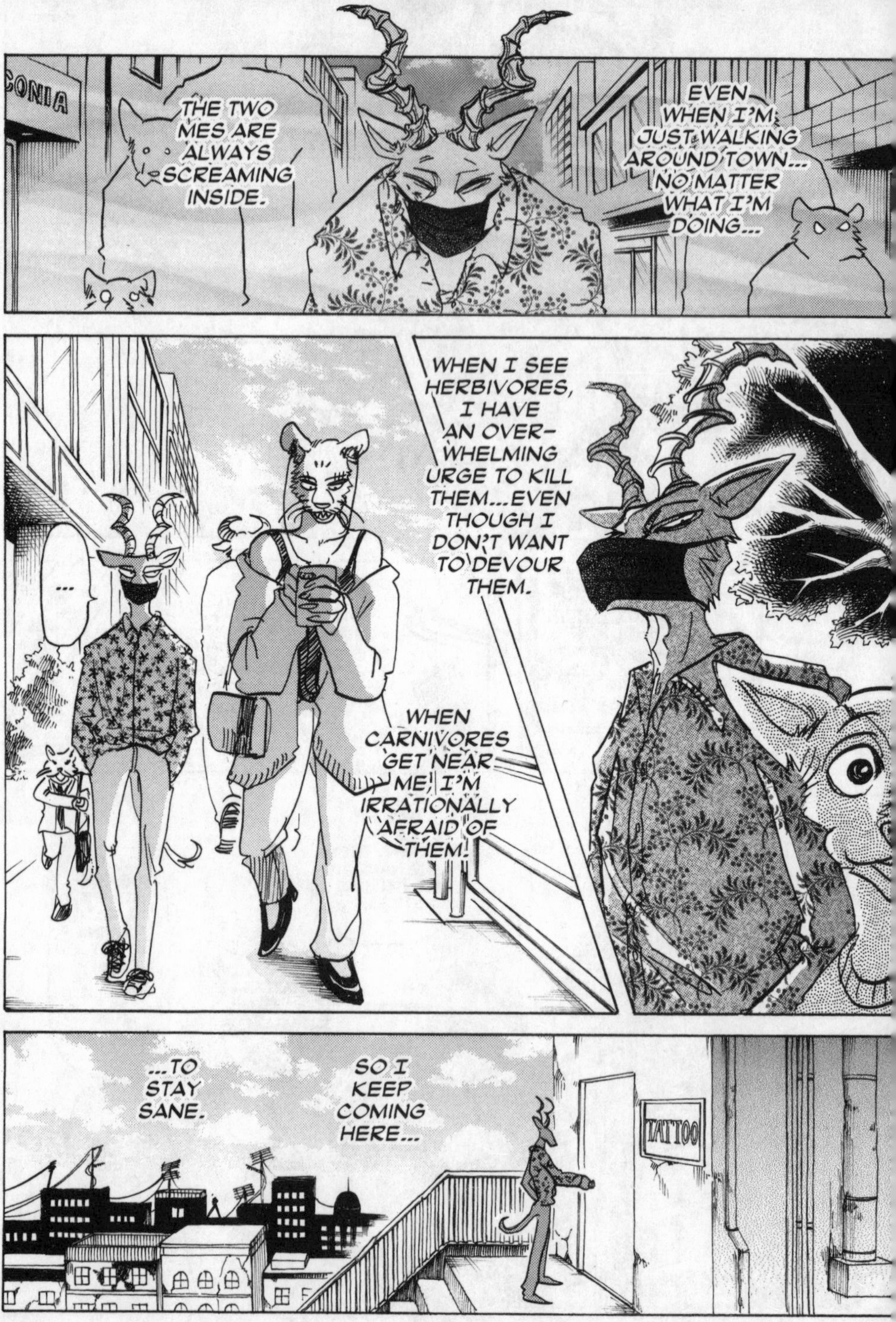
EVEN WHEN I'M JUST WALKING AROUND TOWN... NO MATTER WHAT I'M DOING...
THE TWO MES ARE ALWAYS SCREAMING INSIDE.
WHEN I SEE HERBIVORES, I HAVE AN OVER-WHELMING URGE TO KILL THEM...EVEN THOUGH I DON'T WANT TO DEVOUR THEM.
WHEN CARNIVORES GET NEAR ME, I'M IRRATIONALLY AFRAID OF THEM.
...
TATTOO
SO I KEEP COMING HERE...
...TO STAY SANE.

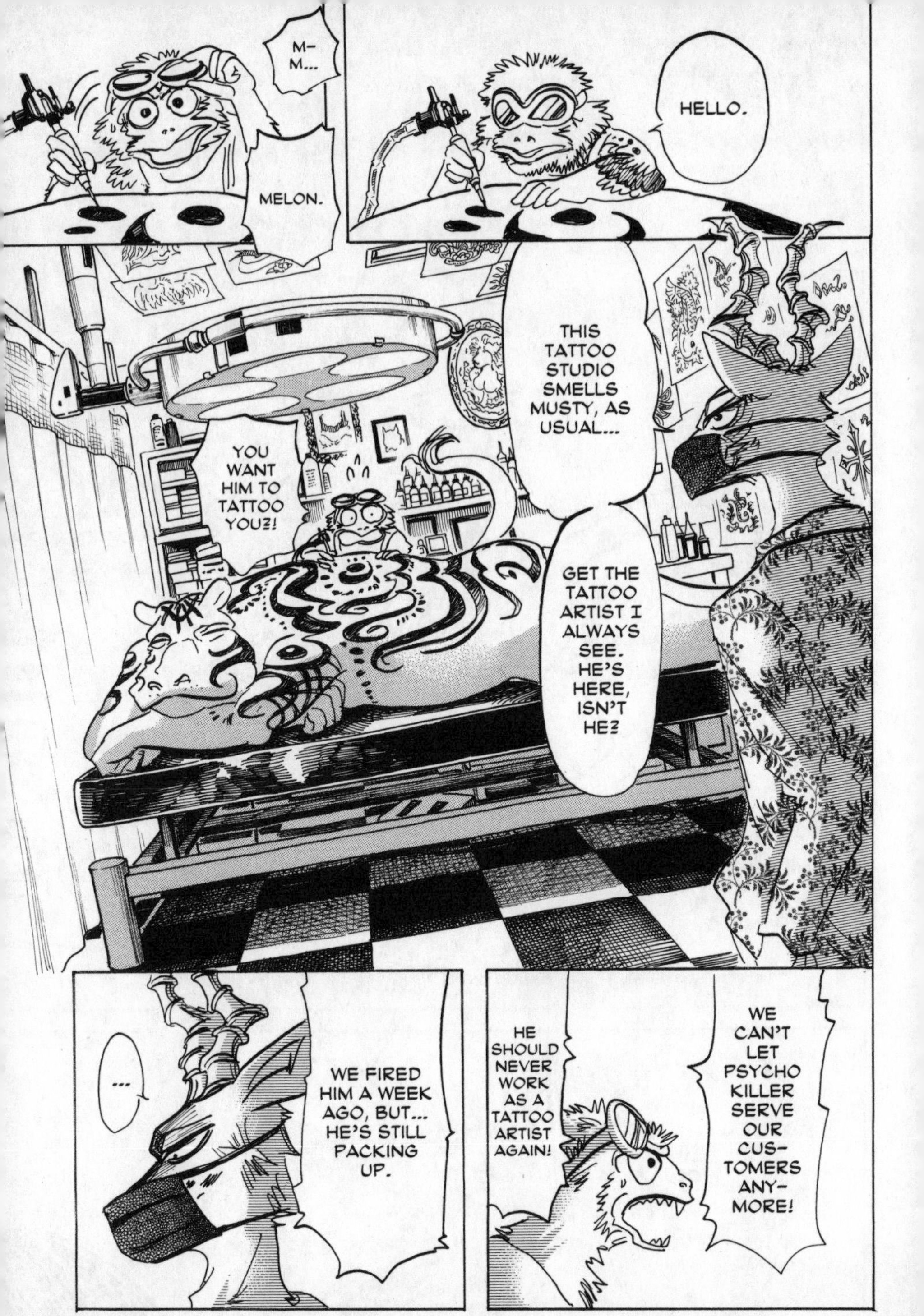
HELLO.
M-M...
MELON.
THIS TATTOO STUDIO SMELLS MUSTY, AS USUAL...
GET THE TATTOO ARTIST I ALWAYS SEE. HE'S HERE, ISN'T HE?
YOU WANT HIM TO TATTOO YOU?!
WE CAN'T LET PSYCHO KILLER SERVE OUR CUS-TOMERS ANY-MORE!
HE SHOULD NEVER WORK AS A TATTOO ARTIST AGAIN!
WE FIRED HIM A WEEK AGO, BUT... HE'S STILL PACKING UP.
...

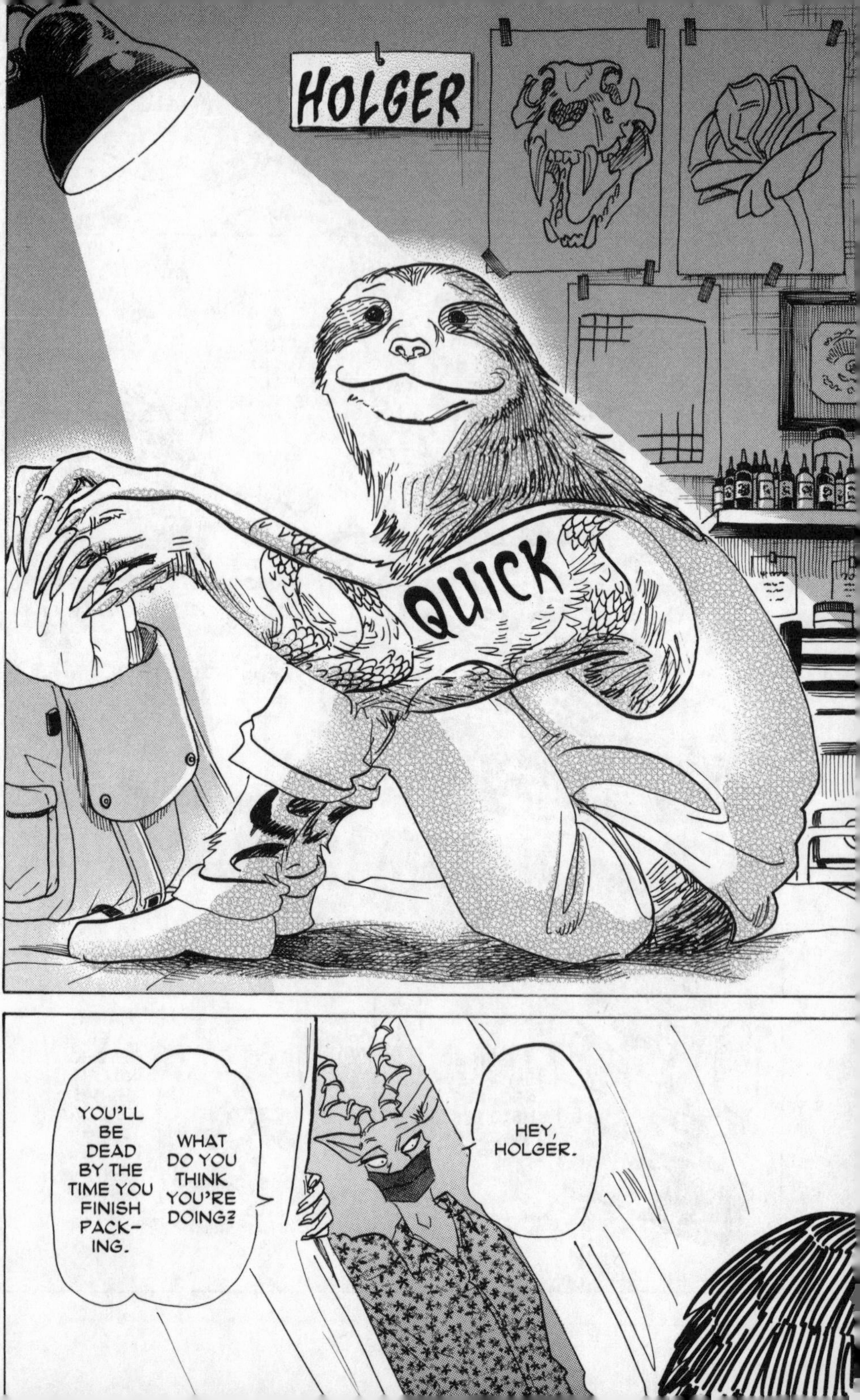
HOLGER
QUICK
HEY, HOLGER.
WHAT DO YOU THINK YOU'RE DOING?
YOU'LL BE DEAD BY THE TIME YOU FINISH PACK-ING.

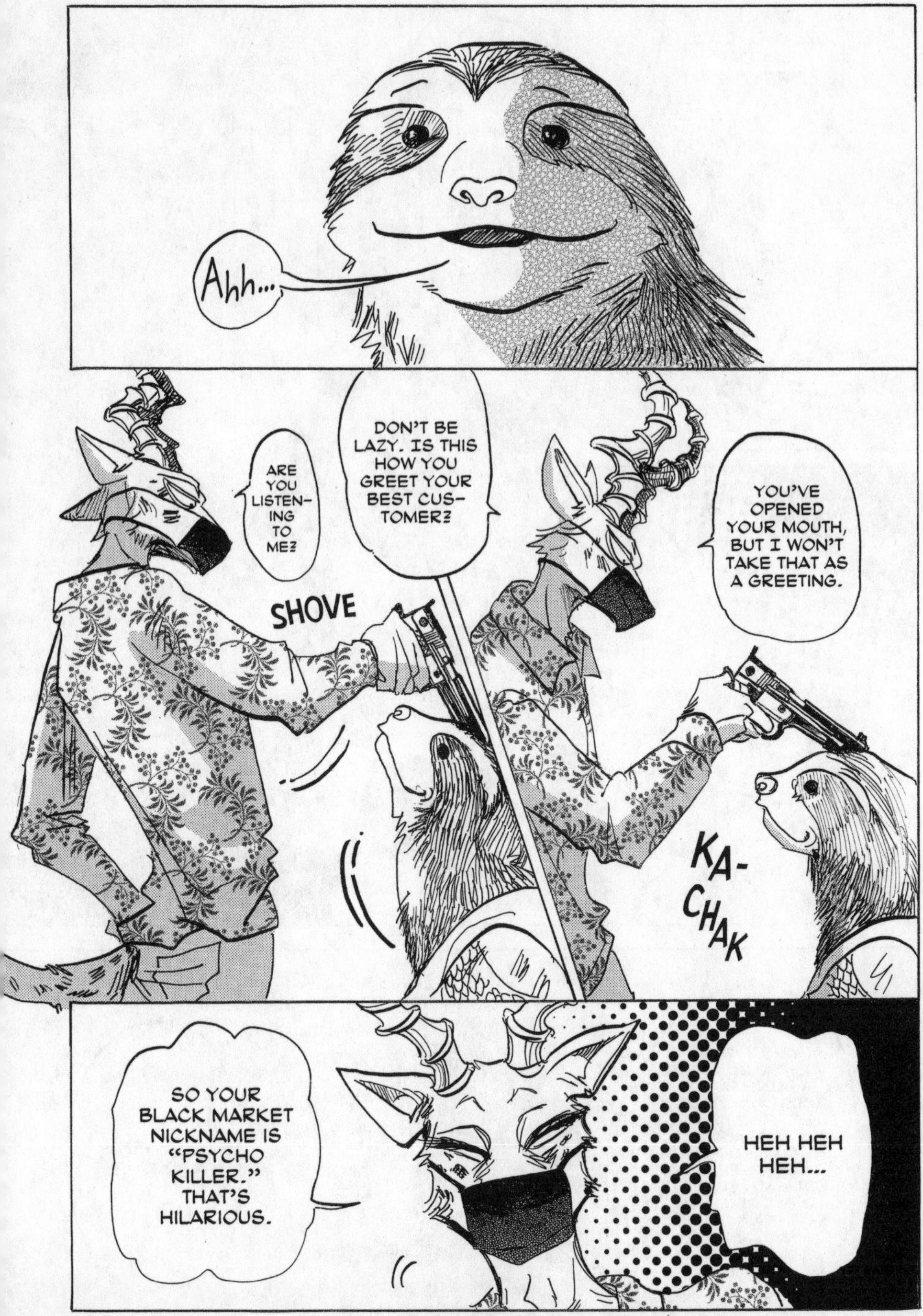
Ahh...
YOU'VE OPENED YOUR MOUTH, BUT I WON'T TAKE THAT AS A GREETING.
KA-CHAK
DON'T BE LAZY. IS THIS HOW YOU GREET YOUR BEST CUS-TOMER?
ARE YOU LISTEN-ING TO ME?
SHOVE
HEH HEH HEH...
SO YOUR BLACK MARKET NICKNAME IS "PSYCHO KILLER." THAT'S HILARIOUS.

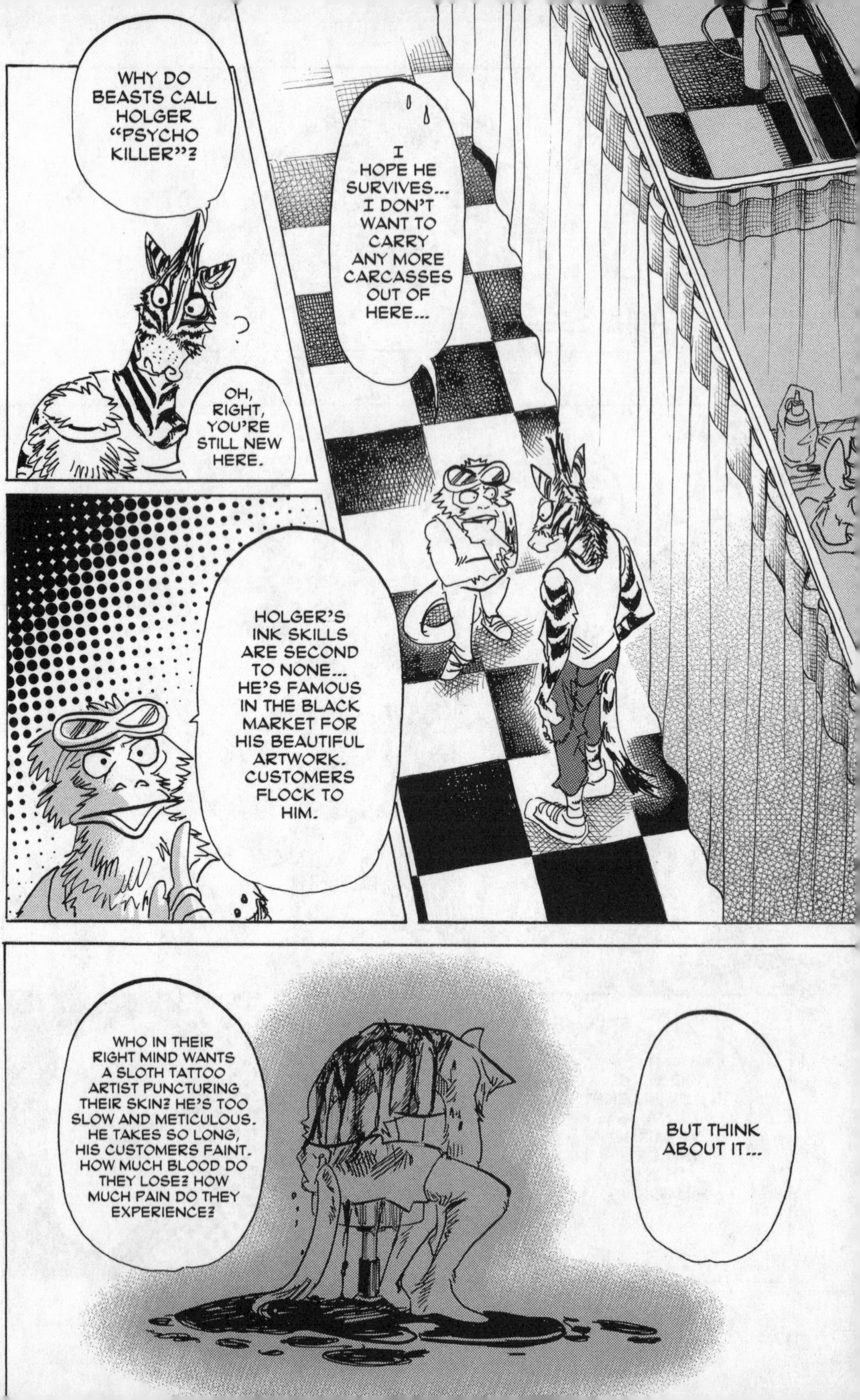
I HOPE HE SURVIVES... I DON'T WANT TO CARRY ANY MORE CARCASSES OUT OF HERE...
WHY DO BEASTS CALL HOLGER "PSYCHO KILLER"?
OH, RIGHT, YOU'RE STILL NEW HERE.
HOLGER'S INK SKILLS ARE SECOND TO NONE... HE'S FAMOUS IN THE BLACK MARKET FOR HIS BEAUTIFUL ARTWORK. CUSTOMERS FLOCK TO HIM.
BUT THINK ABOUT IT...
WHO IN THEIR RIGHT MIND WANTS A SLOTH TATTOO ARTIST PUNCTURING THEIR SKIN? HE'S TOO SLOW AND METICULOUS. HE TAKES SO LONG, HIS CUSTOMERS FAINT. HOW MUCH BLOOD DO THEY LOSE? HOW MUCH PAIN DO THEY EXPERIENCE?

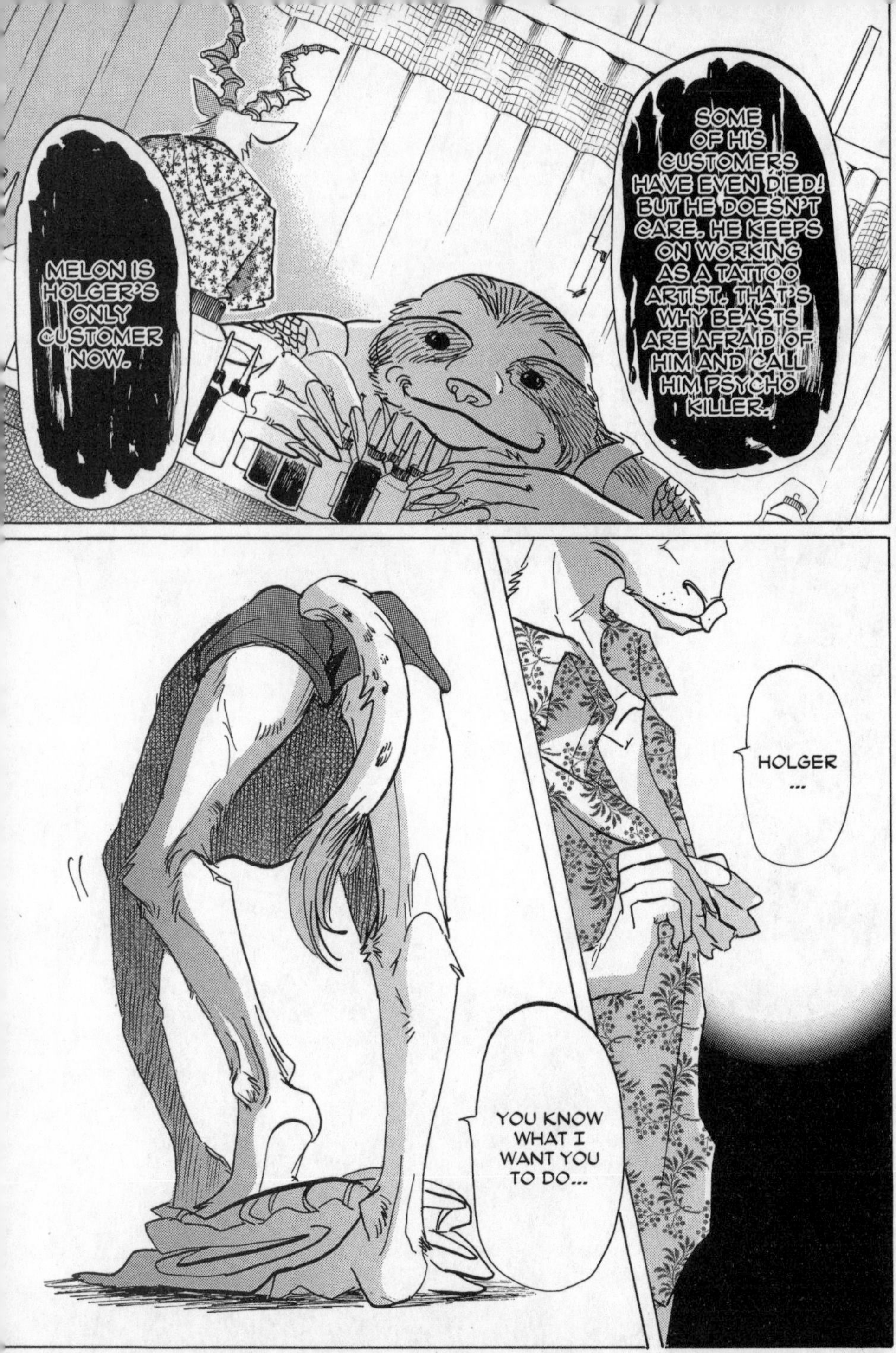
SOME OF HIS CUSTOMERS HAVE EVEN DIED! BUT HE DOESN'T CARE. HE KEEPS ON WORKING AS A TATTOO ARTIST. THAT'S WHY BEASTS ARE AFRAID OF HIM AND CALL HIM PSYCHO KILLER.
MELON IS HOLGER'S ONLY CUSTOMER NOW.
HOLGER...
YOU KNOW WHAT I WANT YOU TO DO...

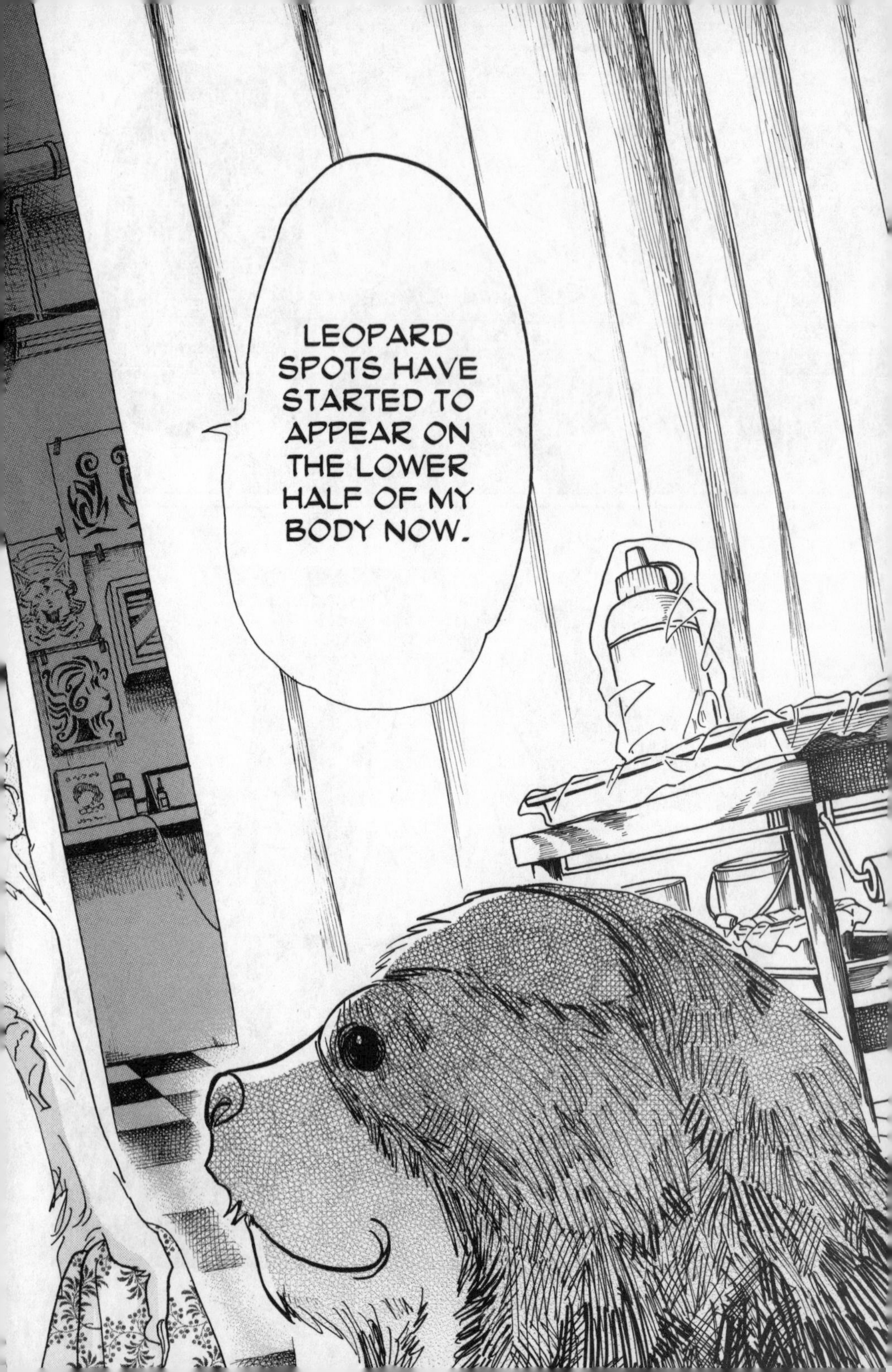
LEOPARD SPOTS HAVE STARTED TO APPEAR ON THE LOWER HALF OF MY BODY NOW.

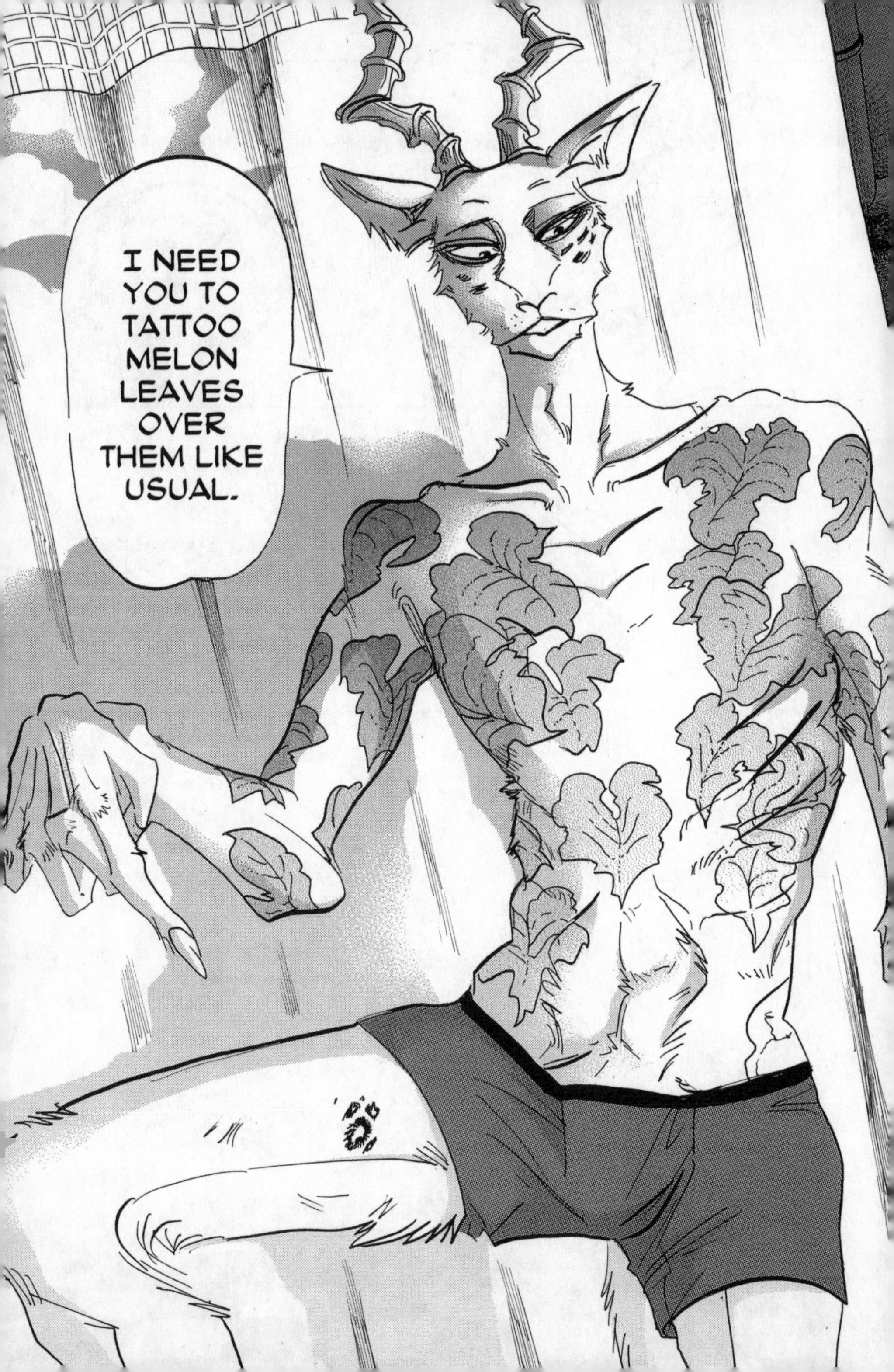
I NEED YOU TO TATTOO MELON LEAVES OVER THEM LIKE USUAL.

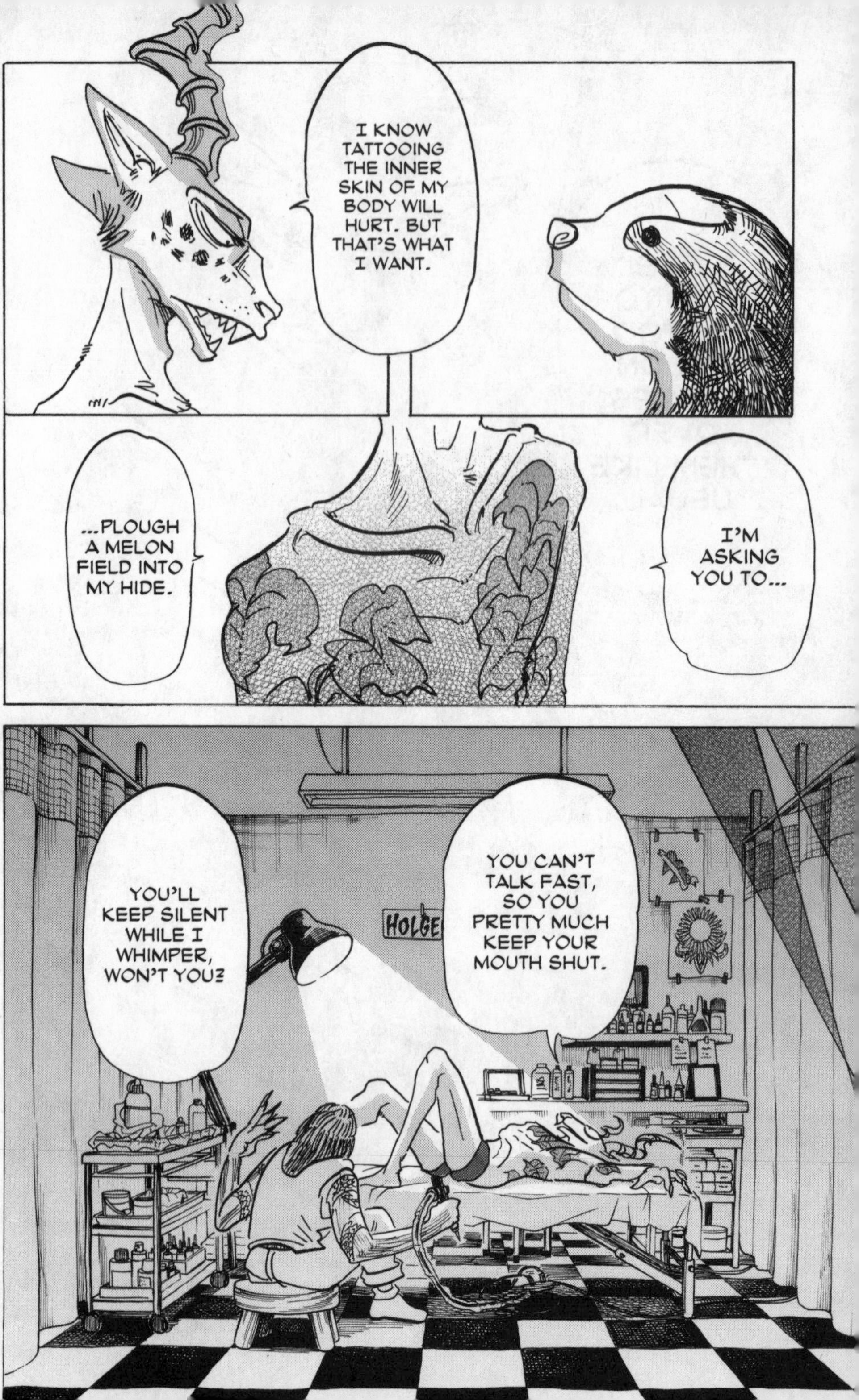
I KNOW TATTOOING THE INNER SKIN OF MY BODY WILL HURT. BUT THAT'S WHAT I WANT.
I'M ASKING YOU TO...
...PLOUGH A MELON FIELD INTO MY HIDE.
YOU CAN'T TALK FAST, SO YOU PRETTY MUCH KEEP YOUR MOUTH SHUT.
YOU'LL KEEP SILENT WHILE I WHIMPER, WON'T YOU?

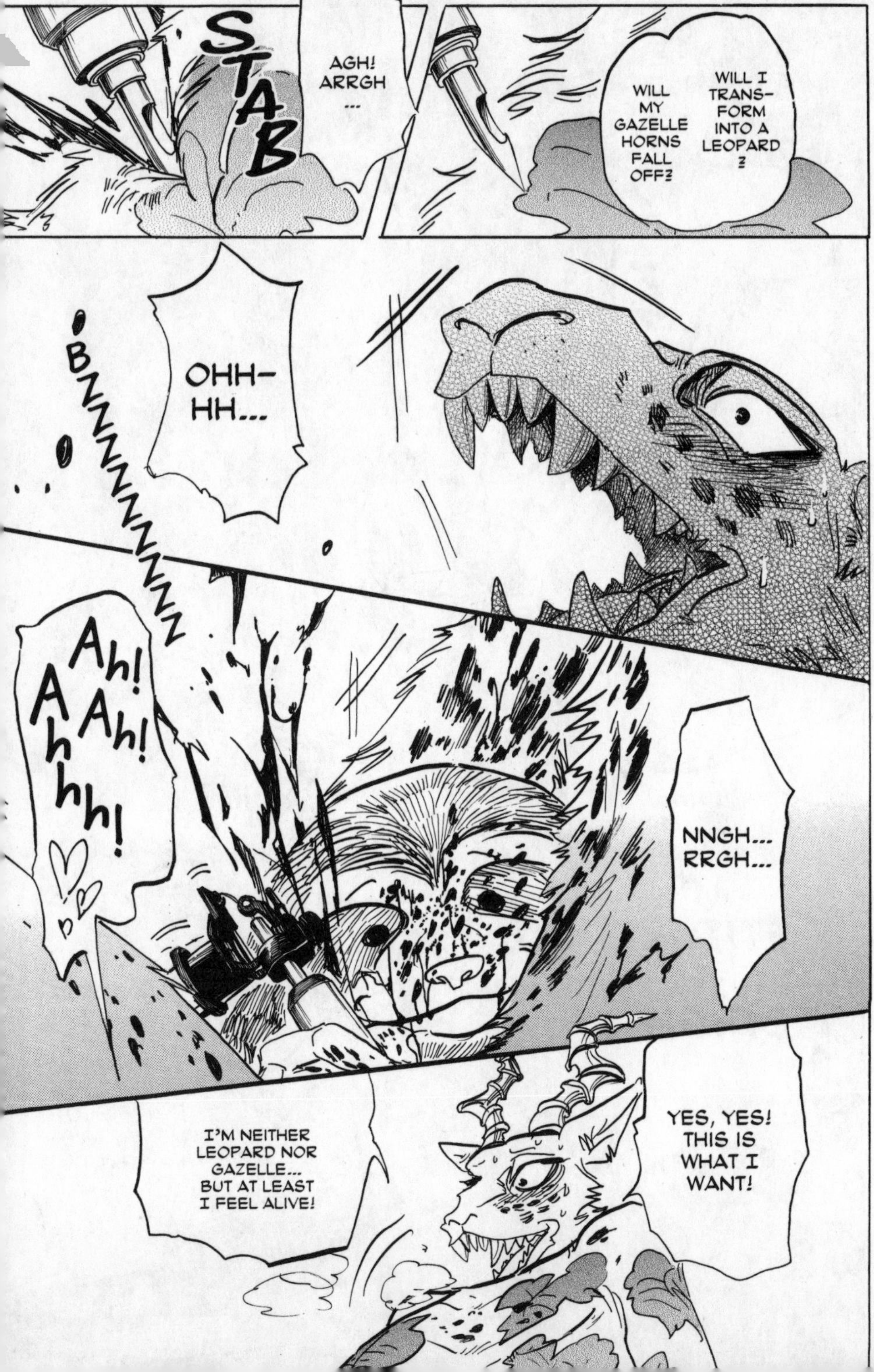
WILL I TRANSFORM INTO A LEOPARD?
WILL MY GAZELLE HORNS FALL OFF?
AGH! ARRGH...
STAB
OHHHH...
BZZZZZZZZZZZZ
NNGH... RRGH...
Ah! Ah! Ahhh! ♡♡♡
YES, YES! THIS IS WHAT I WANT!
I'M NEITHER LEOPARD NOR GAZELLE... BUT AT LEAST I FEEL ALIVE!

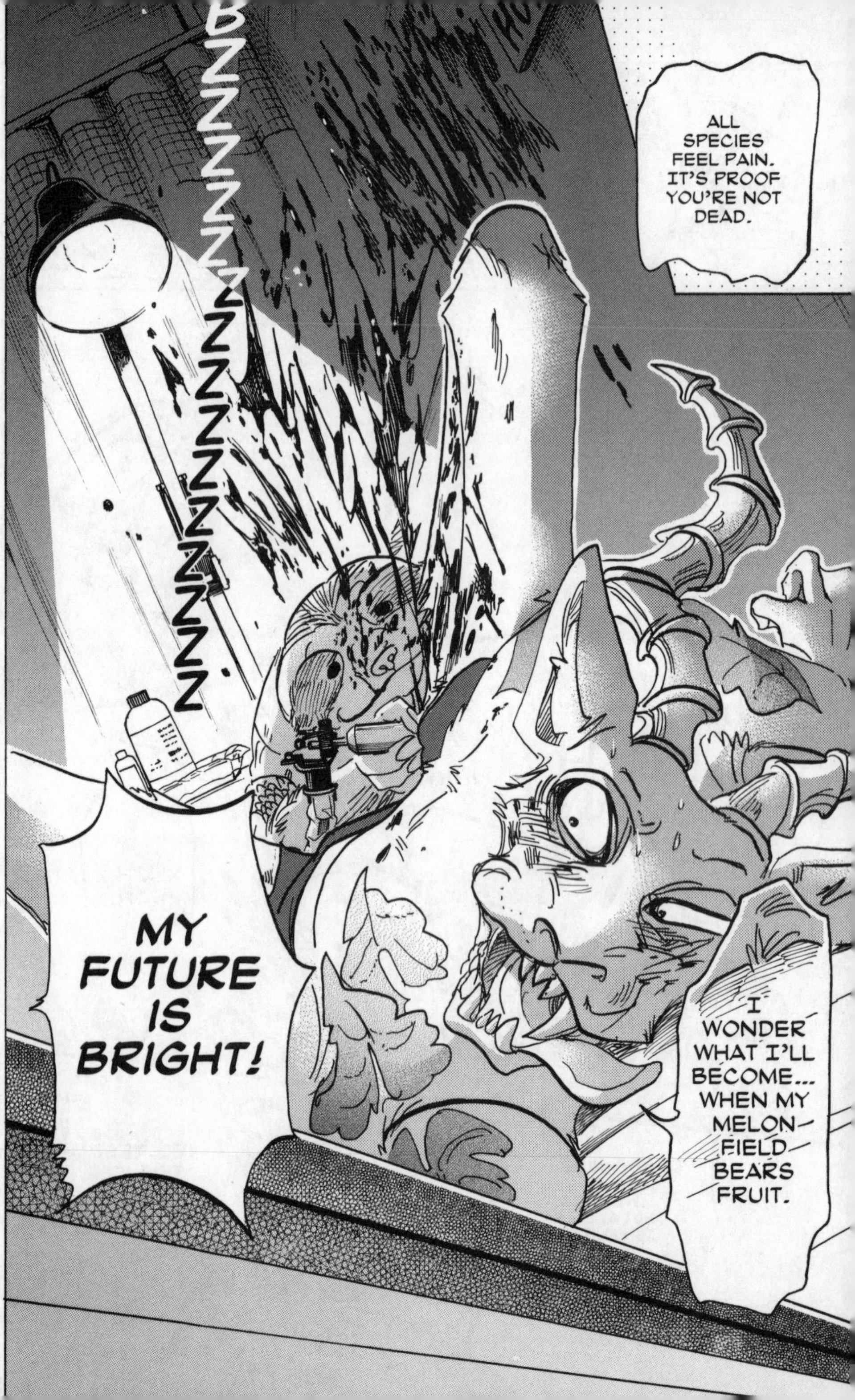
ALL SPECIES FEEL PAIN. IT'S PROOF YOU'RE NOT DEAD.
BZZZZZZZZZZZZZZZZZ
I WONDER WHAT I'LL BECOME... WHEN MY MELON-FIELD BEARS FRUIT.
MY FUTURE IS BRIGHT!

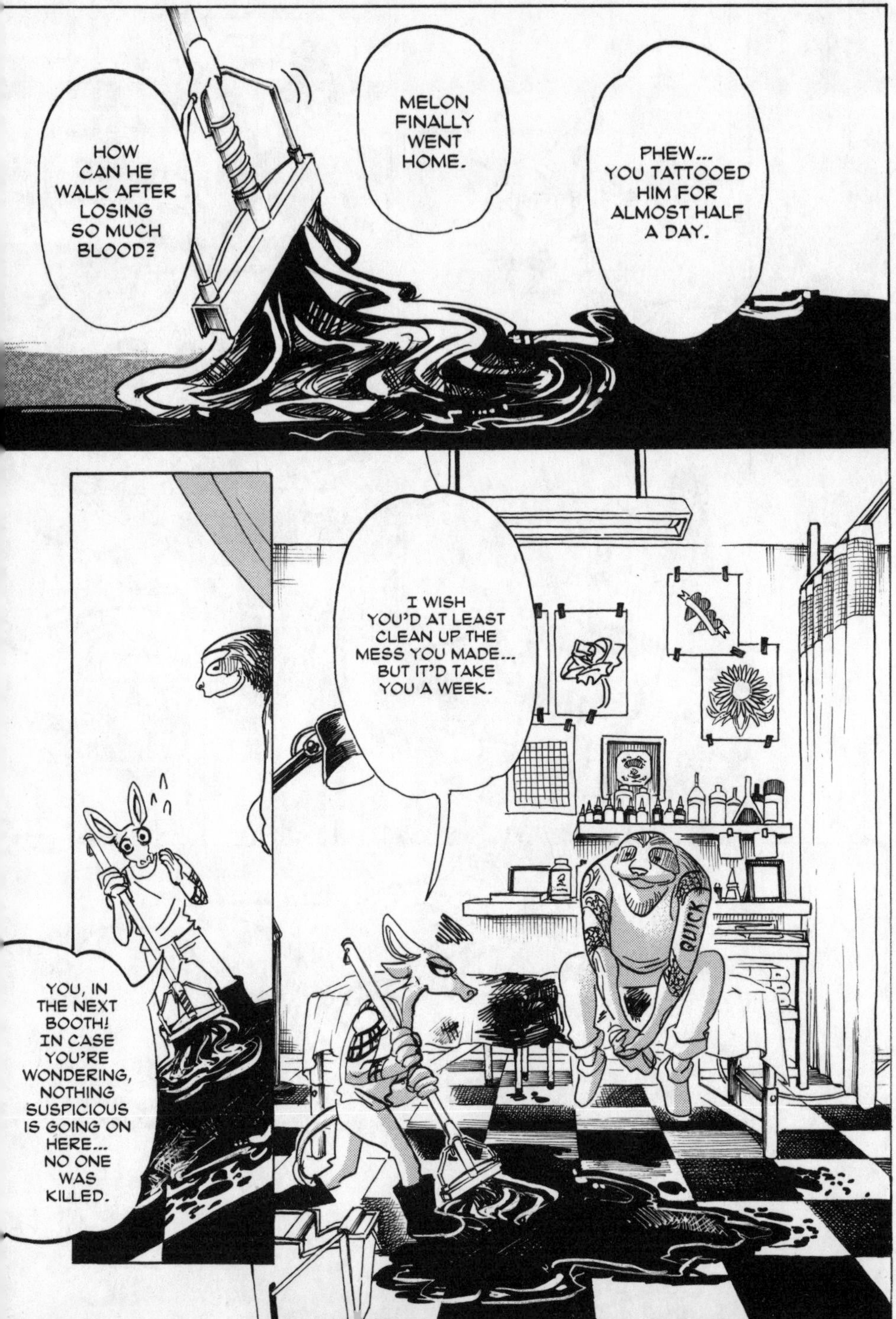
PHEW... YOU TATTOOED HIM FOR ALMOST HALF A DAY.
MELON FINALLY WENT HOME.
HOW CAN HE WALK AFTER LOSING SO MUCH BLOOD?
I WISH YOU'D AT LEAST CLEAN UP THE MESS YOU MADE... BUT IT'D TAKE YOU A WEEK.
QUICK
YOU, IN THE NEXT BOOTH! IN CASE YOU'RE WONDERING, NOTHING SUSPICIOUS IS GOING ON HERE... NO ONE WAS KILLED.

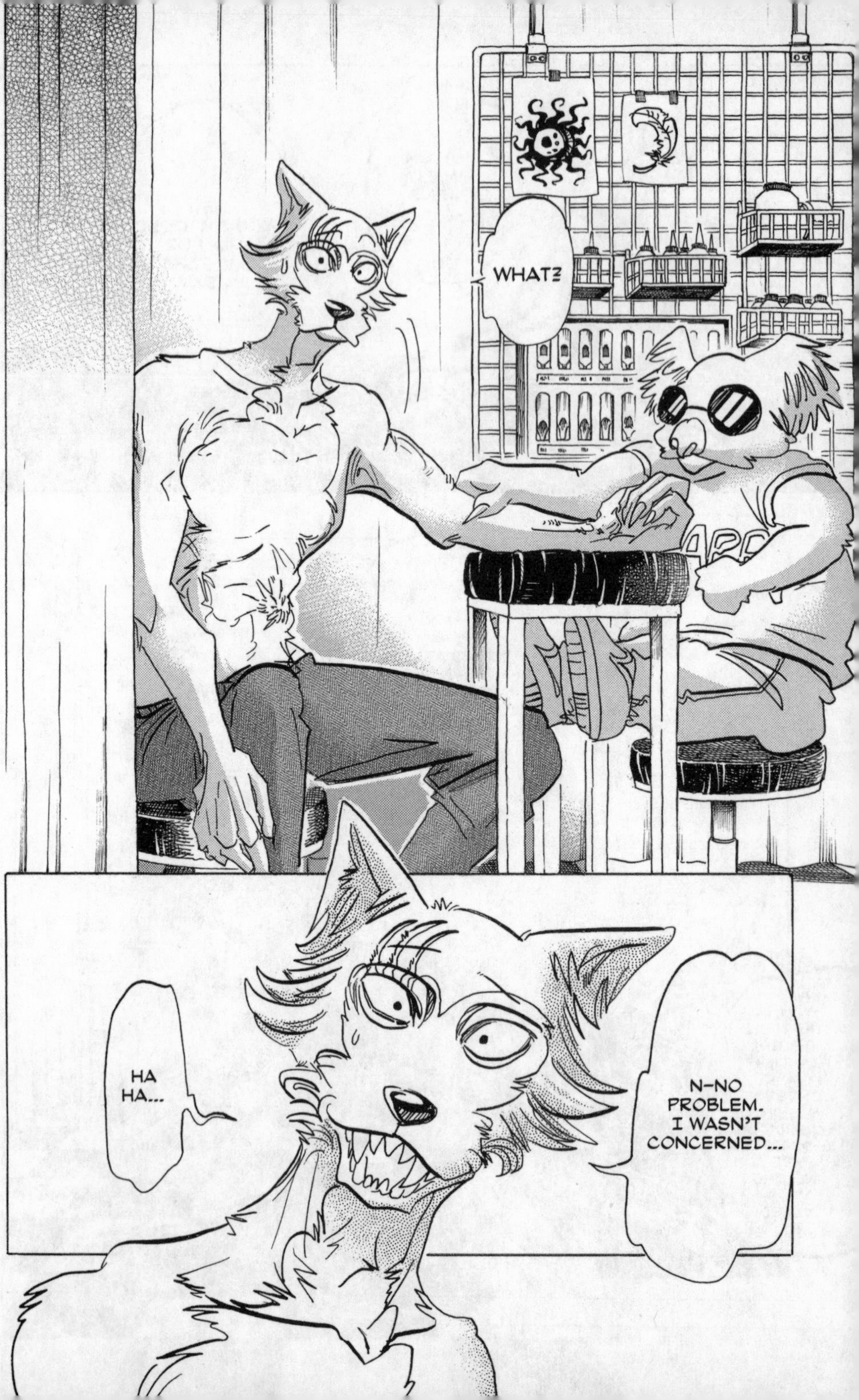
WHAT?
N-NO PROBLEM. I WASN'T CONCERNED...
HA HA...

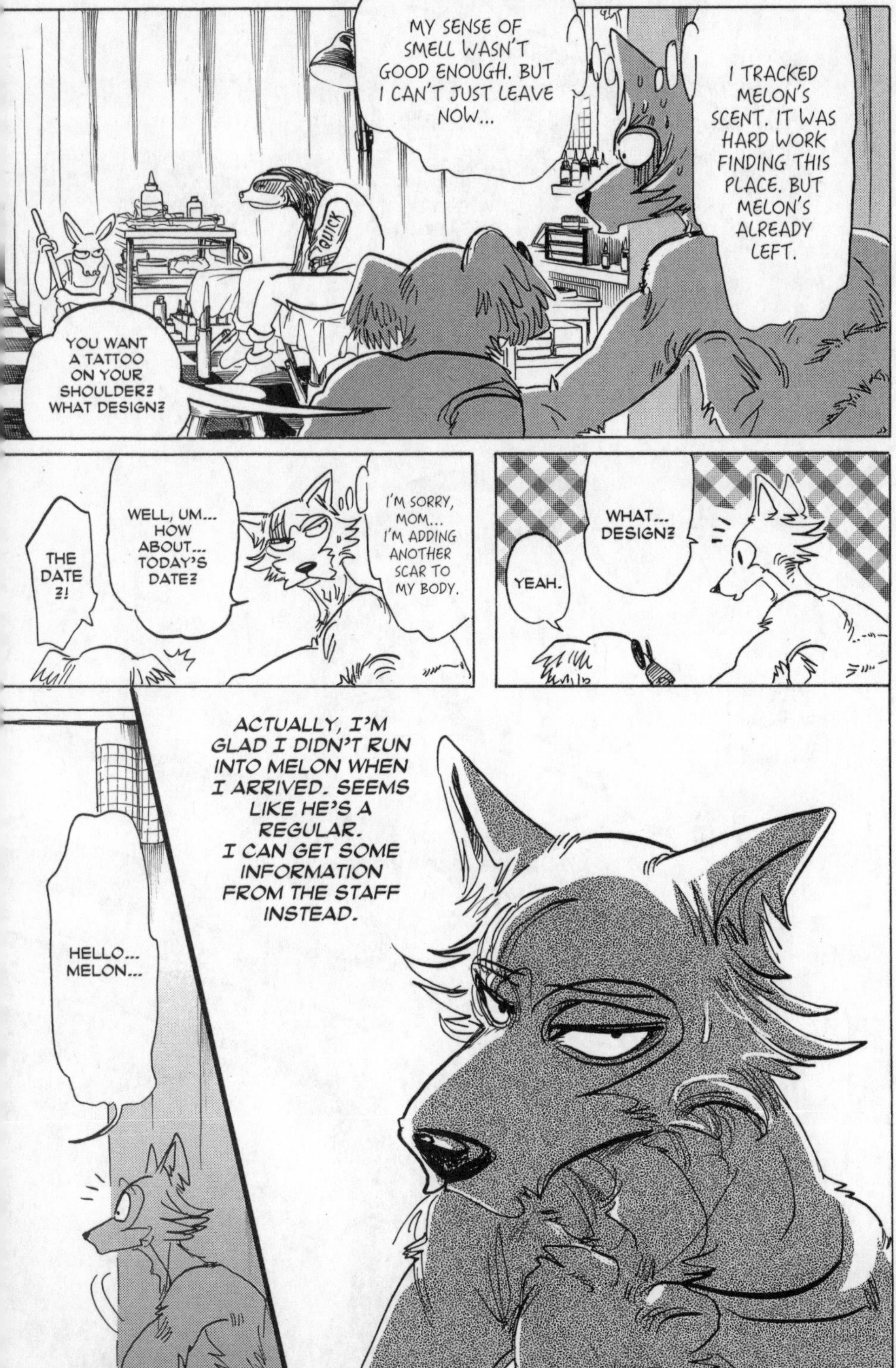
I TRACKED MELON'S SCENT. IT WAS HARD WORK FINDING THIS PLACE. BUT MELON'S ALREADY LEFT.
MY SENSE OF SMELL WASN'T GOOD ENOUGH. BUT I CAN'T JUST LEAVE NOW...
QUICK
YOU WANT A TATTOO ON YOUR SHOULDER? WHAT DESIGN?
WHAT... DESIGN?
YEAH.
I'M SORRY, MOM... I'M ADDING ANOTHER SCAR TO MY BODY.
WELL, UM... HOW ABOUT... TODAY'S DATE?
THE DATE ?!
ACTUALLY, I'M GLAD I DIDN'T RUN INTO MELON WHEN I ARRIVED. SEEMS LIKE HE'S A REGULAR. I CAN GET SOME INFORMATION FROM THE STAFF INSTEAD.
HELLO... MELON...

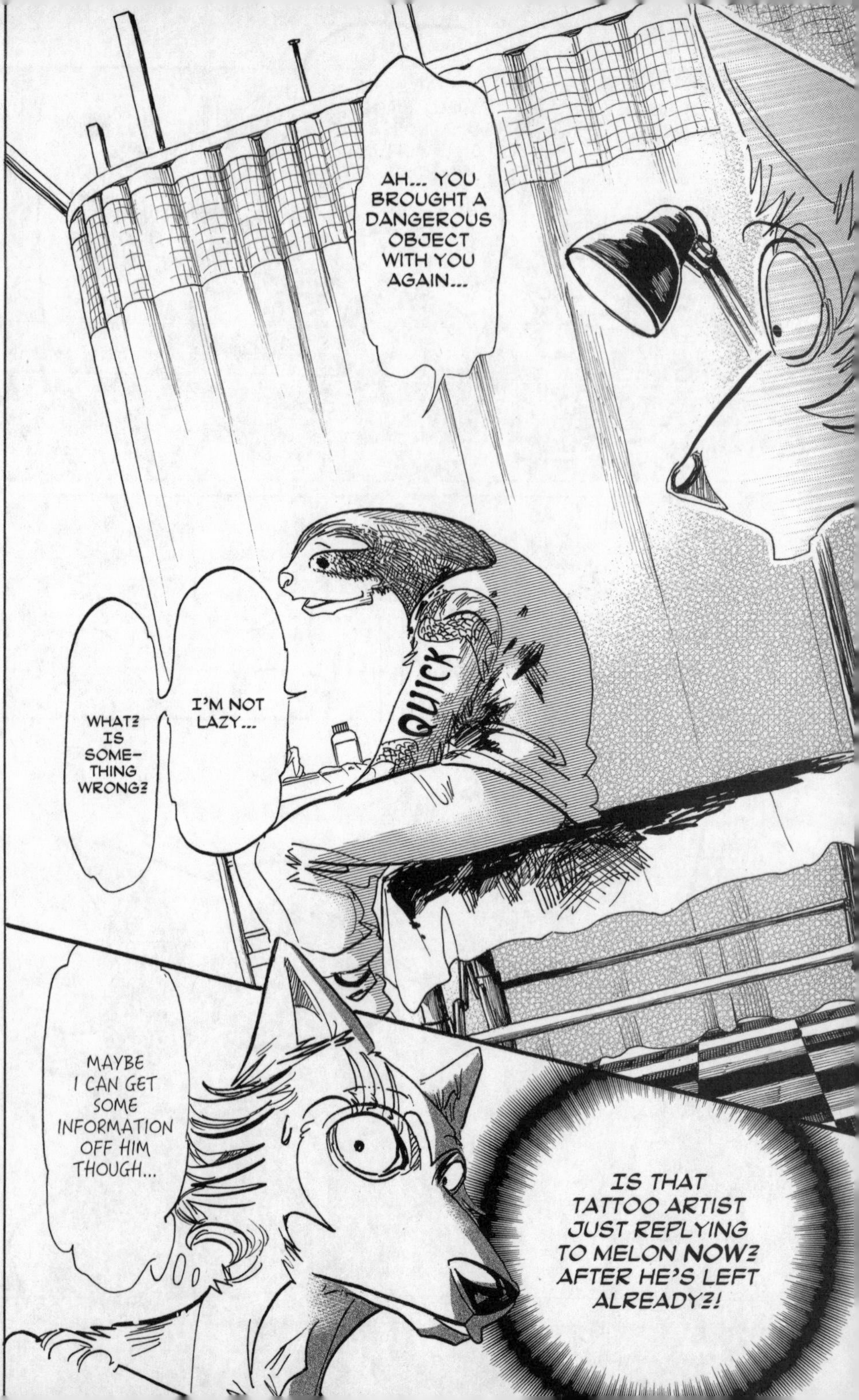
AH... YOU BROUGHT A DANGEROUS OBJECT WITH YOU AGAIN...
QUICK
I'M NOT LAZY...
WHAT? IS SOMETHING WRONG?
IS THAT TATTOO ARTIST JUST REPLYING TO MELON NOW? AFTER HE'S LEFT ALREADY?!
MAYBE I CAN GET SOME INFORMATION OFF HIM THOUGH...

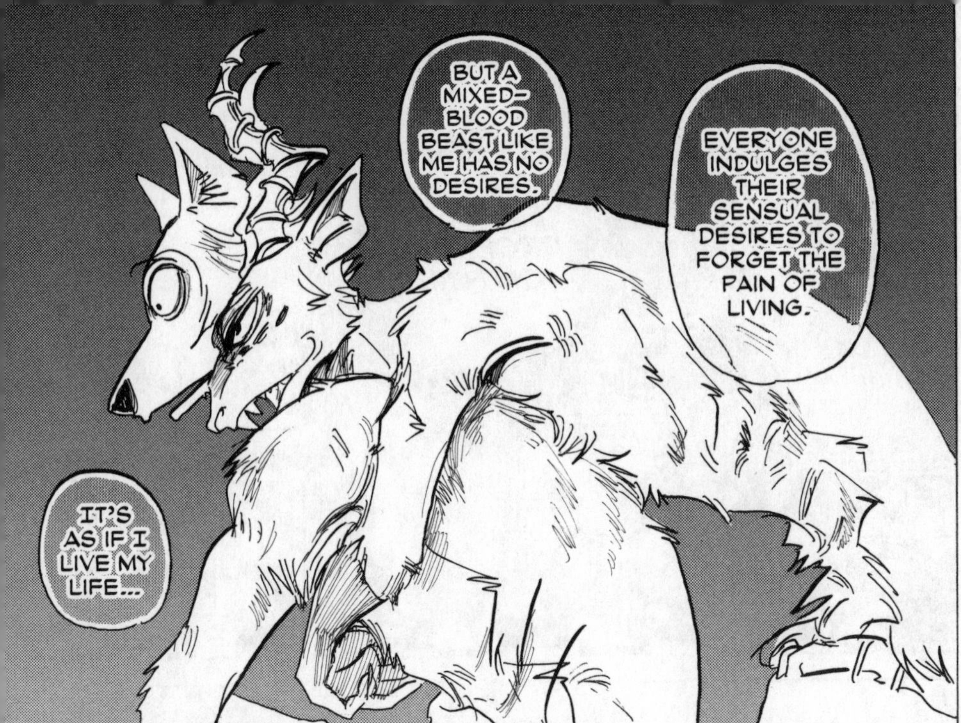
EVERYONE INDULGES THEIR SENSUAL DESIRES TO FORGET THE PAIN OF LIVING.
BUT A MIXED-BLOOD BEAST LIKE ME HAS NO DESIRES.
IT'S AS IF I LIVE MY LIFE...
...WITHOUT A PENIS OR A STOMACH.

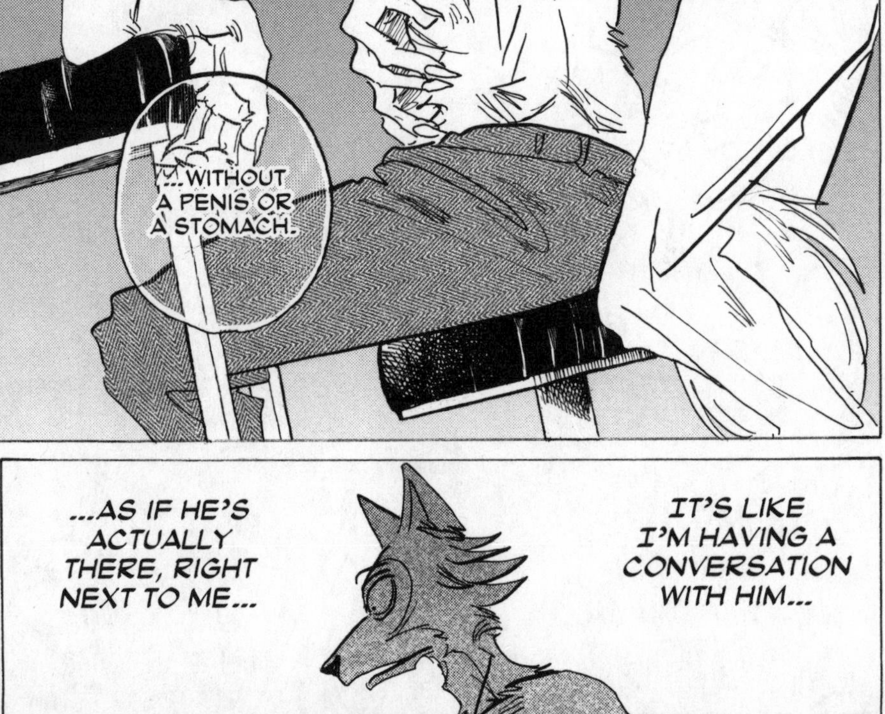
IT'S LIKE I'M HAVING A CONVERSATION WITH HIM...
...AS IF HE'S ACTUALLY THERE, RIGHT NEXT TO ME...

Chapter 140: Training an Actor to Perform Tragedy

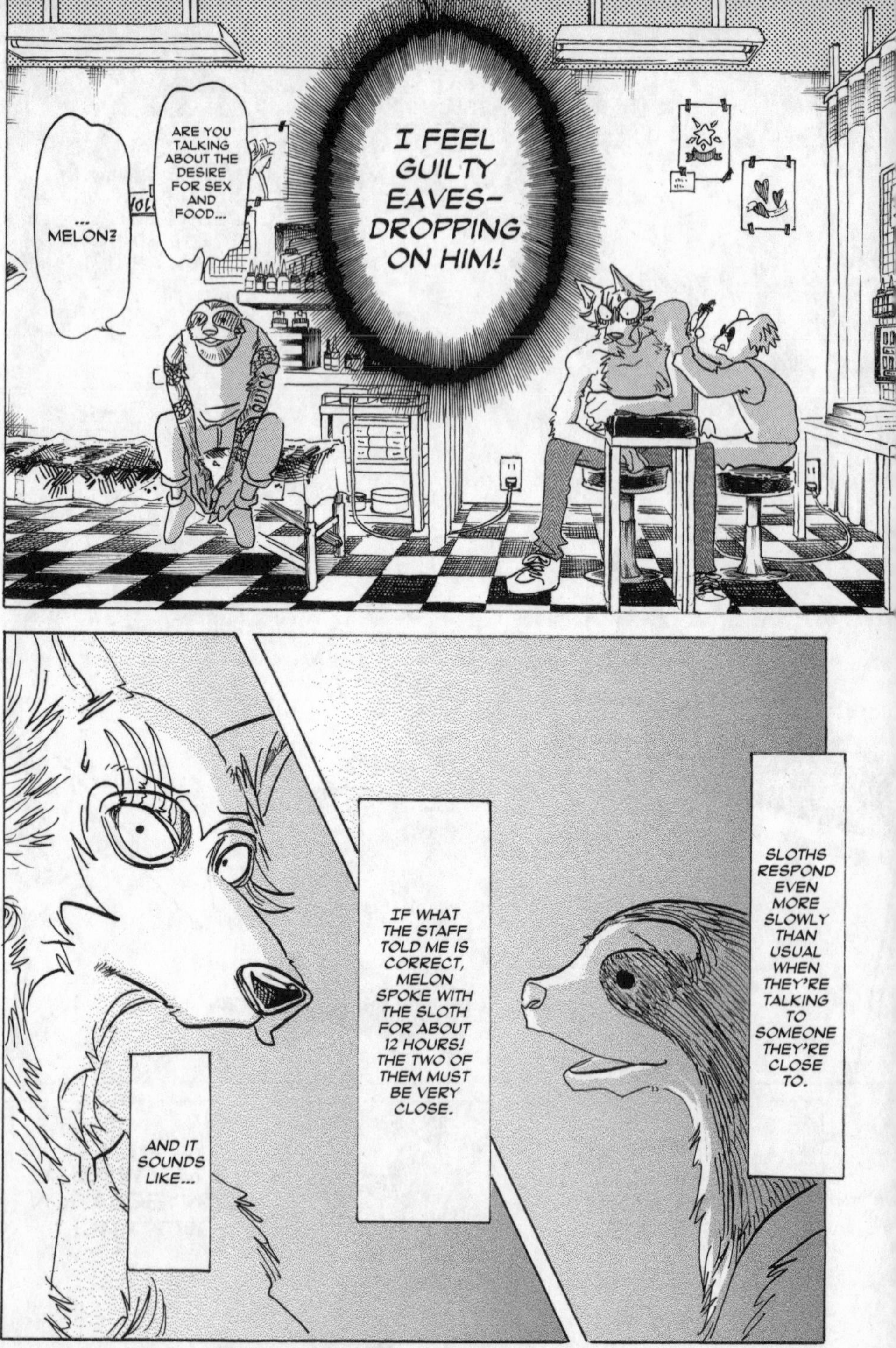
I FEEL GUILTY EAVES-DROPPING ON HIM!
ARE YOU TALKING ABOUT THE DESIRE FOR SEX AND FOOD...
...MELON?
SLOTHS RESPOND EVEN MORE SLOWLY THAN USUAL WHEN THEY'RE TALKING TO SOMEONE THEY'RE CLOSE TO.
IF WHAT THE STAFF TOLD ME IS CORRECT, MELON SPOKE WITH THE SLOTH FOR ABOUT 12 HOURS! THE TWO OF THEM MUST BE VERY CLOSE.
AND IT SOUNDS LIKE...

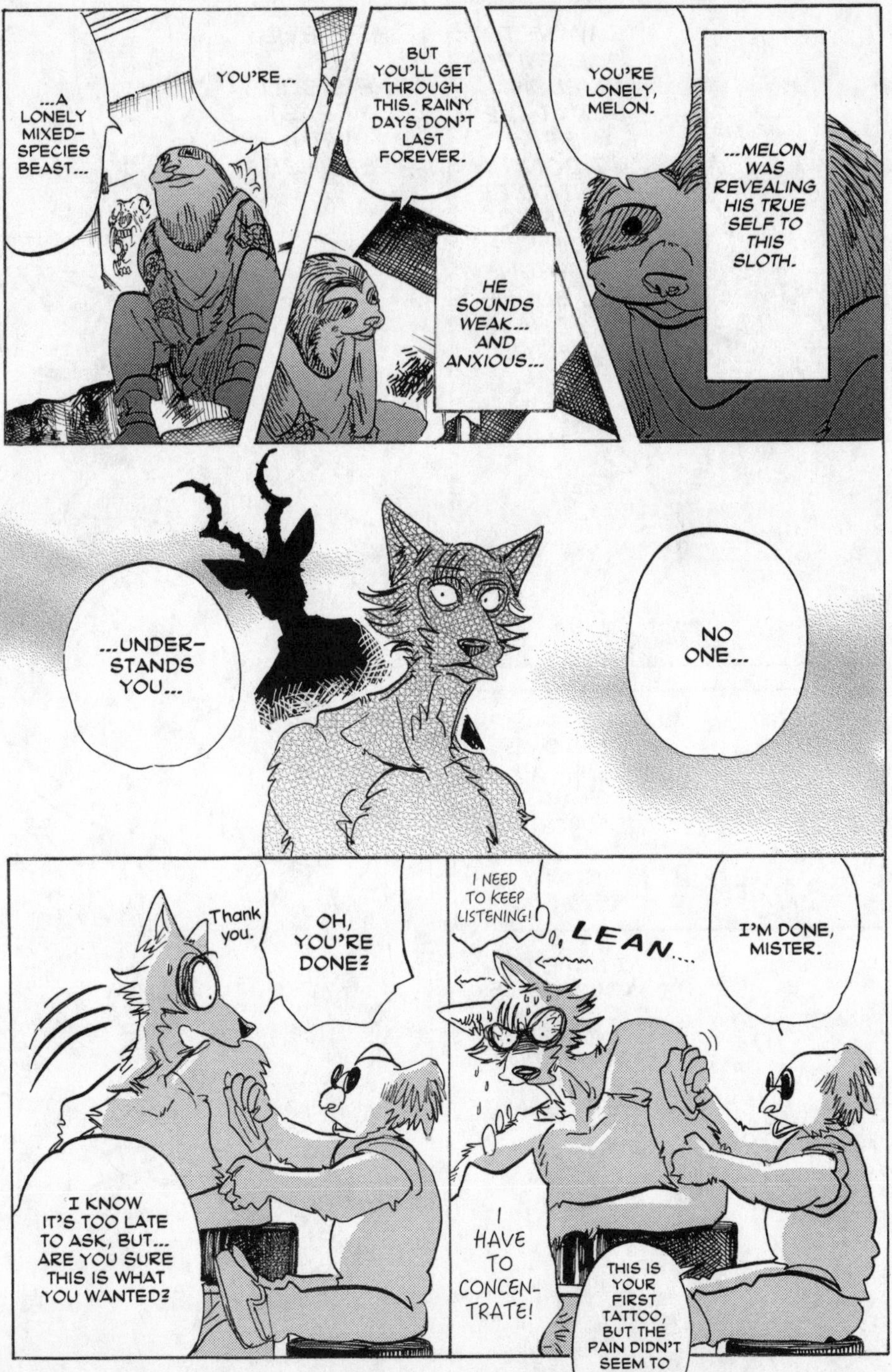

...MELON WAS REVEALING HIS TRUE SELF TO THIS SLOTH.
YOU'RE LONELY, MELON.
BUT YOU'LL GET THROUGH THIS. RAINY DAYS DON'T LAST FOREVER.
HE SOUNDS WEAK... AND ANXIOUS...
YOU'RE...
...A LONELY MIXED-SPECIES BEAST...
NO ONE...
...UNDER-STANDS YOU...
I'M DONE, MISTER.
LEAN...
I NEED TO KEEP LISTENING!
I HAVE TO CONCEN-TRATE!
THIS IS YOUR FIRST TATTOO, BUT THE PAIN DIDN'T SEEM TO BOTHER YOU...
OH, YOU'RE DONE?
Thank you.
I KNOW IT'S TOO LATE TO ASK, BUT... ARE YOU SURE THIS IS WHAT YOU WANTED?

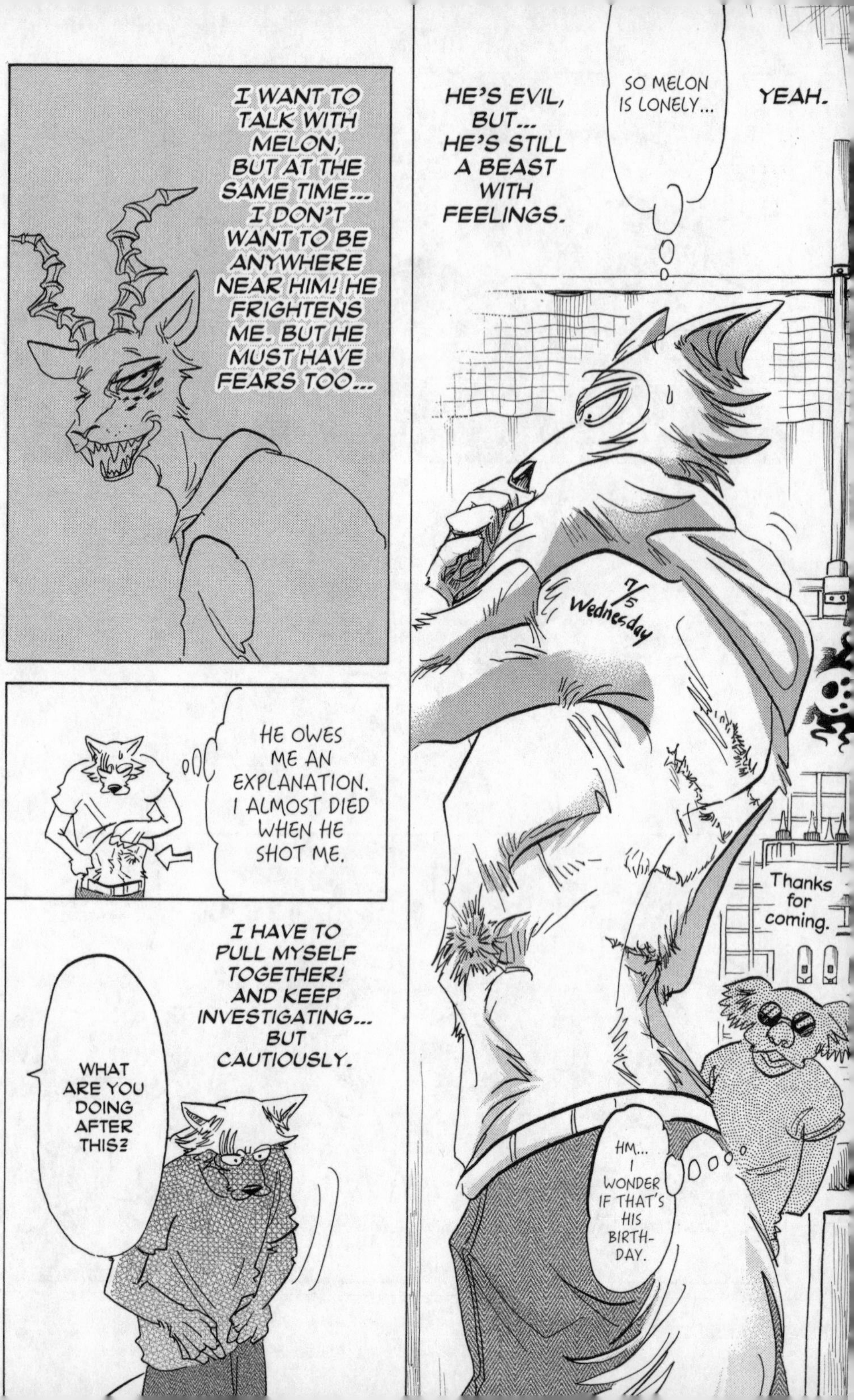
YEAH.
SO MELON IS LONELY...
HE'S EVIL, BUT... HE'S STILL A BEAST WITH FEELINGS.
7/5 Wednesday
Thanks for coming.
HM... I WONDER IF THAT'S HIS BIRTHDAY.
I WANT TO TALK WITH MELON, BUT AT THE SAME TIME... I DON'T WANT TO BE ANYWHERE NEAR HIM! HE FRIGHTENS ME. BUT HE MUST HAVE FEARS TOO...
HE OWES ME AN EXPLANATION. I ALMOST DIED WHEN HE SHOT ME.
I HAVE TO PULL MYSELF TOGETHER! AND KEEP INVESTIGATING... BUT CAUTIOUSLY.
WHAT ARE YOU DOING AFTER THIS?

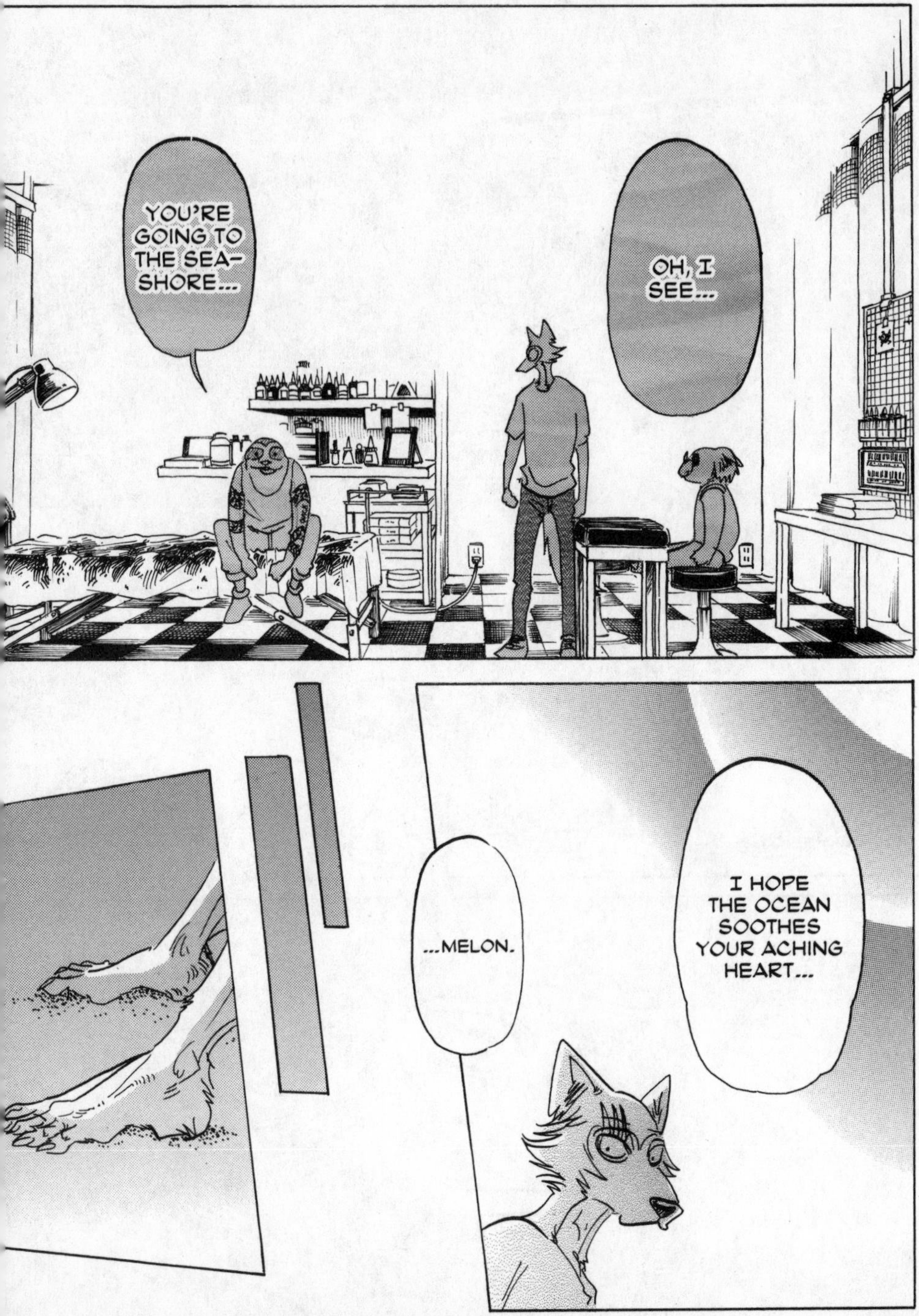
OH, I SEE...
YOU'RE GOING TO THE SEA-SHORE...
I HOPE THE OCEAN SOOTHES YOUR ACHING HEART...
...MELON.

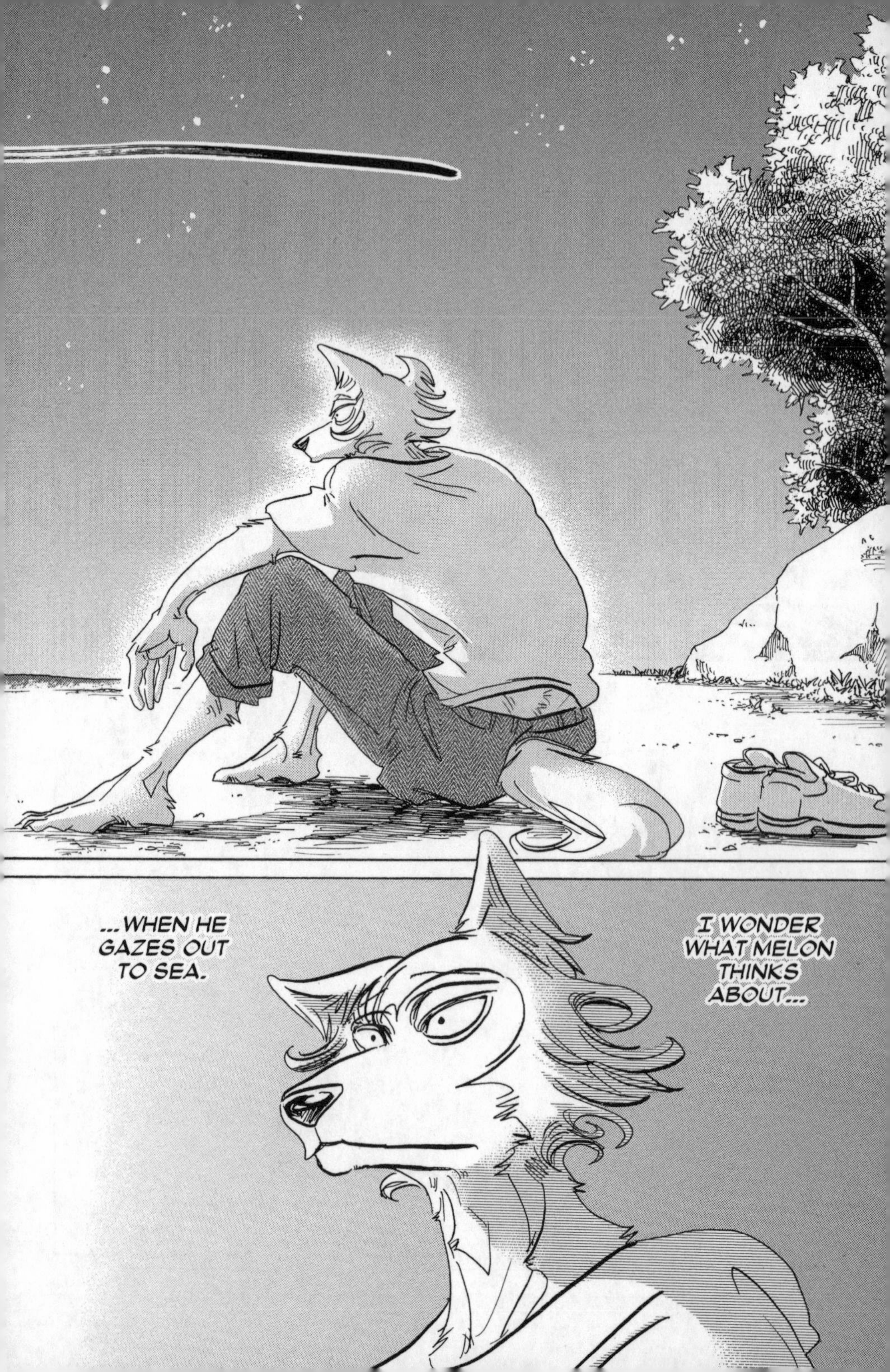
I WONDER WHAT MELON THINKS ABOUT...
...WHEN HE GAZES OUT TO SEA.

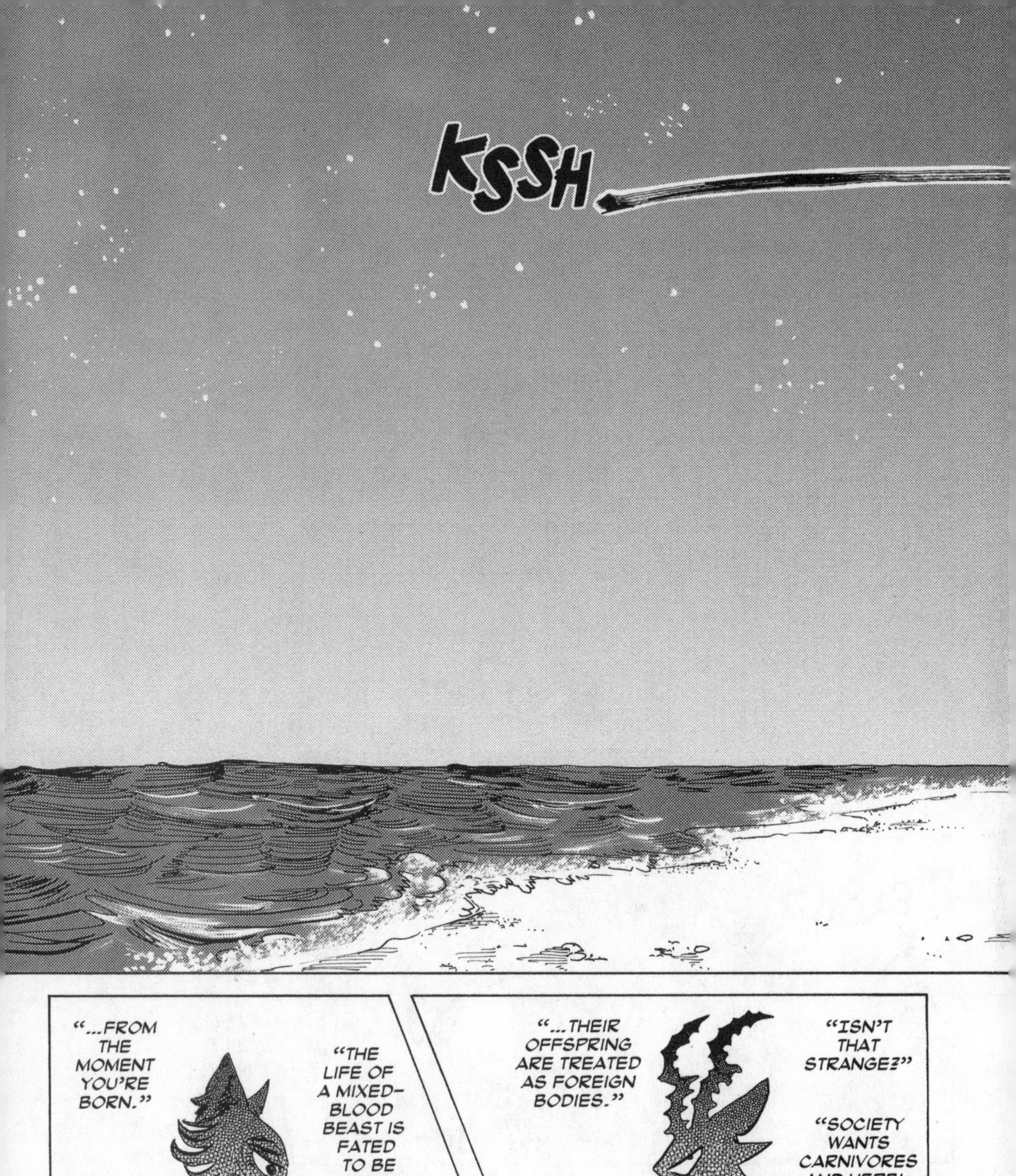
KSSH

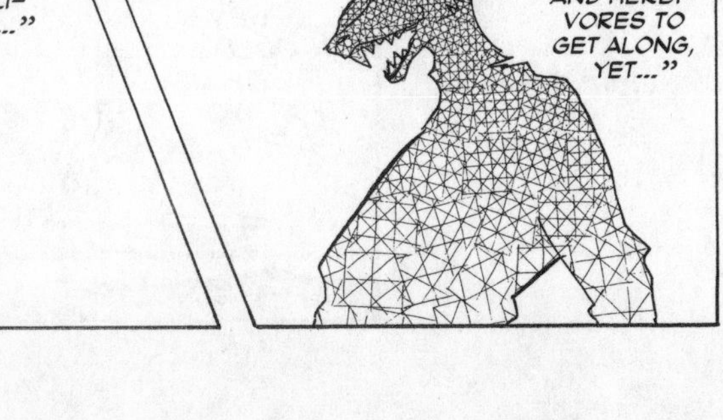
"ISN'T THAT STRANGE?"
"SOCIETY WANTS CARNIVORES AND HERBIVORES TO GET ALONG, YET..."
"...THEIR OFFSPRING ARE TREATED AS FOREIGN BODIES."

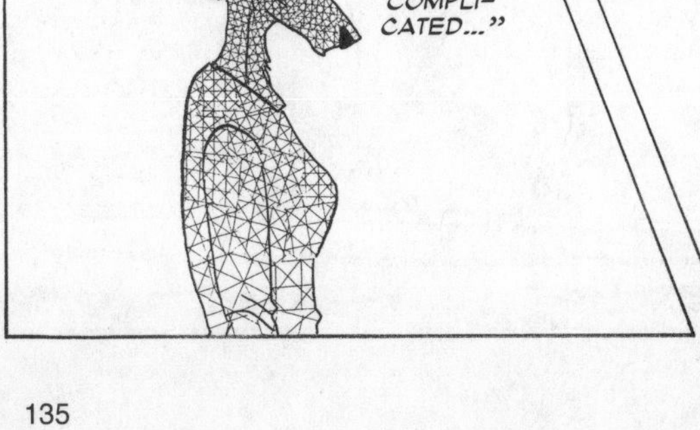
"THE LIFE OF A MIXED-BLOOD BEAST IS FATED TO BE COMPLICATED..."
"...FROM THE MOMENT YOU'RE BORN."

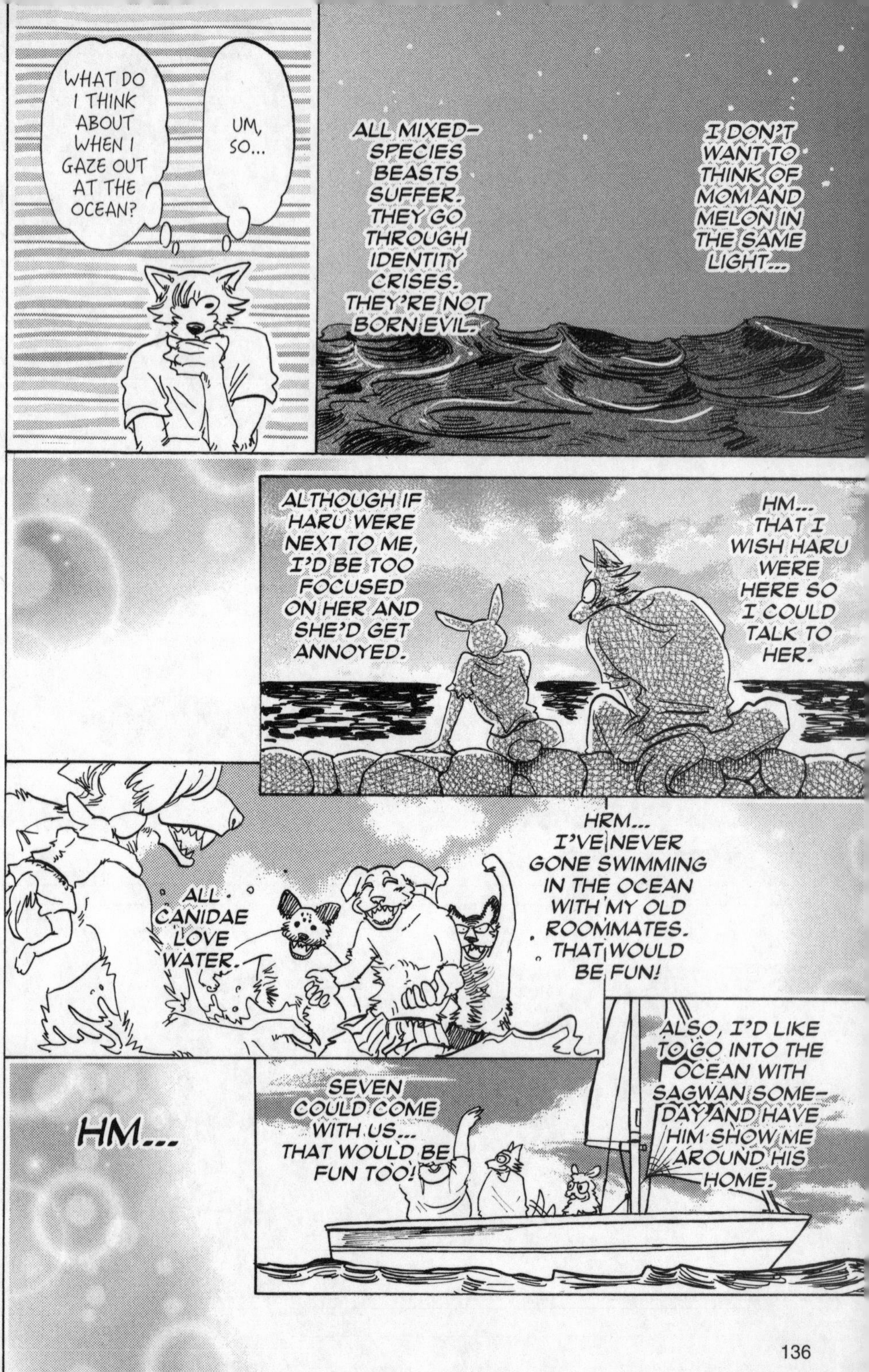
I DON'T WANT TO THINK OF MOM AND MELON IN THE SAME LIGHT...
ALL MIXED-SPECIES BEASTS SUFFER. THEY GO THROUGH IDENTITY CRISES. THEY'RE NOT BORN EVIL.
WHAT DO I THINK ABOUT WHEN I GAZE OUT AT THE OCEAN?
UM, SO...
HM... THAT I WISH HARU WERE HERE SO I COULD TALK TO HER.
ALTHOUGH IF HARU WERE NEXT TO ME, I'D BE TOO FOCUSED ON HER AND SHE'D GET ANNOYED.
HRM... I'VE NEVER GONE SWIMMING IN THE OCEAN WITH MY OLD ROOMMATES. THAT WOULD BE FUN!
ALL CANIDAE LOVE WATER.
ALSO, I'D LIKE TO GO INTO THE OCEAN WITH SAGWAN SOME-DAY AND HAVE HIM SHOW ME AROUND HIS HOME.
SEVEN COULD COME WITH US... THAT WOULD BE FUN TOO!
HM...

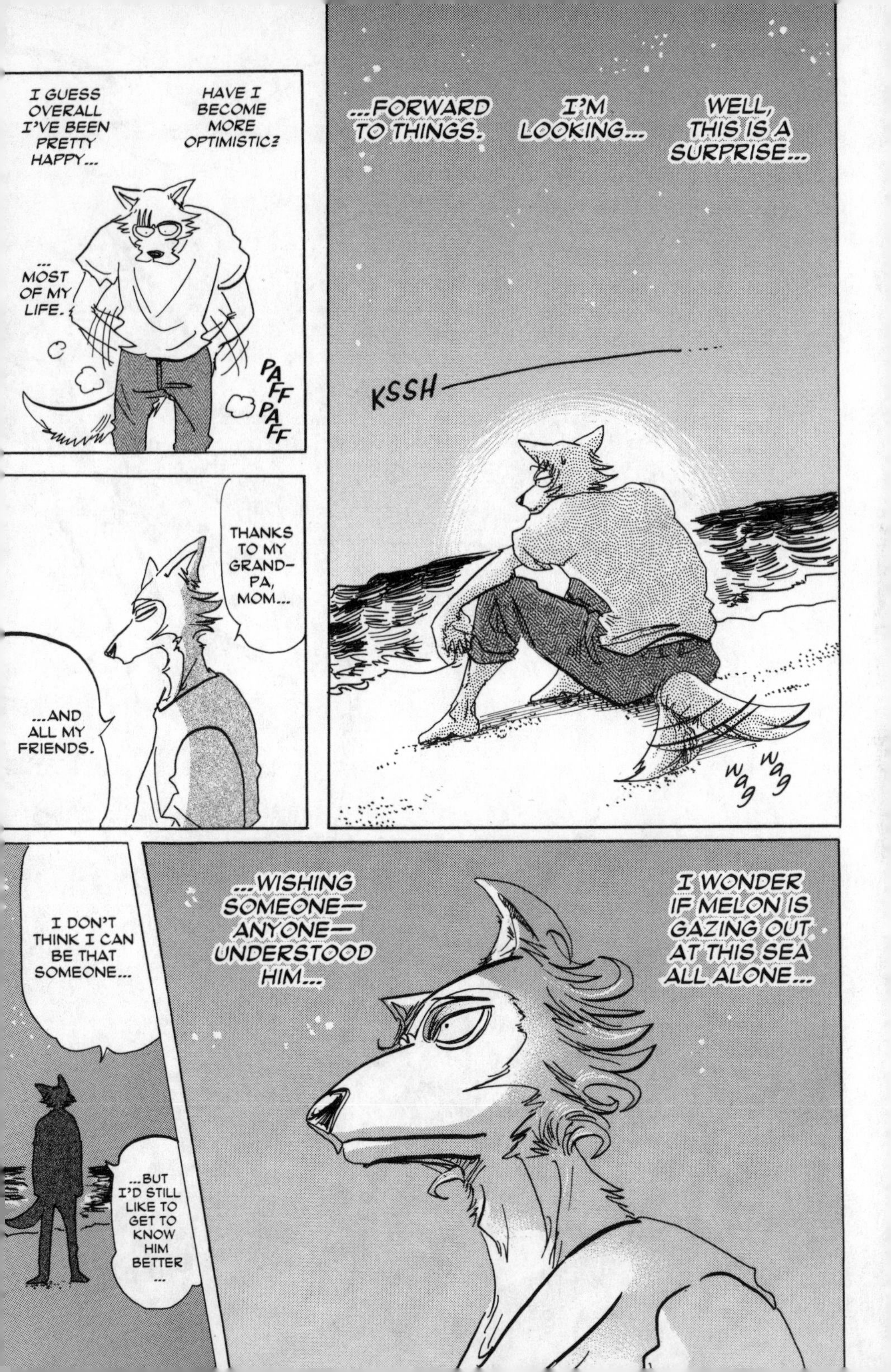
WELL, THIS IS A SURPRISE...
I'M LOOKING...
...FORWARD TO THINGS.
KSSH
wag wag
HAVE I BECOME MORE OPTIMISTIC?
I GUESS OVERALL I'VE BEEN PRETTY HAPPY...
...MOST OF MY LIFE.
PAFF PAFF
THANKS TO MY GRAND-PA, MOM...
...AND ALL MY FRIENDS.
I WONDER IF MELON IS GAZING OUT AT THIS SEA ALL ALONE...
...WISHING SOMEONE—ANYONE—UNDERSTOOD HIM...
I DON'T THINK I CAN BE THAT SOMEONE...
...BUT I'D STILL LIKE TO GET TO KNOW HIM BETTER...

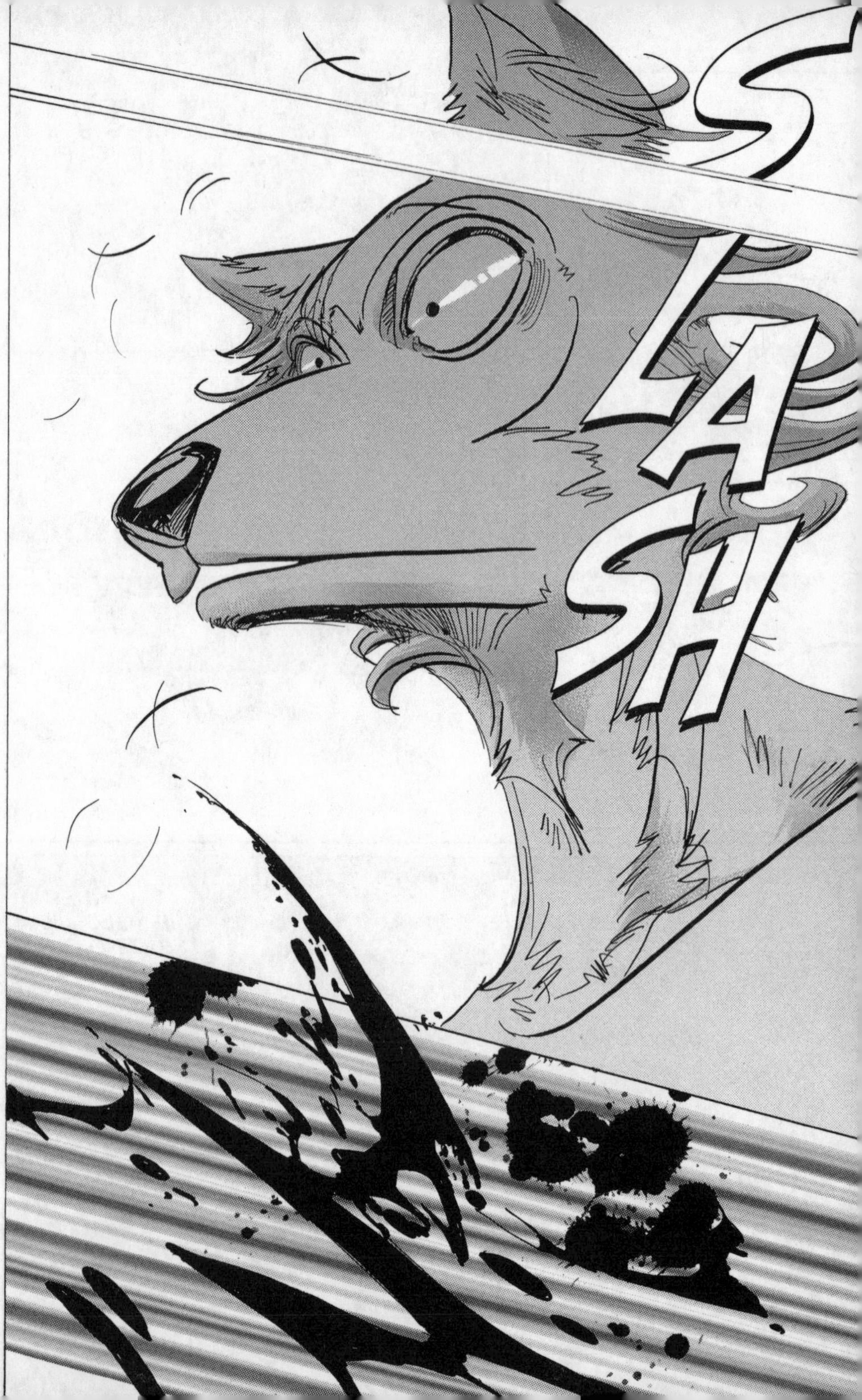
SLASH

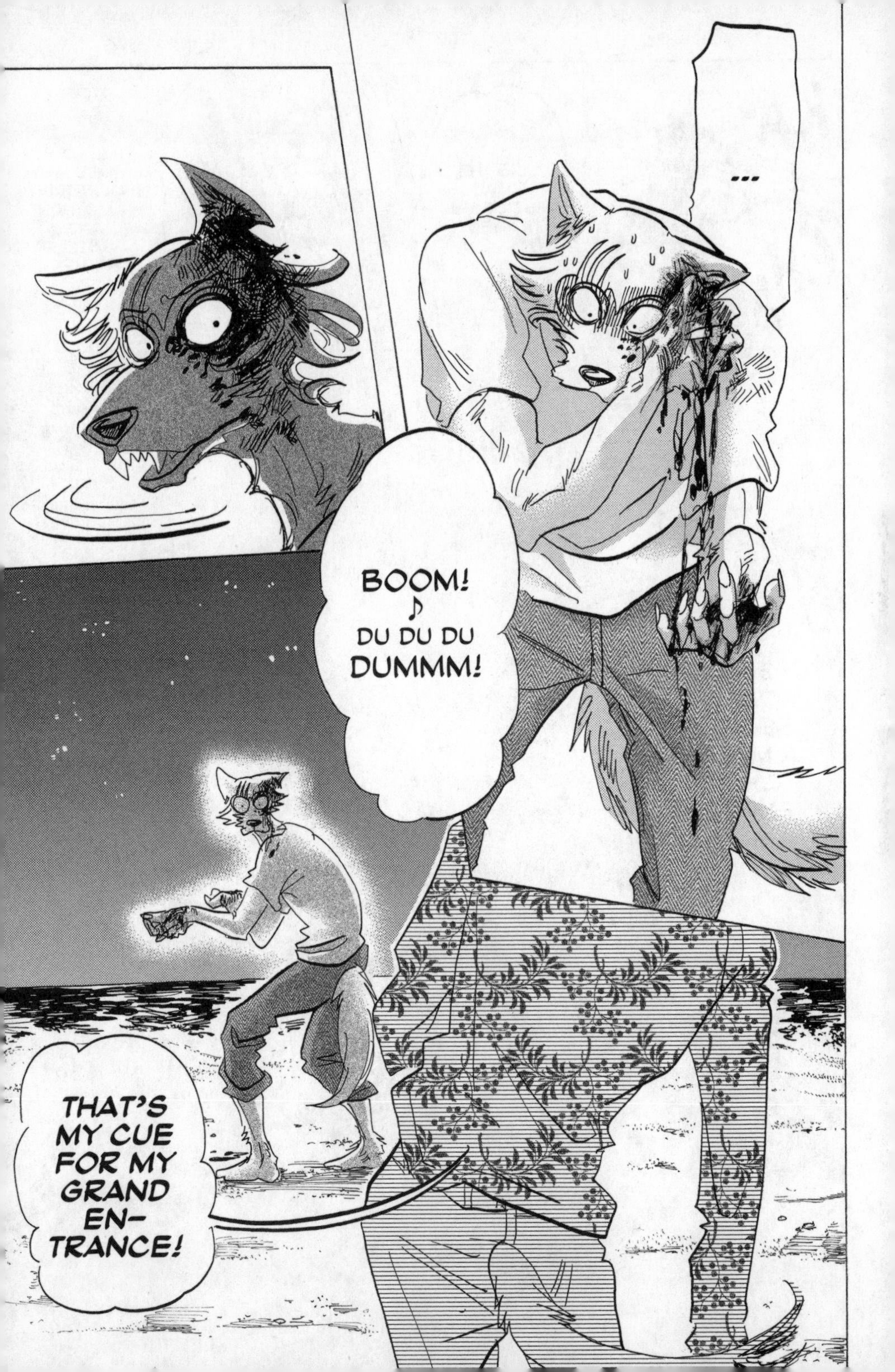
...
BOOM! ♪ DU DU DU DUMMM!
THAT'S MY CUE FOR MY GRAND EN-TRANCE!

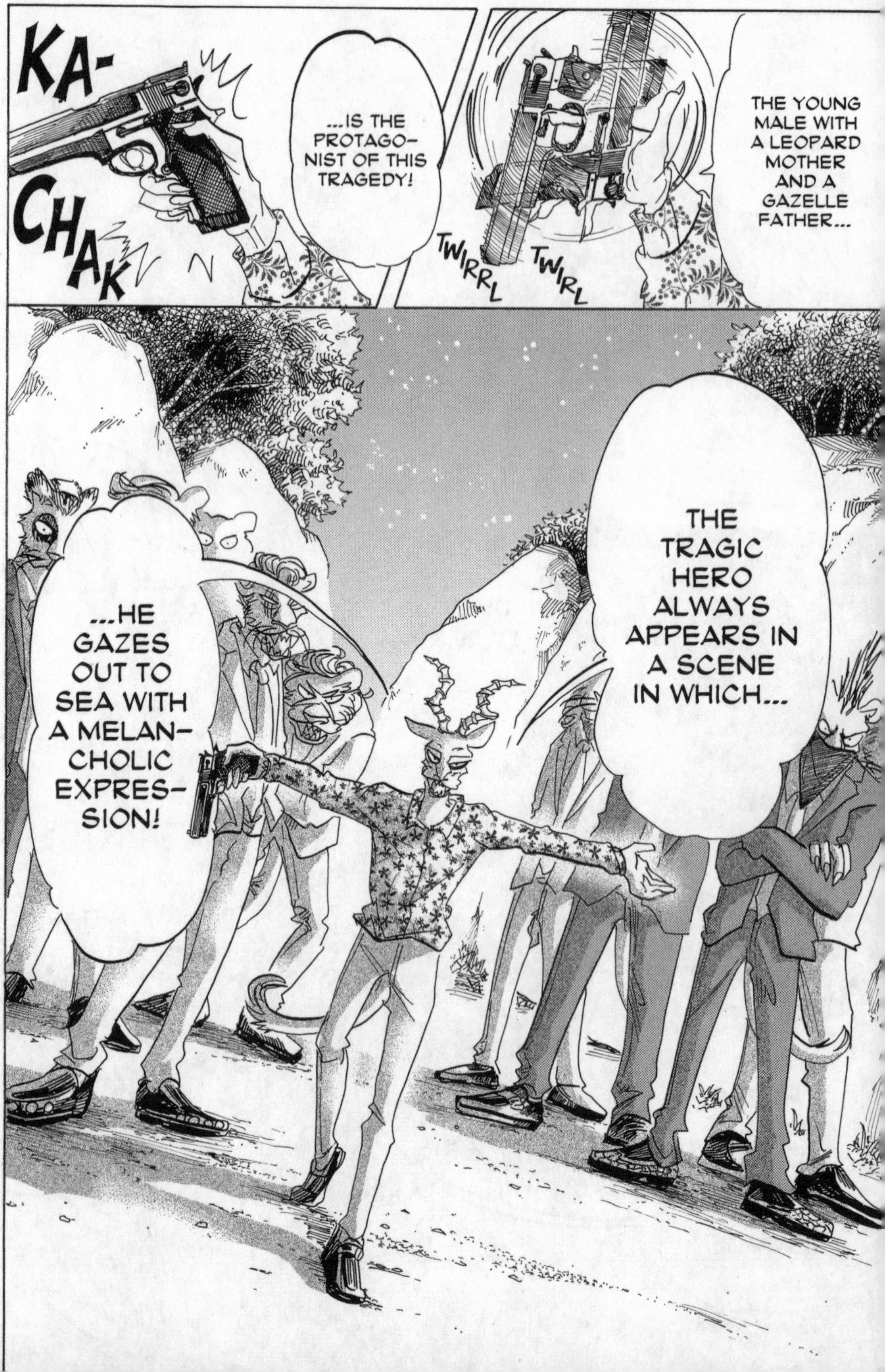
THE YOUNG MALE WITH A LEOPARD MOTHER AND A GAZELLE FATHER...
TWIRRL
TWIRL
...IS THE PROTAGONIST OF THIS TRAGEDY!
KA-CHAK
THE TRAGIC HERO ALWAYS APPEARS IN A SCENE IN WHICH...
...HE GAZES OUT TO SEA WITH A MELANCHOLIC EXPRESSION!

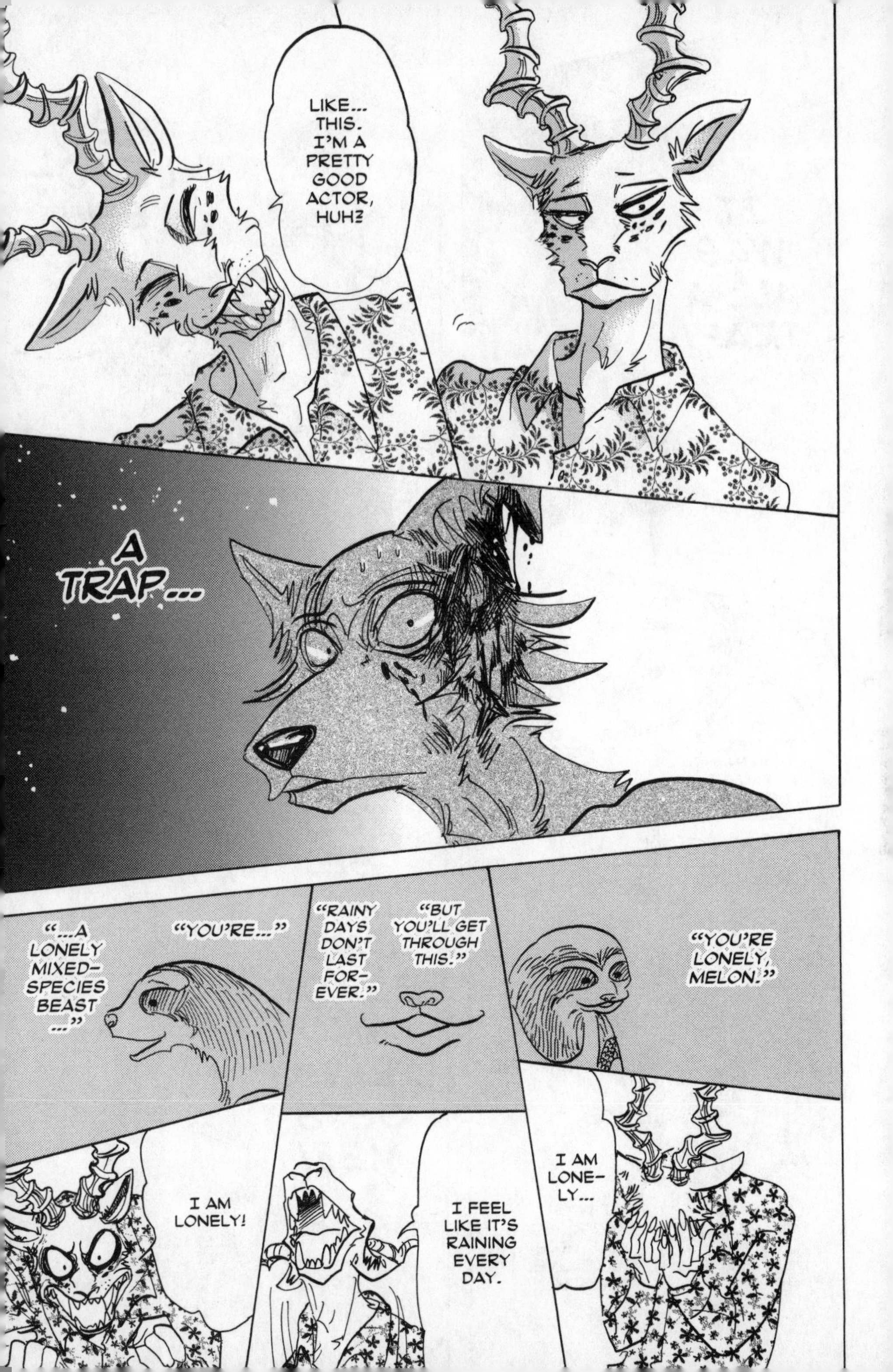
LIKE... THIS. I'M A PRETTY GOOD ACTOR, HUH?
A TRAP...
"YOU'RE LONELY, MELON."
"BUT YOU'LL GET THROUGH THIS."
"RAINY DAYS DON'T LAST FOR-EVER."
"YOU'RE..."
"...A LONELY MIXED-SPECIES BEAST..."
I AM LONE-LY...
I FEEL LIKE IT'S RAINING EVERY DAY.
I AM LONELY!

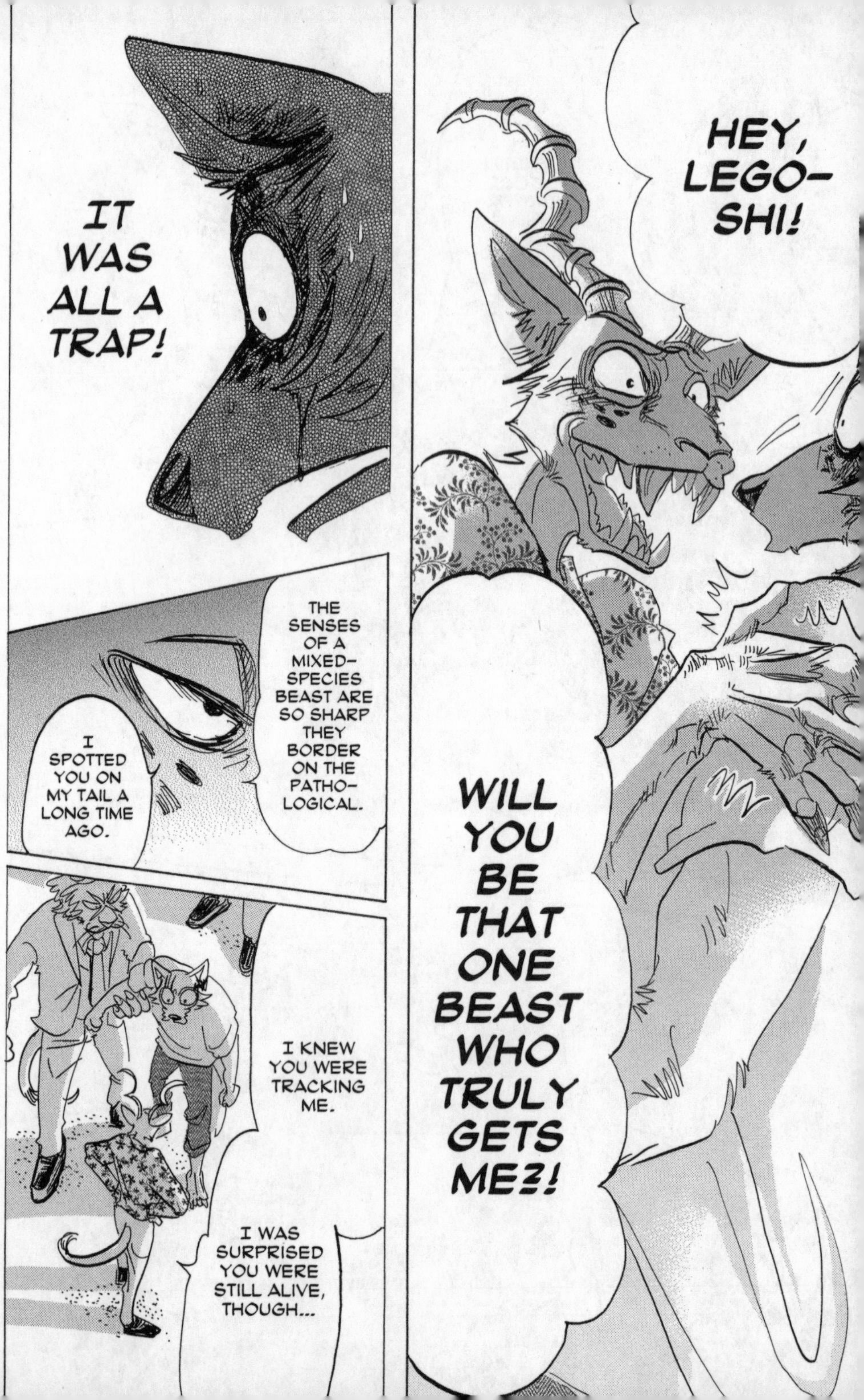
HEY, LEGO-SHI!
WILL YOU BE THAT ONE BEAST WHO TRULY GETS ME?!
IT WAS ALL A TRAP!
THE SENSES OF A MIXED-SPECIES BEAST ARE SO SHARP THEY BORDER ON THE PATHO-LOGICAL.
I SPOTTED YOU ON MY TAIL A LONG TIME AGO.
I KNEW YOU WERE TRACKING ME.
I WAS SURPRISED YOU WERE STILL ALIVE, THOUGH...

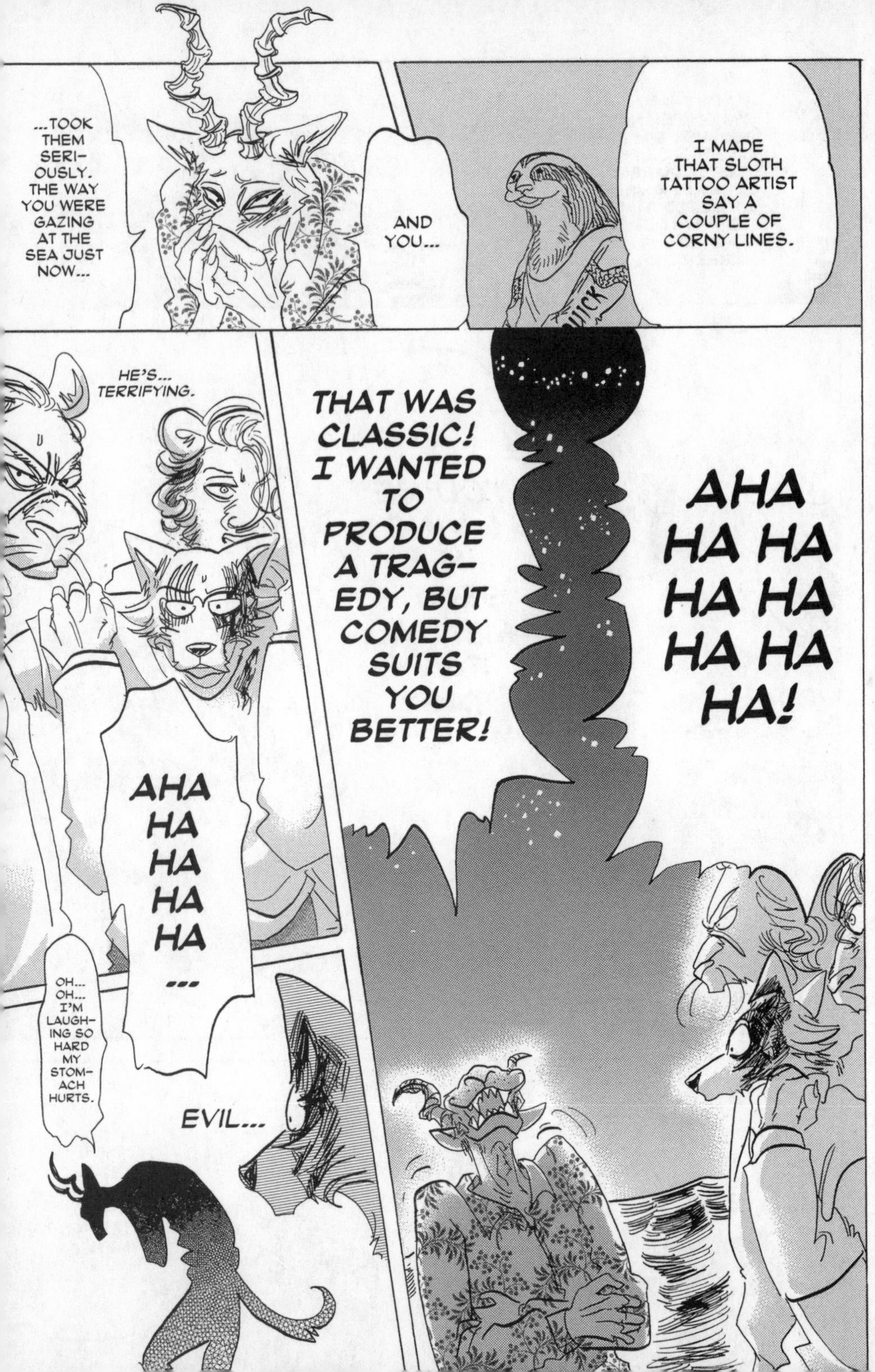
I MADE THAT SLOTH TATTOO ARTIST SAY A COUPLE OF CORNY LINES.
AND YOU...
...TOOK THEM SERIOUSLY. THE WAY YOU WERE GAZING AT THE SEA JUST NOW...
AHA HA HA HA HA HA HA HA!
THAT WAS CLASSIC! I WANTED TO PRODUCE A TRAGEDY, BUT COMEDY SUITS YOU BETTER!
HE'S... TERRIFYING.
AHA HA HA HA HA ...
OH... OH... I'M LAUGHING SO HARD MY STOMACH HURTS.
EVIL...

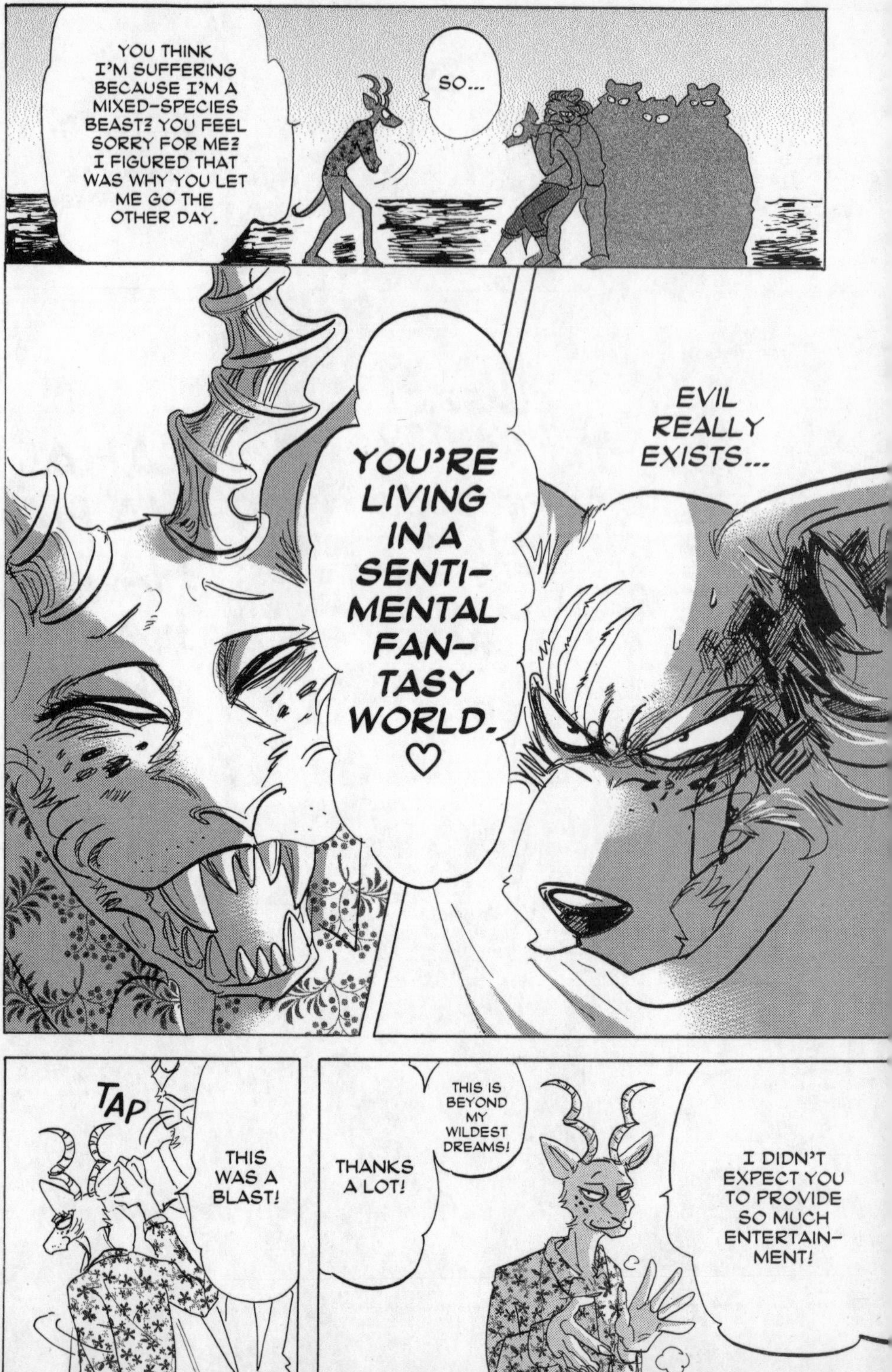
SO...
YOU THINK I'M SUFFERING BECAUSE I'M A MIXED-SPECIES BEAST? YOU FEEL SORRY FOR ME? I FIGURED THAT WAS WHY YOU LET ME GO THE OTHER DAY.
EVIL REALLY EXISTS...
YOU'RE LIVING IN A SENTI-MENTAL FAN-TASY WORLD. ♥
I DIDN'T EXPECT YOU TO PROVIDE SO MUCH ENTERTAIN-MENT!
THIS IS BEYOND MY WILDEST DREAMS!
THANKS A LOT!
THIS WAS A BLAST!
TAP

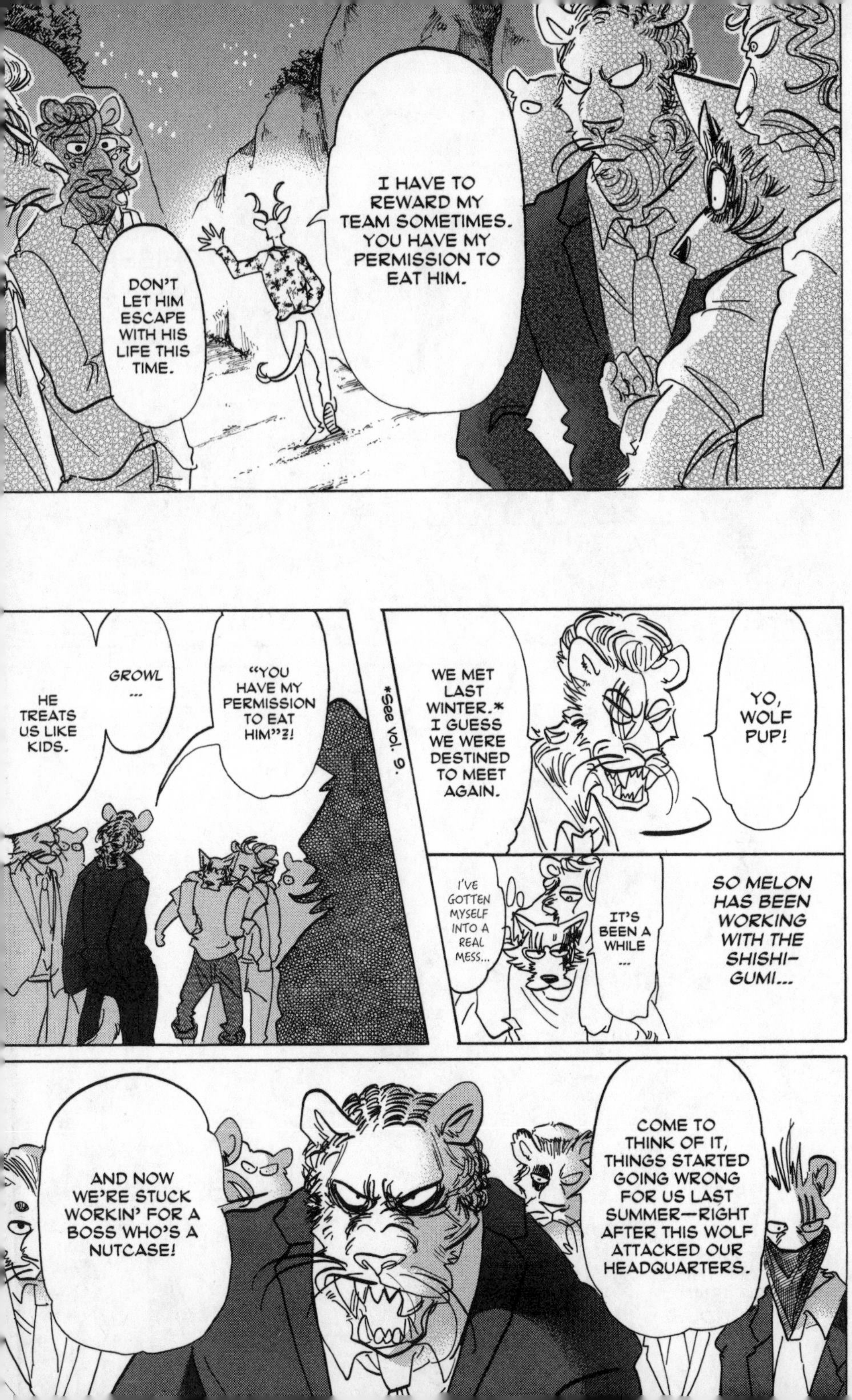
I HAVE TO REWARD MY TEAM SOMETIMES. YOU HAVE MY PERMISSION TO EAT HIM.
DON'T LET HIM ESCAPE WITH HIS LIFE THIS TIME.
YO, WOLF PUP!
WE MET LAST WINTER.* I GUESS WE WERE DESTINED TO MEET AGAIN.
*See vol. 9.
SO MELON HAS BEEN WORKING WITH THE SHISHI-GUMI...
IT'S BEEN A WHILE ...
I'VE GOTTEN MYSELF INTO A REAL MESS...
"YOU HAVE MY PERMISSION TO EAT HIM"?!
GROWL ...
HE TREATS US LIKE KIDS.
COME TO THINK OF IT, THINGS STARTED GOING WRONG FOR US LAST SUMMER—RIGHT AFTER THIS WOLF ATTACKED OUR HEADQUARTERS.
AND NOW WE'RE STUCK WORKIN' FOR A BOSS WHO'S A NUTCASE!

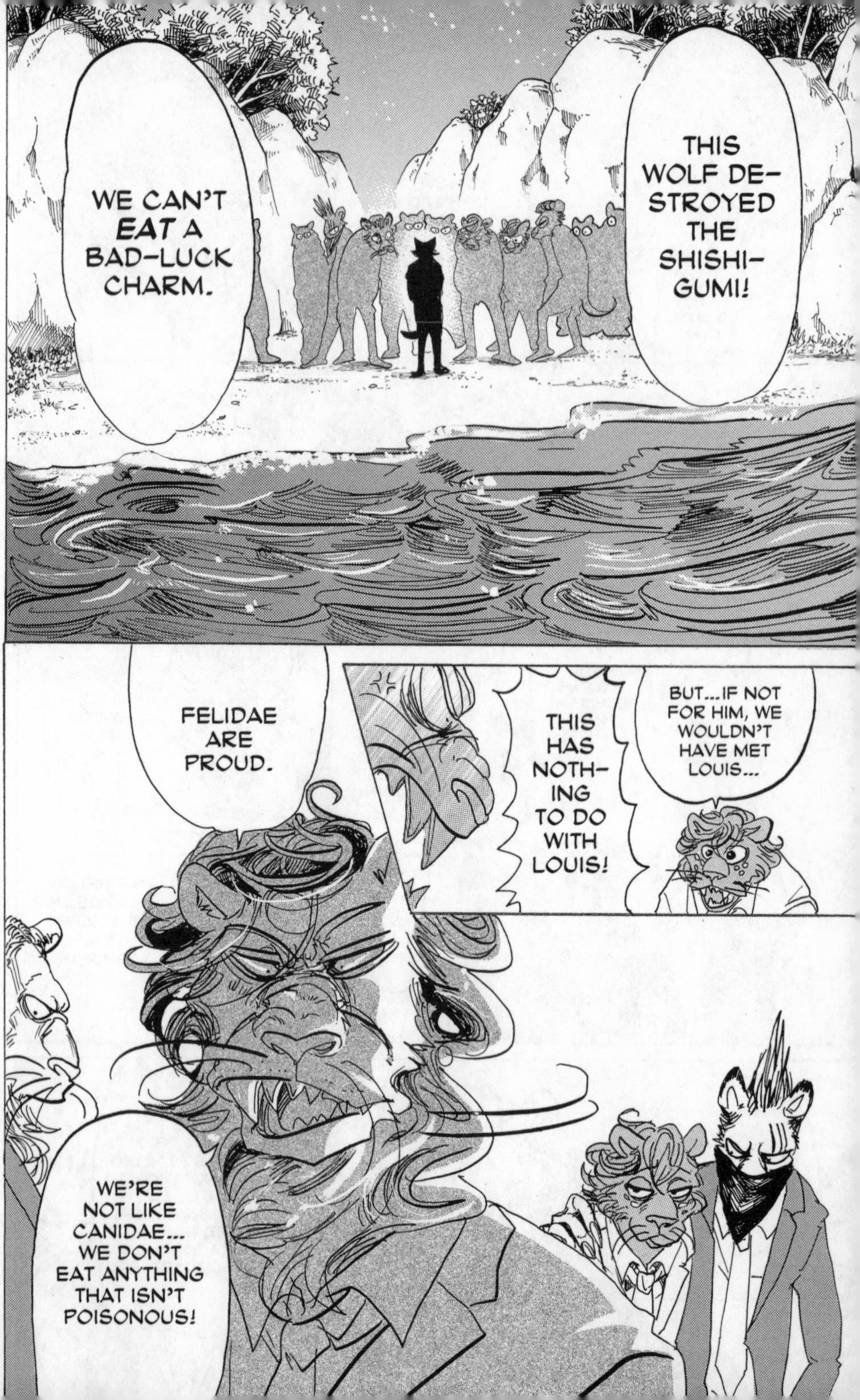
THIS WOLF DESTROYED THE SHISHIGUMI!
WE CAN'T *EAT* A BAD-LUCK CHARM.
BUT...IF NOT FOR HIM, WE WOULDN'T HAVE MET LOUIS...
THIS HAS NOTHING TO DO WITH LOUIS!
FELIDAE ARE PROUD.
WE'RE NOT LIKE CANIDAE... WE DON'T EAT ANYTHING THAT ISN'T POISONOUS!

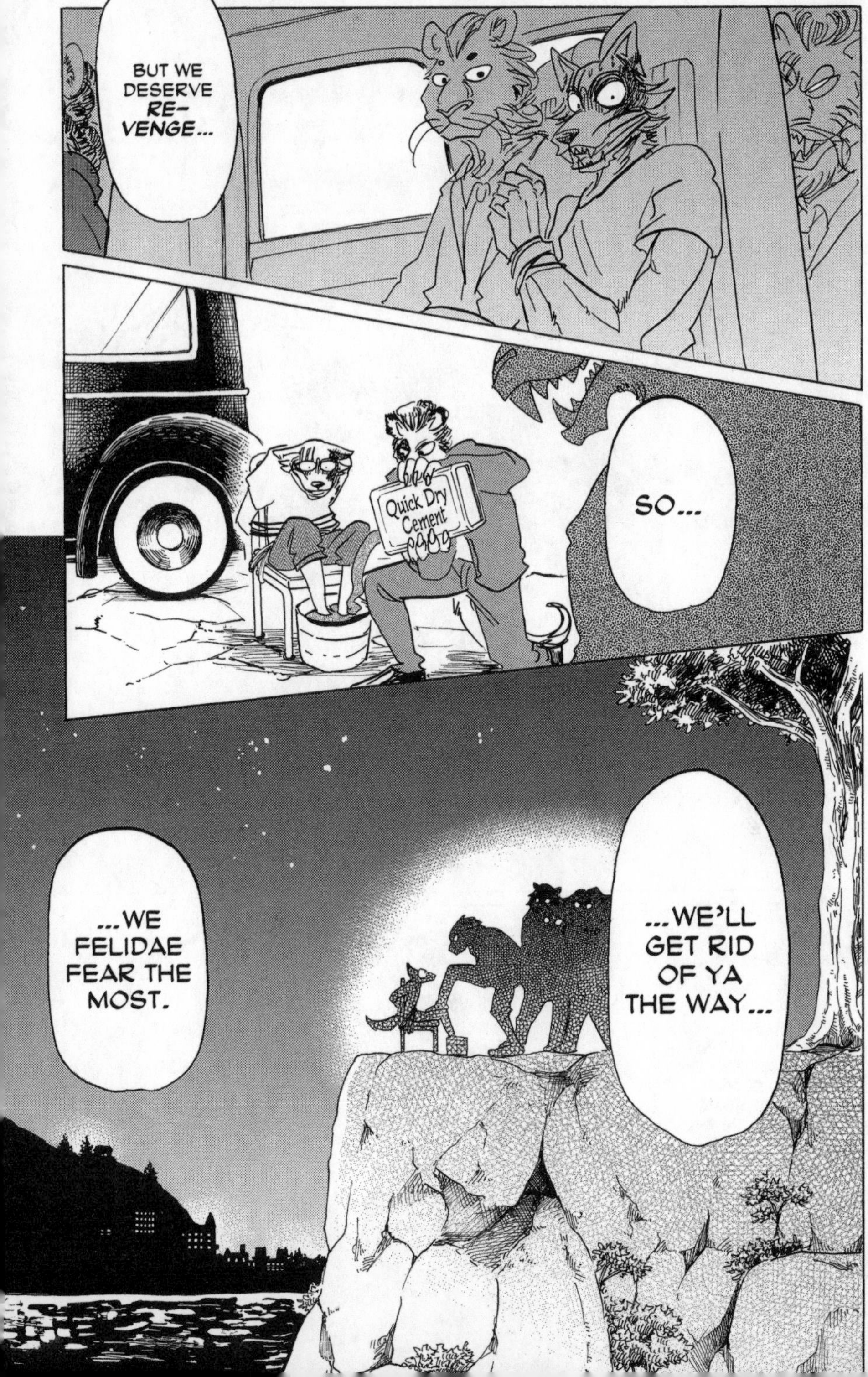
BUT WE DESERVE RE-VENGE...
SO...
Quick Dry Cement
...WE'LL GET RID OF YA THE WAY...
...WE FELIDAE FEAR THE MOST.

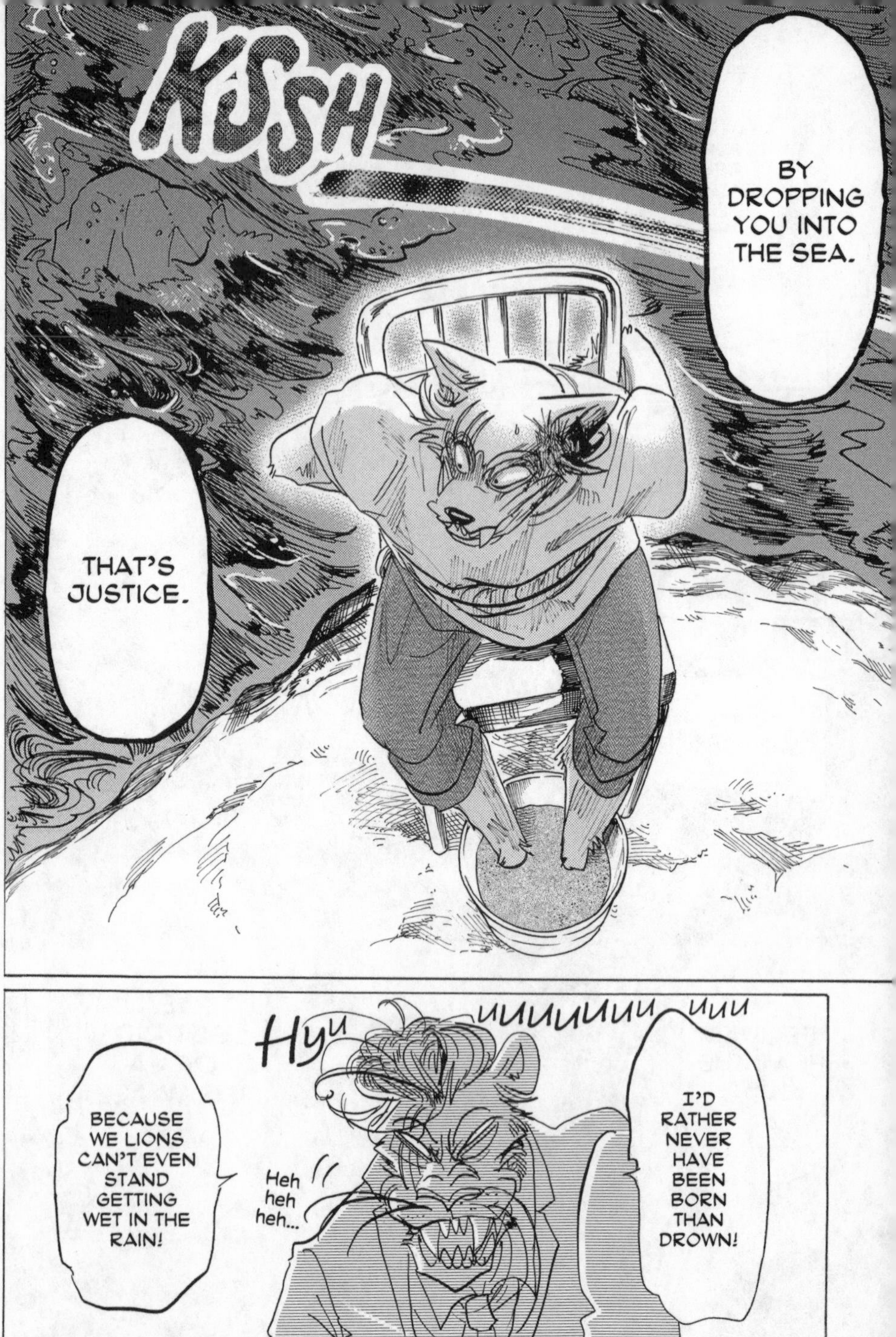
BY DROPPING YOU INTO THE SEA.
KSSH
THAT'S JUSTICE.
I'D RATHER NEVER HAVE BEEN BORN THAN DROWN!
Hyu uuuuuuu uuu
Heh heh heh...
BECAUSE WE LIONS CAN'T EVEN STAND GETTING WET IN THE RAIN!

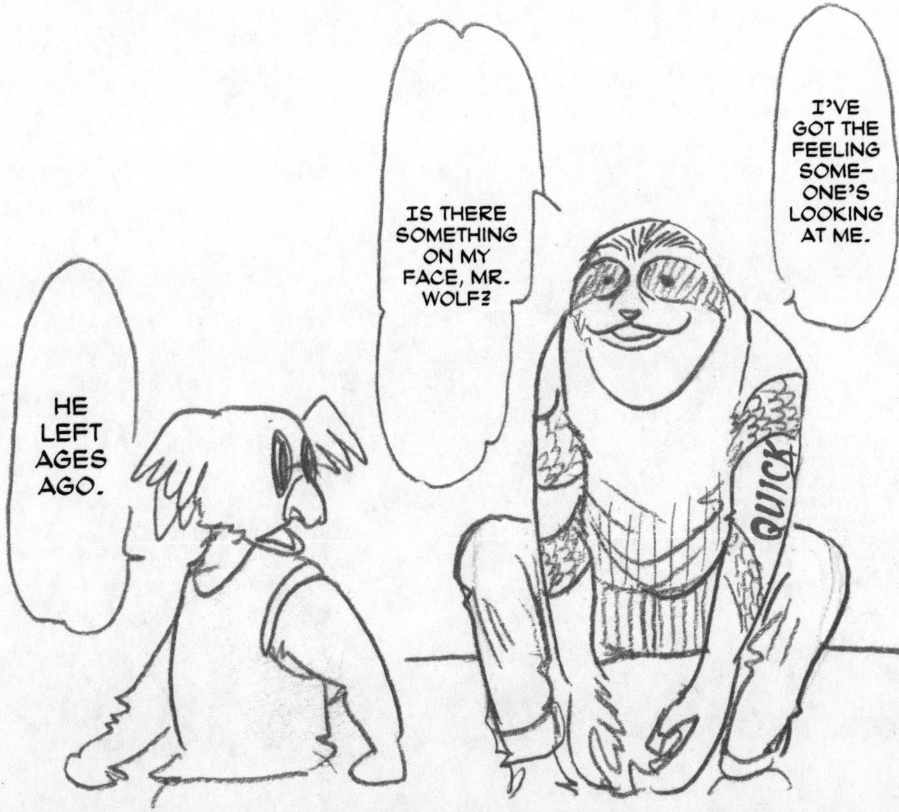
I'VE GOT THE FEELING SOME-ONE'S LOOKING AT ME.
IS THERE SOMETHING ON MY FACE, MR. WOLF?
QUICK
HE LEFT AGES AGO.

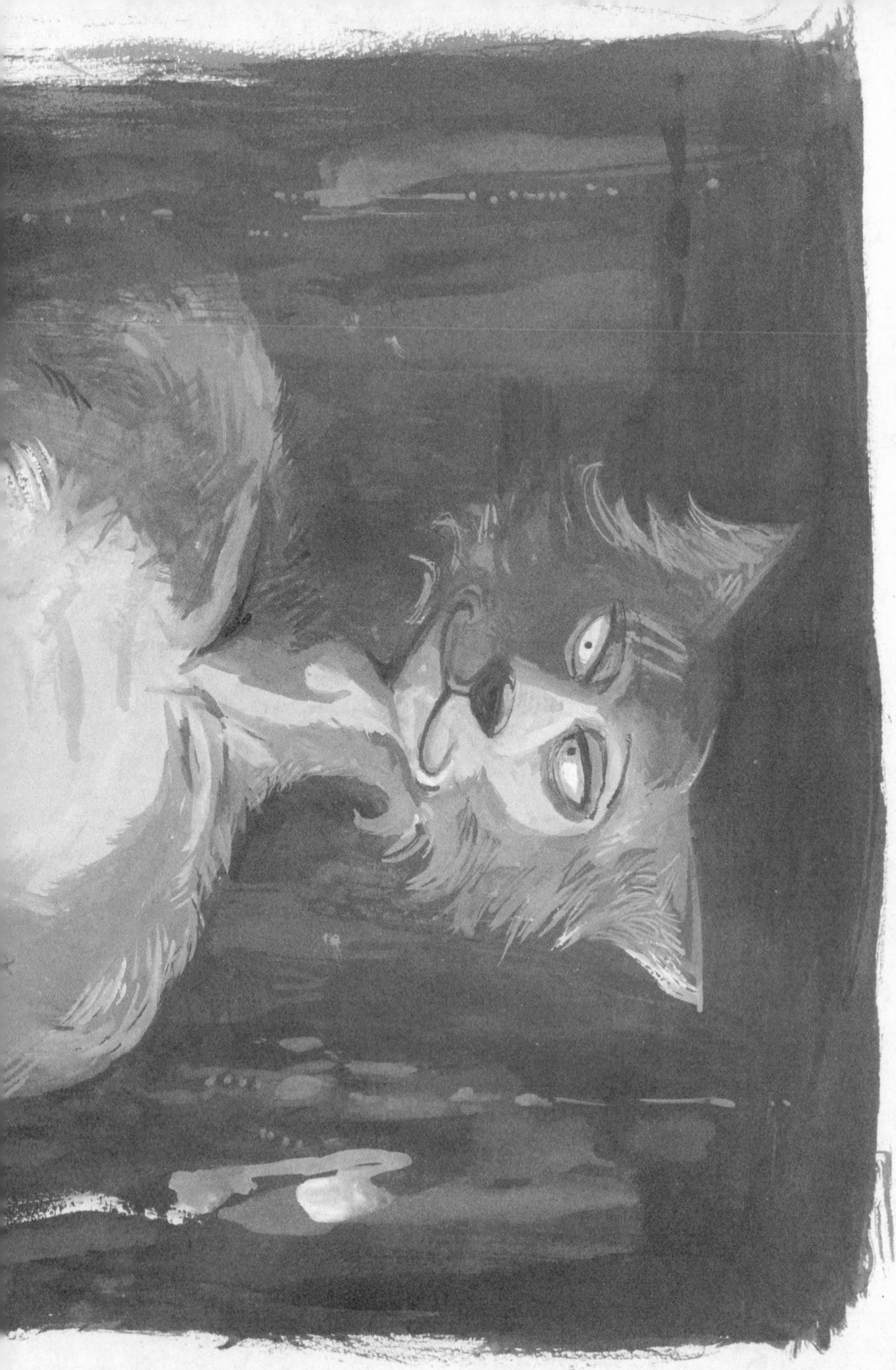

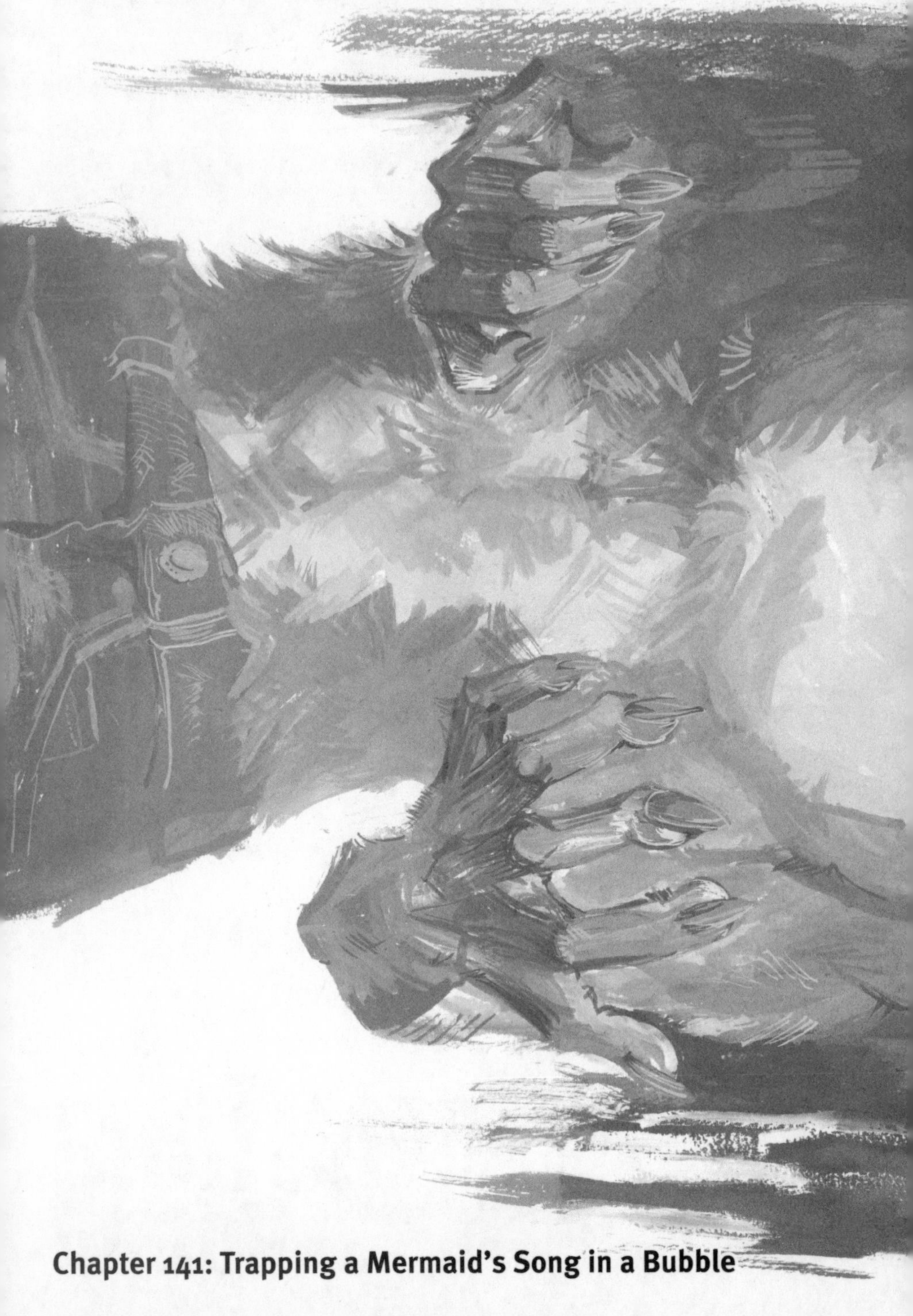

Chapter 141: Trapping a Mermaid's Song in a Bubble

BEASTARS
Vol. 16

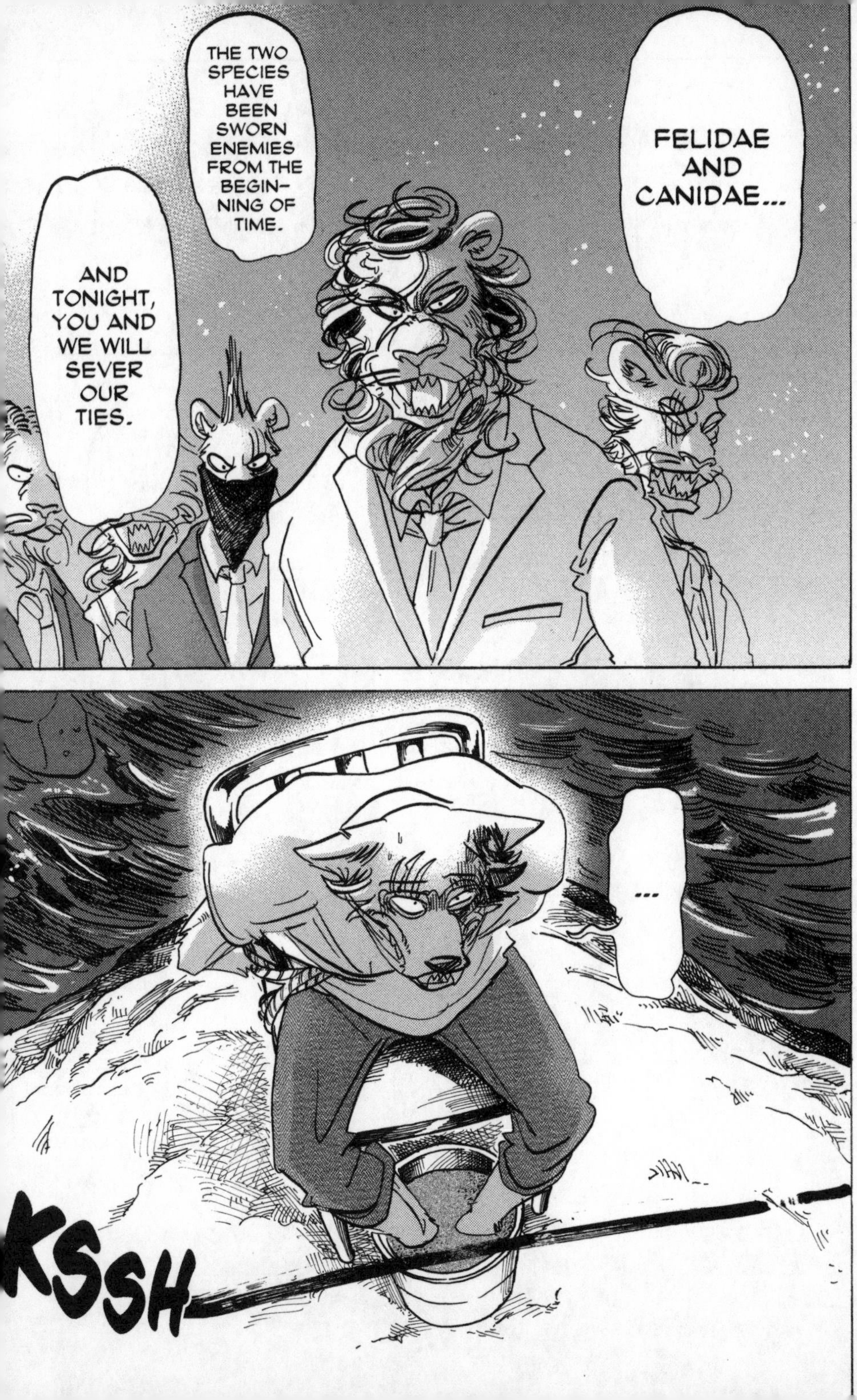
FELIDAE AND CANIDAE...
THE TWO SPECIES HAVE BEEN SWORN ENEMIES FROM THE BEGIN-NING OF TIME.
AND TONIGHT, YOU AND WE WILL SEVER OUR TIES.
...
KSSH

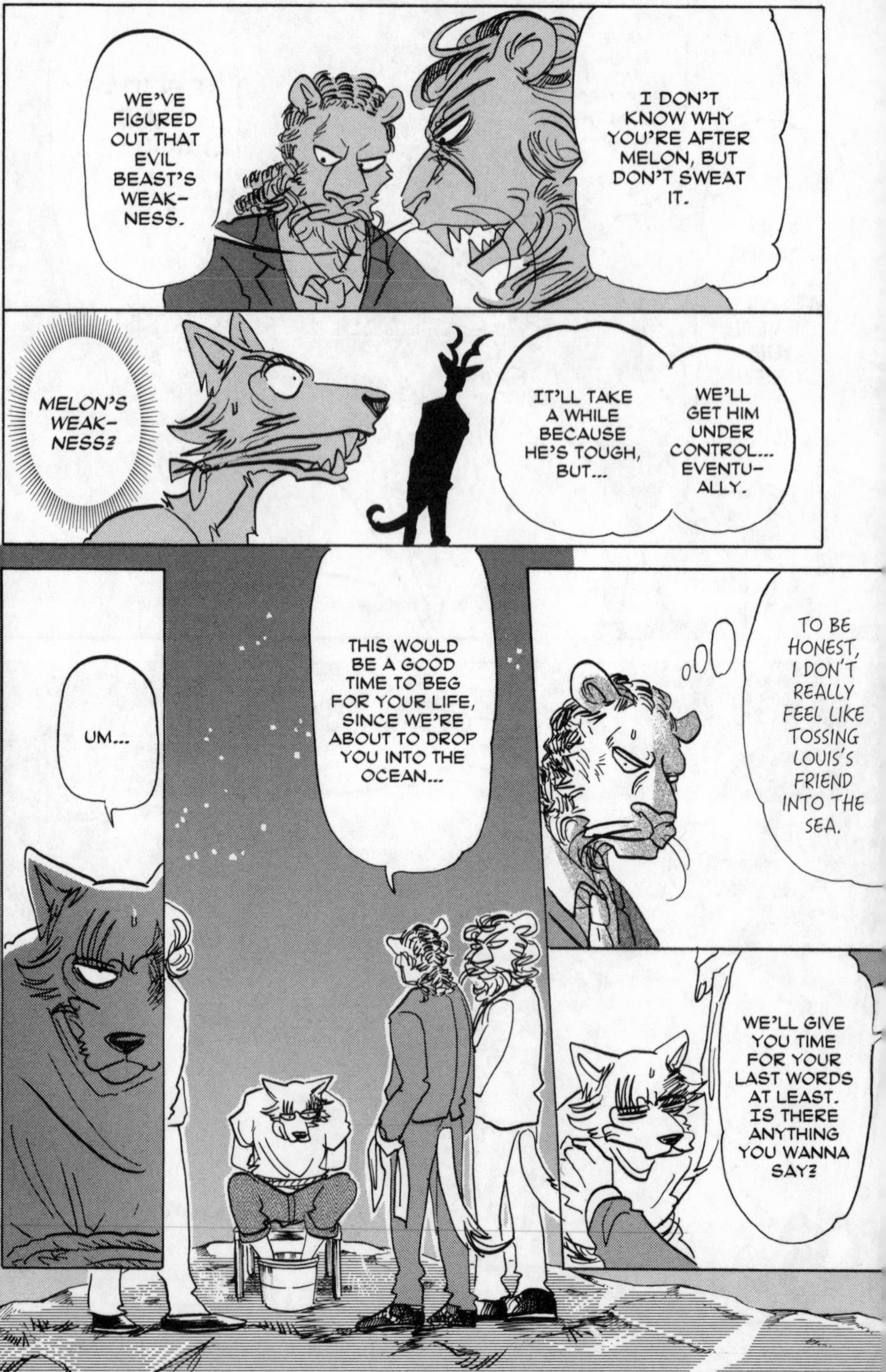
I DON'T KNOW WHY YOU'RE AFTER MELON, BUT DON'T SWEAT IT.
WE'VE FIGURED OUT THAT EVIL BEAST'S WEAK-NESS.
WE'LL GET HIM UNDER CONTROL... EVENTU-ALLY.
IT'LL TAKE A WHILE BECAUSE HE'S TOUGH, BUT...
MELON'S WEAK-NESS?
TO BE HONEST, I DON'T REALLY FEEL LIKE TOSSING LOUIS'S FRIEND INTO THE SEA.
WE'LL GIVE YOU TIME FOR YOUR LAST WORDS AT LEAST. IS THERE ANYTHING YOU WANNA SAY?
THIS WOULD BE A GOOD TIME TO BEG FOR YOUR LIFE, SINCE WE'RE ABOUT TO DROP YOU INTO THE OCEAN...
UM...

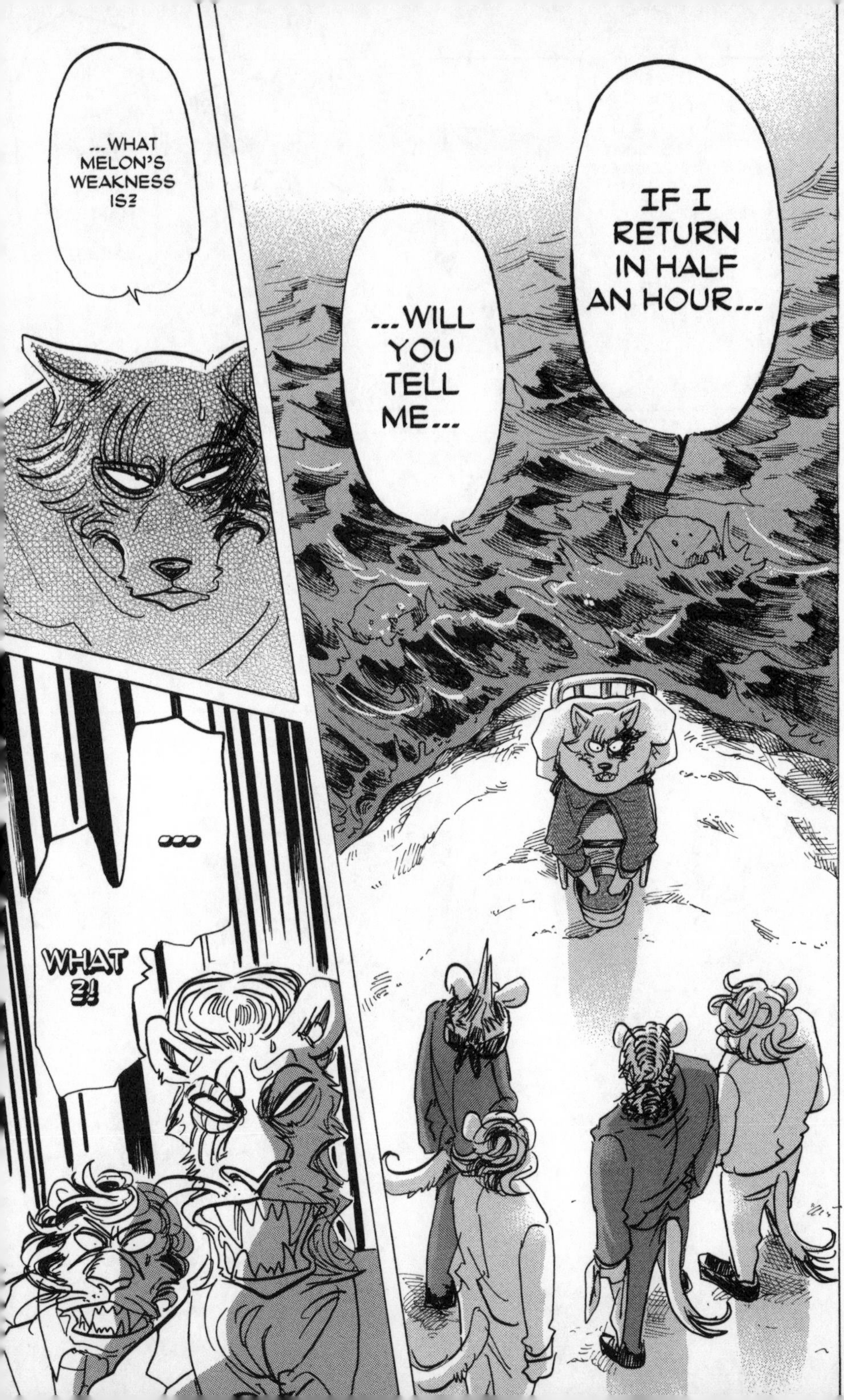
IF I RETURN IN HALF AN HOUR...
...WILL YOU TELL ME...
...WHAT MELON'S WEAKNESS IS?
...
WHAT?!

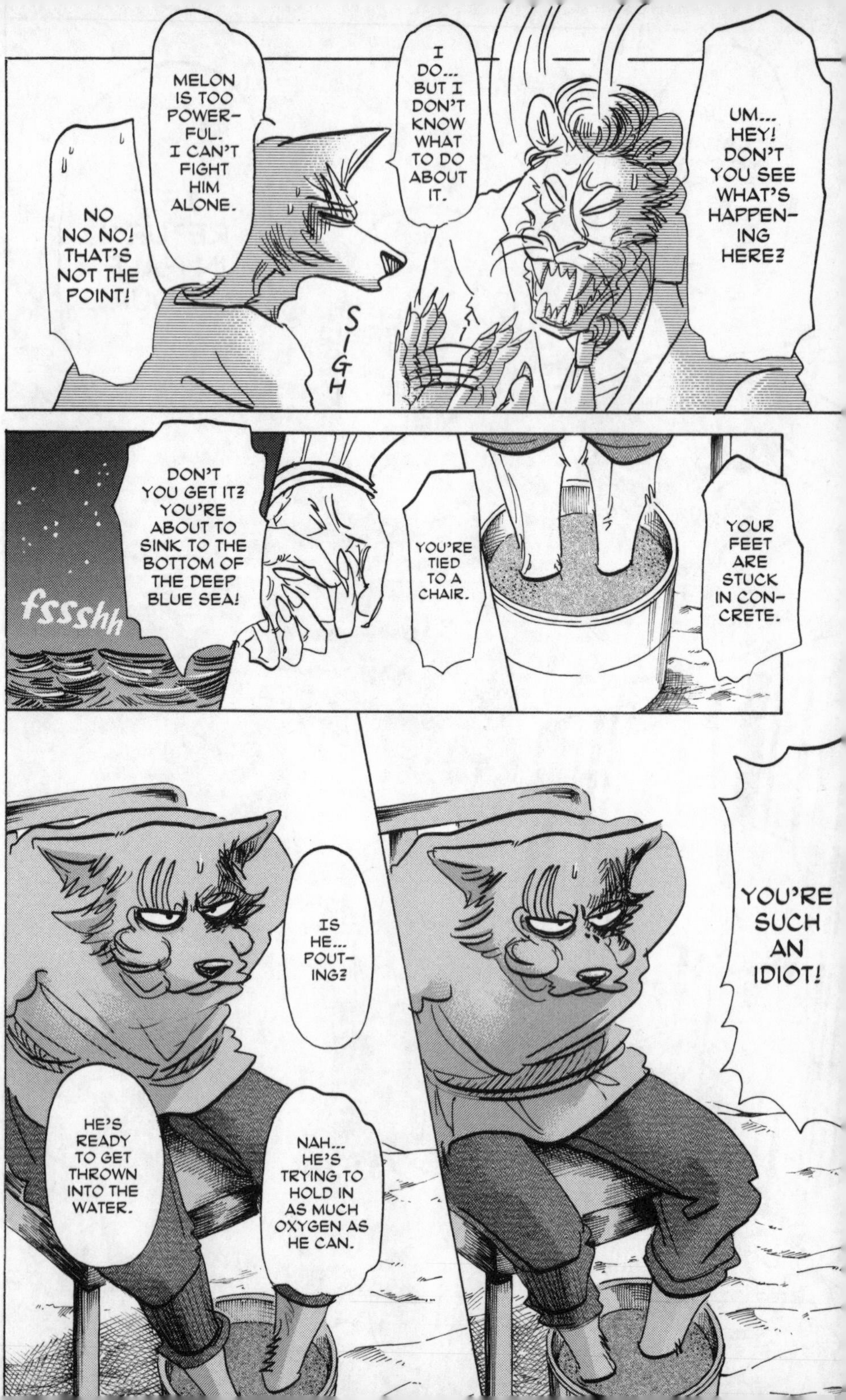

UM... HEY! DON'T YOU SEE WHAT'S HAPPENING HERE?
I DO... BUT I DON'T KNOW WHAT TO DO ABOUT IT.
MELON IS TOO POWERFUL. I CAN'T FIGHT HIM ALONE.
SIGH
NO NO NO! THAT'S NOT THE POINT!
YOUR FEET ARE STUCK IN CONCRETE.
YOU'RE TIED TO A CHAIR.
DON'T YOU GET IT? YOU'RE ABOUT TO SINK TO THE BOTTOM OF THE DEEP BLUE SEA!
fssshh
YOU'RE SUCH AN IDIOT!
IS HE... POUTING?
HE'S READY TO GET THROWN INTO THE WATER.
NAH... HE'S TRYING TO HOLD IN AS MUCH OXYGEN AS HE CAN.

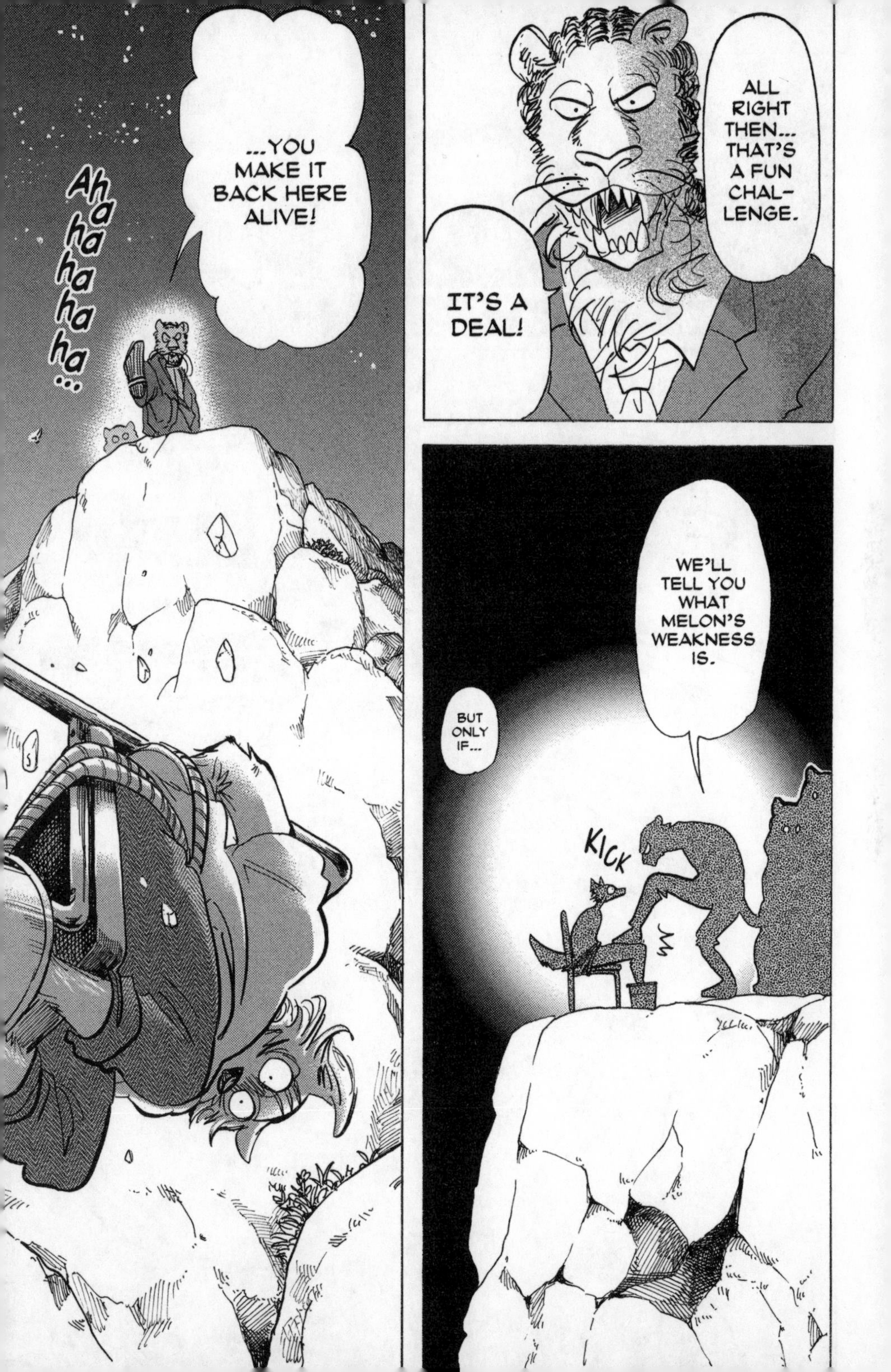
ALL RIGHT THEN... THAT'S A FUN CHAL-LENGE.
IT'S A DEAL!
WE'LL TELL YOU WHAT MELON'S WEAKNESS IS.
BUT ONLY IF...
KICK
...YOU MAKE IT BACK HERE ALIVE!
Ahahahahaha...

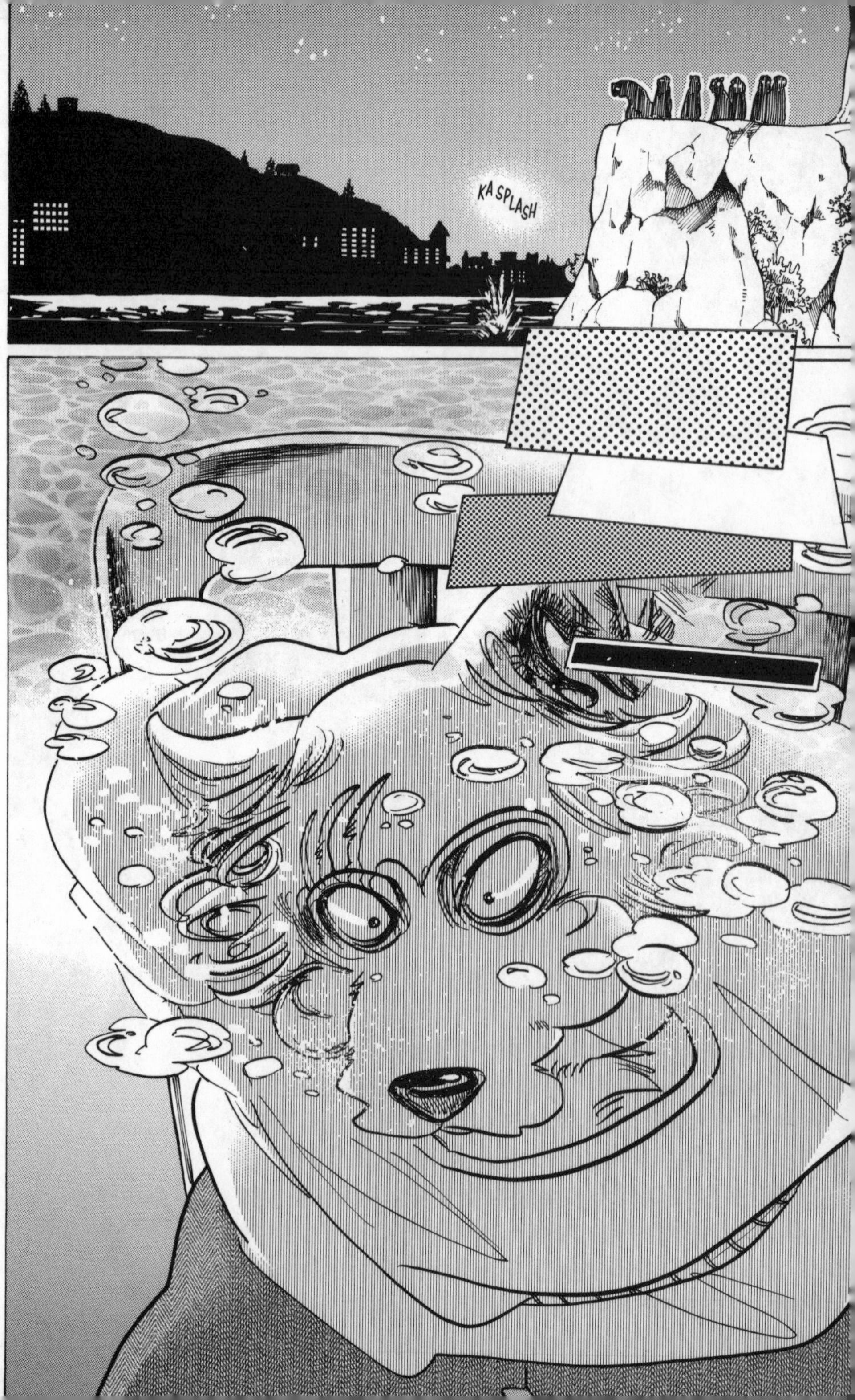
KA SPLASH

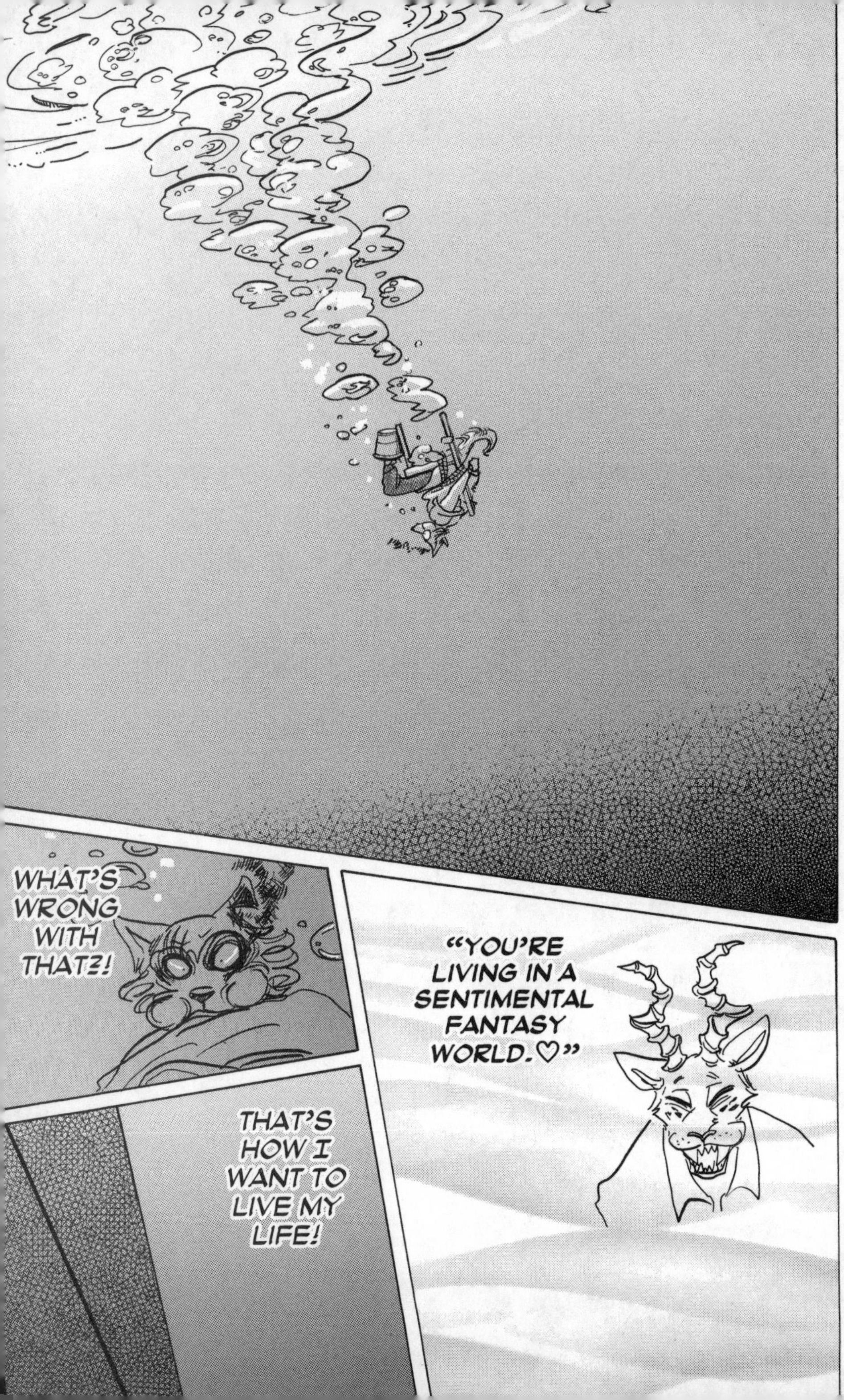
"YOU'RE LIVING IN A SENTIMENTAL FANTASY WORLD.♡"
WHAT'S WRONG WITH THAT?!
THAT'S HOW I WANT TO LIVE MY LIFE!

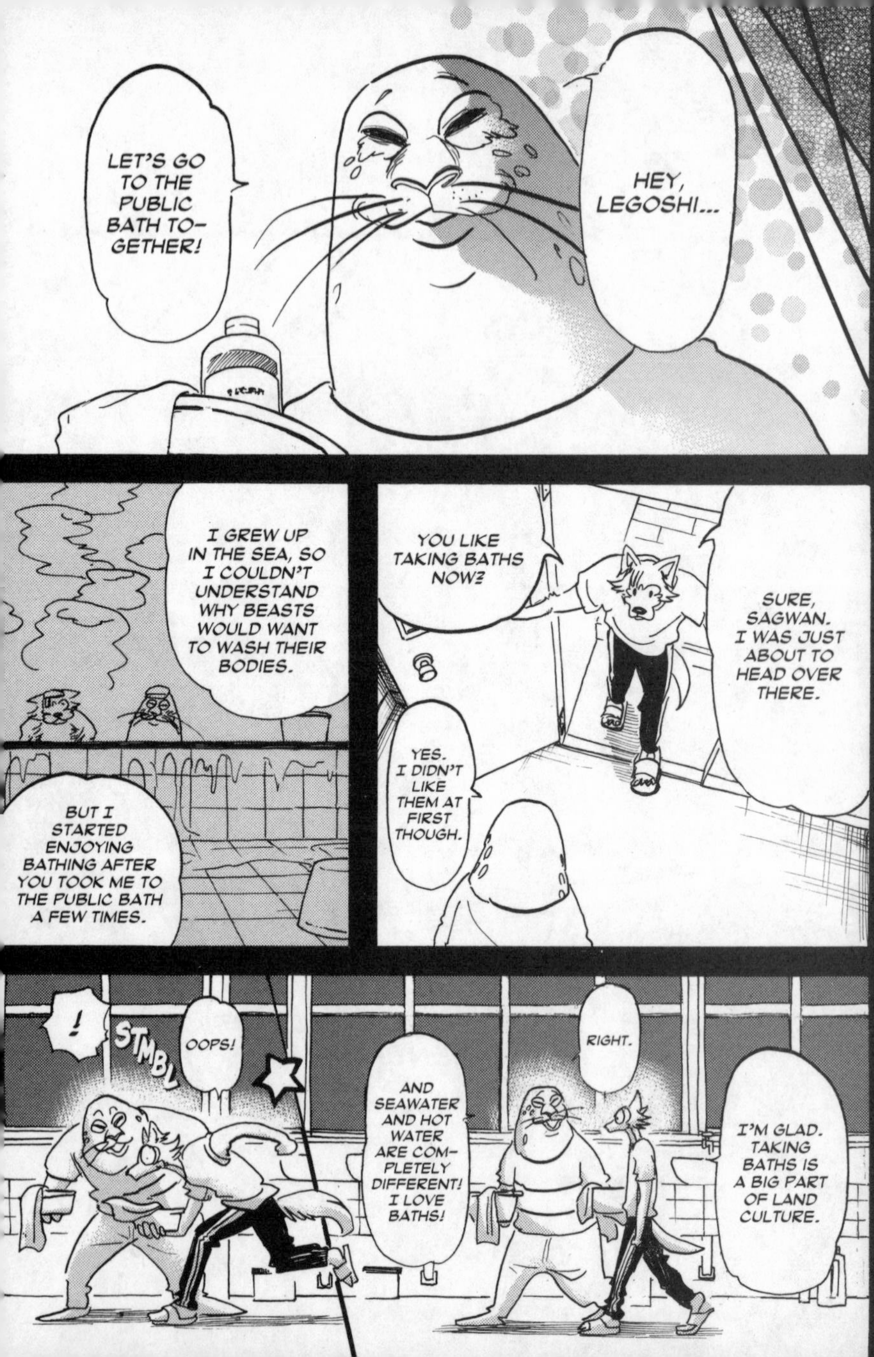
HEY, LEGOSHI...
LET'S GO TO THE PUBLIC BATH TO-GETHER!
SURE, SAGWAN. I WAS JUST ABOUT TO HEAD OVER THERE.
YOU LIKE TAKING BATHS NOW?
YES. I DIDN'T LIKE THEM AT FIRST THOUGH.
I GREW UP IN THE SEA, SO I COULDN'T UNDERSTAND WHY BEASTS WOULD WANT TO WASH THEIR BODIES.
BUT I STARTED ENJOYING BATHING AFTER YOU TOOK ME TO THE PUBLIC BATH A FEW TIMES.
I'M GLAD. TAKING BATHS IS A BIG PART OF LAND CULTURE.
RIGHT.
AND SEAWATER AND HOT WATER ARE COM-PLETELY DIFFERENT! I LOVE BATHS!
OOPS!
!
STMBL

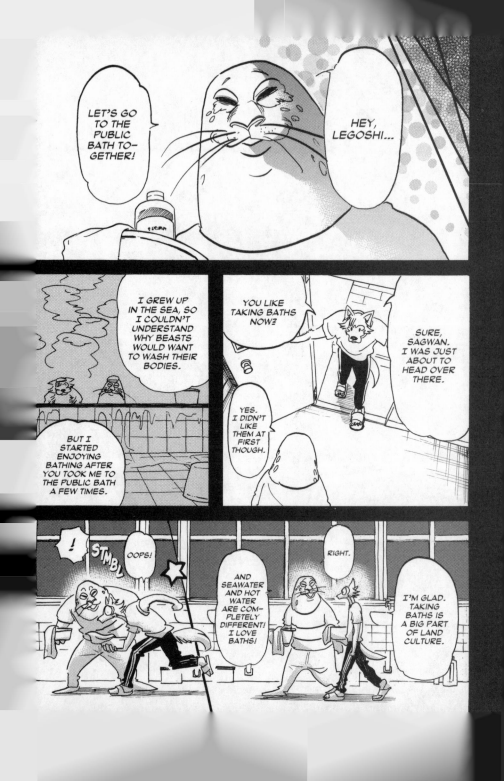

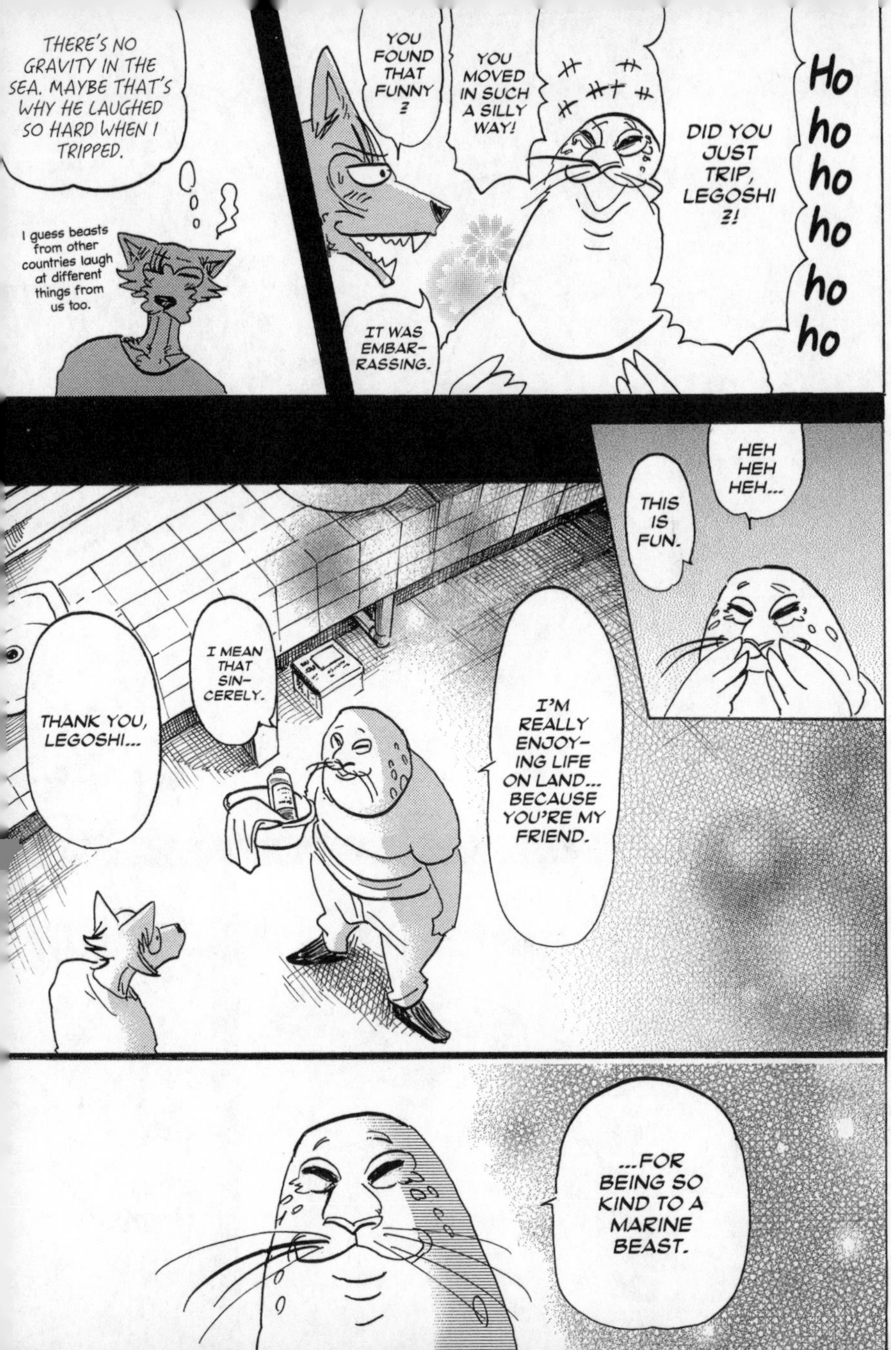

Ho ho ho ho ho ho
DID YOU JUST TRIP, LEGOSHI?!
YOU MOVED IN SUCH A SILLY WAY!
YOU FOUND THAT FUNNY?
IT WAS EMBARRASSING.
THERE'S NO GRAVITY IN THE SEA. MAYBE THAT'S WHY HE LAUGHED SO HARD WHEN I TRIPPED.
I guess beasts from other countries laugh at different things from us too.
HEH HEH HEH...
THIS IS FUN.
I'M REALLY ENJOYING LIFE ON LAND... BECAUSE YOU'RE MY FRIEND.
I MEAN THAT SINCERELY.
THANK YOU, LEGOSHI...
...FOR BEING SO KIND TO A MARINE BEAST.

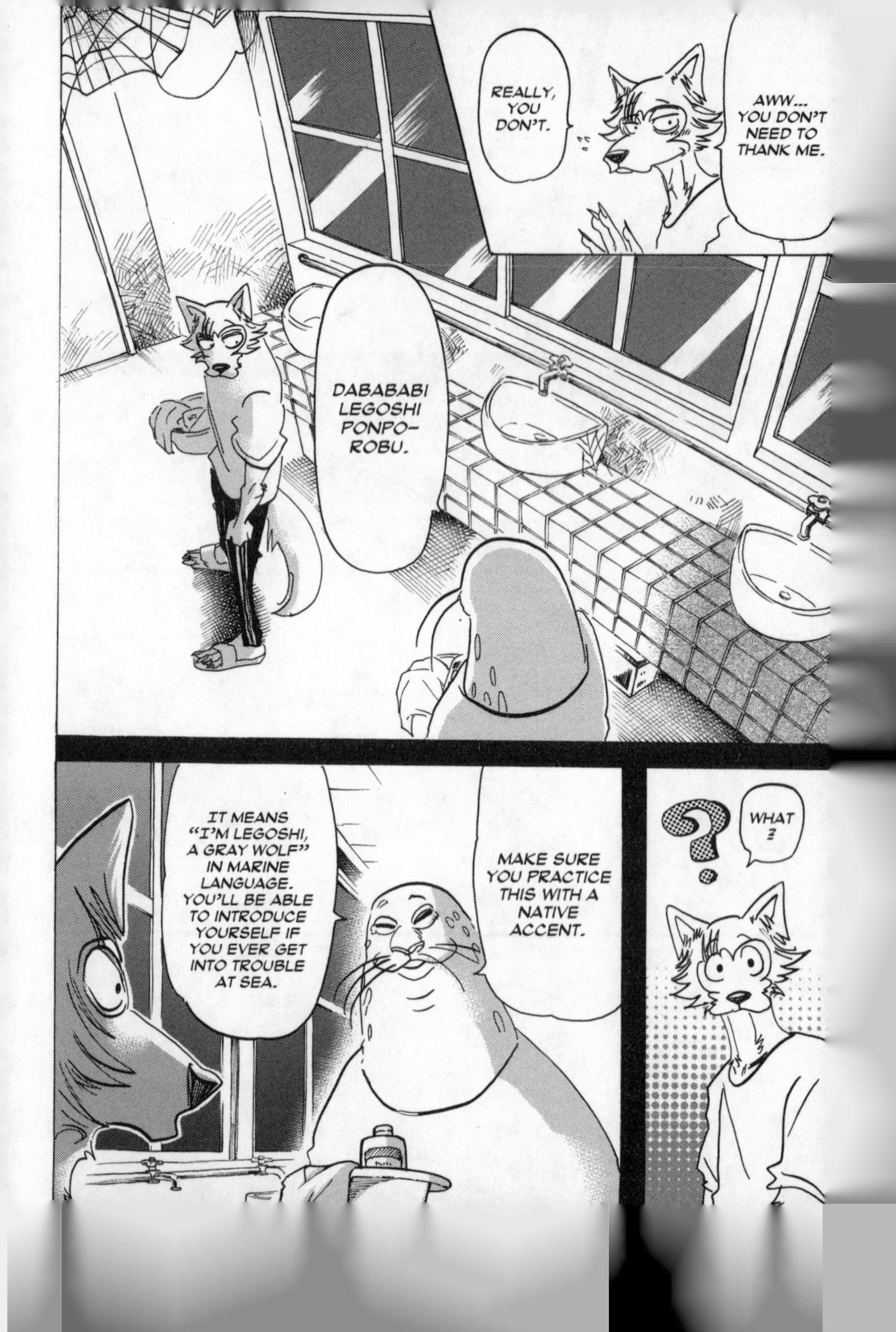
AWW... YOU DON'T NEED TO THANK ME.
REALLY, YOU DON'T.
DABABABI LEGOSHI PONPO-ROBU.
WHAT?
MAKE SURE YOU PRACTICE THIS WITH A NATIVE ACCENT.
IT MEANS "I'M LEGOSHI, A GRAY WOLF" IN MARINE LANGUAGE. YOU'LL BE ABLE TO INTRODUCE YOURSELF IF YOU EVER GET INTO TROUBLE AT SEA.

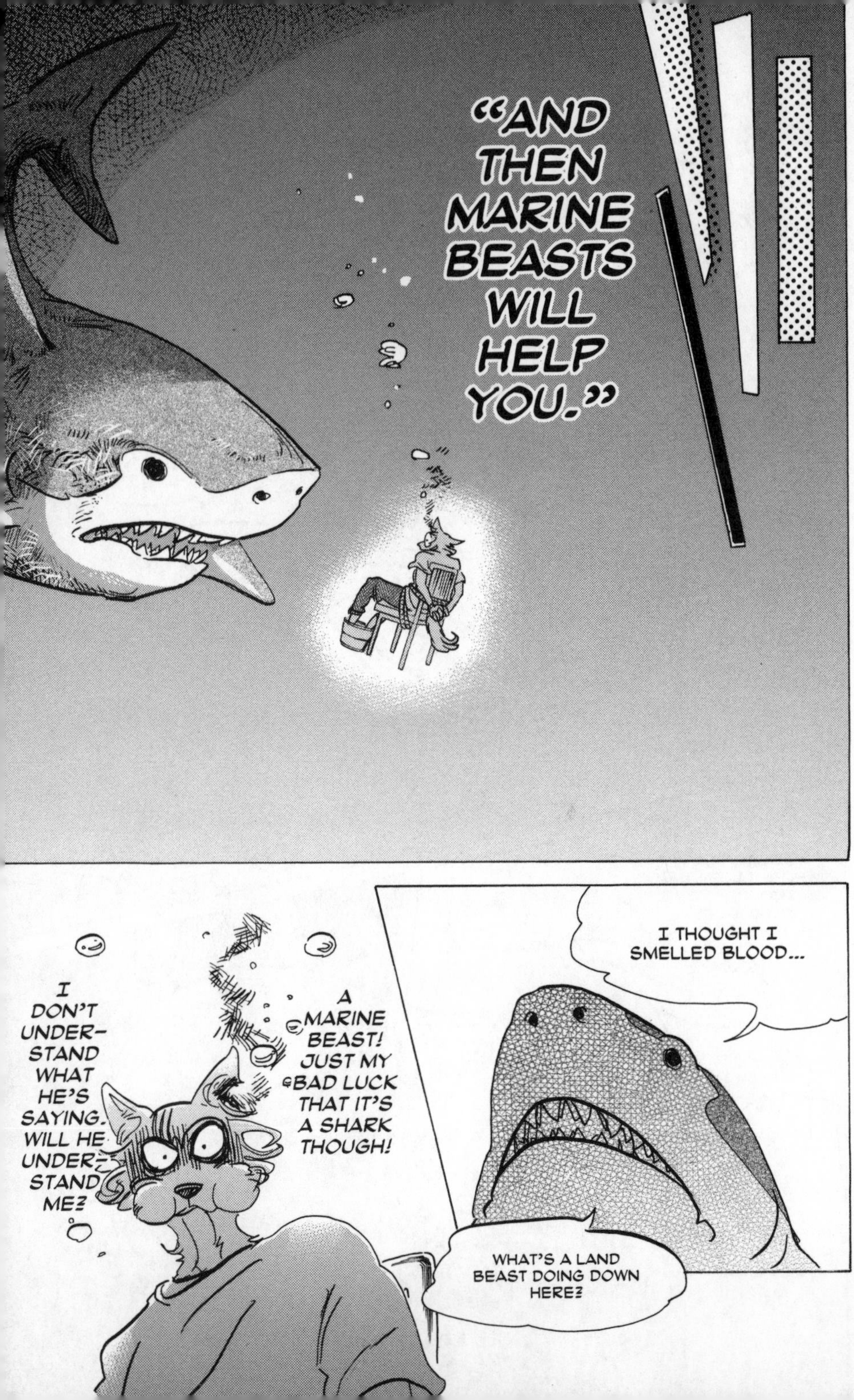
"AND THEN MARINE BEASTS WILL HELP YOU."
I THOUGHT I SMELLED BLOOD...
WHAT'S A LAND BEAST DOING DOWN HERE?
A MARINE BEAST! JUST MY BAD LUCK THAT IT'S A SHARK THOUGH!
I DON'T UNDER-STAND WHAT HE'S SAYING. WILL HE UNDER-STAND ME?

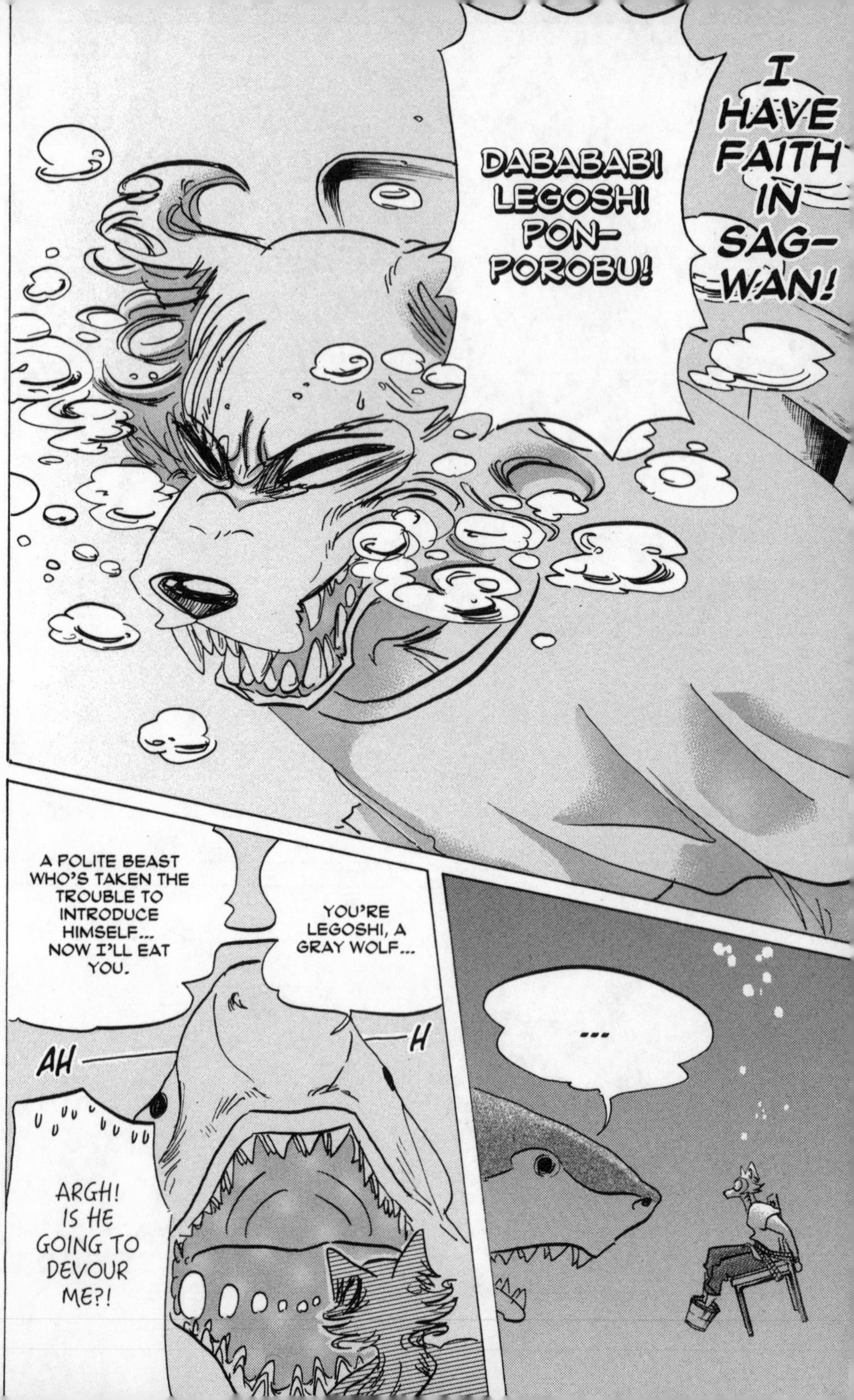
I HAVE FAITH IN SAG-WAN!
DABABABI LEGOSHI PON-POROBU!
...
YOU'RE LEGOSHI, A GRAY WOLF...
A POLITE BEAST WHO'S TAKEN THE TROUBLE TO INTRODUCE HIMSELF... NOW I'LL EAT YOU.
AH—H
ARGH! IS HE GOING TO DEVOUR ME?!

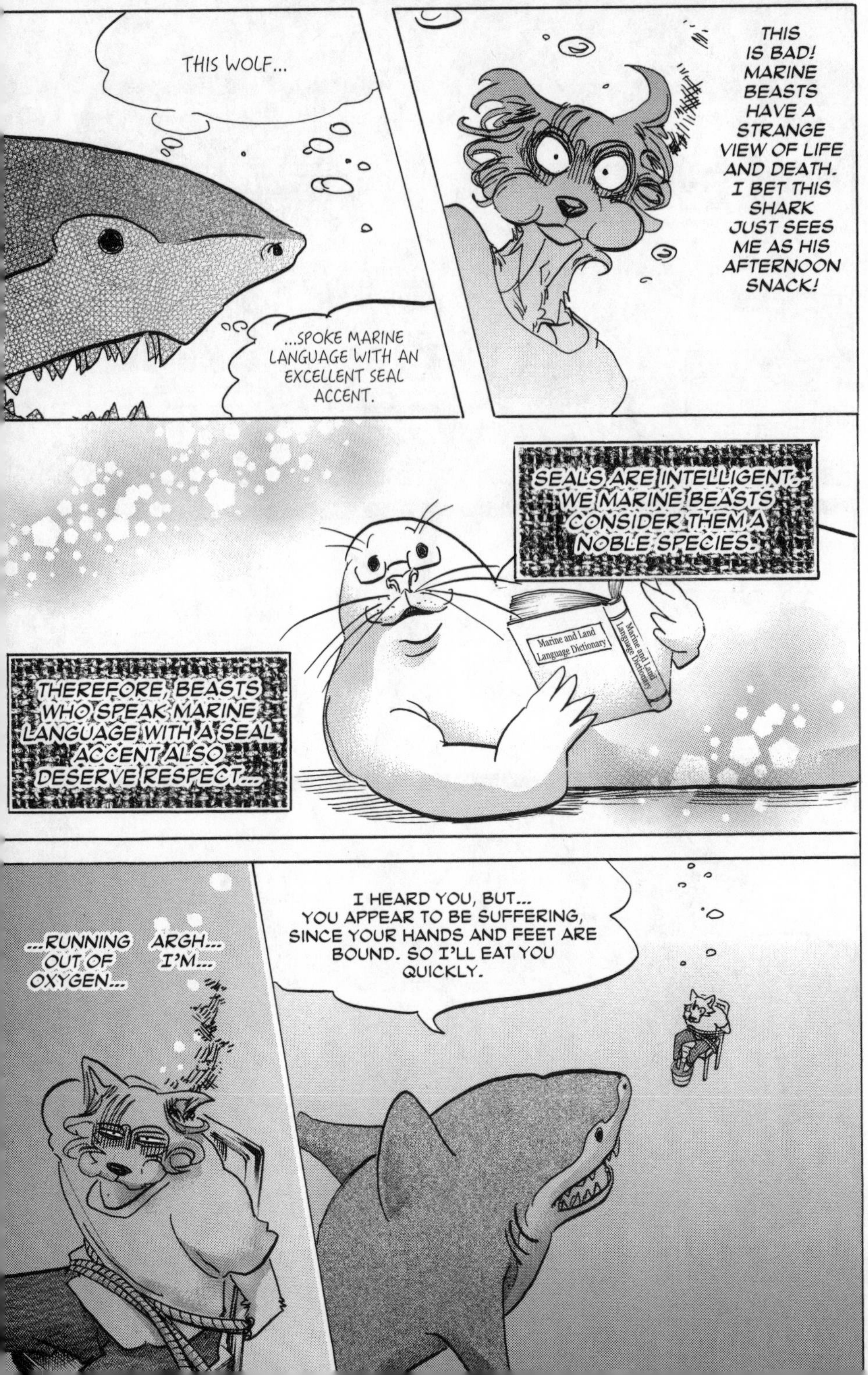
THIS IS BAD! MARINE BEASTS HAVE A STRANGE VIEW OF LIFE AND DEATH. I BET THIS SHARK JUST SEES ME AS HIS AFTERNOON SNACK!
THIS WOLF...
...SPOKE MARINE LANGUAGE WITH AN EXCELLENT SEAL ACCENT.
SEALS ARE INTELLIGENT. WE MARINE BEASTS CONSIDER THEM A NOBLE SPECIES.
Marine and Land Language Dictionary
Marine and Land Language Dictionary
THEREFORE, BEASTS WHO SPEAK MARINE LANGUAGE WITH A SEAL ACCENT ALSO DESERVE RESPECT...
I HEARD YOU, BUT... YOU APPEAR TO BE SUFFERING, SINCE YOUR HANDS AND FEET ARE BOUND. SO I'LL EAT YOU QUICKLY.
ARGH... I'M...
...RUNNING OUT OF OXYGEN...

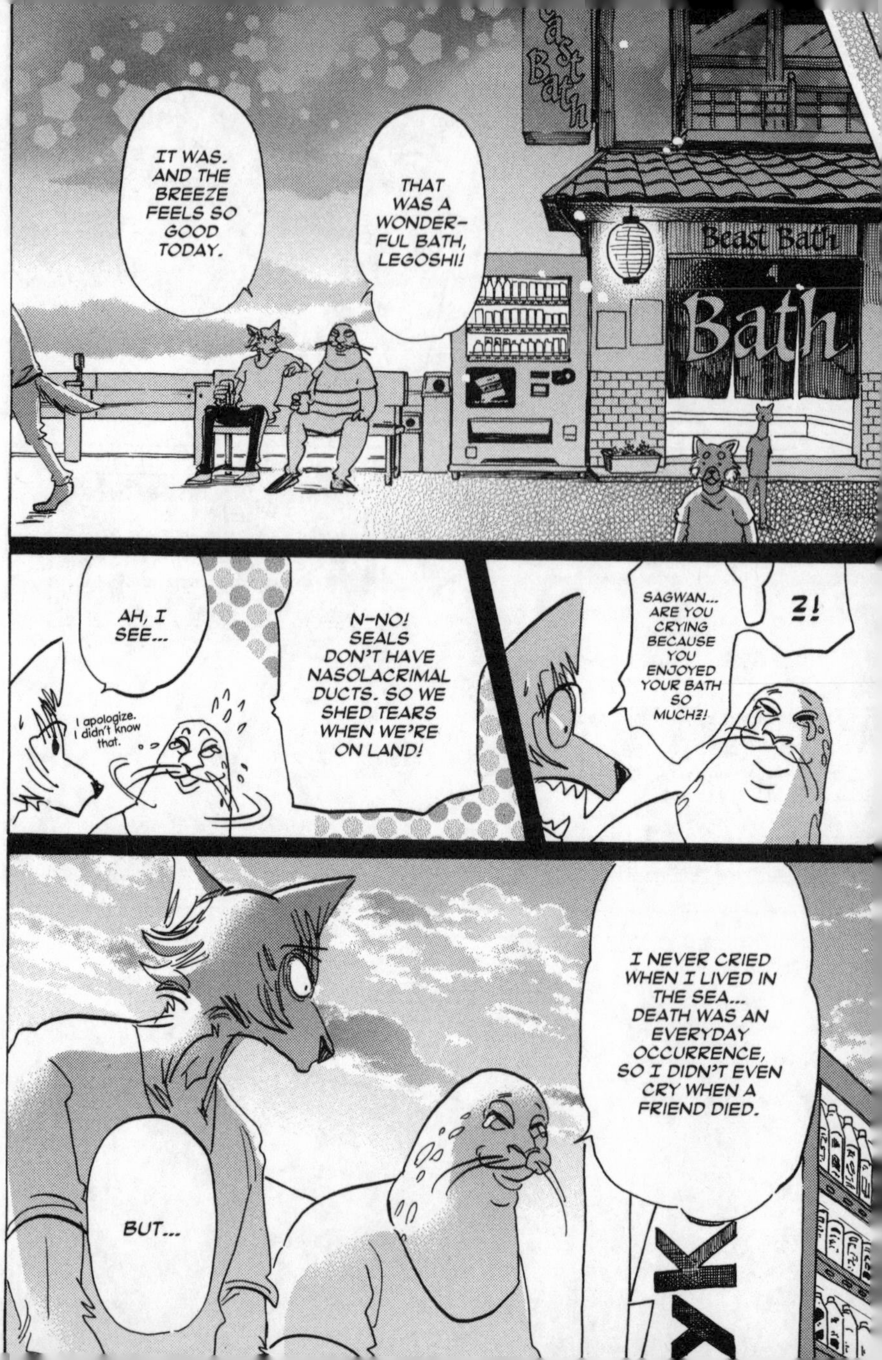
Beast Bath
Beast Bath
Bath
THAT WAS A WONDERFUL BATH, LEGOSHI!
IT WAS. AND THE BREEZE FEELS SO GOOD TODAY.
?!
SAGWAN... ARE YOU CRYING BECAUSE YOU ENJOYED YOUR BATH SO MUCH?!
N-NO! SEALS DON'T HAVE NASOLACRIMAL DUCTS. SO WE SHED TEARS WHEN WE'RE ON LAND!
AH, I SEE...
I apologize. I didn't know that.
I NEVER CRIED WHEN I LIVED IN THE SEA... DEATH WAS AN EVERYDAY OCCURRENCE, SO I DIDN'T EVEN CRY WHEN A FRIEND DIED.
BUT...

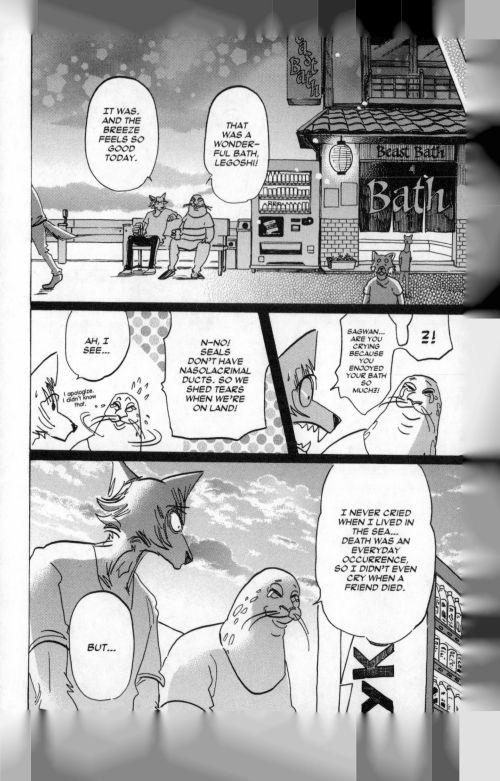

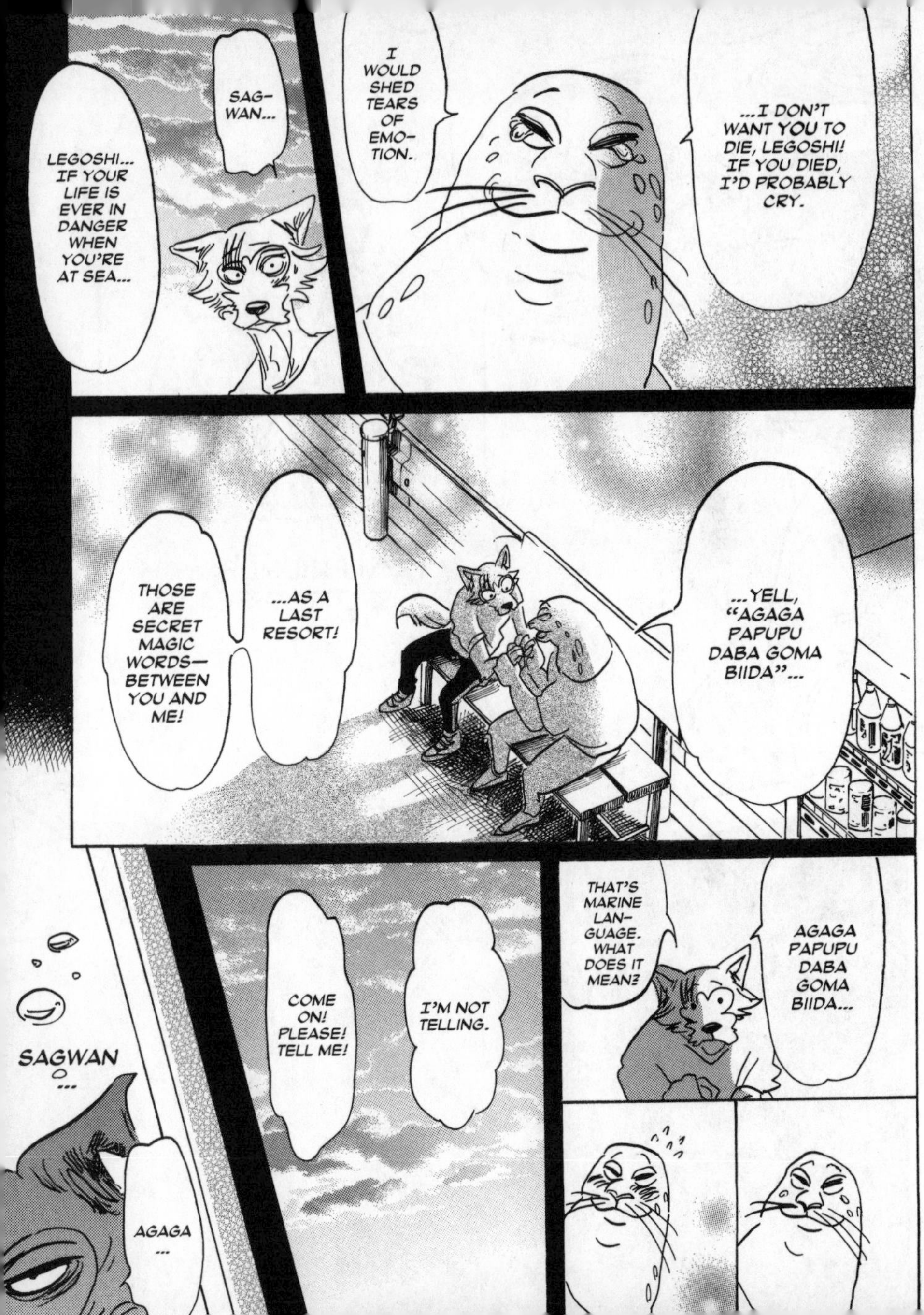
...I DON'T WANT YOU TO DIE, LEGOSHI! IF YOU DIED, I'D PROBABLY CRY.
I WOULD SHED TEARS OF EMOTION.
SAG-WAN...
LEGOSHI... IF YOUR LIFE IS EVER IN DANGER WHEN YOU'RE AT SEA...
...YELL, "AGAGA PAPUPU DABA GOMA BIIDA"...
...AS A LAST RESORT!
THOSE ARE SECRET MAGIC WORDS—BETWEEN YOU AND ME!
AGAGA PAPUPU DABA GOMA BIIDA...
THAT'S MARINE LAN-GUAGE. WHAT DOES IT MEAN?
I'M NOT TELLING.
COME ON! PLEASE! TELL ME!
SAGWAN...
AGAGA...

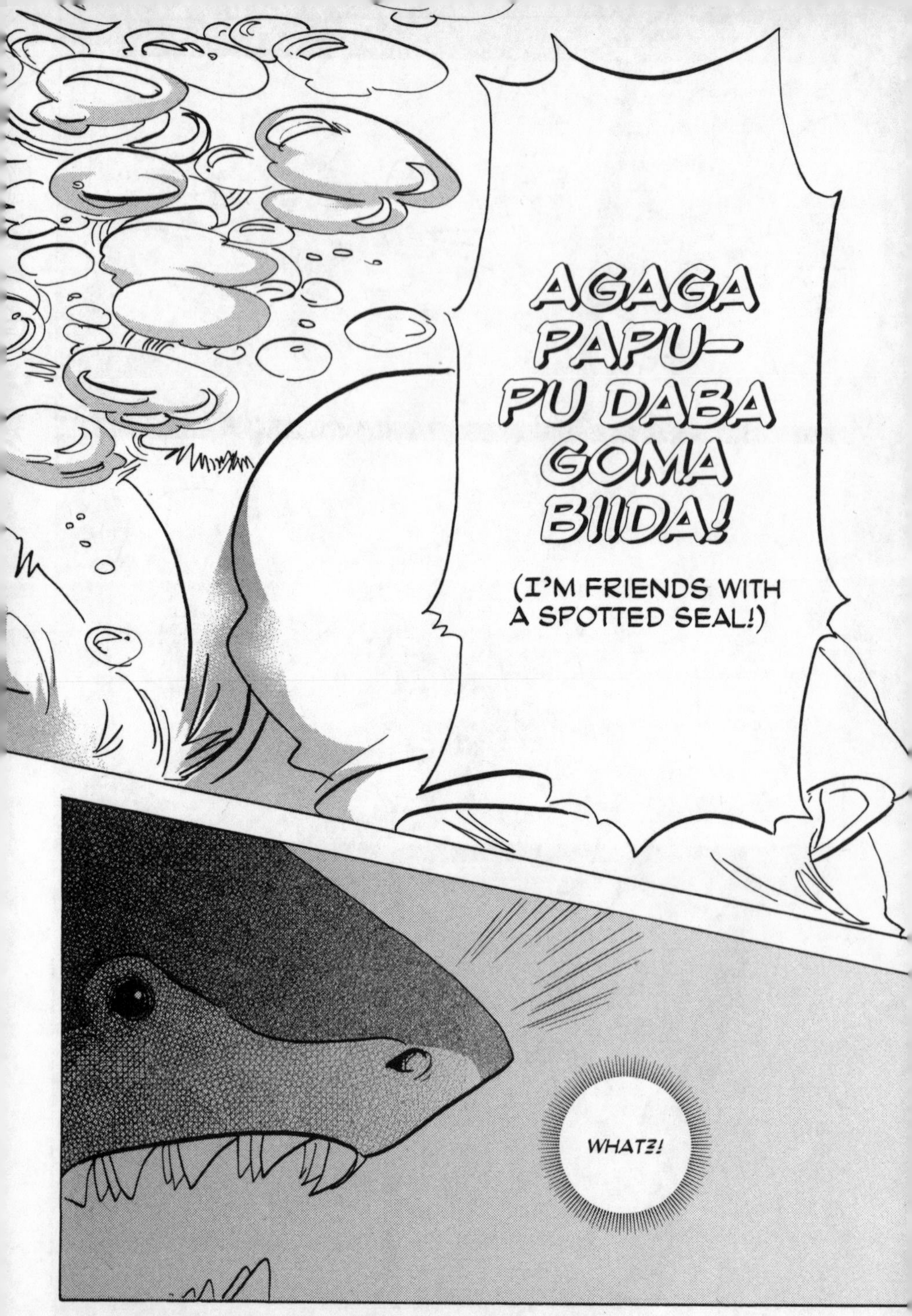
AGAGA PAPU-PU DABA GOMA BIIDA!
(I'M FRIENDS WITH A SPOTTED SEAL!)
WHAT?!

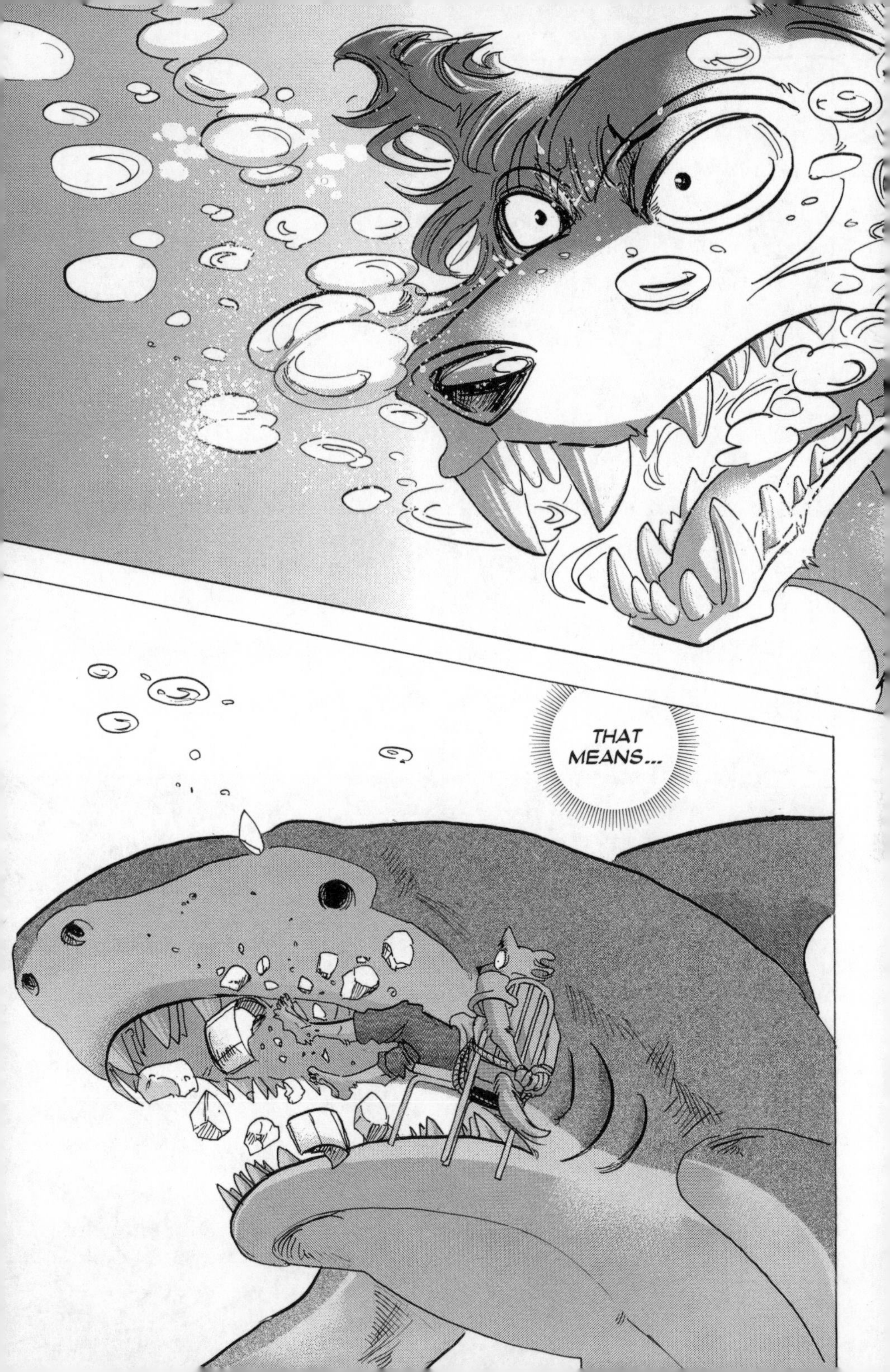
THAT MEANS...

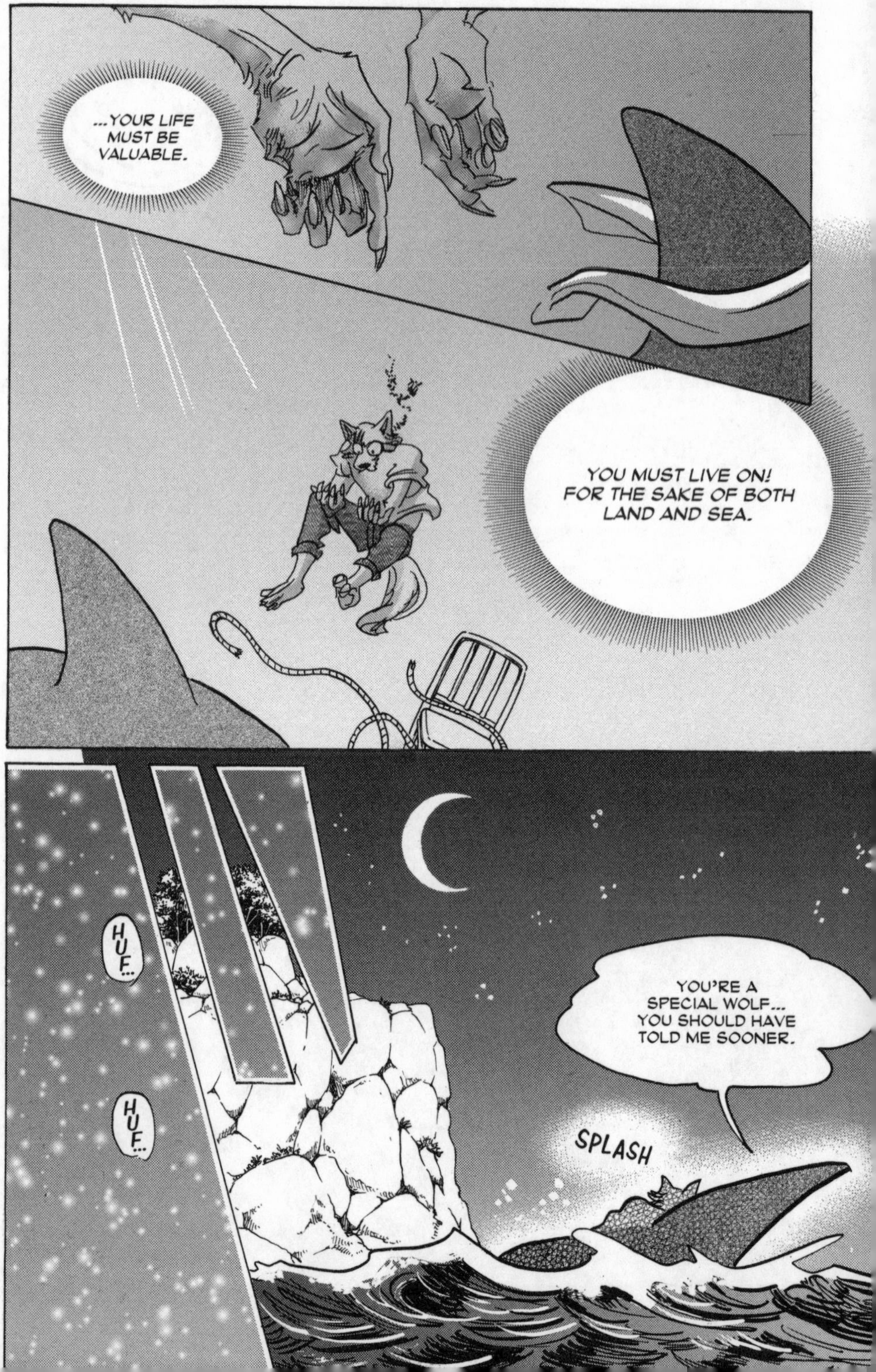
...YOUR LIFE MUST BE VALUABLE.
YOU MUST LIVE ON! FOR THE SAKE OF BOTH LAND AND SEA.
YOU'RE A SPECIAL WOLF... YOU SHOULD HAVE TOLD ME SOONER.
SPLASH
HUF...
HUF...

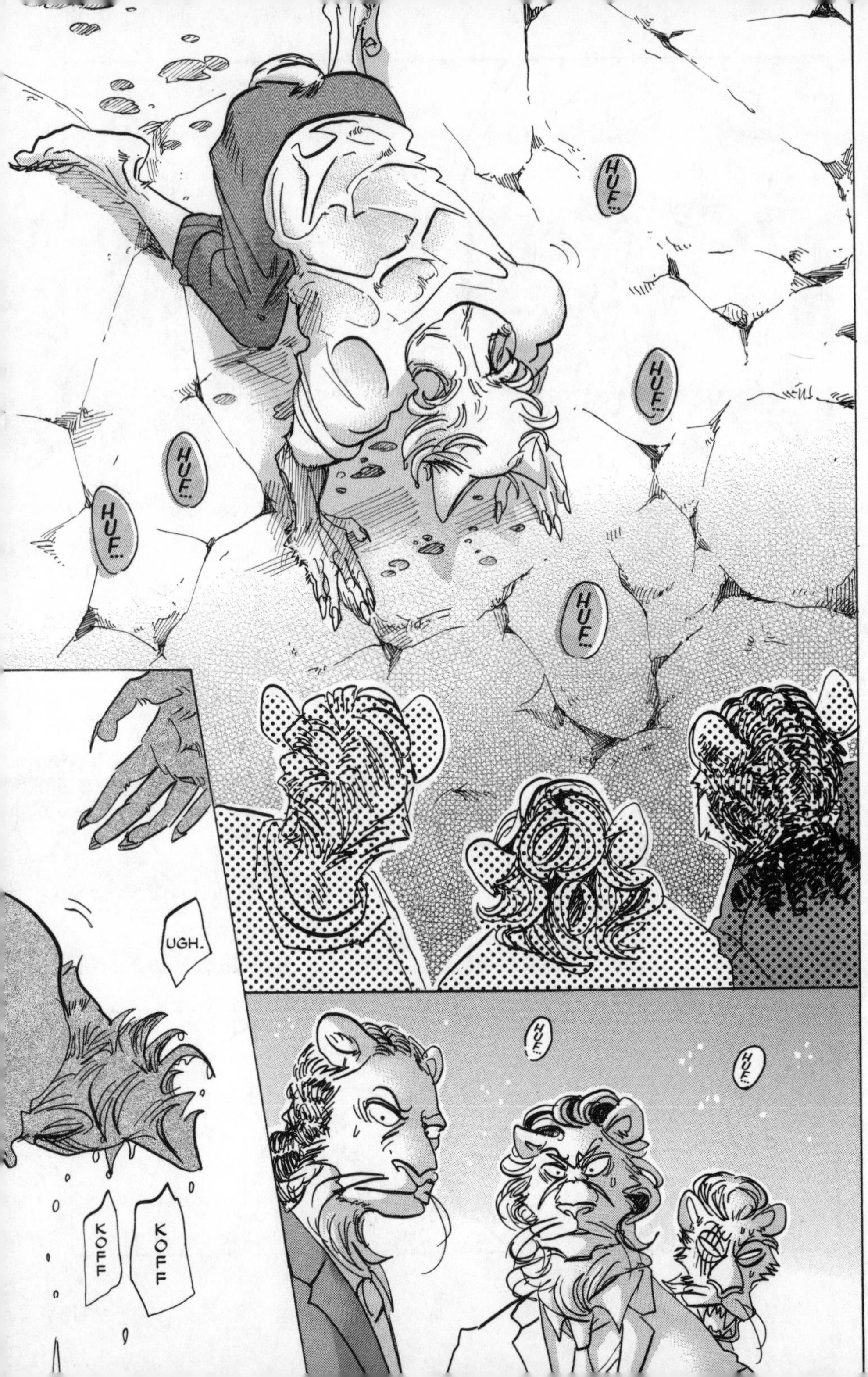
HUF..
HUF..
HUF..
HUF..
HUF..
HUF..
HUF..
UGH.
KOFF
KOFF

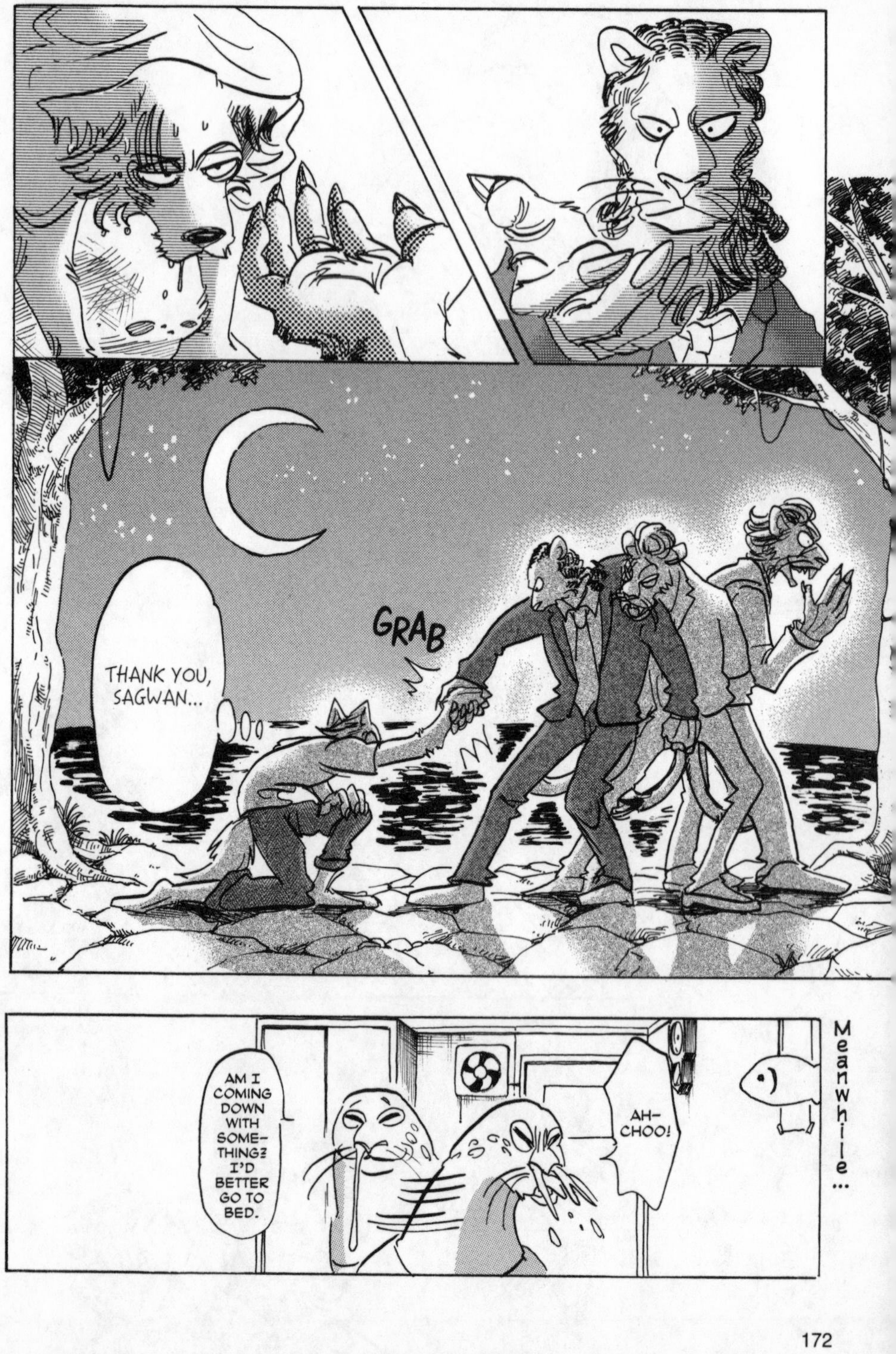
GRAB
THANK YOU, SAGWAN...
Meanwhile...
AH-CHOO!
AM I COMING DOWN WITH SOME-THING? I'D BETTER GO TO BED.

Chapter 142: Beasts Can Live as Long as a Century Now?!

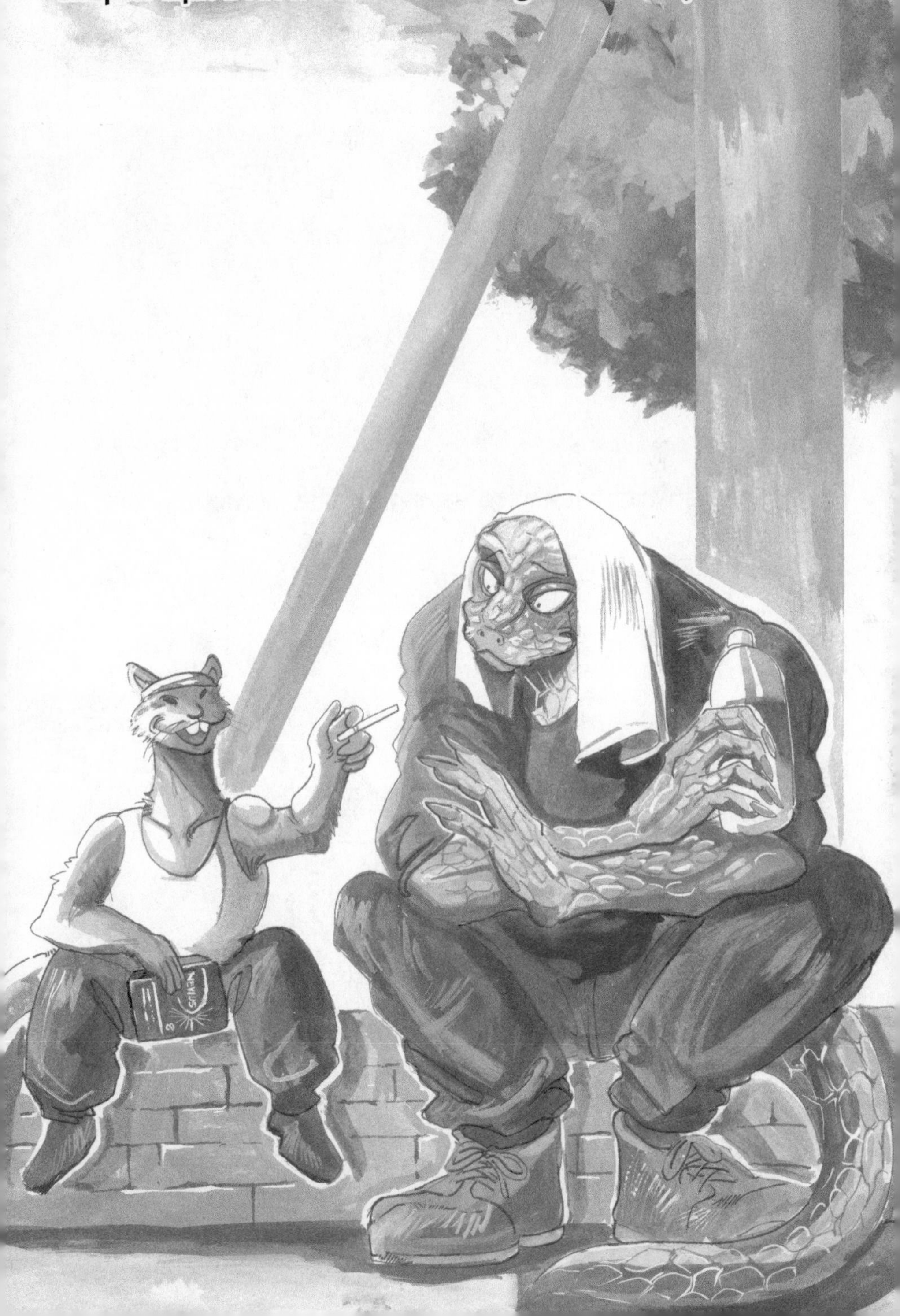

*This is what they were saying on the previous page.

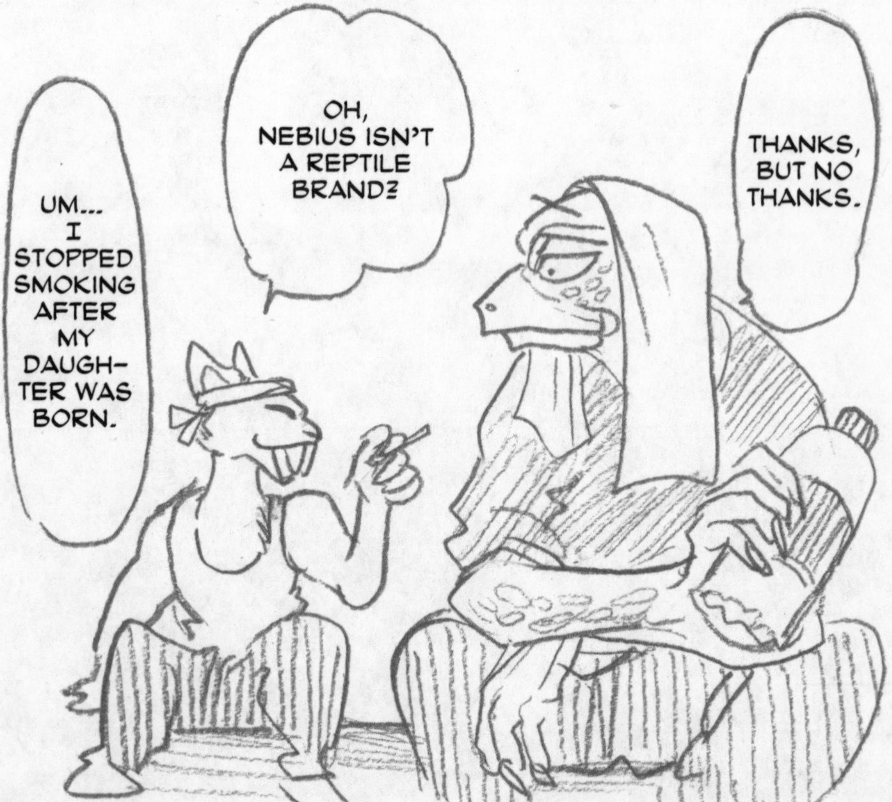
THANKS, BUT NO THANKS.
OH, NEBIUS ISN'T A REPTILE BRAND?
UM... I STOPPED SMOKING AFTER MY DAUGHTER WAS BORN.

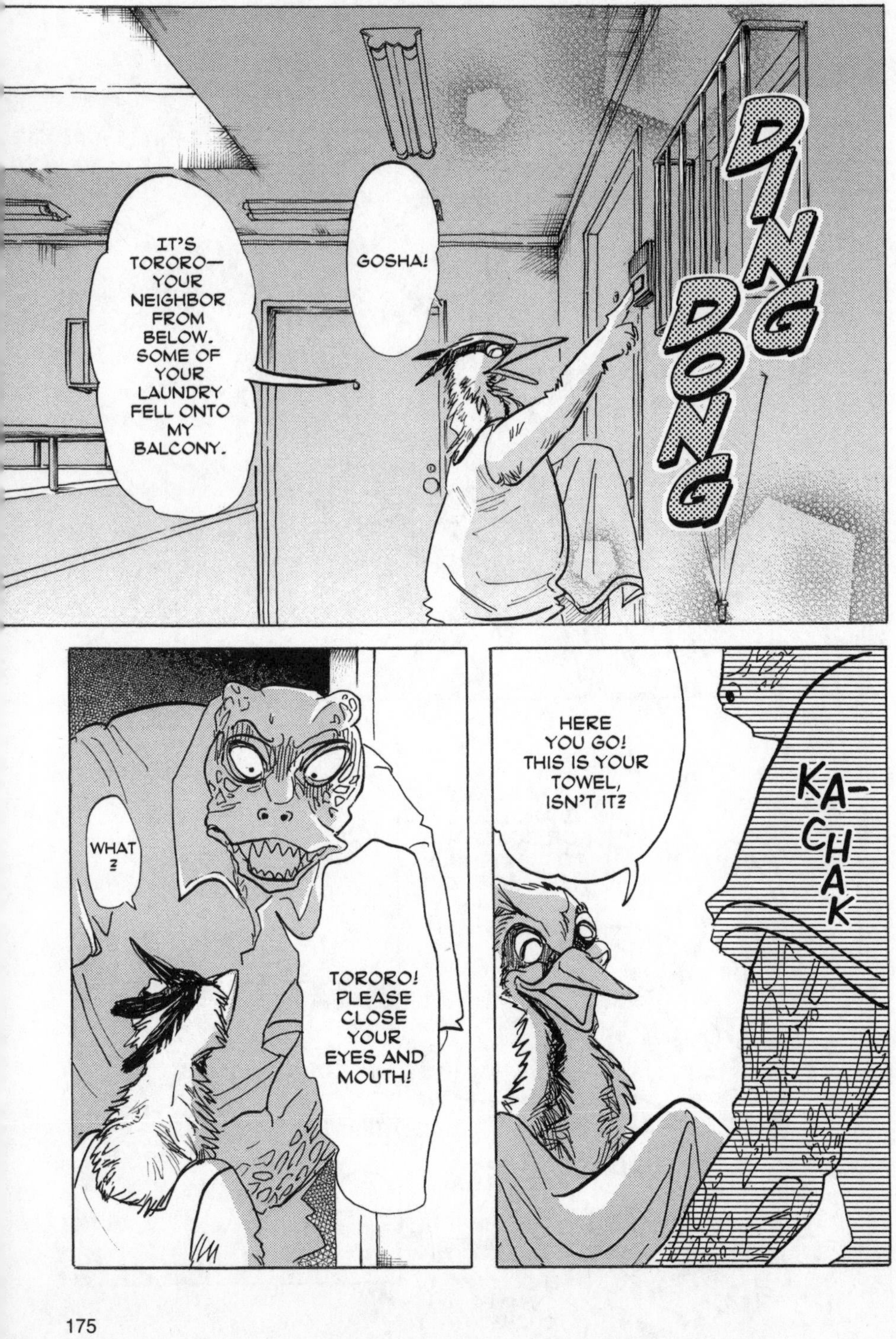
DING DONG
GOSHA!
IT'S TORORO— YOUR NEIGHBOR FROM BELOW. SOME OF YOUR LAUNDRY FELL ONTO MY BALCONY.
KA-CHAK
HERE YOU GO! THIS IS YOUR TOWEL, ISN'T IT?
WHAT?
TORORO! PLEASE CLOSE YOUR EYES AND MOUTH!

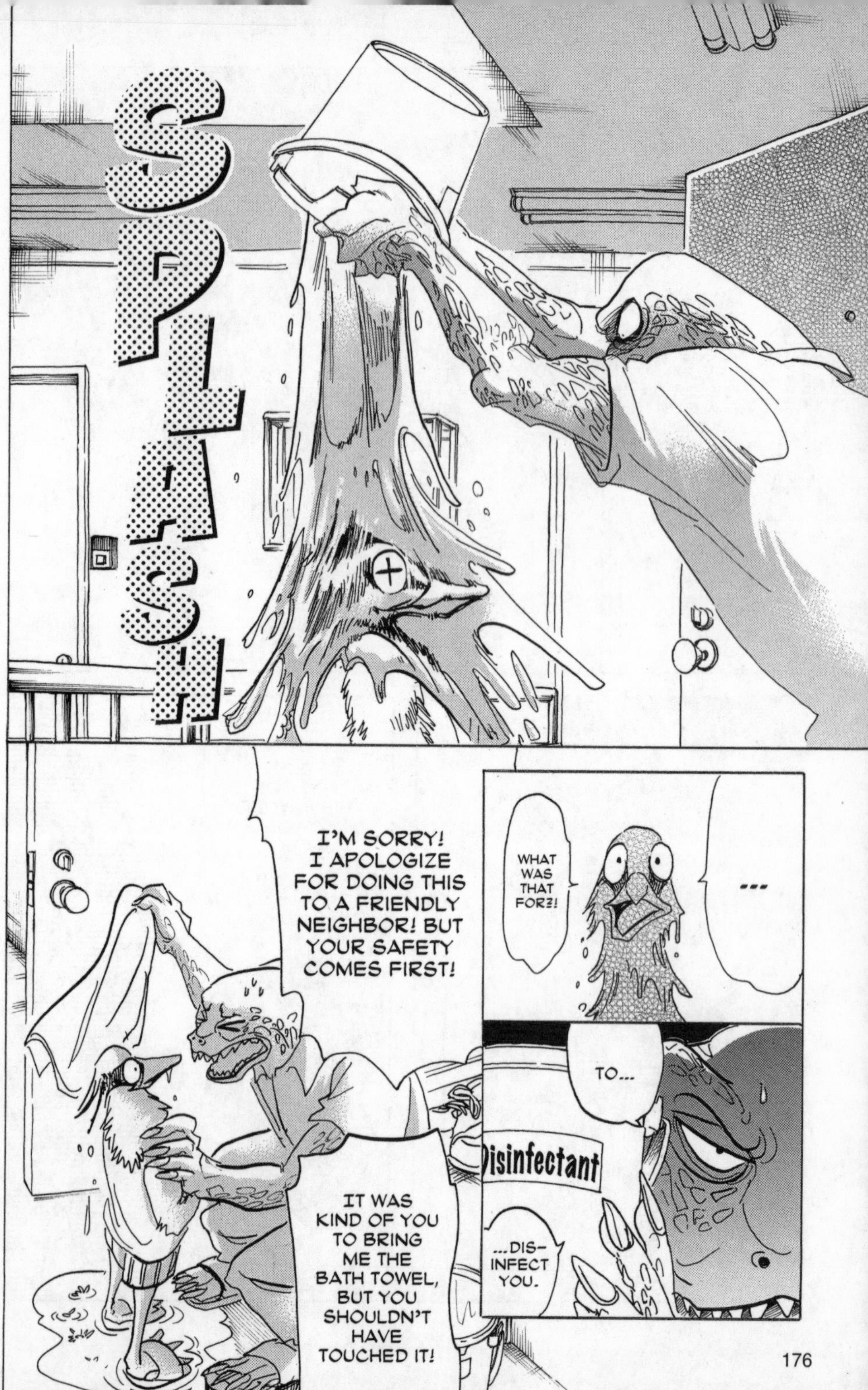
SPLASH
...
WHAT WAS THAT FOR?!
TO...
Disinfectant
...DIS-INFECT YOU.
I'M SORRY! I APOLOGIZE FOR DOING THIS TO A FRIENDLY NEIGHBOR! BUT YOUR SAFETY COMES FIRST!
IT WAS KIND OF YOU TO BRING ME THE BATH TOWEL, BUT YOU SHOULDN'T HAVE TOUCHED IT!

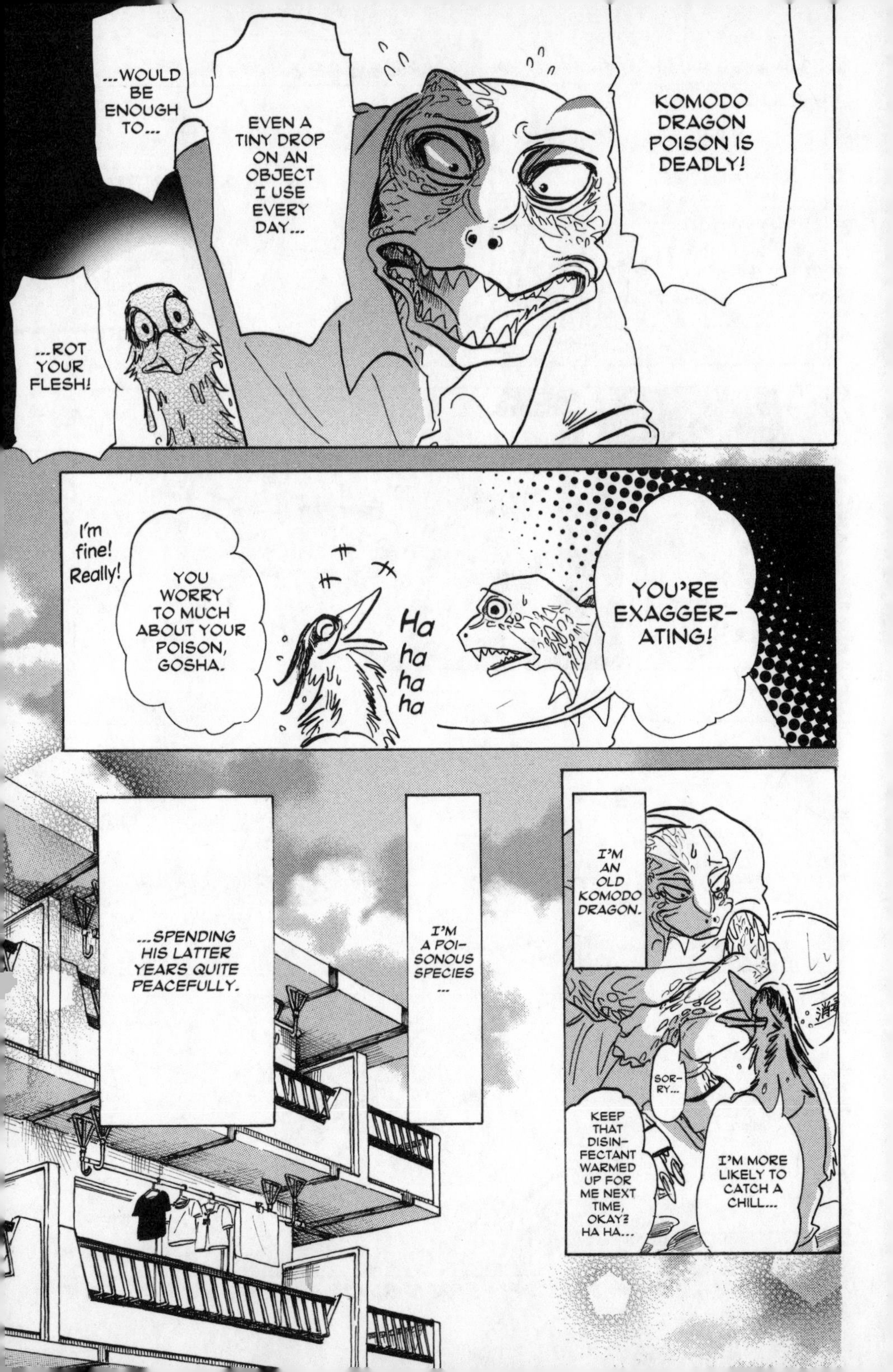
KOMODO DRAGON POISON IS DEADLY!
EVEN A TINY DROP ON AN OBJECT I USE EVERY DAY...
...WOULD BE ENOUGH TO...
...ROT YOUR FLESH!
YOU'RE EXAGGER-ATING!
Ha ha ha ha
YOU WORRY TO MUCH ABOUT YOUR POISON, GOSHA.
I'm fine! Really!
I'M AN OLD KOMODO DRAGON.
I'M MORE LIKELY TO CATCH A CHILL...
SOR-RY...
KEEP THAT DISIN-FECTANT WARMED UP FOR ME NEXT TIME, OKAY? HA HA...
I'M A POI-SONOUS SPECIES ...
...SPENDING HIS LATTER YEARS QUITE PEACEFULLY.

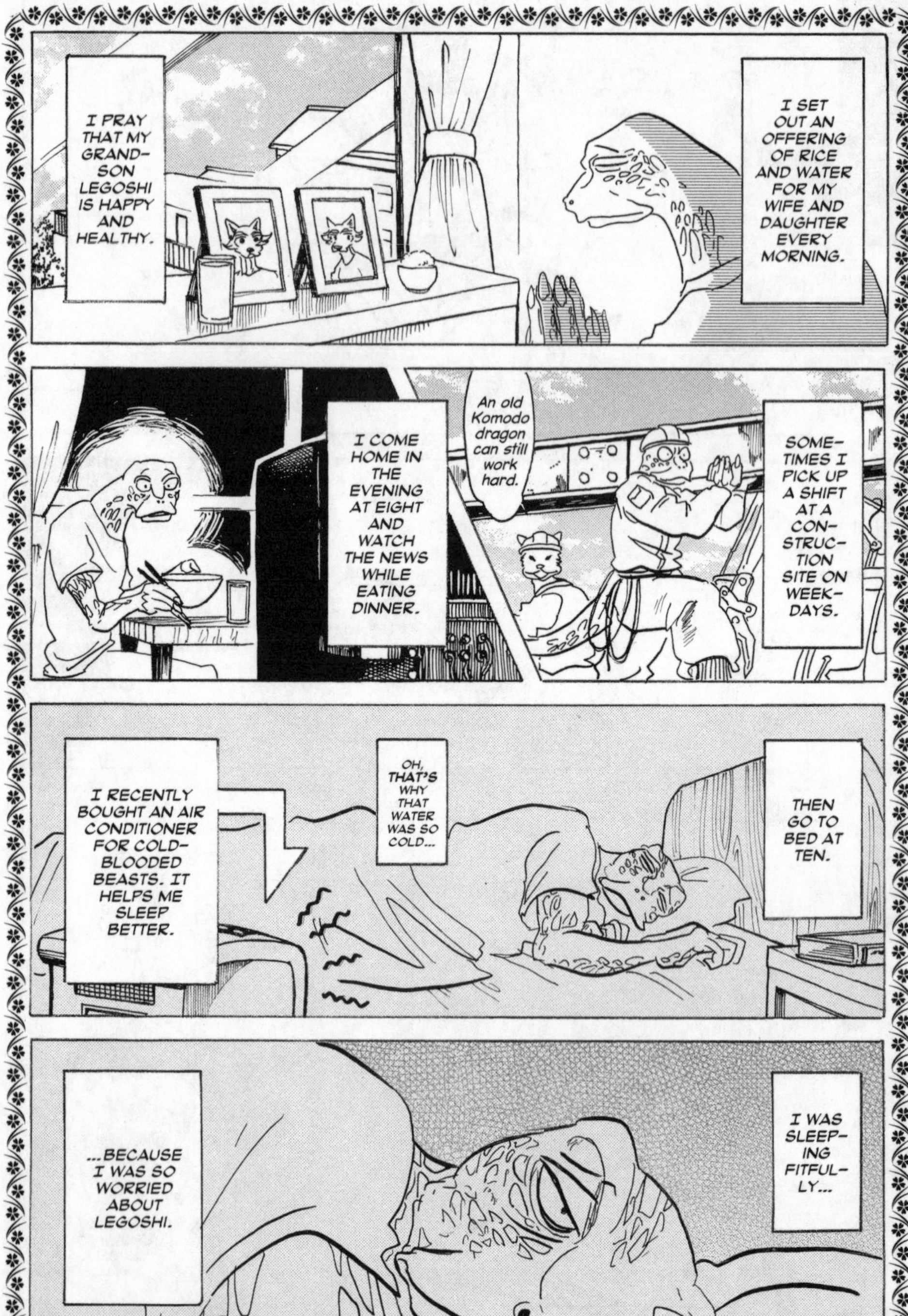
I SET OUT AN OFFERING OF RICE AND WATER FOR MY WIFE AND DAUGHTER EVERY MORNING.
I PRAY THAT MY GRANDSON LEGOSHI IS HAPPY AND HEALTHY.
SOMETIMES I PICK UP A SHIFT AT A CONSTRUCTION SITE ON WEEKDAYS.
An old Komodo dragon can still work hard.
I COME HOME IN THE EVENING AT EIGHT AND WATCH THE NEWS WHILE EATING DINNER.
THEN GO TO BED AT TEN.
OH, THAT'S WHY THAT WATER WAS SO COLD...
I RECENTLY BOUGHT AN AIR CONDITIONER FOR COLD-BLOODED BEASTS. IT HELPS ME SLEEP BETTER.
I WAS SLEEPING FITFULLY...
...BECAUSE I WAS SO WORRIED ABOUT LEGOSHI.

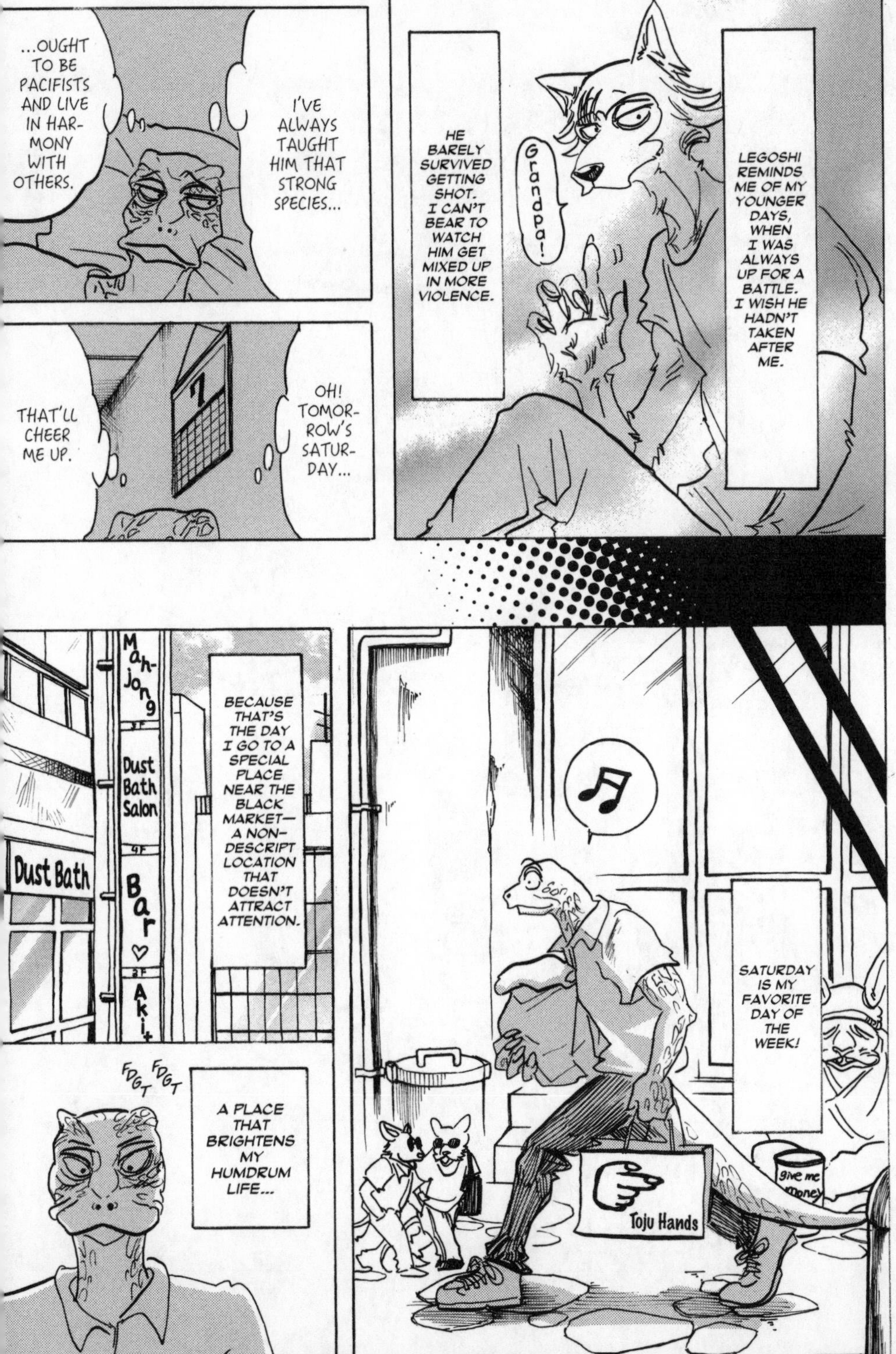
LEGOSHI REMINDS ME OF MY YOUNGER DAYS, WHEN I WAS ALWAYS UP FOR A BATTLE. I WISH HE HADN'T TAKEN AFTER ME.
Grandpa!
HE BARELY SURVIVED GETTING SHOT. I CAN'T BEAR TO WATCH HIM GET MIXED UP IN MORE VIOLENCE.
I'VE ALWAYS TAUGHT HIM THAT STRONG SPECIES...
...OUGHT TO BE PACIFISTS AND LIVE IN HARMONY WITH OTHERS.
OH! TOMORROW'S SATURDAY...
THAT'LL CHEER ME UP.
SATURDAY IS MY FAVORITE DAY OF THE WEEK!
Toju Hands
give me money
BECAUSE THAT'S THE DAY I GO TO A SPECIAL PLACE NEAR THE BLACK MARKET—A NONDESCRIPT LOCATION THAT DOESN'T ATTRACT ATTENTION.
Mah-jong
Dust Bath Salon
Bar ♡
Dust Bath
FDGT FDGT
A PLACE THAT BRIGHTENS MY HUMDRUM LIFE...

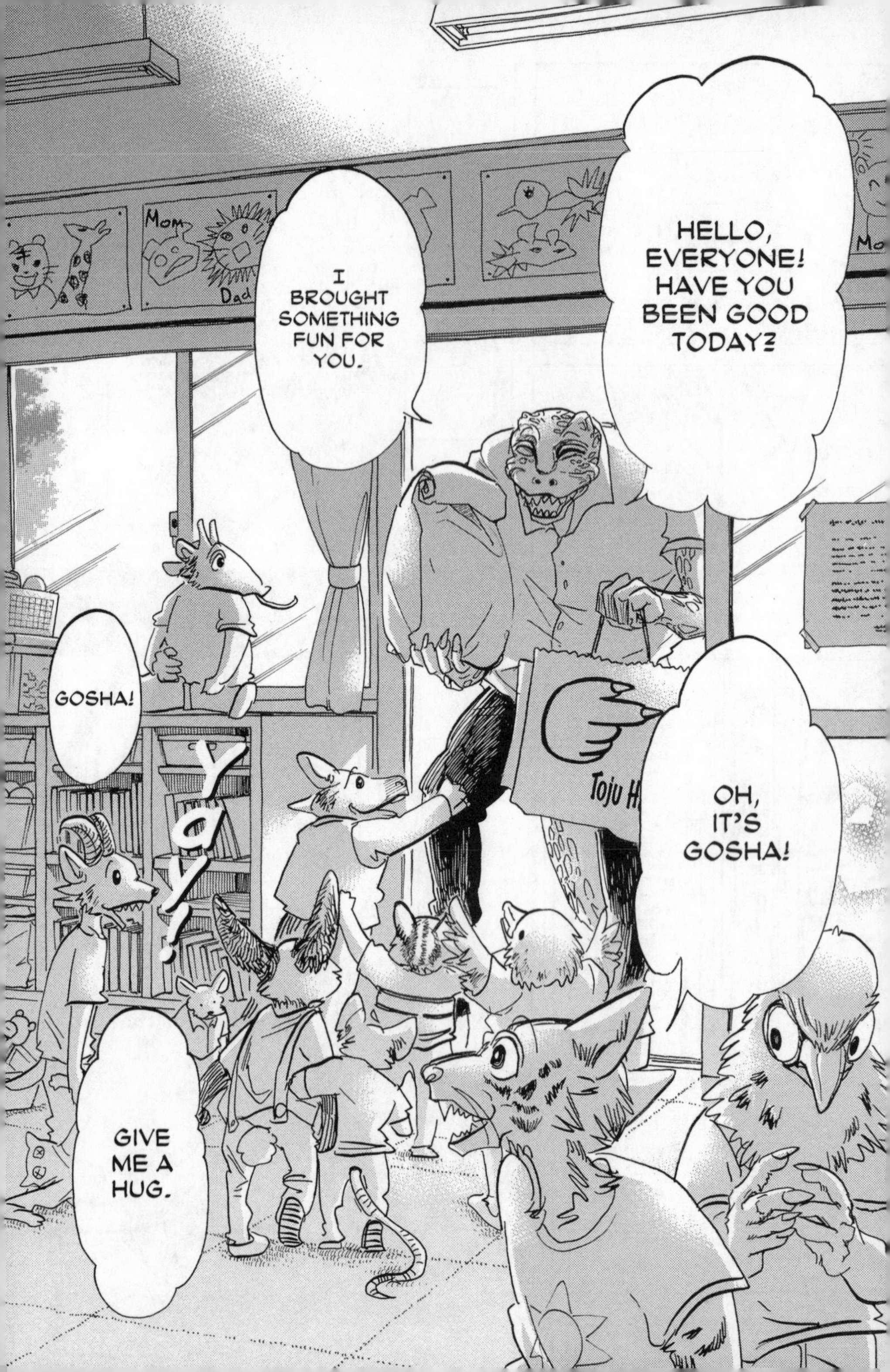

HELLO, EVERYONE! HAVE YOU BEEN GOOD TODAY?
I BROUGHT SOMETHING FUN FOR YOU.
Mom
Dad
OH, IT'S GOSHA!
GOSHA!
YAY!!
GIVE ME A HUG.

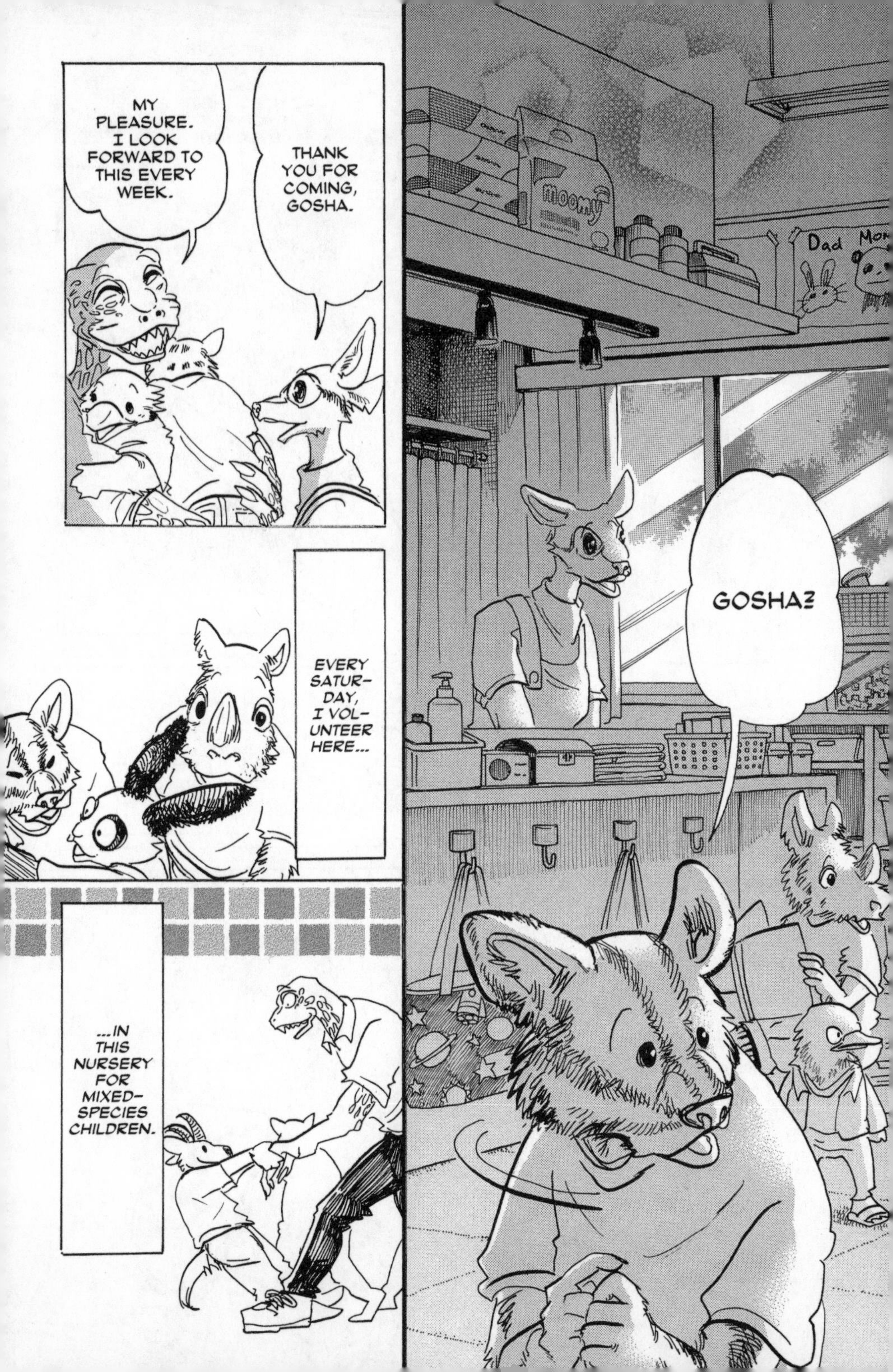
moomy
Dad
GOSHA?
THANK YOU FOR COMING, GOSHA.
MY PLEASURE. I LOOK FORWARD TO THIS EVERY WEEK.
EVERY SATURDAY, I VOLUNTEER HERE...
...IN THIS NURSERY FOR MIXED-SPECIES CHILDREN.

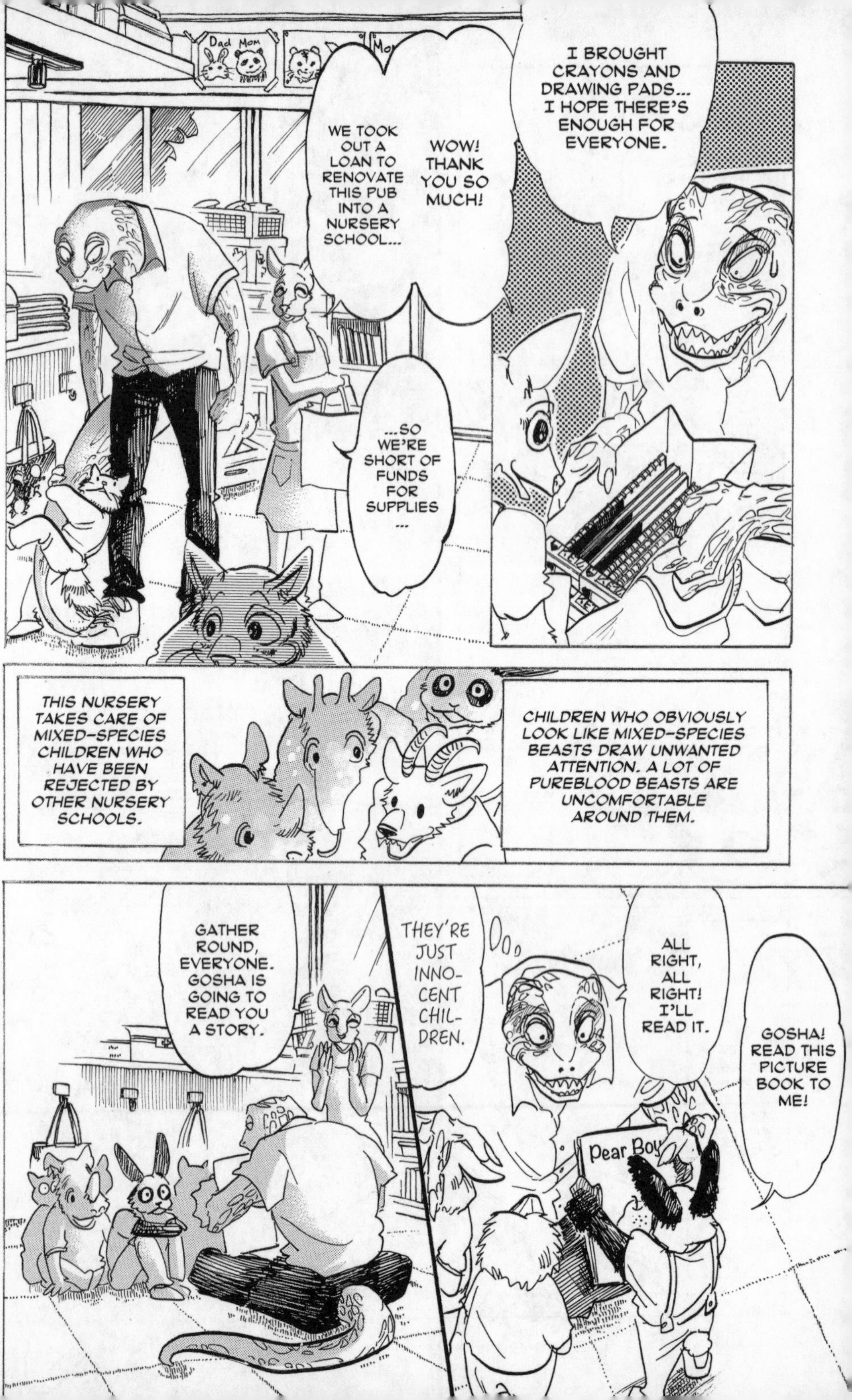
I BROUGHT CRAYONS AND DRAWING PADS... I HOPE THERE'S ENOUGH FOR EVERYONE.
Dad Mom
WOW! THANK YOU SO MUCH!
WE TOOK OUT A LOAN TO RENOVATE THIS PUB INTO A NURSERY SCHOOL...
...SO WE'RE SHORT OF FUNDS FOR SUPPLIES ...
CHILDREN WHO OBVIOUSLY LOOK LIKE MIXED-SPECIES BEASTS DRAW UNWANTED ATTENTION. A LOT OF PUREBLOOD BEASTS ARE UNCOMFORTABLE AROUND THEM.
THIS NURSERY TAKES CARE OF MIXED-SPECIES CHILDREN WHO HAVE BEEN REJECTED BY OTHER NURSERY SCHOOLS.
GOSHA! READ THIS PICTURE BOOK TO ME!
ALL RIGHT, ALL RIGHT! I'LL READ IT.
Pear Boy
THEY'RE JUST INNOCENT CHILDREN.
GATHER ROUND, EVERYONE. GOSHA IS GOING TO READ YOU A STORY.

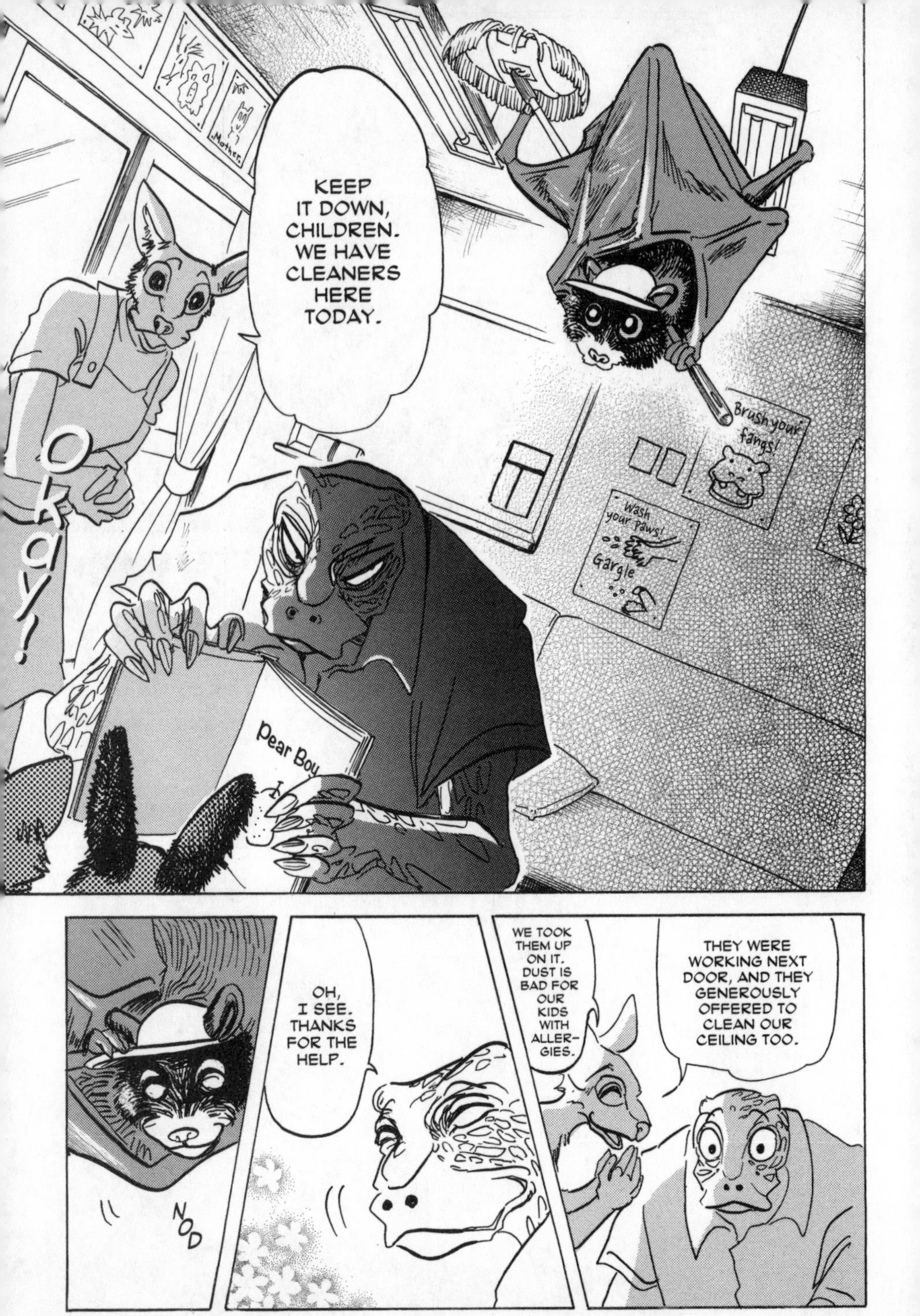
KEEP IT DOWN, CHILDREN. WE HAVE CLEANERS HERE TODAY.
Brush your fangs!
Wash your Paws!
Gargle
Mother.
Okay!
Pear Boy
THEY WERE WORKING NEXT DOOR, AND THEY GENEROUSLY OFFERED TO CLEAN OUR CEILING TOO.
WE TOOK THEM UP ON IT. DUST IS BAD FOR OUR KIDS WITH ALLER-GIES.
OH, I SEE. THANKS FOR THE HELP.
NOD

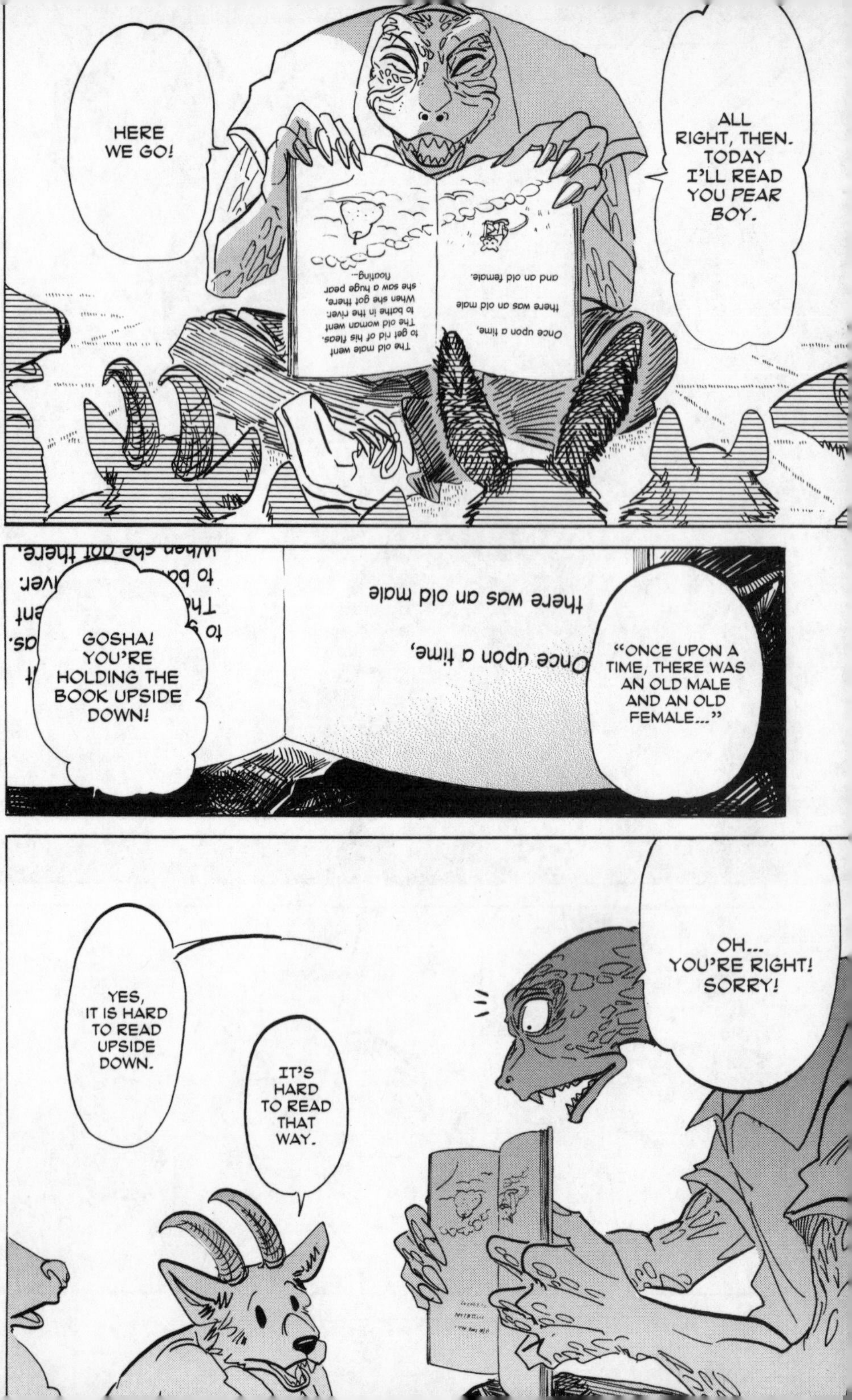
ALL RIGHT, THEN. TODAY I'LL READ YOU *PEAR BOY*.
HERE WE GO!
Once upon a time, there was an old male and an old female.
The old male went to get rid of his fleas. The old woman went to bathe in the river. When she got there, she saw a huge pear floating...
"ONCE UPON A TIME, THERE WAS AN OLD MALE AND AN OLD FEMALE..."
Once upon a time, there was an old male
GOSHA! YOU'RE HOLDING THE BOOK UPSIDE DOWN!
OH... YOU'RE RIGHT! SORRY!
IT'S HARD TO READ THAT WAY.
YES, IT IS HARD TO READ UPSIDE DOWN.

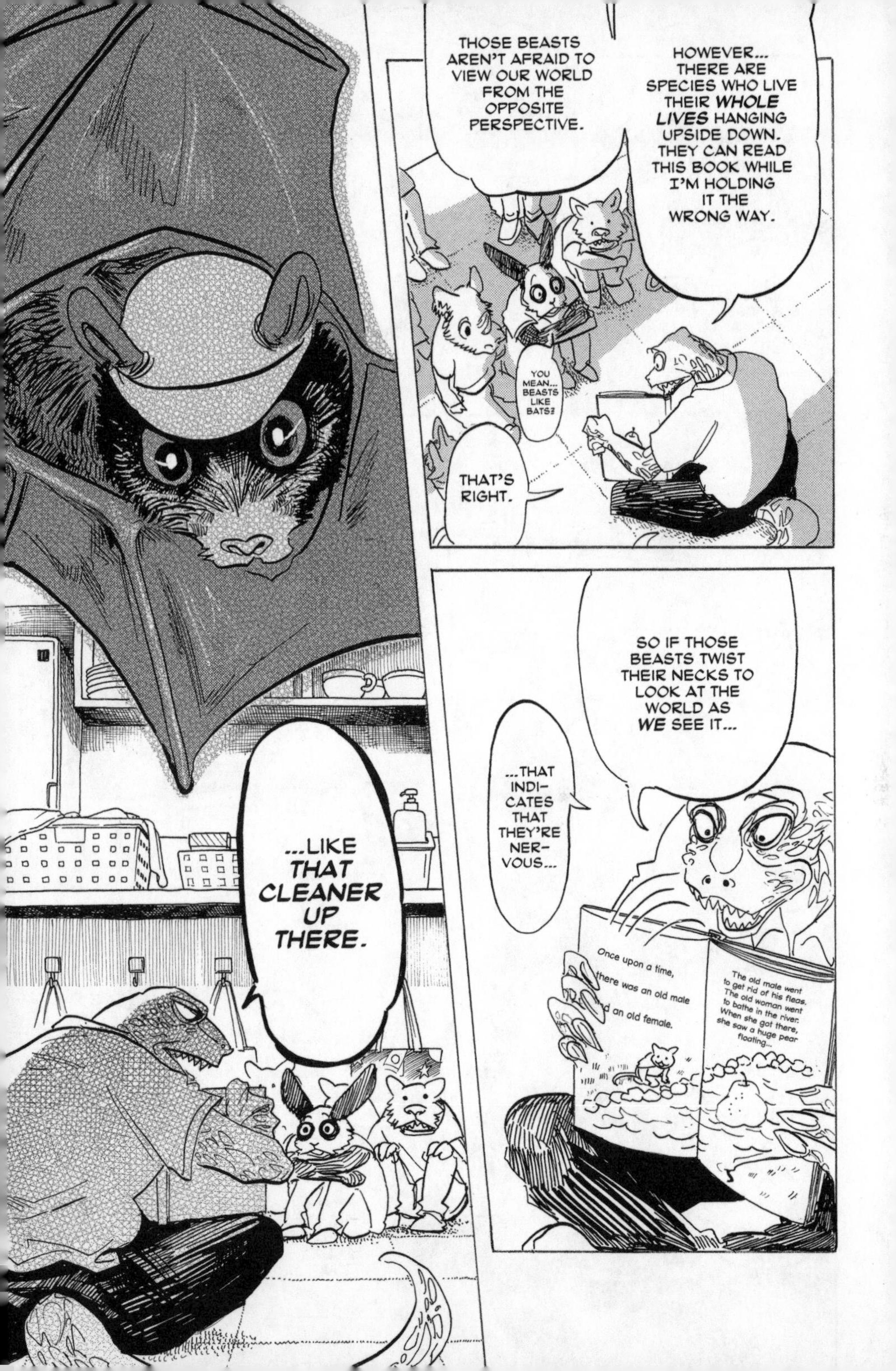
HOWEVER... THERE ARE SPECIES WHO LIVE THEIR WHOLE LIVES HANGING UPSIDE DOWN. THEY CAN READ THIS BOOK WHILE I'M HOLDING IT THE WRONG WAY.
THOSE BEASTS AREN'T AFRAID TO VIEW OUR WORLD FROM THE OPPOSITE PERSPECTIVE.
YOU MEAN... BEASTS LIKE BATS?
THAT'S RIGHT.
SO IF THOSE BEASTS TWIST THEIR NECKS TO LOOK AT THE WORLD AS WE SEE IT...
...THAT INDICATES THAT THEY'RE NERVOUS...
Once upon a time, there was an old male and an old female.
The old male went to get rid of his fleas. The old woman went to bathe in the river. When she got there, she saw a huge pear floating...
...LIKE THAT CLEANER UP THERE.

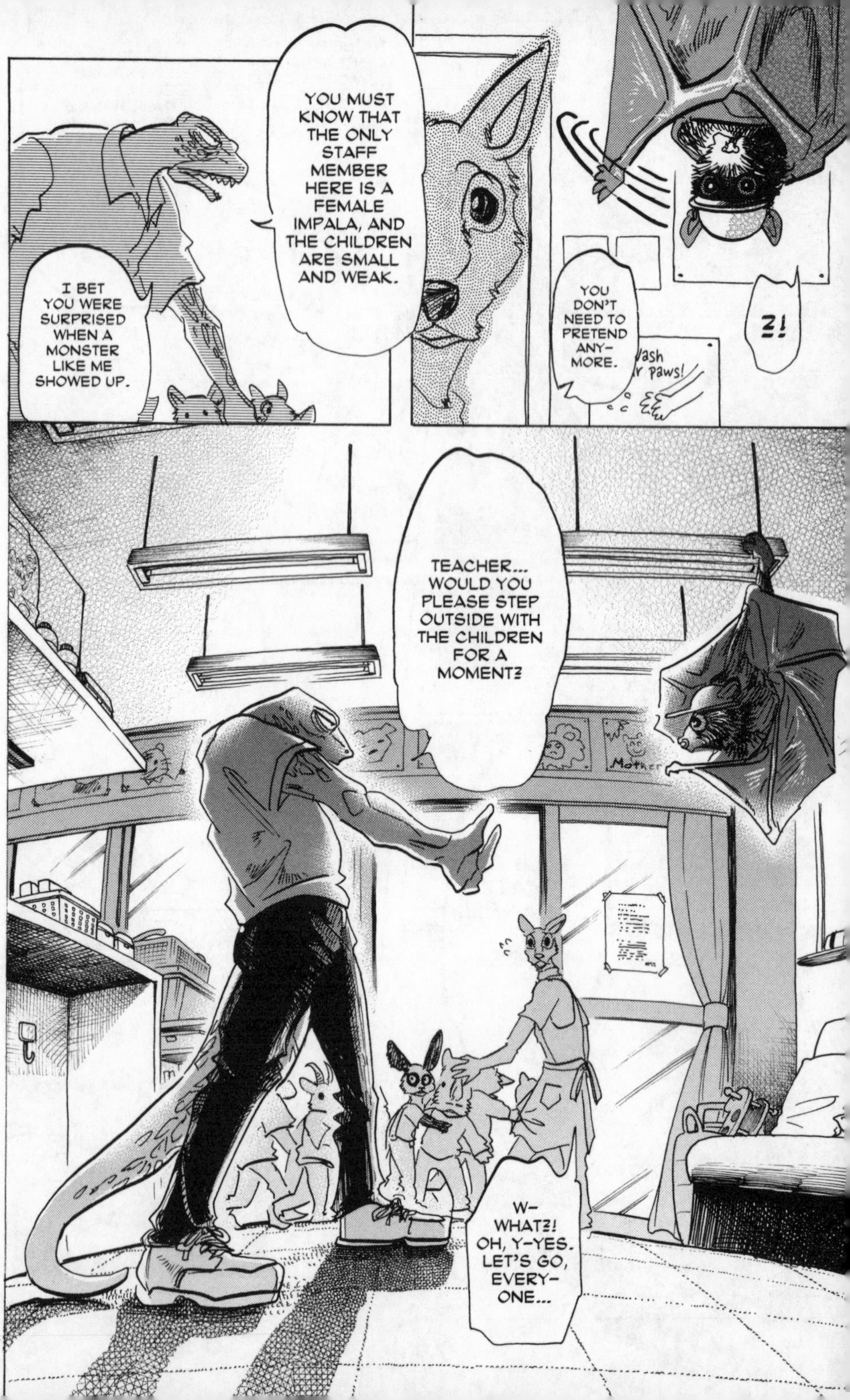
?!
YOU DON'T NEED TO PRETEND ANYMORE.
YOU MUST KNOW THAT THE ONLY STAFF MEMBER HERE IS A FEMALE IMPALA, AND THE CHILDREN ARE SMALL AND WEAK.
I BET YOU WERE SURPRISED WHEN A MONSTER LIKE ME SHOWED UP.
TEACHER... WOULD YOU PLEASE STEP OUTSIDE WITH THE CHILDREN FOR A MOMENT?
Mother
W-WHAT?! OH, Y-YES. LET'S GO, EVERY-ONE...

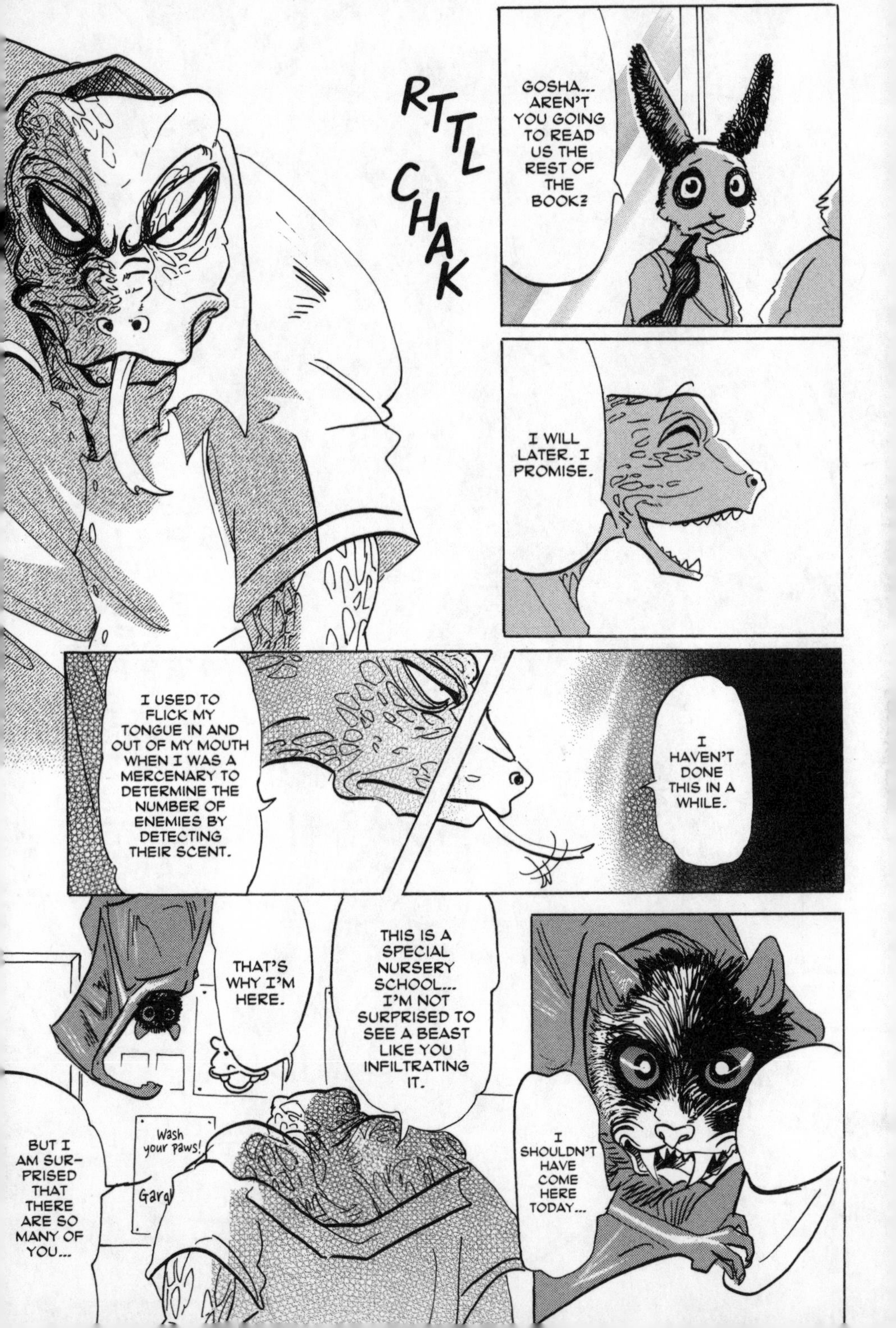
GOSHA... AREN'T YOU GOING TO READ US THE REST OF THE BOOK?
I WILL LATER. I PROMISE.
RTTL CHAK
I HAVEN'T DONE THIS IN A WHILE.
I USED TO FLICK MY TONGUE IN AND OUT OF MY MOUTH WHEN I WAS A MERCENARY TO DETERMINE THE NUMBER OF ENEMIES BY DETECTING THEIR SCENT.
I SHOULDN'T HAVE COME HERE TODAY...
THIS IS A SPECIAL NURSERY SCHOOL... I'M NOT SURPRISED TO SEE A BEAST LIKE YOU INFILTRATING IT.
THAT'S WHY I'M HERE.
Wash your paws!
BUT I AM SUR-PRISED THAT THERE ARE SO MANY OF YOU...

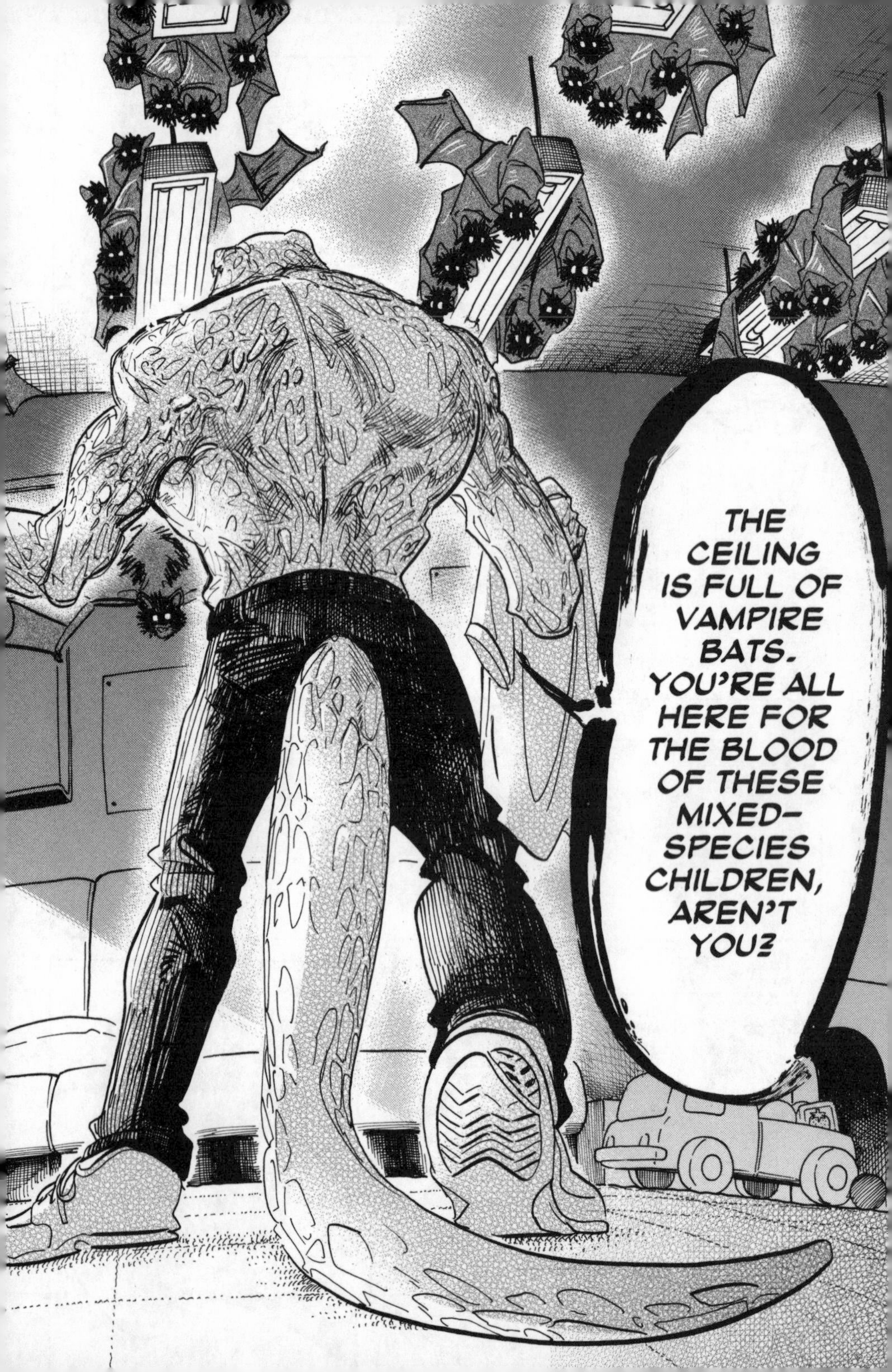
THE CEILING IS FULL OF VAMPIRE BATS. YOU'RE ALL HERE FOR THE BLOOD OF THESE MIXED-SPECIES CHILDREN, AREN'T YOU?

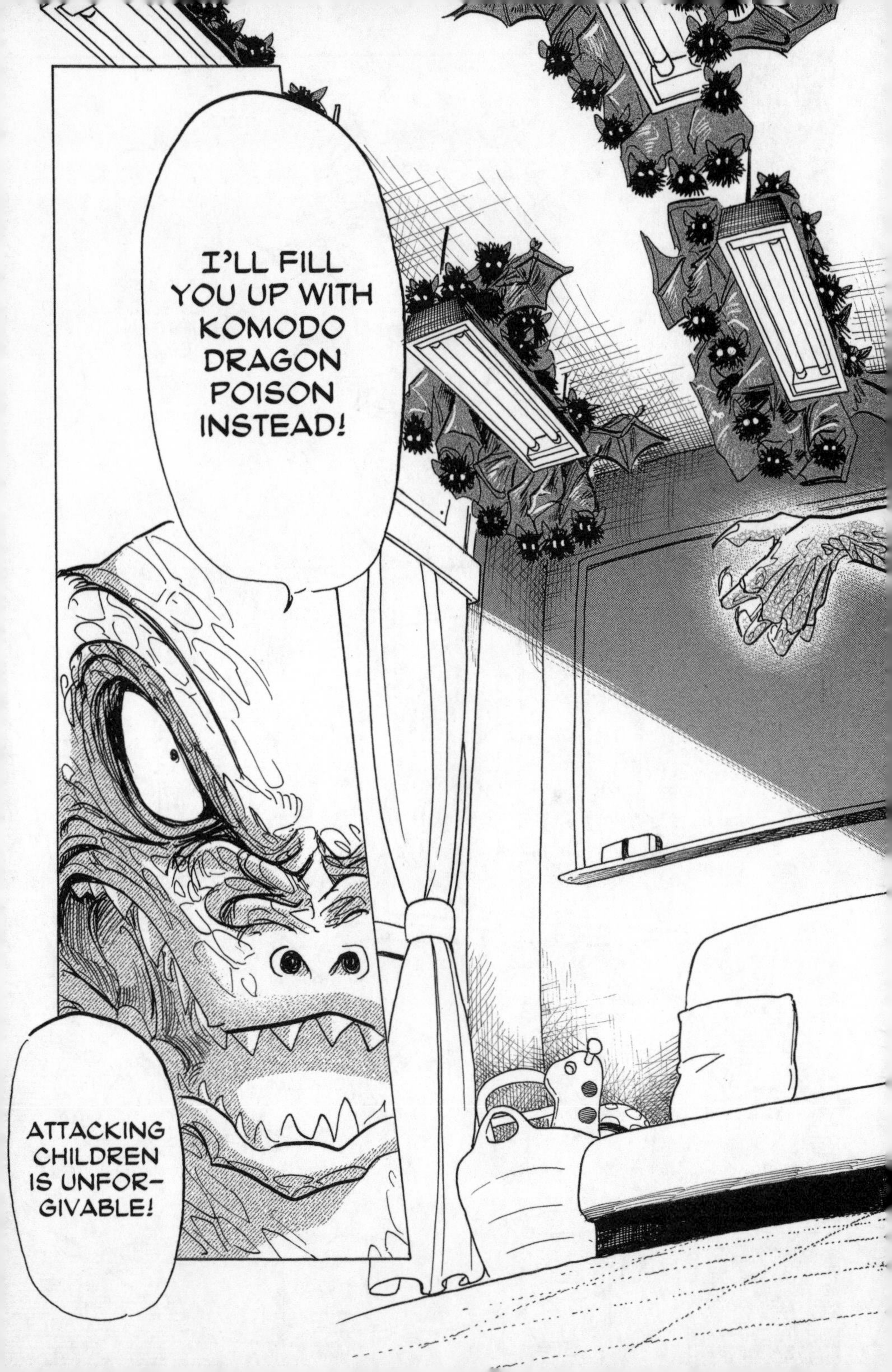
I'LL FILL YOU UP WITH KOMODO DRAGON POISON INSTEAD!
ATTACKING CHILDREN IS UNFOR-GIVABLE!

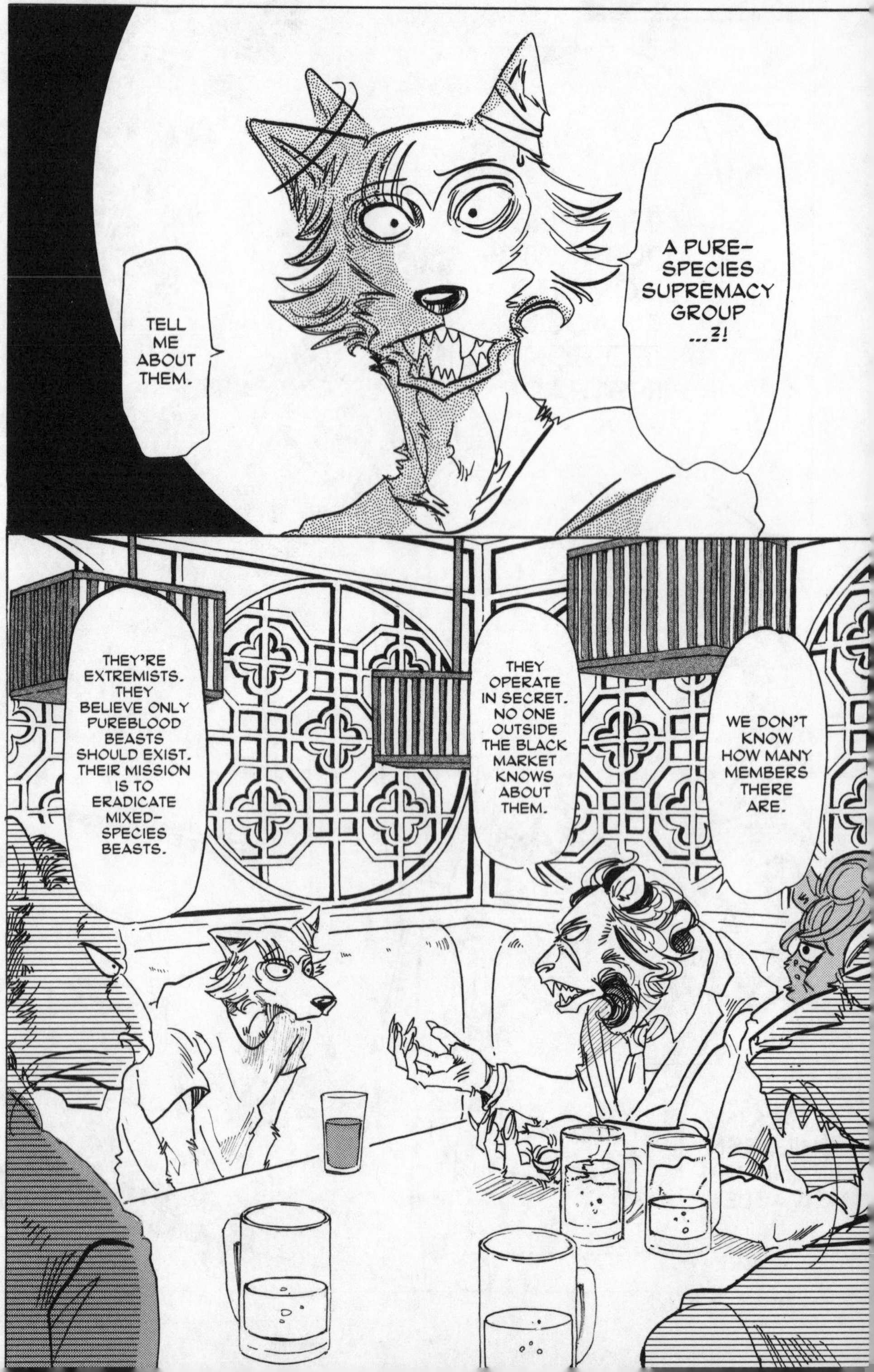
A PURE-SPECIES SUPREMACY GROUP ...?!
TELL ME ABOUT THEM.
WE DON'T KNOW HOW MANY MEMBERS THERE ARE.
THEY OPERATE IN SECRET. NO ONE OUTSIDE THE BLACK MARKET KNOWS ABOUT THEM.
THEY'RE EXTREMISTS. THEY BELIEVE ONLY PUREBLOOD BEASTS SHOULD EXIST. THEIR MISSION IS TO ERADICATE MIXED-SPECIES BEASTS.

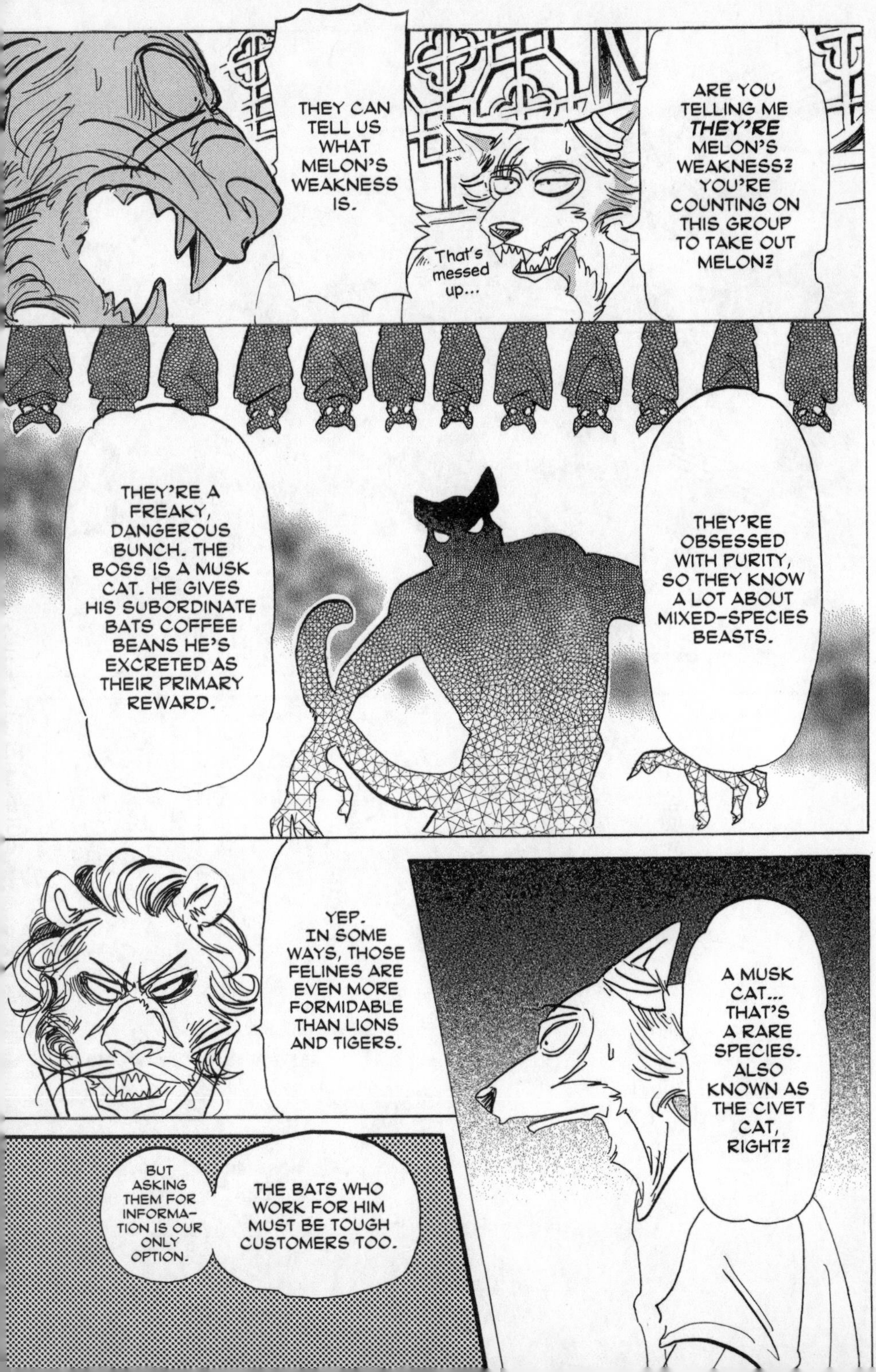
ARE YOU TELLING ME *THEY'RE* MELON'S WEAKNESS? YOU'RE COUNTING ON THIS GROUP TO TAKE OUT MELON?
That's messed up...
THEY CAN TELL US WHAT MELON'S WEAKNESS IS.
THEY'RE OBSESSED WITH PURITY, SO THEY KNOW A LOT ABOUT MIXED-SPECIES BEASTS.
THEY'RE A FREAKY, DANGEROUS BUNCH. THE BOSS IS A MUSK CAT. HE GIVES HIS SUBORDINATE BATS COFFEE BEANS HE'S EXCRETED AS THEIR PRIMARY REWARD.
A MUSK CAT... THAT'S A RARE SPECIES. ALSO KNOWN AS THE CIVET CAT, RIGHT?
YEP. IN SOME WAYS, THOSE FELINES ARE EVEN MORE FORMIDABLE THAN LIONS AND TIGERS.
THE BATS WHO WORK FOR HIM MUST BE TOUGH CUSTOMERS TOO.
BUT ASKING THEM FOR INFORMATION IS OUR ONLY OPTION.

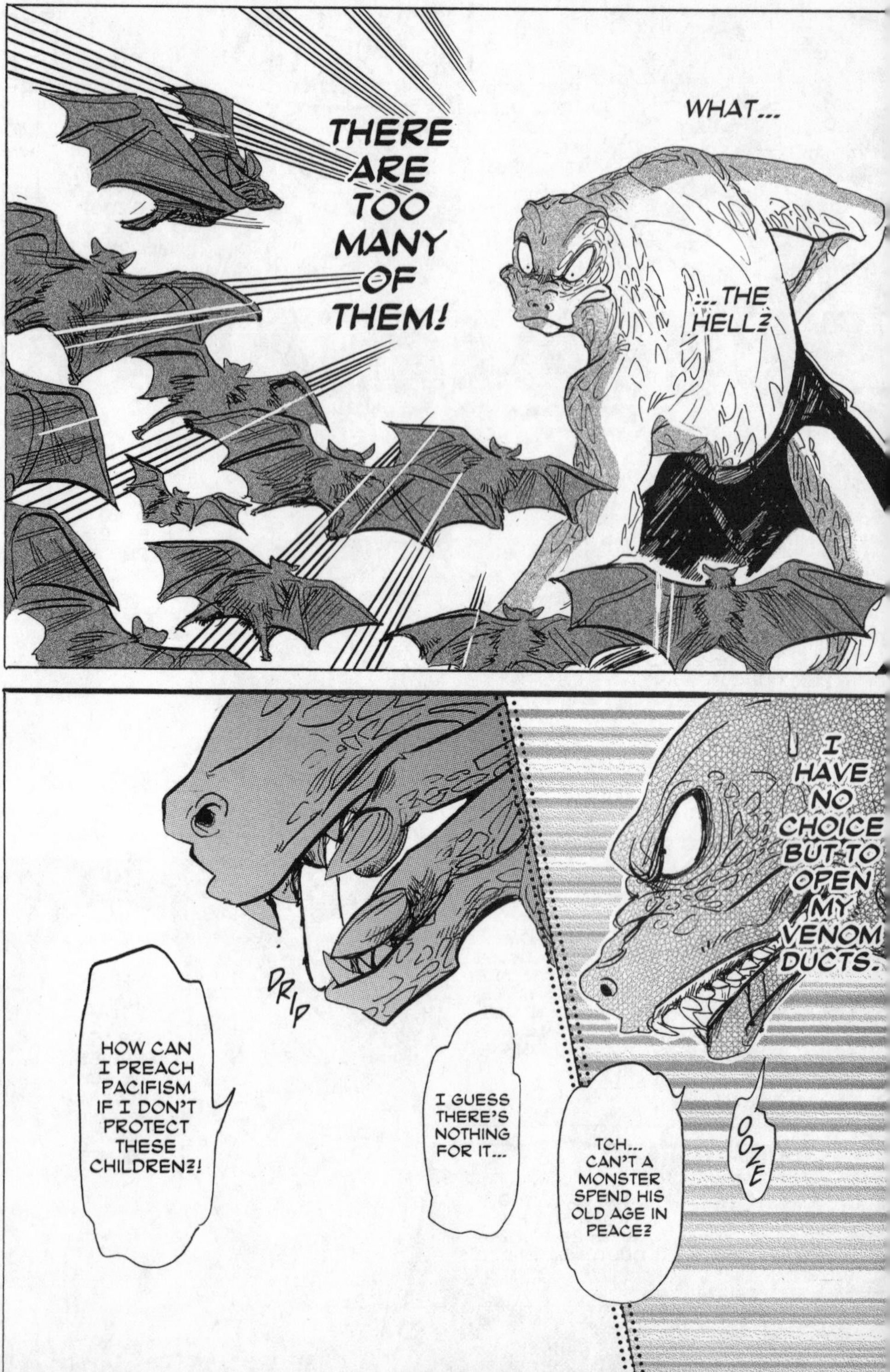
WHAT...
...THE HELL?
THERE ARE TOO MANY OF THEM!
I HAVE NO CHOICE BUT TO OPEN MY VENOM DUCTS.
OOZE
TCH... CAN'T A MONSTER SPEND HIS OLD AGE IN PEACE?
DRIP
I GUESS THERE'S NOTHING FOR IT...
HOW CAN I PREACH PACIFISM IF I DON'T PROTECT THESE CHILDREN?!

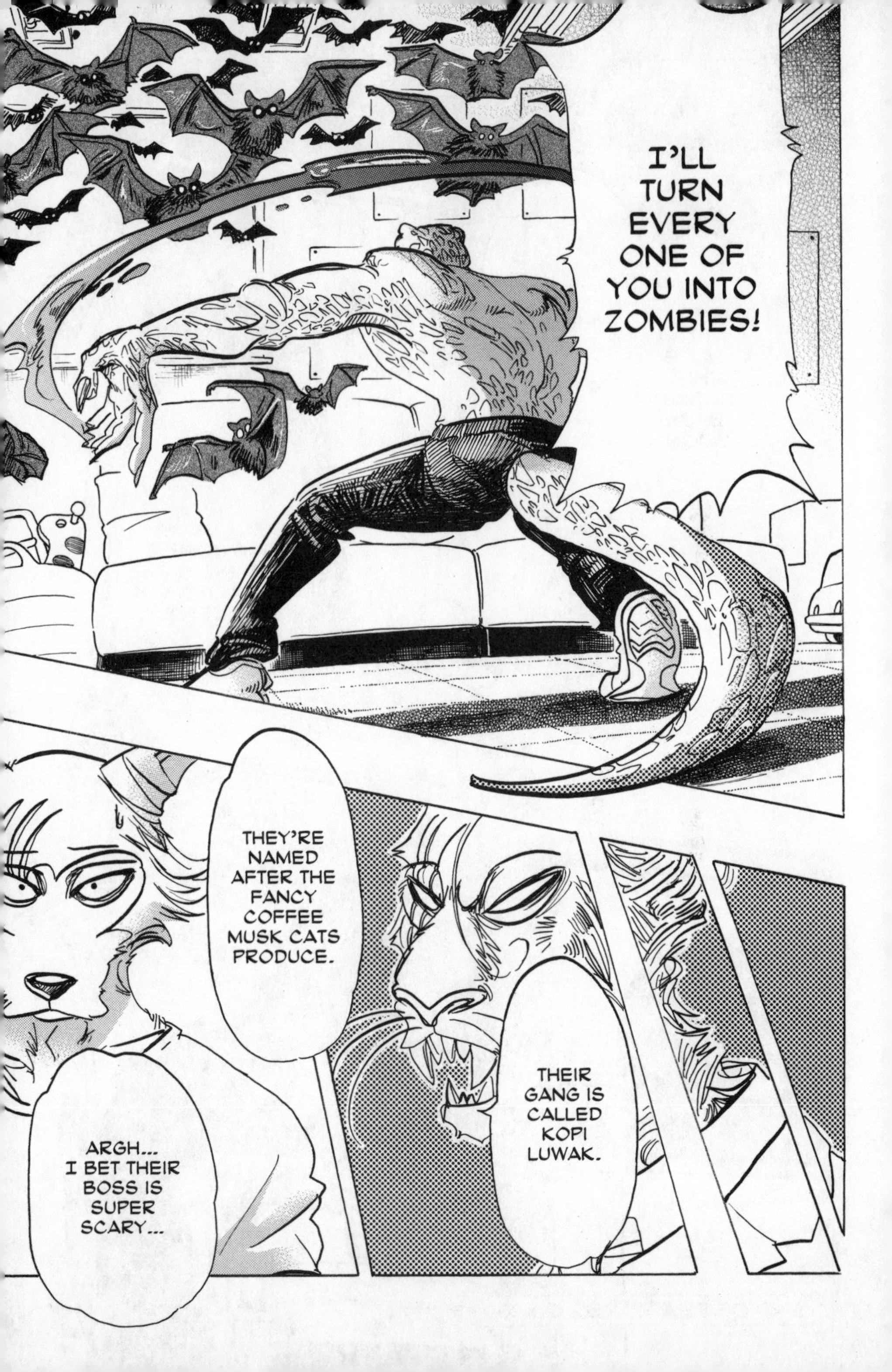
I'LL TURN EVERY ONE OF YOU INTO ZOMBIES!
THEIR GANG IS CALLED KOPI LUWAK.
THEY'RE NAMED AFTER THE FANCY COFFEE MUSK CATS PRODUCE.
ARGH... I BET THEIR BOSS IS SUPER SCARY...

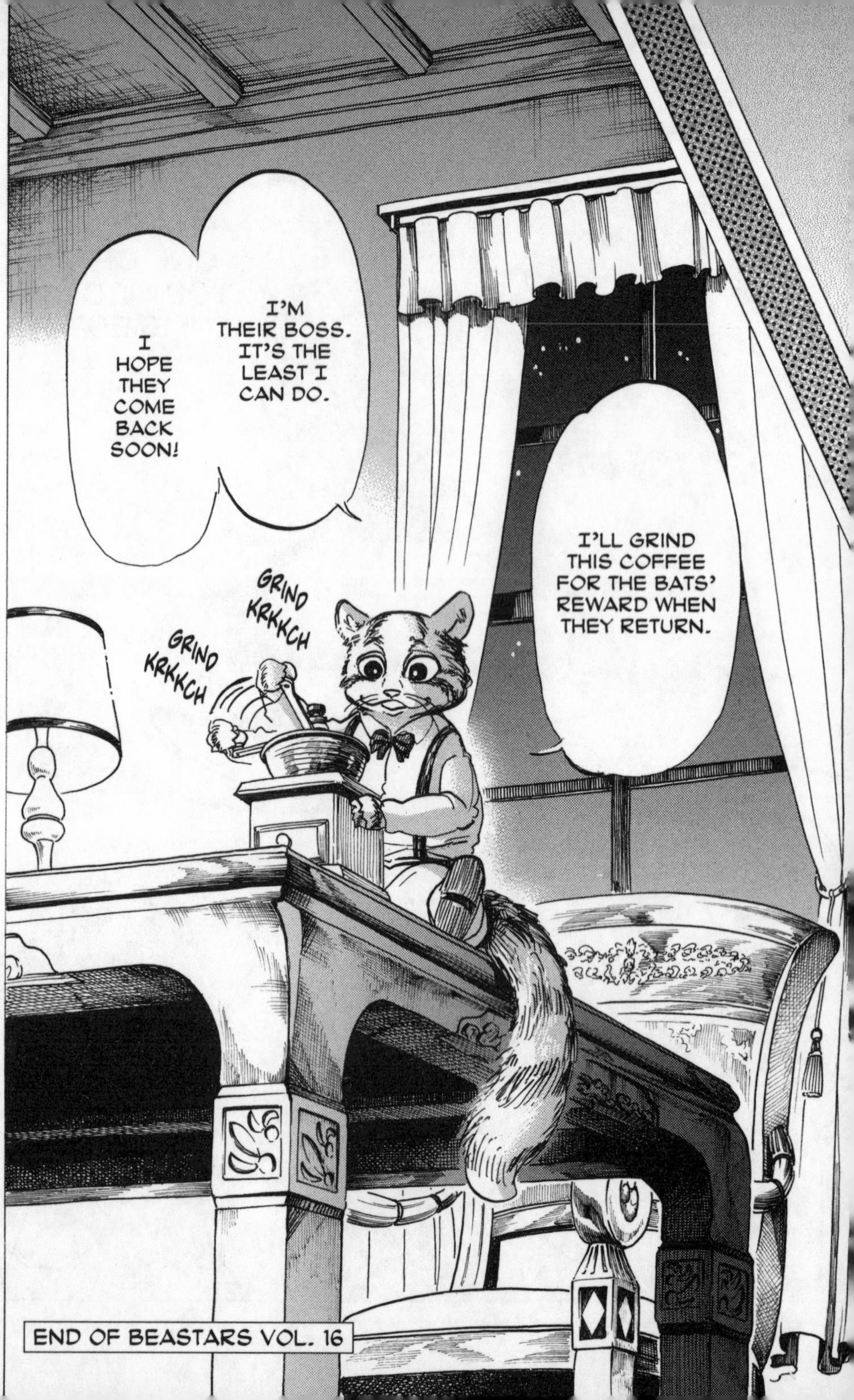
I'LL GRIND THIS COFFEE FOR THE BATS' REWARD WHEN THEY RETURN.
I'M THEIR BOSS. IT'S THE LEAST I CAN DO.
I HOPE THEY COME BACK SOON!
GRIND KRKKCH
GRIND KRKKCH
END OF BEASTARS VOL. 16

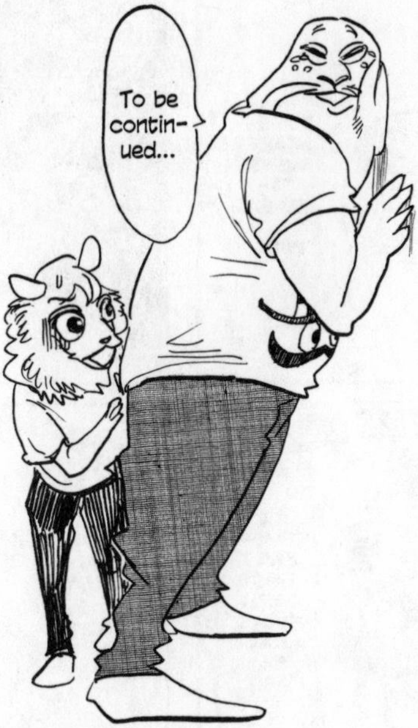
To be contin-ued...

A Funny Anecdote from Chapter 136

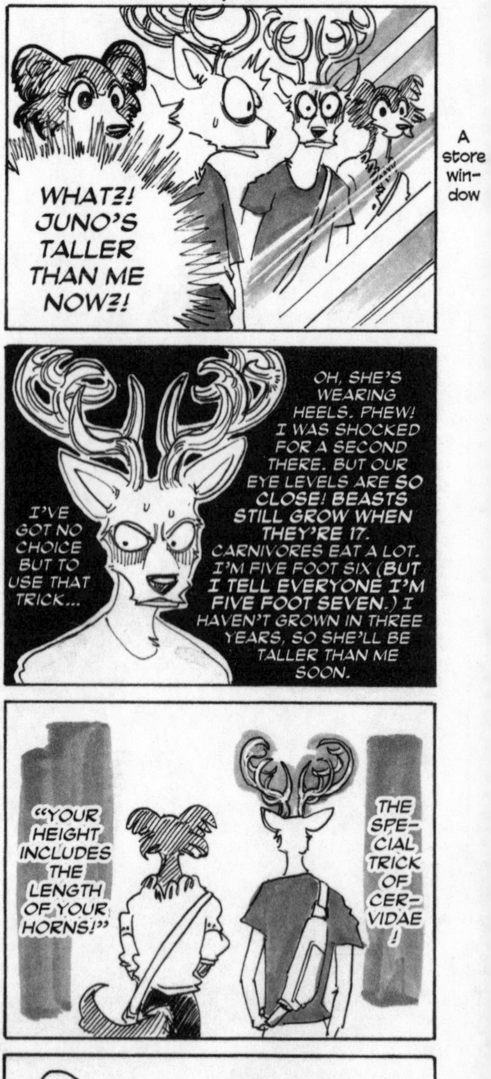

A store window
WHAT?! JUNO'S TALLER THAN ME NOW?!
OH, SHE'S WEARING HEELS. PHEW! I WAS SHOCKED FOR A SECOND THERE. BUT OUR EYE LEVELS ARE SO CLOSE! BEASTS STILL GROW WHEN THEY'RE 17. CARNIVORES EAT A LOT. I'M FIVE FOOT SIX (BUT I TELL EVERYONE I'M FIVE FOOT SEVEN.) I HAVEN'T GROWN IN THREE YEARS, SO SHE'LL BE TALLER THAN ME SOON.
I'VE GOT NO CHOICE BUT TO USE THAT TRICK...
THE SPECIAL TRICK OF CERVIDAE!
"YOUR HEIGHT INCLUDES THE LENGTH OF YOUR HORNS!"
LOUIS, DO YOU HAVE ANY PLANS AFTER THIS?

*Continues on p. 9 of ch. 136.

The Inside Story of Chapter 141

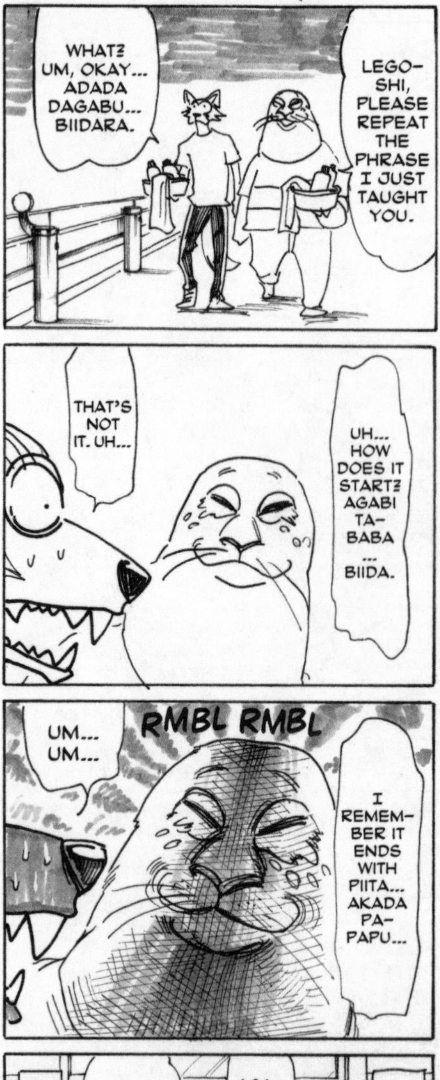

LEGOSHI, PLEASE REPEAT THE PHRASE I JUST TAUGHT YOU.
WHAT? UM, OKAY... ADADA DAGABU... BIIDARA.
UH... HOW DOES IT START? AGABI TABABA... BIIDA.
THAT'S NOT IT. UH...
I REMEMBER IT ENDS WITH PIITA... AKADA PAPAPU...
RMBL RMBL
UM... UM...
Several days later...
Let me hear!!
AGAGA?
PAPUPU DABA GOMA BIIDA!
It's as if Sagwan has become Legoshi's mentor now.
?

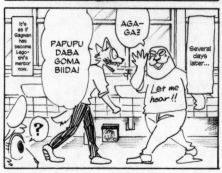

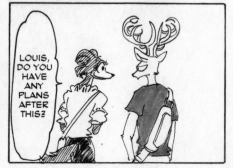

BEASTARS SCRATCHED screentones and PLAIN screentones

I'm not sure if you readers are interested in a how-to about such detailed techniques, but here goes... I absolutely love determining a well-defined light source in a panel and putting shadows on the characters!

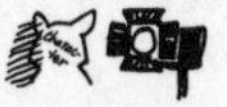
← Like this

Maybe it's because I learned how interesting lighting is when I studied filmmaking in college. In manga, screentone is used to produce shadows.

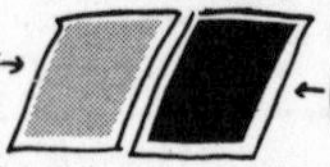
No. 61
No. 65
Screentones look like this.
The screentone business isn't doing too well lately because most manga artists are switching to digital...
I want to keep them in business!

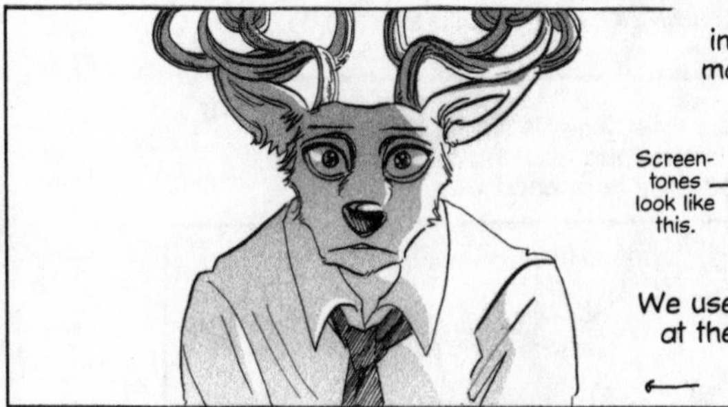

We use two types of screentones at the BEASTARS workplace.

← The first one is the screentone as is. These screentones aren't scratched.

I do almost all of this work myself. That's because I'm not good at the scratching... Scraping screentones with a small blade requires a lot of training and practice. My assistants are experts at it.

Even just a little bit of scratching makes the character look more three-dimensional and the drawing very polished!

I apply the plain screentones while my assistants are busy with other work. I don't disklike the task. Weirdly, I enjoy the stress of cutting them precisely. There's so much to learn about screentone work!

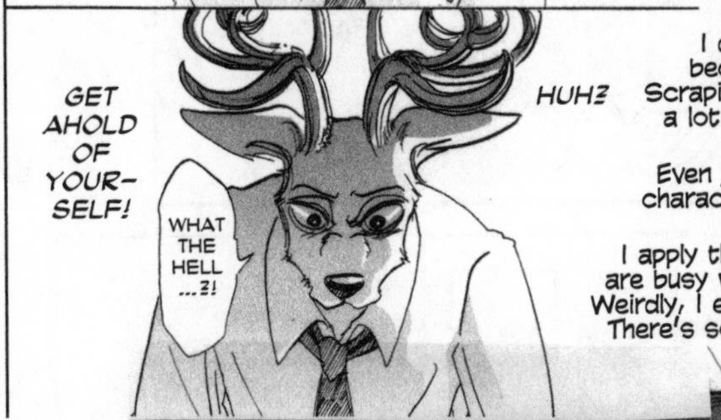
HUH?
GET AHOLD OF YOURSELF!
WHAT THE HELL ...?!

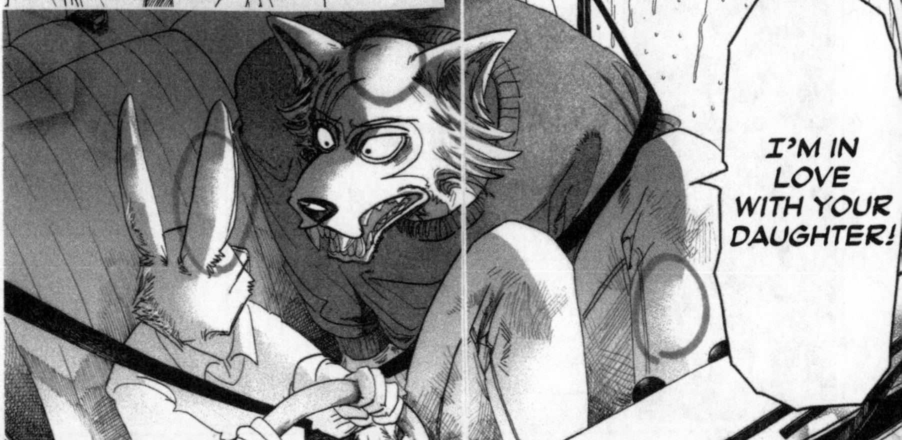
I'M IN LOVE WITH YOUR DAUGHTER!

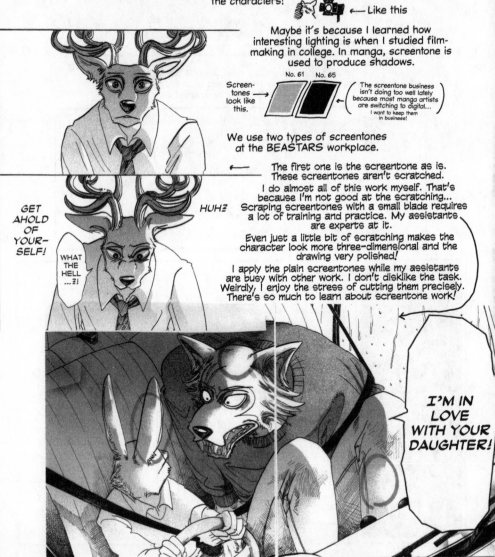

What Happened when BEASTARS Became an Anime

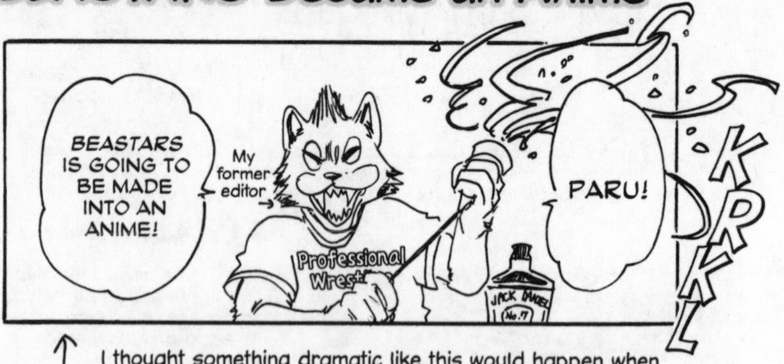
KRKL
PARU!
BEASTARS IS GOING TO BE MADE INTO AN ANIME!
My former editor
Professional Wrest
JACK DANIEL No.7

I thought something dramatic like this would happen when your editor tells you your manga is going to be an anime. But what actually happened was...

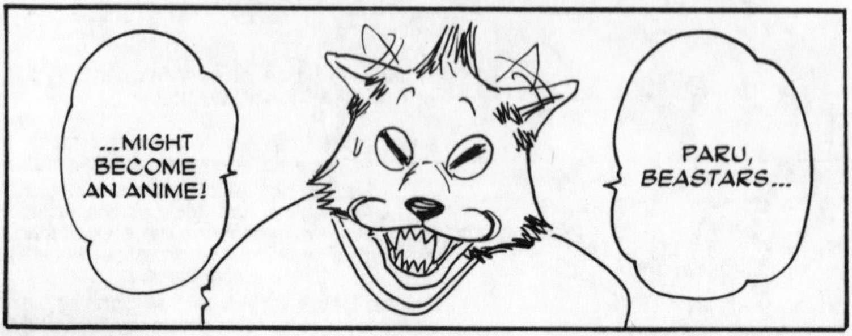
PARU, BEASTARS...
...MIGHT BECOME AN ANIME!

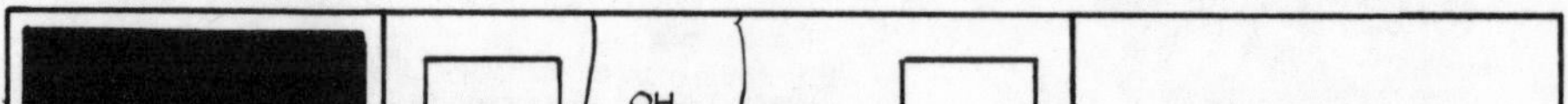
I'd heard that plans to turn a manga into another medi-um, like anime, often fall apart.
OH... REALLY?
So I kept telling myself not to get too excited.
However... before I knew it...

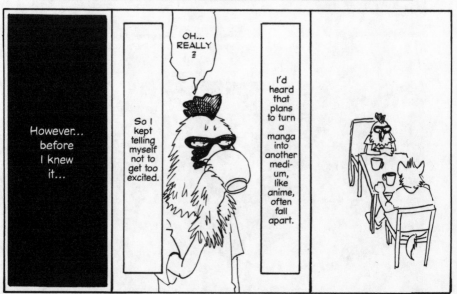

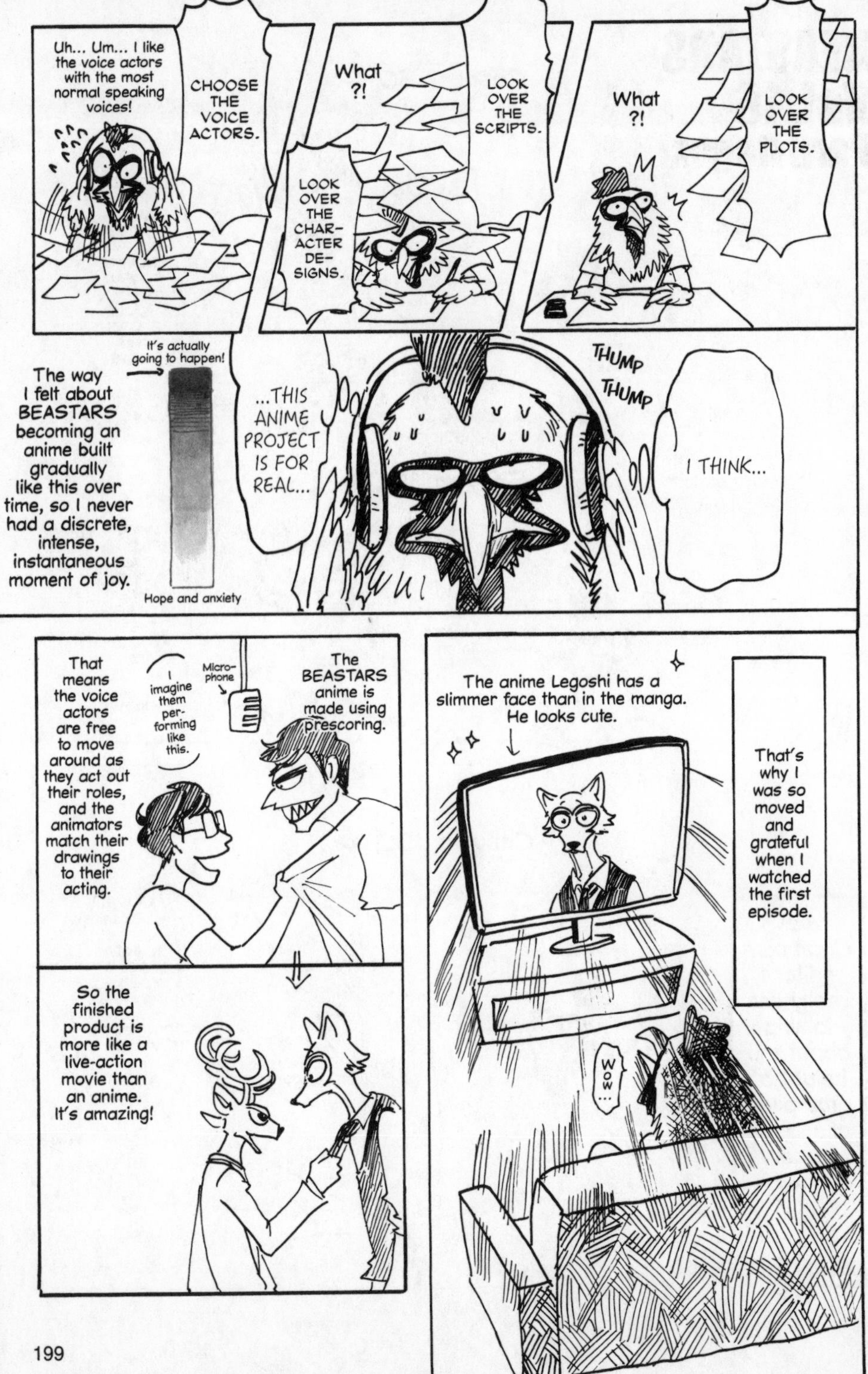
LOOK OVER THE PLOTS.
What ?!
LOOK OVER THE SCRIPTS.
What ?!
LOOK OVER THE CHAR-ACTER DE-SIGNS.
CHOOSE THE VOICE ACTORS.
Uh... Um... I like the voice actors with the most normal speaking voices!
I THINK...
THUMP
THUMP
...THIS ANIME PROJECT IS FOR REAL...
It's actually going to happen!
The way I felt about BEASTARS becoming an anime built gradually like this over time, so I never had a discrete, intense, instantaneous moment of joy.
Hope and anxiety
That's why I was so moved and grateful when I watched the first episode.
The anime Legoshi has a slimmer face than in the manga. He looks cute.
WOW...
The BEASTARS anime is made using prescoring.
Micro-phone
I imagine them per-forming like this.
That means the voice actors are free to move around as they act out their roles, and the animators match their drawings to their acting.
So the finished product is more like a live-action movie than an anime. It's amazing!

BEASTARS
Vol. 16
Paru Itagaki

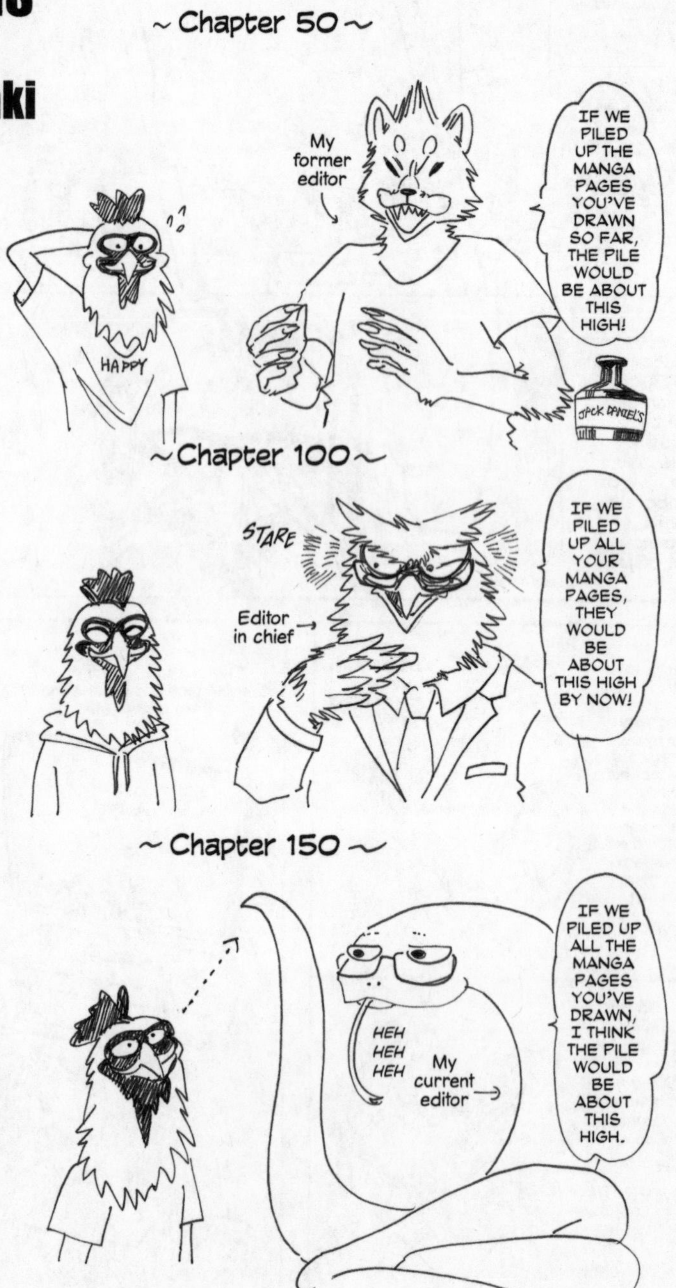

~Chapter 50~
IF WE PILED UP THE MANGA PAGES YOU'VE DRAWN SO FAR, THE PILE WOULD BE ABOUT THIS HIGH!
JACK DANIEL'S
My former editor
HAPPY
~Chapter 100~
IF WE PILED UP ALL YOUR MANGA PAGES, THEY WOULD BE ABOUT THIS HIGH BY NOW!
STARE
Editor in chief
~Chapter 150~
IF WE PILED UP ALL THE MANGA PAGES YOU'VE DRAWN, I THINK THE PILE WOULD BE ABOUT THIS HIGH.
My current editor
HEH HEH HEH

Weekly Champion editors really like talking about the height of my pile of manga pages.

I'm going to record what I was thinking when I was drawing *Beastars*, something like the "inside story."

This is about chapter 100, "When the Train Is Packed" (volume 12). I have strong feelings about this chapter, partly because 100 is a round number. Seven's heart was shattered because she'd been discriminated against and harassed at her workplace for a very long time. There's a scene near the end of the chapter where she taps her cheek three times in front of Legoshi. In the *Beastars* world, this is equivalent to committing suicide. It meant she was asking Legoshi to eat her.

This scene was inspired by a personal experience.

The incident occurred when I was in high school. I had a quarrel with a friend over something trivial, and the friend stopped talking to me for a long time. Like Seven, I wasn't aware at first that my heart had been shattered. I had trouble sleeping at night, and I hated going to school every day.

I was sitting in the train on the way home from school one day when a man with a large build and glassy eyes came and stood in front of me. All of a sudden I thought, "I wish this man would kidnap me." I was hoping my friend would worry about me if I were kidnapped. But the main reason is that I wanted to run away from my problems. I was so desperate that I looked the man straight in the eye. I even smiled slightly at him. (What the hell was I doing?!) Come to think of it, I was making assumptions about this man as well as disrespecting him. I regretted my actions. That's why I had Legoshi rebuke Seven by saying "You're being disrespectful" and then push her out of the train.

I thought being a female high school student made me special somehow. I felt like a victim because a friend was ignoring me. Then there was the thrill of seducing (did that count as seducing?) someone of the opposite sex on a crowded train. I thought I was tired of life, but I wasn't really. All of that made me fall into the trap of such self-centered behavior.

I don't think I've ever behaved as badly and creepily since then. I wonder why this memory of the unpleasantness that people possess inside has remained in my heart for such a long time. The incident on the train was over in a flash. It happened almost ten years ago, yet it left a lasting impression on me. Am I indulging in this memory and falling into the trap of self-absorption even now? (If that's true, I really, really suck.)

I was hoping I'd eventually be able to sublimate this creepy and intense experience by incorporating it into my manga. That's why I drew chapter 100. Seven isn't as creepy as I was. And she has to deal with problems way more serious than mine. I think that's why this chapter didn't turn out to be uncomfortable to read.

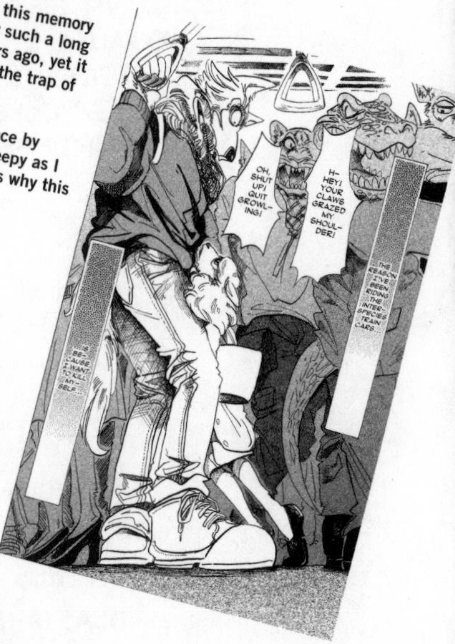
THE REASON I'VE BEEN RIDING THE INTER-SPECIES TRAIN CARS...
H-HEY! YOUR CLAWS GRAZED MY SHOULDER!
OH, SHUT UP! QUIT GROWLING!
IS BECAUSE I WANT TO KILL MYSELF...

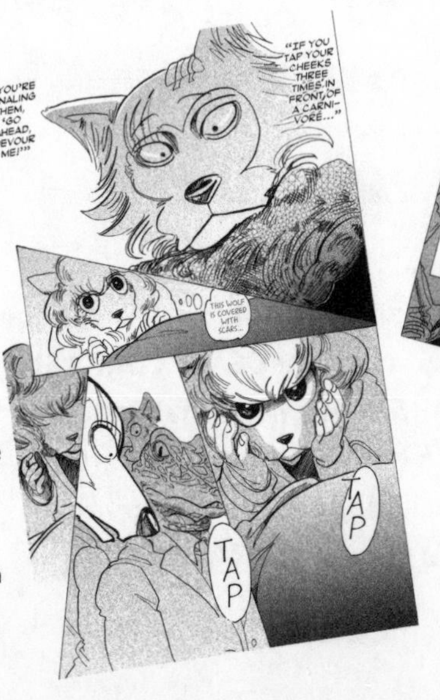
"IF YOU TAP YOUR CHEEKS THREE TIMES IN FRONT OF A CARNIVORE..."
"...YOU'RE SIGNALING THEM, 'GO AHEAD, DEVOUR ME!'"
THIS WOLF IS COVERED WITH SCARS...
TAP
TAP

I typed the above on my PC because I thought, "Handwriting all that will be a pain!" But now it looks like a nasty anonymous letter. Printed text seems more bitter than handwritten text somehow. That's weird. I guess I've discovered something. (There's no bitterness in what I wrote though...)

WHEN PEOPLE USED TO ASK ME WHY I STILL
DREW MY MANGA 100 PERCENT BY HAND, I
COULDN'T GIVE THEM A CLEAR-CUT ANSWER
BECAUSE I DIDN'T KNOW WHY MYSELF.
BUT RECENTLY I REALIZED IT'S BECAUSE
TOOLS YOU CAN TOUCH AND FEEL ARE
INTRINSICALLY SATISFYING.

PARU ITAGAKI

Paru Itagaki began her professional
career as a manga author in 2016 with the
short story collection **BEAST COMPLEX**.
BEASTARS is her first serialization.
BEASTARS has won multiple awards in
Japan, including the prestigious 2018
Manga Taisho Award.

BEASTARS
VOL. 16
VIZ Signature Edition

Story & Art by
Paru Itagaki

Translation/Tomo Kimura
English Adaptation/Annette Roman
Touch-Up Art & Lettering/Susan Daigle-Leach
Cover & Interior Design/Yukiko Whitley
Editor/Annette Roman

Printed in the U.S.A.

Published by VIZ Media, LLC
P.O. Box 77010
San Francisco, CA 94107

10 9 8 7 6 5 4 3 2 1
First printing, January 2022

VIZ MEDIA
viz.com

VIZ SIGNATURE
vizsignature.com

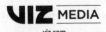

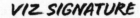

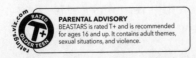

COMING IN VOLUME 17...

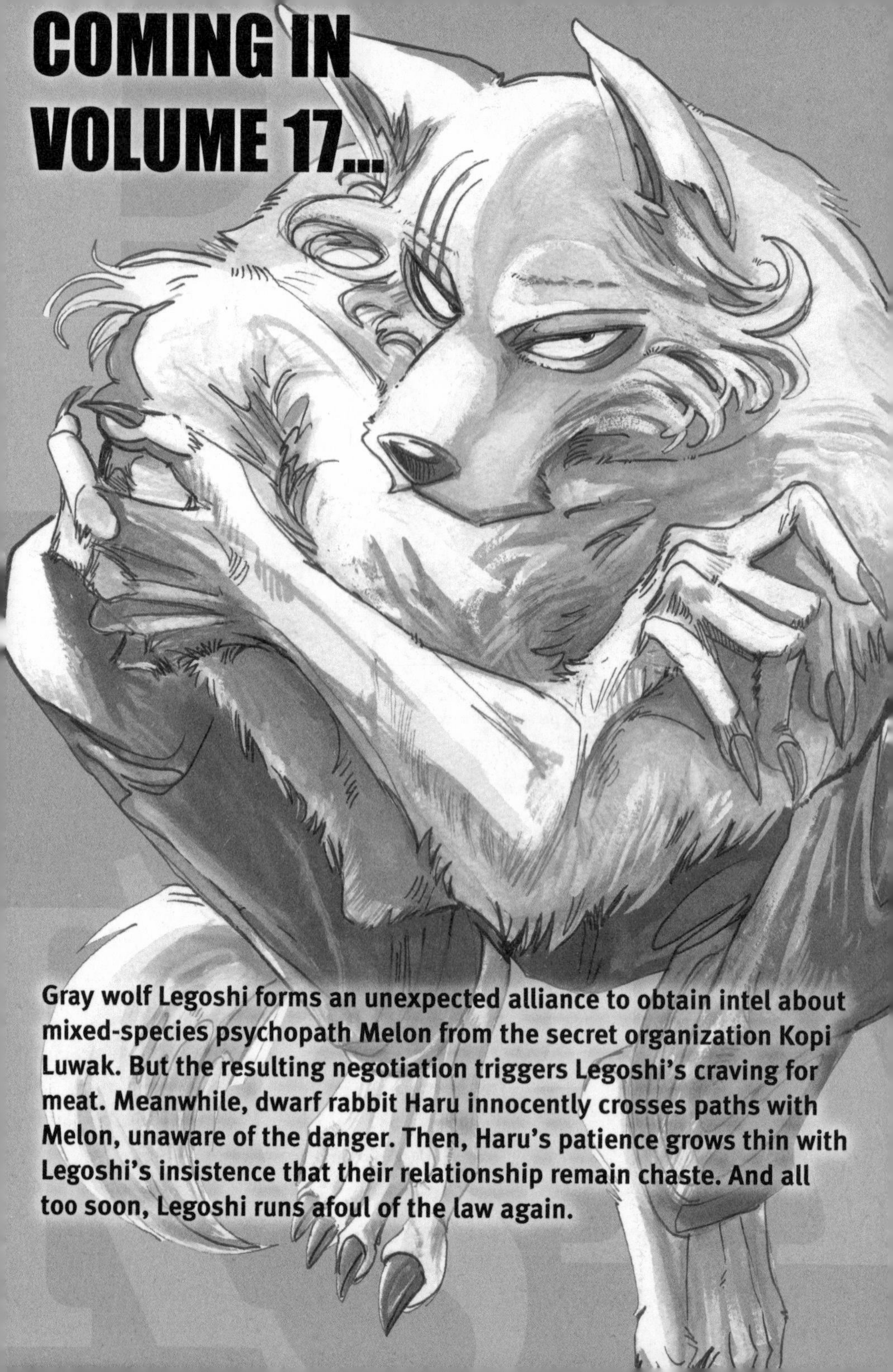

Gray wolf Legoshi forms an unexpected alliance to obtain intel about mixed-species psychopath Melon from the secret organization Kopi Luwak. But the resulting negotiation triggers Legoshi's craving for meat. Meanwhile, dwarf rabbit Haru innocently crosses paths with Melon, unaware of the danger. Then, Haru's patience grows thin with Legoshi's insistence that their relationship remain chaste. And all too soon, Legoshi runs afoul of the law again.

CHILDREN OF THE WHALES

In this postapocalyptic fantasy, a sea of sand swallows everything but the past.

In an endless sea of sand drifts the Mud Whale, a floating island city of clay and magic. In its chambers a small community clings to survival, cut off from its own history by the shadows of the past.

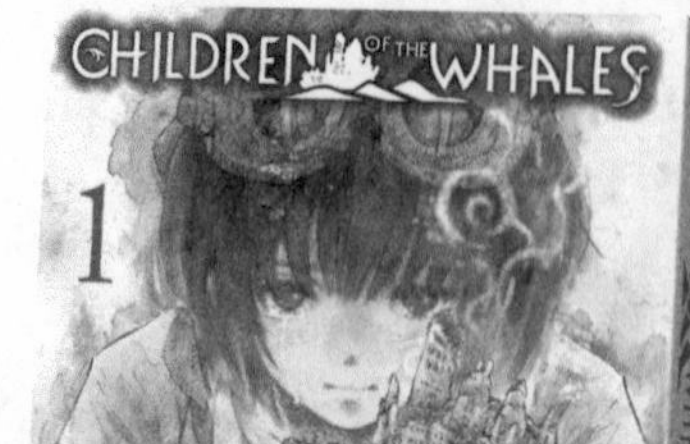

CHILDREN OF THE WHALES
1
CHILDREN OF THE WHALES
1
ABI UMEDA
VIZ

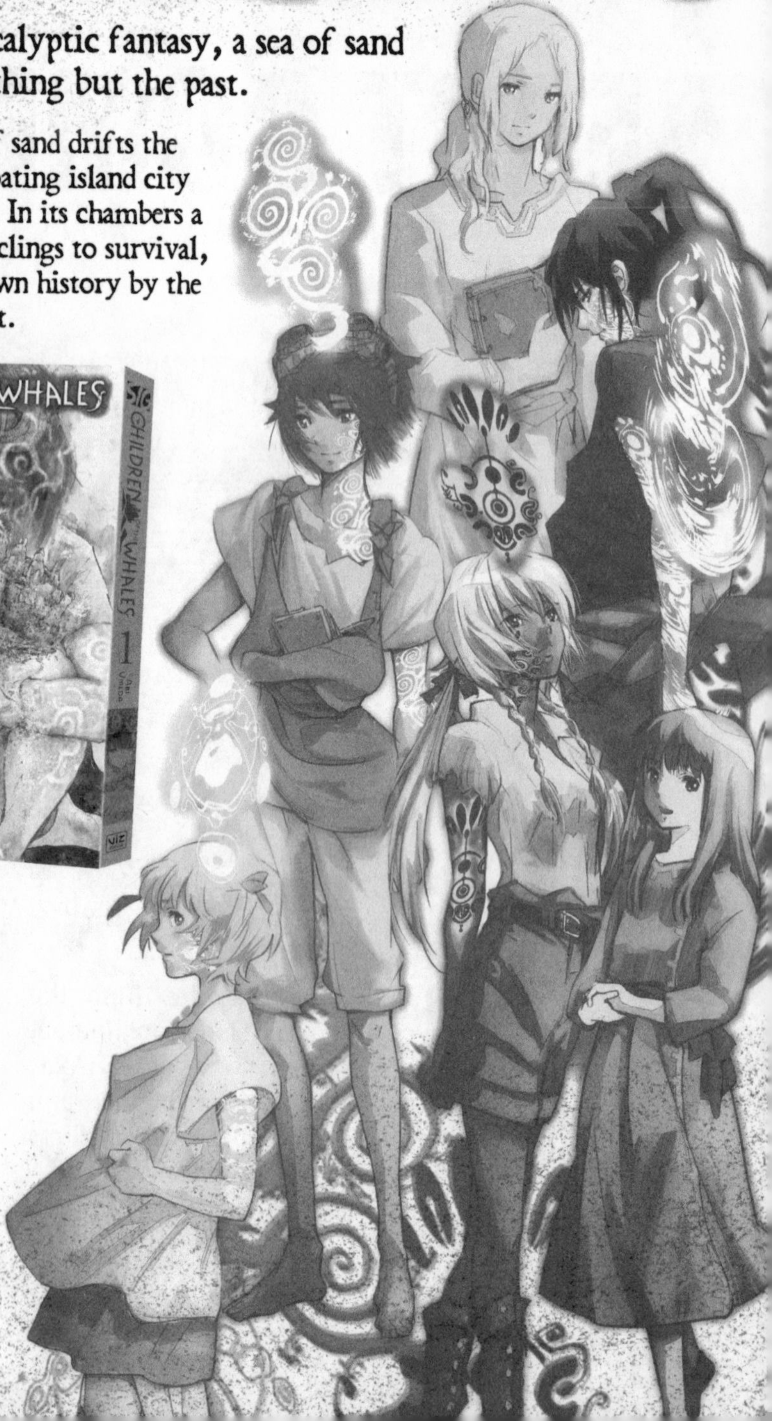

viz.com

RATED T+ OLDER TEEN

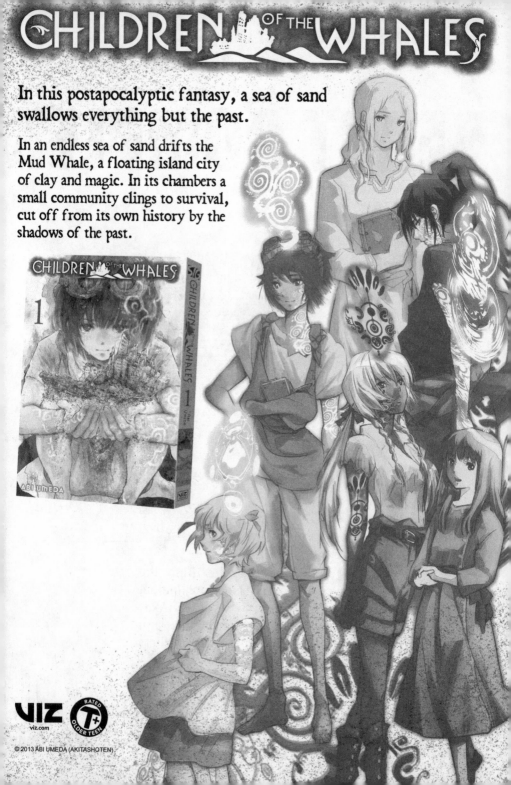

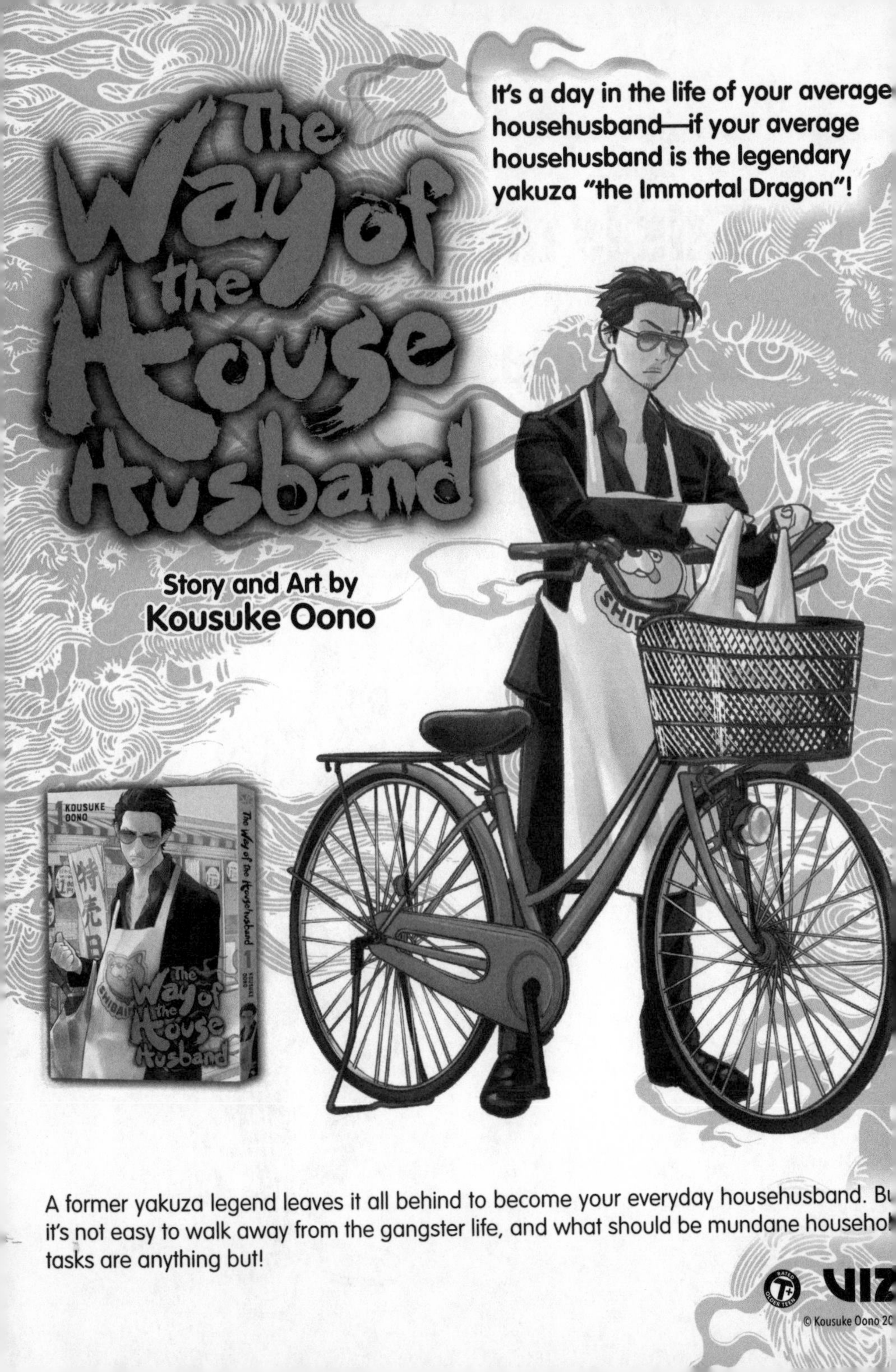
The Way of the House Husband
It's a day in the life of your average househusband—if your average housebusband is the legendary yakuza "the Immortal Dragon"!
Story and Art by
Kousuke Oono
KOUSUKE OONO
The Way of the Househusband
1
The Way of the House Husband
A former yakuza legend leaves it all behind to become your everyday househusband. Bu
it's not easy to walk away from the gangster life, and what should be mundane househo
tasks are anything but!
VIZ
© Kousuke Oono 20

This is the last page.

BEASTARS reads from right to left to preserve the orientation of the original Japanese artwork.